AF446836

FLASH FOCUS

PRESIDENTIAL ELECTIONS
1788–2000

VOLUME 1

an imprint of

SCHOLASTIC

www.scholastic.com/librarypublishing

Set ISBN 0-7172-5935-8
Volume ISBN 0-7172-5934-X

Library of Congress Cataloging-in-Publication Data
Flash focus
      p. cm.
   Includes bibliographical references and index.
   Contents: Vol. 1. Presidential elections, 1788–2000 – v. 2. Political
Parties – v. 3. The Supreme Court – v. 4. Equal rights under law.
   ISBN 0-7172-5935-8 (set : alk. paper)
      1. United States--Politics and government--Juvenile literature. I.
Grolier (Firm)

JK40.F58 2004
320.473--dc22

                                              2004042417

For information, address the publisher:
Scholastic Library Publishing,
Old Sherman Turnpike, Danbury, Connecticut 06816

Printed and bound in Thailand.

Contents

How Presidents Are Chosen: The Constitution

The Constitution provides that the president and vice president be chosen by an "electoral college." The total number of electors equals the total number of senators (two from each state) plus the total number of representatives, determined on the basis of population. Each state chooses as many electors as it has senators and representatives combined. The Constitution does not specify how states choose electors. The electoral college does not meet as a group. Rather, in each state the electors cast their ballots for president and the results are sent to the Senate, to be counted in the presence of the Senate and the House of Representatives. Over time, states have used different methods of selecting its electors, and details of how the system operates have changed significantly since the Constitution was adopted by the states in 1788.

Several reasons have been put forth to justify the indirect election of the president, rather than the direct election by popular vote. One argument is that the system gives less populated states slightly greater representation than very large states—all states start with three electoral votes (two senators plus at least one representative), regardless of population. Another argument is that the Founding Fathers distrusted common people with the choice of president. A third argument is that the electoral college preserved an advantage held by states with significant numbers of slaves. Each slave (none of whom could vote), counted for six-tenths of a person in determining the number of representatives and thus the number of electors. This formula boosted the number of electors coming from slave-holding states in the South. A direct popular vote in which slaves could not participate would have eliminated this advantage.

Choosing the First Three Presidents

In the original form adopted in 1789, the Constitution made no mention of a popular vote in choosing presidential electors. The only restriction was that no elector could be a senator or representative, or hold official office. Each elector wrote two names on his ballot, one of which had to be someone from a different state, without indicating a preference for president and vice president or even a "first choice" and "second choice." Each state then sent a list of names to the Senate, with the number of votes received by each one. The Constitution provided for several possible outcomes:

The person receiving the greatest number of votes was named president, so long as he received votes from a majority of the electors. The person with the second greatest number of votes was named vice president.

If two people were tied, and each received votes from a majority of electors, the House of Representatives chose between them, one to become president and the other to become vice president.

If no one received votes from a majority of electors, the top five names were submitted to the House of Representatives, which chose among the five for the next president with each state having one vote. Of the remaining four candidates, the one with the greatest number of electoral votes automatically became vice president.

If two of the remaining four received the same number of electoral votes, the Senate chose the next vice president.

The 12th Amendment

The original method worked smoothly in 1789 and 1792 to select George Washington as president, and again in 1796 to elect John Adams as president. In 1800, two candidates—Thomas Jefferson of Virginia and Aaron Burr of New York—each received 73 electoral votes in the first round. The Democratic-Republican party had intended Jefferson to become president and Bur to become vice president. But in repeated votes in the House of Representatives over five days, neither Jefferson or Burr won a majority. Finally, on the 36th ballot, Jefferson was chosen president and Burr vice president, thanks to political maneuvering by Alexander Hamilton, who opposed Jefferson's political principles but despised Burr, his chief rival in New York state politics, even more.

In the wake of this imbroglio, the twelfth amendment was proposed in 1803 and ratified the following year. The amendment modified the procedure. Instead of listing two names without distinction, the electors created two sets of ballots, one for president and one for vice president. The rules for choosing a president remained the same, except that the presidential ballots were counted separately from the vice presidential ballots. As before, the person who received the most presidential votes was elected president, so long as he had received a majority of the electoral votes cast. If no one received a majority, the House of Representatives was to choose among the top three, with each state casting one vote. This provision has been used only twice: once to elect Thomas Jefferson in 1804, and once to elect John Quincy Adams in 1824. If the House could not decide by March 4 of the year following the election, the sitting vice president became president. On the vice presidential ballots, if no one received a majority of electoral votes, the Senate chose between the top two.

The Popular Vote

Article II of the Constitution did not specify how presidential electors were to be chosen. Initially the process was a mixture of popular votes and appointments by legislatures. Following adoption of the Constitution in June, 1788, the Continental Congress specified that presidential electors be chosen on January 7, 1789. In four states (Connecticut, New Jersey, Georgia, and South Carolina) the legislature chose the electors without a popular vote. In two states (New Hampshire and Massachusetts), the legislature chose electors from among candidates elected by popular vote. Four states (Delaware, Pennsylvania, Maryland, and Virginia) chose presidential electors entirely by popular votes. Of the remaining three states, Vermont and Rhode Island had not yet ratified the new Constitution, and New York had not passed an election law in time to participate in the first presidential election. Electors met on February 4, 1789.

In 1792, nine state legislatures chose the electors and the remaining six states put the choice to a popular vote (although records of the popular vote for president were not kept before 1824). As late as 1876, the legislature in the newly admitted state of Colorado chose its presidential electors, although all other states chose electors by popular vote.

The Constitution has never contained a clause specifying that presidential electors be picked by popular vote, although the 14th and 20th Amendments specify that the right to vote cannot be limited by race, previous state of servitude (covering former slaves) or for women.

Other Amendments

In addition to the Twelfth Amendment, there have been three other amendments to the Constitution affecting the election of presidents.

The **Twentieth Amendment** was adopted in 1933, changing the date that presidents took office from March to January. In 1789, travel and communications took time, so it made sense to wait several months from the time electors cast their ballots, and the Congress tabulated them, until the day the president could be present in the capital to take office. By tradition (though not by the Constitution) presidents took office in March after elections in November. By the twentieth century, it made no practical sense for the former president, who may have been voted out of office as early as November, to remain in power for another four months. The Twentieth Amendment provided that the new president take office on January 20.

The **Twenty-Second Amendment,** adopted in 1951, limits one person to two terms as president. George Washington served two terms in office, then declined a third term. By so doing, he established a firm tradition that presidents would not serve more than two terms, although this was not a matter of law. In 1940, Franklin D. Roosevelt broke with this tradition and ran for a third term, and for a fourth term in 1944. (Roosevelt died in office in 1945.) The notion of one man running for office indefinitely made some Americans uncomfortable, and consequently the Twenty-second Amendment was adopted in 1951. It provided that no one could be elected for more than two terms. It also provided that anyone who served as

president for more than two years (for instance, a vice president who took office on the death or resignation of a president) could run for only one full term. (Someone who replaced a president for less than two years could still run for two full terms.) The effect of the amendment was to limit one person's time in office to a maximum of ten years (for example, an acting president not more than two years, plus election to two four-year terms).

The **Twenty-fifth Amendment,** adopted in 1967, dealt with the contingency of a president being incapacitated while in office, either by ill health or for some other reason, such as war or a catastrophe. The amendment also dealt with the issue of a vacancy in the vice presidency. Under the amendment, the vice president becomes president in case of death, resignation, or removal from office of the president. In case of a vacancy in the vice presidency (as had happened when the president died in office, for example), the president nominates a replacement who is subject to confirmation by both the Senate and the House of Representatives. The amendment also allows a president to declare to the Senate and House that he is temporarily unable to carry out his duties, in which case the vice president becomes the acting president.

Section four of the amendment describes the procedure when a majority of a president's cabinet decides the president is unable to carry out the duties of the office. Woodrow Wilson, for example, suffered a stroke eighteen months before the end of his second term, leading many to wonder whether he was capable of acting as president, or whether people around him, including his wife, were stepping in for him. The amendment states:

Section 4. Whenever the vice president and a majority of either the principal officers of the executive departments [the cabinet officers] or of such other body as Congress may by law provide, transmit to the president pro tempore of the Senate and the Speaker of the House of Representatives their written declaration that the president is unable to discharge the powers and duties of his office, the vice president shall immediately assume the powers and duties of the office as acting president.

Thereafter, when the president transmits to the president pro tempore of the Senate and the Speaker of the House of Representatives his written declaration that no inability exists, he shall resume the powers and duties of his office unless the vice president and a majority of either the principle officers of the executive department or of such other body as Congress may by law provide, transmit within four days to the president pro tempore of the Senate and the Speaker of the House of Representatives their written declaration that the president is unable to discharge the powers and duties of his office. Thereupon Congress shall decide the issue, assembling within forty-eight hours for that purpose if not in session. If the Congress within twenty-one days after receipt of the latter written declaration, or, if Congress is not in session within twenty-one days after Congress is required to assemble, determines by two-thirds vote of both Houses that the president is unable to discharge the powers and duties of his office, the vice president shall continue to discharge the same as acting president; otherwise, the president shall resume the powers and duties of his office.

The provisions of the Twenty-fifth Amendment were implemented soon after it was adopted. When Vice President Spiro Agnew resigned on October 10, 1973, President Richard Nixon nominated Representative Gerald Ford of Michigan to succeed Agnew. The House and Senate confirmed Ford as vice president in December, 1973. Eight months later, on August 9, 1974, Nixon resigned as president and Ford succeeded him the same day. In turn, Ford nominated Nelson Rockefeller as vice president; he was confirmed by both houses of Congress on December 19, 1974, marking the first time that neither the president nor the vice president had been elected to either office.

1789
George Washington

The first presidential election under the newly adopted Constitution, which installed George Washington as the first president, bore little resemblance to any later election. The choice of the former commander of America's Revolutionary War forces to be the first president seemed to be a foregone conclusion at the end of the Constitutional Convention. Indeed, Washington's prestige as a commanding general had helped persuade some delegates to accept the idea of a strong chief executive officer under the new Constitution.

The convention finished on September 17, 1787, after which delegates returned home to campaign for ratification of the constitution over the next nine months. In June, 1789, New Hampshire became the ninth state to ratify the Constitution, which meant that two-thirds of the states of the confederation had agreed and that the document was in force. New Hampshire's ratification enabled the process of choosing a president to proceed. There was little doubt or debate that Washington, who had served as chairman of the Constitutional Convention, would be chosen.

The procedure for the first election had been specified by the Continental Congress: Presidential electors should be chosen in the separate states on the same day, January 7, 1789, and meet a month later, on February 4, to cast their ballots. As of January 7, however, Vermont and Rhode Island had not yet ratified the Constitution (and were thus ineligible to cast votes) and New York's legislature had not passed a law covering the choice of electors. Consequently, only ten states participated in choosing the first president.

The method of choosing the first presidential electors was a mixture of popular elections and elections carried out by state legislatures. Delaware, Pennsylvania, Maryland, and Virginia selected electors by popular vote. The state legislatures of Connecticut, New Jersey, Georgia, and South Carolina chose their electors, with no popular vote. In New Hampshire and Massachusetts the legislature chose electors from among people elected by popular vote. In no sense was there a campaign for the presidency; to the contrary, Washington appeared reluctant to accept the office. Nor was there any semblance of political parties in 1789.

The chosen electors met in their respective states on February 4, 1789. Each elector wrote two names on his ballot without specifying which was for president and which for vice president. (This system was changed by the Twelfth Amendment, adopted in 1804, under which electors began voting separately for president and vice president.) The states tabulated the votes and sent them to the Senate, where the results from all the states were counted on April 6, 1789 in the presence of nine

FlashFocus: 1789

Candidates

There were no formal candidates in 1789, the first time a President had been chosen under the new Constitution that had been ratified in June, 1788. Each presidential elector listed two names on his ballot, without specifying which name was meant to be President and which Vice President. The name with the greatest number of votes was elected President and the runner-up was Vice President, so long as the winner received votes from a majority of the electors.

George Washington, the military leader of the colonies in the Revolutionary War, received one vote from each of the 69 electors who cast votes on February 4, 1789, and became the first President.

John Adams of Massachusetts, who played a key role in drafting the new Constitution, received 34 votes and became the first Vice President.

Other names listed by electors included **John Jay** (9 votes), **R. H. Harrison** (6), **John Rutledge** (6), and **John Hancock** (4). Ten other men received symbolic votes.

Issues

The Federal system. The new Constitution gave the central government much more power than the previous Articles of Confederation, and in effect ceded authority to the new institution.

Office of the president. Some people who were concerned about giving too much power to a distant central government also worried that the new office of the President could turn into a *de facto* monarch. The Constitution did not impose any limits on how long the President could serve, although it did call for new elections every four years.

Outcome

Electoral College

Washington	69 ✓	(President)
Adams	34 ✓	(Vice President)
Others	44	

Tabulations of popular votes were not kept until 1824.

senators. (Despite the name "electoral college," presidential electors have never gathered as a group in one place to vote.)

The results were unambiguous: Washington received 69 votes, one from each elector who cast a vote. John Adams of Massachusetts received 34 elector votes, the second highest total, and became the first vice president. The names of other prominent individuals listed on electors' ballots (not necessarily

FlashFocus: George Washington

1st President, 1789–1797

Born: February 22, 1732, Westmoreland County, Virginia
Died: December 14, 1799, Mount Vernon, Virginia
Family: Son of Augustine Washington, a prosperous planter, and Mary Ball Washington; married Martha Dandridge Custis, a wealthy widow
Education: Little formal education; tutored in various subjects
Military career: Washington fought with the British in the French and Indian War (1754–58), served as commander-in-chief of the Virginia militia, and was commander-in-chief of the Continental army during the American Revolutionary War (1775–83). The fact that he was able to transform his untrained, undisciplined, unequipped, and underfed men into an effective fighting force increased his reputation dramatically.
Political career: Member of the Virginia House of Burgesses (1759–69); delegate to the First and Second Continental Congresses (1774–75)

Washington led the Virginia delegation to the Constitutional Convention in 1787 and was elected its presiding officer. Upon ratification of the new Constitution, he was elected president of the new country unanimously on February 4, 1789.

Washington was inaugurated on April 30, 1789. Ever dignified, he was as mindful of his legacy in the office as he was of his leadership of the new nation. He generally favored a strong central government. His support of plans for the assumption of states' debts and for an excise tax put him out of favor with the Jeffersonian Democrats.

Washington was elected to a second term in 1792. He steered a course of neutrality in the war between England and France and promoted the acceptance of a formal peace with England.

Washington insisted that the new nation think of itself as independent but not isolationist, and that its destiny was separate from Europe's. Although he was troubled by the partisanship he saw emerging, when he left office in 1797 the United States was truly united.

He died at Mount Vernon, Virginia, on December 14, 1799.

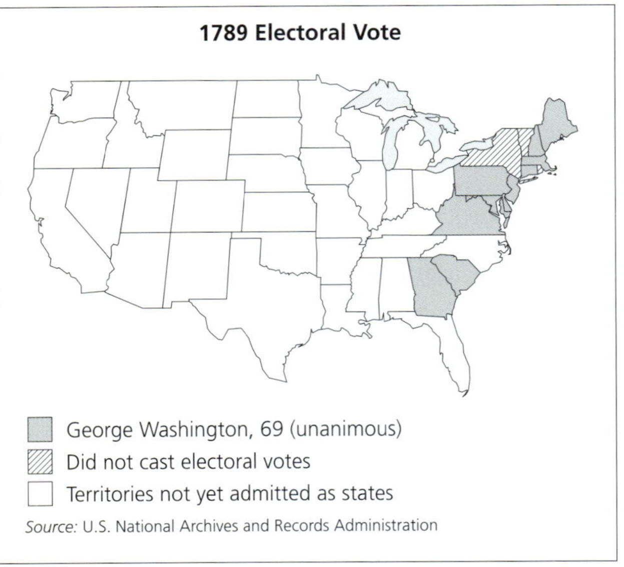

Benjamin Lincoln of Massachusetts (1), and Edward Telfair of Georgia (1). Two electors from Maryland and one from Virginia did not vote at all.

Washington was sworn into office as the first president of the United States on April 30, 1789.

More Information

▶ Faber, Doris. *The Birth of a Nation: The Early Years of the United States.* New York: Scribner, 1989.

▶ Kitzman, Marvin. *The Making of the President 1789: The Unauthorized Campaign Biography.* New York: Harper & Row, 1989.

▶ Rozell, Mark J., William D. Pederson and Frank J. Williams, eds. *George Washington and the Origins of the American Presidency.* Westport, Connecticut: Praeger, 2000.

▶ Yoder, Carolyn P., ed. *George Washington, the Writer: A Treasury of Letters, Diaries and Public Documents.* Honesdale, Pennsylvania: Boyds Mills Press, 2003.

On the Web

▶ Washington, George. "First Inaugural Address, Thursday, April 30, 1789." *Inaugural Addresses of the Presidents of the United States.* Washington, D.C.: U.S. Government Printing Office, 1989; Bartleby.com, 2001. **http://www.bartleby.com/124/pres13.html.**

▶ ———. *The Papers of George Washington.* Links to a variety of online documents from the life of George Washington. **http://gwpapers.virginia.edu/index.html.**

"presidential" votes) included John Jay of New York (9), Robert H. Harrison of Maryland (6), John Rutledge of South Carolina (6), John Hancock of Massachusetts (4), George Clinton of New York (3), Samuel Huntington of Connecticut (2), John Milton of Georgia (2), James Armstrong of Pennsylvania (1),

1792
George Washington

Reelection of George Washington in 1792 for a second term was unanimous and uncontested, much like the first presidential election in 1789. Washington received 132 electoral votes. Vice President John Adams received 77 and served a second term as vice president.

Five states cast electoral votes for the first time: Kentucky, New York, North Carolina, Rhode Island, and Vermont.

But behind the numeric results lay growing political divisions that would come out into the open in 1796 in the form of party politics.

The Context

Much of Washington's first term (1789–93) was occupied with establishing the executive branch of government and establishing diplomatic relations with England, the former colonial ruler, and France, which was in the midst of turmoil because of the French Revolution in 1789.

Setting up the government, including establishing departments that would later turn into cabinet posts, soon underscored basic differences in philosophy that separated prominent politicians.

One group led by Alexander Hamilton, Washington's treasury secretary, believed the new Constitution had been adopted precisely because the United States need to establish a strong central government that would dominate the individual states. Hamilton also advocated policies, such as establishing a central bank, that would ally the government with urban business interests, which in that era primarily meant foreign trade and finance. Hamilton had persuaded Congress to take on the debts of the states, dating from the Revolution, partly as a means of establishing the financial legitimacy of the new government.

An opposing group, led by Secretary of State Thomas Jefferson, distrusted the central government, believing that the essence of the new American experiment lay in small independent farmers. Jefferson and his political allies saw only a limited role for the new federal government, largely confined to international issues.

By 1792, these divisions were obvious to everyone, despite pleas by Washington in particular to avoid partisan politics.

The Campaign

There was no presidential campaign in 1792. To the contrary, both the Federalists and anti-Federalists implored Washington to continue in office for a second term. Washington had not intended to serve beyond four years. At age 60 his health was declining and he longed for a restful retirement on his farm at Mount Vernon, Virginia. But Washington saw the rising political discord, especially between Hamilton and Jefferson, who told Washington: "Your being at the helm will be more than an answer to every argument that can be used to alarm and lead the people in any quarter into violence and secession. North and South will hang together if they have you to hang on."

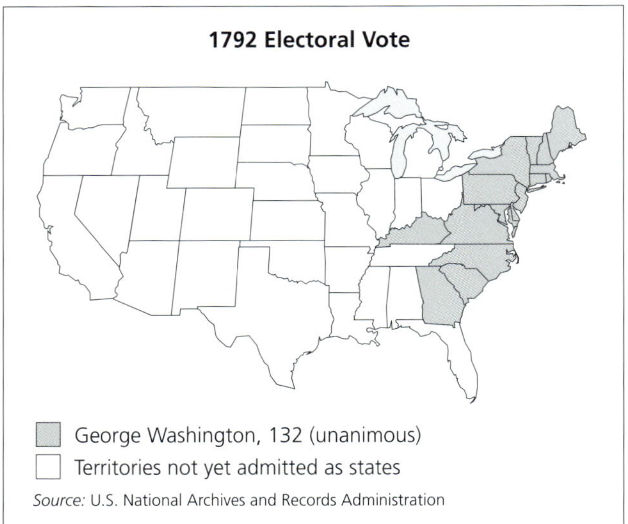

Source: U.S. National Archives and Records Administration

See also: George Washington, p. 6; John Adams, p. 10; Aaron Burr, p. 14.

It was a prophetic statement. The differences between Jefferson and Hamilton had already begun to suggest a split along regional lines: the largely rural South versus the more mercantile North, although this split was must less obvious in 1792 than it became decades later.

Thus 1792 became perhaps the only election in U.S. history in which the choice of vice president became the focal point. The Federalists backed the incumbent vice president, John Adams of Massachusetts, although Hamilton was not enthusiastic about him. Even though the anti-Federalists' main source of political strength was in the agrarian southern states, in 1792 they backed the governor of New York, George Clinton, for vice president. Their enthusiasm waned, however, as a result of the New York gubernatorial election held in the spring of 1792. In that election, Federalist John Jay received more popular votes than Clinton. Some votes were thrown out on a technicality, leaving Clinton the victor. Some dissident anti-

Federalists turned away from Clinton and toward Revolutionary War hero Aaron Burr (see p. 14), also of New York.

The Outcome

Although electors simply cast two votes without indicating a preference for president and vice president, it was widely recognized that the presidency was intended for Washington. Every elector who voted cast one vote for Washington, making him the unanimous choice for the second election in a row.

The second set of 132 electoral votes became, in effect, the vice presidential election.

As in 1789 John Adams of Massachusetts received the second highest number of votes (77), which assured him a second term as vice president—an office he professed to detest. In second place was the unofficial anti-Federalist candidate, Clinton of New York, with 50 votes. Jefferson of Virginia got four electoral votes and Burr received one.

More Information

▶ Alden, John Richard. *George Washington: A Biography*. Baton Rouge: Louisiana State University Press, 1984.

▶ Nordham, George Washington. *The Age of Washington: George Washington's Presidency, 1789–1797*. Chicago: Adams Press, 1989.

▶ Randall, Willard Sterne. *George Washington: A Life*. New York: Henry Holt & Co., 1998.

▶ Smith, Richard Norton. *Patriarch: George Washington and the New American Nation*. Boston: Houghton Mifflin Co., 1993.

On the Web

▶ Washington, George. "Second Inaugural Address, Monday, March 4, 1793." *Inaugural Addresses of the Presidents of the United States*. Washington, D.C.: U.S. Government Printing Office, 1989; Bartleby.com, 2001. **http://www.bartleby.com/124/pres14.html.**

▶ ———. "The Papers of George Washington." Links to a variety of online documents from the life of George Washington. **http://gwpapers.virginia.edu/index.html.**

1796
John Adams vs. Thomas Jefferson

Choosing a successor to George Washington in 1796 was a completely different process than electing the first president. While the choice of Washington had been unanimous in 1789 and again in 1792, the election of 1796 looked much more like modern party contests.

In many respects this was the first "true" election, as it came to be understood. It pitted the sitting vice president, John Adams, against Thomas Jefferson, former secretary of state and author of the Declaration of Independence.

The Context

Washington's presidency, and the process of setting up the new federal government, had served to obscure differences that deeply divided the country into two main camps, the Federalists and the anti-Federalists (who began calling themselves Democratic-Republicans). Two sets of issues separated them: the role and nature of the federal government, and relations between the United States and the two great European rivals of the era, France and England.

The Federalists, represented in the 1796 election by John Adams but primarily led by Alexander Hamilton, the first treasury secretary under Washington, advocated a strong central government aligned with business interests in cities, mostly in the northern states. Hamilton had played a major role in setting up the financial systems needed to conduct business, notably establishment of a national bank, which enabled the government to have a major role in the economy by issuing a form of currency called bank notes (certificates that could be exchanged for gold on deposit at the bank). Hamilton also moved successfully to have the new federal government take over the debts incurred by separate states to pay for the Revolutionary War, a move intended to establish the creditworthiness of the new government.

The anti-Federalists, led by Thomas Jefferson, had a very different vision for the young democracy: a nation based on independent farmers and small tradesmen, with whom the government would have little involvement. The Anti-Federalists saw no mandate in the new Constitution for expanding the role of government into such areas as finance and banking.

These competing ideas took on a regional flavor as well. The Federalists were strongest in the northern states; the anti-Federalists were strongest in the South and West (at that time, the West was western Pennsylvania and Ohio). Their competing visions had been dramatized in 1794 during the so-called Whiskey Rebellion.

To help finance Hamilton's agreement to take over states' debts, the Washington administration passed an excise tax (one that is paid on goods or transactions) on whiskey, which was

FlashFocus: 1796

Candidates

John Adams & Charles Pinckney, Federalist
Thomas Jefferson & Aaron Burr, Democratic-Republican

Issues

Federalism. Neither Adams nor Jefferson, both prominent politicians during the Revolutionary War, were formally affiliated with a political party. However, the beginnings of the modern two-party system could be seen in the alignment of the two leading candidates. Adams was linked to the Federalists, who favored a strong central government and business and merchant interests. Jefferson was liked to the anti-Federalists, sometimes called Democratic-Republicans, who favored a weaker central government and were aligned with rural interests.

Whiskey Rebellion. In 1794, farmers in Western Pennsylvania refused to pay a federal tax on whiskey and attacked government agents trying to collect it. Washington led 12,000 soldiers to Pennsylvania to crush this first challenge to the authority of the federal government.

French Revolution. Establishment of a republic in France through a violent revolution continued to divide Americans. Adams and the Federalists deplored the violence that had taken place in France, as many aristocrats and their sympathizers had been executed. Jefferson applauded the Revolution's republican principles. The issue became even more relevant during Adams' administration with passage of the Alien and Sedition Acts.

Jay's Treaty. The 1794 treaty with Britain establishing normal trade relations and freedom of navigation on the Mississippi River (still west of U.S. territory at the time) was attacked as too favorable to Britain, partly because it did not stop forced drafting ("impressments") of American sailors onto British navy ships.

Outcome

Electoral College

Adams	71 ✓	(President)
Jefferson	69	(Vice President)
Pinckney	59	
Burr	30	

Popular voting results were not kept until 1824. Until 1804, electors voted for two names without distinguishing between president and vice president. The candidate with the most votes became president, provided he received a majority of votes; the candidate with the second highest total became vice president.

See also: Thomas Jefferson, p. 13.

FlashFocus: John Adams

2nd President, 1797–1801

Born: October 30, 1735, Braintree, Massachusetts
Died: July 4, 1826, Quincy, Massachusetts
Family: Son of John Adams, a farmer, and Susanna Boylston; married Abigail Smith
Education: Harvard University
Political career: Delegate to First Continental Congress, 1774–77; served on diplomatic missions to both France and England; vice president, 1789–97

Adams was a firebrand without the violence. He first gained notice for the protest he wrote against the Stamp Act of 1765. This, and his approval of the Boston Tea Party, placed him among the more radical colonial leaders of the time. At the Continental Congress, he was among the first to advocate independence and among the foremost in advocating freedom. In 1777 he offered the resolution that established the new American flag.

In 1777 he was part of a mission to France and in 1785 he was appointed the first minister to England. He resigned the post in 1788 and the next year was elected America's first vice president under George Washington. He chafed in the role, complaining of feeling useless and insignificant.

He took office as the second president in 1797, with Thomas Jefferson, his main political rival, as his vice president. The French and British were at war, and France was interfering with American shipping. Should the United States go to war against France, or try to broker a peace? Differing opinions caused political rifts and personal alienations. For a time "war fever" reigned as the country smarted from the "XYZ Affair," in which France refused to receive American diplomats unless they first paid a bribe. Adams' desire was for peace, which put him at odds with his cabinet and many Federalists

Due in part to the divisions in the Federalist Party, Adams lost the 1800 presidential election to Thomas Jefferson.

He retired to his farm, where he died in 1826.

largely produced by western farmers from their grain. Westerners were also the main users of whiskey, so the tax fell heaviest on rural areas. In 1794 some farmers in western Pennsylvania refused to pay the whiskey tax and attacked government agents trying to collect it. In response, President Washington, aided by Hamilton, led an army of 12,000 men into western Pennsylvania to restore order and enforce collection of the tax.

The focus of the debate over foreign relations was the French Revolution. In July, 1789, just as the new federal government was being organized, a revolution in Paris overthrew King Louis XVI and established a republic—government based on the will of the people instead of on a monarch or hereditary aristocracy. Jefferson, who had been the U.S. envoy to Paris and secretary of state under Washington until 1794, supported the French Revolution. He argued that the two republics, France and the United States, were natural allies, and

also remembered that the Americans had received crucial help from France (albeit the French monarchy) during its revolution against England.

The Federalists, on the other hand, were disturbed by the French revolution, and particularly by the large-scale execution of French aristocrats and many others who supported them. In their view, the French Revolution looked like the rule of a mob, and entirely incompatible with an orderly society in which wealth was protected by government.

During the election, debate centered on Jay's Treaty of 1794. John Jay, a leading Federalist, had negotiated a Treaty of Amity Commerce and Navigation with Britain. It gave the United States unrestricted navigation of the Mississippi River, as well as free trade between the two countries. In some ways it was an extension and confirmation of the peace treaty that ended the Revolutionary War. On the other hand Jay's Treaty did not protect American sailors from being forced into duty on British navy ships ("impressment"), and it left in place restrictions on American trade with British possessions in the Caribbean. Democratic-Republicans strongly criticized the agreement as being too one-sided in favor of Britain, which was engaged in a long struggle with France over the French Revolution. The French government also viewed the treaty as tilting towards Britain, and later launched an undeclared naval war against the United States.

The Campaign

Political parties were a new phenomenon in the United States, and lacked formal structures for designating candidates. Nevertheless it was widely acknowledged—although not formally—that Vice President John Adams was the candidate of the Federalists, and Thomas Jefferson was the candidate of the anti-Federalists who began calling themselves Democratic-Republicans. Charles Pinckney of South Carolina, a former governor, was acknowledged as the unofficial vice presidential candidate of the Federalists, and Senator Aaron Burr of New York as the Democratic-Republican vice presidential preference.

On September 19, 1796, Washington's Farewell Address was printed in the *American Daily Advertiser*, published in Philadelphia. With that, the campaign was off and running. The only candidate who actively campaigned was Aaron Burr, who visited the New England states in an effort to undercut Federalist strength in that region. None of the other three worked openly, setting a precedent for presidential candidates to be seen to let the office seek them. Moreover, Adams and Jefferson had been leaders during the revolution and, however different their political views in 1796, maintained mutual respect and admiration. Campaigning was conducted instead by their supporters through pamphlets, newspapers, and speeches.

Democratic-Republican partisans viciously attacked Adams as being pro-British and accused him of plotting to become an American monarch. Adams was labeled "His Rotundity," a play on his supposed monarchical tendencies and on his stature—he was relatively short and stout. Attacks extended to George Washington who, although widely admired for his role in the

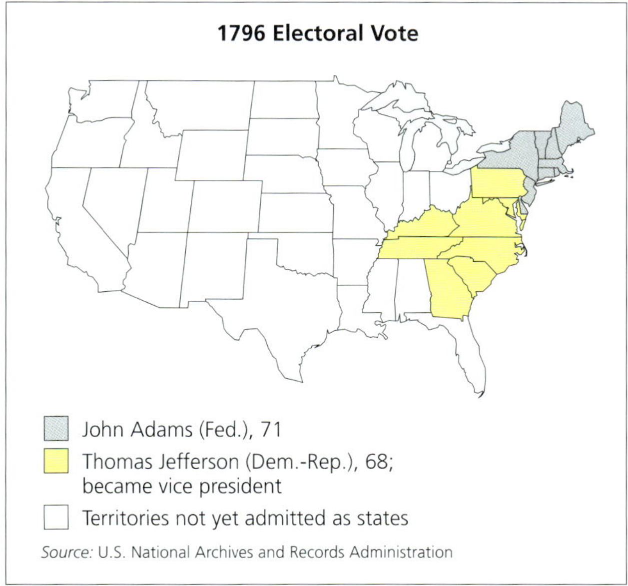

Source: U.S. National Archives and Records Administration

Revolution, had been associated with the policies advocated by Hamilton.

The Federalist attacks on Thomas Jefferson were, if anything, even more vicious. Federalists grimly predicted that a Jefferson presidency would lead to chaos. Others claimed that Jefferson was a philosopher who would be incapable of administering the government. The French ambassador to the United States, Pierre Adet, openly campaigned for Jefferson—an unusually open effort by a foreign country to influence another country's election.

In the midst of these attacks, Alexander Hamilton entered the fray in an attempt to influence the election. Hamilton, a native of the Caribbean island of Nevis and therefore ineligible to become president, did not care for John Adams. He preferred Charles Pinckney of South Carolina, believing that Pinckney would be easier to manipulate, and tried to persuade a few Federalist candidates for elector to vote for Pinckney and someone else besides Adams. Upon hearing about this effort, champions of Adams in New England (the seat of Adams' political strength) took a similar counter-measure, urging Federalist electors to vote for Adams and someone besides Pinckney.

The Outcome

In the election, six states chose electors by popular vote, and in ten states the legislature chose the electors. There were 138 electors altogether, with 70 votes required for a majority. (Under the original Constitution, a president needed not only the greatest number of votes, but also a majority of votes.) The electors gathered in their respective states to vote on the first Wednesday of December, 1796, although their ballots were not tabulated by Congress for more than two months, on the second Wednesday of February.

During the waiting period, it became clear that Jefferson would not receive 70 votes, partly because he would not get all 63 electors from the southern states. It was also assumed that the state legislatures of New York, New Jersey, and Delaware, controlled by Federalists, would not elect Democratic-Republican electors.

On the other hand, it was a question as to whether Adams would receive the necessary 71 votes to win a majority. Since electors cast two votes without designating which vote was for president and which for vice president, it seemed possible that Pinckney could win if enough Federalist electors followed Hamilton's urgings and withheld their votes for Adams. However, by the end of December it was evident that Adams would win exactly seventy-one electoral votes, the minimum needed for election, and Jefferson sent a letter of congratulations.

When the electoral ballots were opened before the Congress on February 8, 1797, the totals were: Adams 71, Jefferson 68, Pinckney 59, Burr 30. Perhaps as a result of Hamilton's efforts to promote Pinckney, nine other men received a total of 48 electoral votes. In the states outside New England that chose electors by popular vote, Jefferson had won more than eighty percent of the electors—an indication of things to come.

Two electoral votes in particular proved critical for Adams. He won one vote from Virginia, considered Jefferson territory, and one from North Carolina, also a Jefferson stronghold. In Virginia, voters in western counties rejected the large planters of the eastern part of the state (such as Jefferson); in North Carolina, commercial interests along the coast succeeded in carrying one vote for Adams. Had those two votes gone the other way, Jefferson would have had 70 votes to Adams' 69.

The actual result meant that Adams became president and his arch political foe Jefferson became vice president, setting the stage for a rematch four years later.

More Information

▶ McCullough, David. *John Adams.* New York: Simon & Schuster, 2002.

▶ Ryerson, Richard Alan, ed. *John Adams and the Founding of the Republic.* Boston: Massachusetts Historical Society, 2001.

▶ Sharp, James Roger. *American Politics in the Early Republic: The New Nation in Crisis.* New Haven: Yale University Press, 1993.

▶ Simon, James F. *What Kind of Nation: Thomas Jefferson, John Marshall, and the Epic Struggle to Create a United States.* New York: Simon & Schuster, 2002.

On the Web

▶ *The Adams Papers,* Massachusetts Historical Society. Multiple resources related to the family of John Adams, the second president, and his son, John Quincy Adams, the sixth president. **http://www.masshist.org/adams_editorial/.**

▶ Adams, John. "Inaugural Address, March 4, 1797." *Inaugural Addresses of the Presidents of the United States.* Washington, D.C.: U.S. Government Printing Office, 1989; Bartleby.com, 2001. **http://www.bartleby.com/124/pres15.html.**

▶ Ferling, John. "1796: The First Real Election." Originally published in *American History* magazine, December 1996. **http://americanhistory.about.com/library/prm/blfirstelection1.htm.**

1800
Thomas Jefferson (Democratic-Republican)
vs. John Adams (Federalist)

FlashFocus: 1800

Candidates

John Adams, Charles Cotesworth Pinckney, John Jay, Federalist

Thomas Jefferson, Aaron Burr, Democratic-Republican

In 1800, there were no vice presidential candidates. Each elector had two votes which did not distinguish between president and vice president. Under the Constitution the candidate with the most votes became president; the candidate with the second-highest total became vice president.

Issues

States rights. Federalists believed in the supremacy of the federal government; Democratic-Republicans believed the federal government represented a "compact" among the states, which retained the ultimate power.

Alien and Sedition Acts. The Federalist congress in 1798 passed four laws nominally designed to protect the United States from foreign interference, but in fact aimed against the Democratic-Republicans. One act, the Sedition Act, outlawed criticism of the government, the president or the Congress. In response, the Federalists encouraged Kentucky and Virginia to pass resolutions declaring the acts in violation of the Constitution and therefore unenforceable.

Religion. Federalists, who reviled Jefferson, attacked the Democratic-Republican candidate as an atheist (he wasn't) and urged the public to vote for a Christian candidate, thereby challenging the new Constitution's strict separation of church and state.

Outcome

Electoral College

Jefferson	73
Burr	73
Adams	65
Pinckney	64
Jay	1

House of Representatives

Jefferson	**10 ✓**
Burr	4

In 1800, each elector had two votes. The votes did not distinguish between president and vice president. The electoral college vote was a tie between Jefferson and Burr for 36 ballots. Finally, Alexander Hamilton, a leading Federalist, persuaded the New York delegation to withhold its votes, giving Jefferson the presidency and Burr the vice presidency. The confusing outcome led directly to adoption of the Twelfth Amendment to the Constitution, in effect for 1804, in which each elector was given one vote for president and one for vice president.

The election of 1800 was referred to as the "revolution" of 1800 by Thomas Jefferson because it marked the transfer of power from the Federalists and John Adams to their bitter political foes, the Democratic-Republicans led by Jefferson. The election concluded a bitter campaign in which the role of political parties was brought to the forefront. The unique outcome of the election—it was eventually decided by the House of Representatives—underscored a weakness in the original formula for selecting a president and led directly to adoption of the Twelfth Amendment to the Constitution in 1803, which still governs the way presidents are elected.

The Context

The election took place in the context of bitter divisions between the two sides over the relationship between the federal government and the states and over the fundamental nature of American democracy.

The Federalists had controlled the White House since George Washington became president in 1789. Washington was not formally a Federalist, but was generally supportive of their positions, which emphasized a strong central government. Many Federalists mistrusted popular democracy, fearing that undereducated common people might easily be led astray and citing as their example the French Revolution of 1789, which had resulted in the execution of the king and many aristocrats. Instead, the Federalists favored rule by the elite, meaning the wealthy, represented by urban merchants in the northeast.

Thomas Jefferson, leader of the Democratic-Republican opposition, was especially alarming to Federalists. The author of the Declaration of Independence ("... all men are created equal ..."), he had long been sympathetic to the French Revolution. He saw a nation of ordinary farmers as the best protectors of individual freedoms. In Jefferson's view the wealthy merchant class could not be trusted, and city-dwelling workers were too dependent on their employers to exercise independent judgment in political affairs.

The issue of government power versus individual rights was highlighted in 1798 when Federalists pushed through the Alien and Sedition Acts. The United States was engaged in an undeclared war with France over the issue of trading with England, against whom France was at war. France believed that the Jay's Treaty of 1794 (see p. 10) had aligned the United States with Britain, violating an earlier treaty of alliance with France. In retaliation, the French navy had started seizing American merchant ships as a form of economic warfare. Efforts by President Adams to negotiate a settlement in the conflict had been rebuffed by the French foreign minister, who sent agents referred to as X, Y and Z in a written message, even though their names were well known. These agents insinuated that they expected a bribe in exchange for negotiating with the United States—the so-called XYZ Affair.

In this context, Federalists had adopted the Naturalization Act that required immigrants to wait fourteen years (instead of five) before voting, thereby trying to cut into immigrants' support for the Democratic-Republicans. The Alien Act and the Alien Enemies Act gave the president the power to expel foreigners judged hostile to the national government (although Adams never exercised this power). Finally, the Sedition Act had outlawed criticism of the government, the Congress or the president. The administration applied the Sedition Act to prosecute several Democratic-Republican newspaper editors, several of whom were convicted.

Opposing the Federalists were the Democratic-Republicans led by Thomas Jefferson, the vice president under Adams, his chief political rival. Jefferson had lost the 1796 election to Adams by just two electoral votes (see p. 9). He chafed under Federalist policies toward France, and was concerned about the Federalist attitude regarding civil liberties. He was ready for the rematch.

By prohibiting public criticism of the government the Sedition Act boldly ignored the First Amendment's guarantee of freedom of speech and of the press. In November 1798, prompted by Jefferson and the Democratic-Republicans, the Kentucky legislature adopted a resolution declaring that the federal government was simply a compact among the states, and that its powers were limited to what was written in the constitution. States had the right to decide whether federal laws were constitutional, and if states found that federal laws violated the constitution, they had the right to declare such laws "altogether void and of no force." A similar resolution was adopted by the Virginia state legislature in December, 1798.

The Campaign

The campaign of 1800 was exceptionally bitter. The Sedition Act, still in force, muted some criticism of President Adams and his government, but no such restrictions were placed on statements about Thomas Jefferson.

One writer in the *Commercial Appeal,* a New York paper owned by Noah Webster, predicted that victory by Jefferson would result in catastrophe. Jefferson would "tumble the financial system of the country into ruin at one stroke," bring about "universal bankruptcy and beggary," and send veterans of the revolutionary war "starving in the streets or living on the cold and precarious supplies of charity," the paper claimed. The attacks on Jefferson were really by way of defending the Federalists' close ties with businessmen and merchants.

Other Federalists attacked Jefferson's religious views, and accused him of leading a crusade against all religions, Christianity in particular. The president of Yale University, clergyman Timothy Dwight, demanded from his pulpit: "Can serious and reflecting men look about them and doubt that, if

Jefferson is elected, those morals which protect our lives from the knife of the assassin, which guard the chastity of our wives and daughters from seduction and violence, defend our property from plunder and devastation, and shield our religion from contempt and profanation, will not be trampled upon? For what end? That our churches may become temples of reason, the Bible cast into a bonfire, and that we may see our wives and daughters the victims of legal prostitution?" The *Gazette of the United States,* the chief newspaper of the Federalist party, told its readers to ask themselves: "Shall I continue in allegiance to God, and a Religious President, or impiously declare for Jefferson and No God!"

The religious issue went beyond mere campaign rhetoric. The Constitution clearly stated, in Article VI, Section 3, that "no religious test shall ever be required as a qualification to any

FlashFocus: Aaron Burr

Candidate for Vice President, 1800

Born: February 6, 1756, Newark, New Jersey

Died: September 14, 1836, Staten Island, New York

Family: Son of Aaron Burr, president of the College of New Jersey (Princeton University) and Esther Edwards, daughter of the famous Puritan preacher Jonathan Edwards; married Theodosia Prevost

Education: College of New Jersey (Princeton)

Political career: After the Revolutionary War, Burr became a successful lawyer with a reputation for charm and womanizing. In 1791 he was elected to the Senate from New York. Burr occupied a middle ground between the Federalists led by John Adams and Alexander Hamilton and the Anti-Federalists led by Thomas Jefferson.

Burr was defeated for the Senate in 1796 and became a member of the New York legislature the next year. He lost a bid for reelection over his political support for a company in which he held a personal interest. Undeterred, Burr agreed to help Jefferson carry New York against Federalist John Adams in 1800 in exchange for being named Jefferson's vice presidential running mate.

At the time, presidential electors voted for two names without designating a president and vice president. Jefferson and Burr tied with 73 votes each, sending the election to the House of Representatives (one vote per state). Burr remained silent rather than encouraging the House to choose Jefferson as president. The two men remained tied each until Alexander Hamilton persuaded New York's Federalists to withhold their vote, making Jefferson the president and Burr the vice president.

In 1804 Burr ran for governor of New York. Hamilton strongly opposed him and on July 11, 1804 the two men fought a duel over some remarks attributed to Hamilton; Hamilton was fatally wounded.

Burr launched a plan to carve a new nation from Spanish territory in the Southwest, with himself as the president. He set off towards New Orleans with 100 men in August, 1806, but when he realized his plans had become known, he fled toward Spanish Florida. He was arrested and charged with treason, but was acquitted on a technicality at a trial presided over by John Marshall, chief justice of the Supreme Court.

Burr spent four years in Europe before returning to New York and reestablishing his law practice, but his reputation was shattered and Burr gradually declined into poverty. He died on September 14, 1836, in Staten Island, New York.

office or public trust. . . ." Yet some Federalists seemed to imply that only an orthodox Christian could be trusted to be president. To Jefferson and others, the Federalist attacks seemed to challenge not just Jefferson, but the strict separation of church and state as well. (Later in life, Jefferson said he was a Unitarian, believing in God but not in the divinity of Jesus.)

Other Federalist writers seized upon Jefferson's reputed affair with a slave, Sally Hemings, and accused him of being fathering several children by her. Federalists regularly referred to Jefferson's "Congo Harem" at his Virginia estate.

Federalist judges appointed by Adams did not hesitate to jail critics, ranging from newspaper editors to ordinary citizens. One drunk was jailed for threatening to fire his musket even if the ball (bullet) "went up John Adams' a—."

Although constrained by threat of jail under the Sedition Act, Democratic-Republicans fought against the Federalists with similar virulence. One writer accused John Adams of sending an emissary to Europe to obtain a mistress.

More telling, perhaps, was the fact that many Federalists lacked enthusiasm for Adams. In May 1800, Adams had dismissed half his cabinet ministers when he found they were taking orders from Hamilton rather than himself. During the campaign, Hamilton denounced Adams as unfit for office and tried to replace him with Charles C. Pinckney of South Carolina.

Despite the undeclared naval war with France, and passions aroused by the XYZ Affair, foreign affairs ended up playing a minor role in the election. With the rise of Napoléon Bonaparte in France, Jefferson's enthusiasm for the French Revolution had cooled, and neither side emphasized the continued unwilling involvement of the United States in the struggle between England and France.

The Outcome

When the electoral college votes were tabulated, both Thomas Jefferson and his official Democratic-Republican vice presidential running mate, Aaron Burr of New York, had each received 73 votes (70 were needed to win), against 65 for John Adams, 64 for the Federalist Charles C. Pinckney and one vote for John Jay, who was also a Federalist.

The outcome was striking on two counts. Of his 73 electoral votes, Jefferson received 53 from southern states with extensive slave populations. At least some of these electoral votes could be attributed to the fact that in apportioning representation in Congress (and thus, electoral votes), every five slaves counted as three people—a scheme deliberately adopted to give Southern states a greater voice in the federal government without challenging the status of slaves.

The Constitution had provided that electors simply list two names on their ballots without specifying which was to be president and which to be vice president. In case of a tie vote, the House of Representatives was to choose, with each state having a single vote. But when the electoral college met to break the tie between Jefferson and Burr, the House of Representatives was still controlled by Federalists who had been elected in 1798.

Over the span of a week, the House voted 36 times without changing the result. For his part, Burr was unwilling to surrender the chance to become president.

Finally, Alexander Hamilton, sworn political enemy of both Jefferson and Burr, decided that as much as he disliked Jeffer-

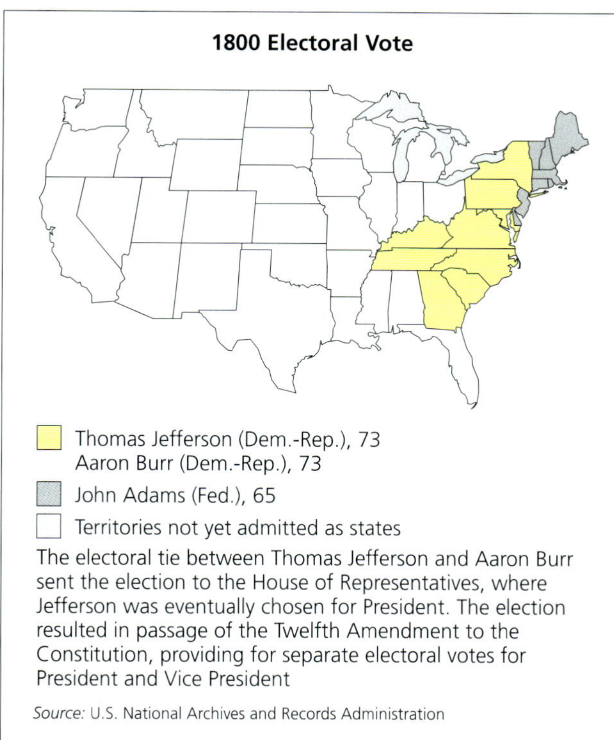

Thomas Jefferson (Dem.-Rep.), 73
Aaron Burr (Dem.-Rep.), 73

John Adams (Fed.), 65

Territories not yet admitted as states

The electoral tie between Thomas Jefferson and Aaron Burr sent the election to the House of Representatives, where Jefferson was eventually chosen for President. The election resulted in passage of the Twelfth Amendment to the Constitution, providing for separate electoral votes for President and Vice President

Source: U.S. National Archives and Records Administration

Quincy, Massachusetts and retirement from public life. His departure marked the last time a Federalist would occupy the White House.

More Information

▶ Appleby, Joynce. *Thomas Jefferson.* New York: Times Books, 2003.

▶ Kennedy, Roger. *Burr, Hamilton and Jefferson: A Study in Character.* New York: Oxford University Press, 2000.

▶ Melton, Buckner F., Jr. *Aaron Burr: Conspiracy to Treason.* New York: Wiley, 2002.

▶ Sharp, James R. *American Politics in the Early Republic: The New Nation in Crisis.* New Haven: Yale University Press, 1993.

▶ Van der Linden, Frank. *The Turning Point. Jefferson's Battle for the Presidency.* Washington: R. B. Luce,1962.

▶ Weisberger, Bernard A. *America Afire: Jefferson, Adams and the Revolutionary Election of 1800.* New York: William Morrow, 2000.

Periodicals

▶ Collinson, Simon. "President or King?" *History Today,* November, 2002, p. 9.

On the Web

▶ Jefferson, Thomas. "First Inaugural Address, Wednesday, March 4, 1801." *Inaugural Addresses of the Presidents of the United States.* Washington, D.C.: U.S. Government Printing Office, 1989; Bartleby.com, 2001. **http://www.bartleby.com/ 124/pres16.html.**

▶ Parton, James. "The Presidential Election of 1800." *The Atlantic,* July 1873. **http://www.theatlantic.com/politics/ policamp/parton.htm.**

▶ Stromberg, Joseph. "The Election of 1800." Ludwig von Mises Institute. **http://www.mises.org/fullstory.asp?control=582.**

▶ U.S. Constitution: Twelfth Amendment. **http://caselaw. lp.findlaw.com/data/constitution/amendment12/ #annotations.**

son's policies, he detested and distrusted Burr even more. Hamilton arranged for New York's delegation to switch its vote to Jefferson instead of their native son, Burr, giving Thomas Jefferson the vote he needed to win the election. As a direct result of the drama, the Twelfth Amendment was enacted in time for the next presidential election. The amendment provided for separate votes for president and vice president (see p. 1).

On the morning of his inauguration, March 4, 1801, Thomas Jefferson had breakfast as usual in his boarding house, then walked to the ceremony. John Adams was not to be found—he had boarded a coach at four o'clock that morning, bound for

1804
Thomas Jefferson (Democratic-Republican)
vs. Charles C. Pinckney (Federalist)

FlashFocus: 1804

Candidates

Thomas Jefferson & James Madison, Democratic-Republican

Charles Cotesworth Pinckney & Rufus King, Federalist

Issues

Louisiana Purchase. Federalists criticized Jefferson's acquisition of French territory as not having been authorized by the Constitution. Politically, Federalists feared that the new territory would attract settlers and dilute the influence of the Federalists. But the acquisition, which guaranteed navigation from the Mississippi River through the port of New Orleans and into the Caribbean, was widely popular.

Small government. Jefferson's ideal was a small central government, and he reduced slightly the number of presidential appointees, while leaving steady the number of government clerks and postal workers.

National debt. Even with the Louisiana Purchase, Jefferson had insisted on reducing the national debt (which had included Revolutionary War debts of the states taken on by the new federal government) from $80 million to $57 million.

Sally Hemings. Desperate for an issue on which to attack Jefferson, some Federalists seized on rumors that the president had an affair with a slave, Sally Hemings. Publicly the president refused to comment on the charges, although he privately denied them.

Barbary pirates. Jefferson sent the Navy to the Mediterranean coast off Africa to rescue American merchant ships and sailors seized by the Pasha of Tripoli for their refusal to pay a tribute in exchange for free passage.

Outcome

Electoral College

Jefferson	162 ✓
Pinckney	14

Results of the popular vote were not kept until 1824.

The election of 1804 was in sharp contrast to the election of 1800. After four years in office, Thomas Jefferson was no longer a feared and controversial figure. On the other hand, the Federalists had lost their most prominent defender, Alexander Hamilton, who had died in a duel, and the party already showed signs of its eventual demise in the wake of Jeffersonian democracy.

The Context

Jefferson's first term had been widely successful. The country was at peace and its economy was steadily growing. Three of Jefferson's policies in particular gave him a strong base of political support: repeal of unpopular excise taxes (internal taxes, as opposed to tariffs, on such items as whiskey, first imposed during the Washington administration in 1791); confrontation with the so-called Barbary pirates in North Africa; and the Louisiana Purchase.

Jefferson had managed to reduce the federal government's debt even after spending $15 million for the Louisiana Purchase. He had also repealed the Alien and Sedition Acts of 1798 (see p. 12) and pardoned the ten individuals still in jail after having been found guilty by partisan Federalist judges for having violated the laws.

Jefferson had pursued policies in line with his vision of a limited popular government based on small, independent farmers. He had slightly reduced the number of government presidential appointees (316 in all) while leaving intact the federal government's staff of 700 clerical employees and 3,000 postal workers. He reduced the size of the standing army in favor of a popular militia—part-time voluntary citizen-soldiers, similar to the National Guard in the twenty-first century—in keeping with his vision of a democracy protected by citizens rather than a large, formal army characteristic of traditional, non-democratic European powers.

As a result of the Napoleonic wars in Europe, Spain had ceded much of its North American territory to France in 1802. Concerned that this might jeopardize freedom of American shipping down the Mississippi River, through the port of New Orleans, and into the Caribbean, Jefferson tried to purchase New Orleans. To his surprise, Napoleon agreed to sell all French holdings in the Louisiana Territory for $15 million, or about four cents an acre. The territory included the port of New Orleans plus a large swath of land that later became Louisiana, Arkansas, Missouri, Iowa, part of Minnesota, most of North Dakota, South Dakota, most of Montana, most of Wyoming, the eastern half of Colorado, the northwest corner of New Mexico, much of Oklahoma, and the northern part of Texas.

The Constitution did not specifically authorize such a move by the president, but Jefferson seized on the chance to nearly double U.S. territory. It opened western land for settlement and effectively removed one of the three European powers with holdings in North America, leaving England and Spain.

Jefferson also instilled national pride by directing action against the Barbary pirates, Muslim states along North Africa's Mediterranean coast that had demanded payments from European and American merchant ships in exchange for safe passage. American ships had paid the tributes since 1784, but when the Pasha of Tripoli increased his demands in 1801, American ships refused to pay. In retaliation, several ships and their crews were taken hostage. Jefferson sent the Navy and Marines to Tripoli to rescue the hostages in 1805, shortly after the election and negotiate an end to the practice.

One other event in 1804 also affected presidential politics. Alexander Hamilton, a leading Federalist, died in a pistol duel against vice president Aaron Burr in July, 1804.

The Democratic-Republicans

In February, 1804, a group of over 100 Democratic-Republican representatives met in Washington and nominated Jefferson for reelection. It was the first formal party nomination in the country's short history, and the decision by the congressmen was unanimous.

Party politics were still relatively new, and in this case largely based on the personality and policies of Thomas Jefferson. Instead of the incumbent vice president, Aaron Burr, the Democratic-Republicans designated New York Governor George Clinton as vice president, at Jefferson's suggestion.

The Federalists

The looming election found the Federalists in disarray. Having dominated the country since adoption of the new Constitution in 1788, the Federalists found themselves without a powerful national leader after the death of Hamilton and the retirement of John Adams (who had, in any case, been estranged from many Federalists in the waning months of his administration.)

While most Americans supported the Louisiana Purchase, some Federalists saw it as a diminution of their political strength in the Northeast. In particular, a group of Federalists nicknamed the Essex Junto (because many members came from Essex County, Massachusetts, north of Boston) began wondering out loud whether New England and perhaps New York State should withdraw from the United States and form a separate nation that might include parts of Canada. The Junto was not popular, even among Federalists, and hurt the Federalist cause in the election.

In July, 1804, the Federalists lost one of their most persuasive leaders, Hamilton, in a pistol duel with Aaron Burr, the vice president who had already been abandoned by Jefferson (and who later would be charged with treason). The two men had been enemies at least since Burr defeated Hamilton's father-in-law in a race for a Senate seat from New York in 1792. Burr challenged Hamilton to a duel over a comment by Hamilton during Burr's campaign for governor of New York. Hamilton was fatally wounded.

Unlike the Democratic-Republicans, the Federalist members of Congress did not hold a formal nominating caucus. Instead, Charles C. Pinckney of South Carolina, who had been John Adams' candidate for vice president in 1800, became the nominee somewhat informally. He ran with Rufus King, a Federalist senator from New York, as candidate for vice president.

Pinckney lacked a coherent base of support due to the lack of formality of his nomination and, as the Essex Junto demonstrated, regional differences between the Northeast and South.

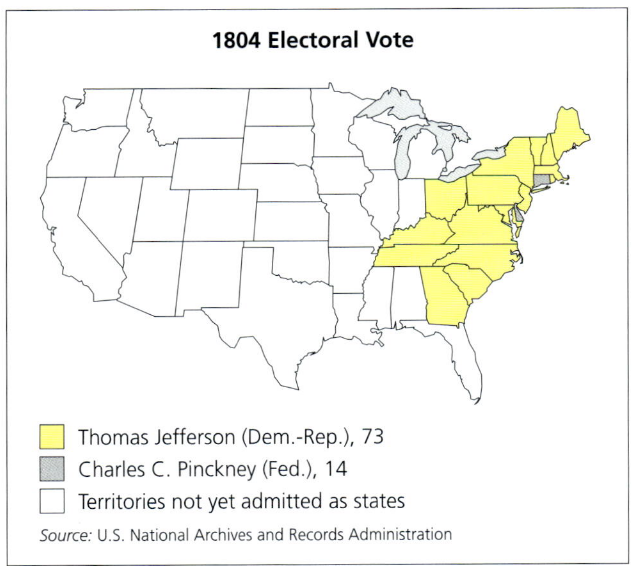

Source: U.S. National Archives and Records Administration

The Campaign and Outcome

Fearing loss of influence when the newly acquired Louisiana territory was integrated into the country, the Federalists led their charge with opposition to Jefferson's purchase. They argued there was no provision in the Constitution to justify such a move. It was a political disaster for the Federalists, however, since the purchase had been widely very popular.

Desperate, the Federalists attempted to focus on the alleged affair between Jefferson and one of his slaves, Sally Hemings. Jefferson refused to comment on the allegations except to publicly deny them. In any case the issue did not catch on with the public.

On his side, Jefferson referred to the Federalists as a "prigarchy," meaning rule by people who observe propriety to an obnoxious extent. The term underscored the emerging image of the Federalists as the party of the overly mannered, semi-aristocratic business class that seemed pitched against the common man.

The election was the first held under the Twelfth Amendment, which specified separate Electoral College ballots for president and vice president. The amendment avoided a repetition of the election of 1800, in which Federalists Jefferson and Burr tied in the Electoral College (see Twelfth Amendment, p. 1).

In 1804, Jefferson scored an overwhelming victory in the Electoral College (no popular vote totals have survived). He and Clinton each received 162 electoral votes, to 14 for Pinckney and his running mate, Rufus King of New York. The Federalists received electoral votes from Connecticut and Delaware, and two votes from Maryland.

More Information

► Ambrose, Stephen E. *Lewis and Clark: Voyage of Discovery.* Washington, DC: National Geographic Society, 1998.

► Simon, James F. *What Kind of Nation: Thomas Jefferson, John Marshall and the Epic Struggle to Create a United States.* New York: Simon & Schuster, 2002.

► Williams, Frances Leigh. *A Founding Family: The Pinckneys of South Carolina.* New York: Harcourt Brace Jovanovich, 1978.

► Zahniser, Marvin R. *Charles Cotesworth Pinckney, Founding Father.* Chapel Hill, NC: The Institute of Early American History and Culture, Williamsburg, Virginia. Published by the University of North Carolina Press, 1967.

On the Web

► Jefferson, Thomas. "Second Inaugural Address, Monday, March 4, 1801." *Inaugural Addresses of the Presidents of the United States.* Washington, D.C.: U.S. Government Printing Office, 1989; Bartleby.com, 2001. **http://www.bartleby.com/124/pres17.html.**

► "Thomas Jefferson 1743–1826." U.S. History.com. **http://www.u-s-history.com/pages/h664.html.**

1808
James Madison (Democratic-Republican) vs. Charles C. Pinckney (Federalist)

James Madison, secretary of state under Thomas Jefferson, was easily elected president in 1808, reflecting both the power and influence of Jefferson and the flagging fortunes of the Federalist party. France, led by Napoléon Bonaparte, and England were are war, and both nations tried to deprive the other of trade with the United States.

Jefferson had imposed a complete trade embargo, barring shipments of U.S. agriculture products to Europe, or the import of manufactured goods. The embargo failed to persuade either England or France to change course, but it did impose economic hardship on American merchants, especially in New England and New York. The embargo became the principal issue in the campaign of 1808.

The Candidates

The campaign for the Democratic-Republican nomination began in early January 1808, when a group of Democratic-Republican legislators met and endorsed James Madison as the next president. Madison had been secretary of state throughout the eight years of Thomas Jefferson's administration, and was Jefferson's designated favorite to succeed him in the White House in 1809. But not all Democratic-Republicans were prepared to go along with Jefferson, and the election of 1808 consisted largely of rival factions of Jefferson's party maneuvering for different candidates.

Madison was the leading candidate and was preferred by those Democratic-Republicans loyal to Jefferson. Another faction of the party in New York backed George Clinton, Jefferson's vice president, while some anti-Jefferson Democratic-Republicans in Virginia backed James Monroe, recently returned from Britain where he had been the U.S. ambassador. Some enemies of Madison distrusted his credentials as a Democratic-Republican, remembering his role in writing the Constitution in 1788, and joining the nation's two leading Federalists, Alexander Hamilton and John Jay, in promoting its adoption. Both Clinton and Monroe apparently were annoyed that Jefferson had not consulted them or included them in deliberations on government policy. Some party members, led by John Randolph of Virginia, were largely motivated by an intense dislike for Jefferson, which they carried onto his presumed favorite, Madison.

None of the three men—Madison, Monroe or Clinton—allowed himself to be seen actively participating in what amounted to a three-way contest waged in various newspapers. Jefferson, too, had said he would remain neutral, although most Democratic-Republicans thought he favored Madison.

In January 1808, a group of Democratic-Federalist congressmen held a meeting (a "caucus") and endorsed Madison by a vote of 83 for Monroe and three for Clinton. The same caucus voted in favor of Clinton for vice president, with 79 votes for the New Yorker to nine votes spread among three New England candidates. However, sixty other Democratic-Federalist members of Congress refused to attend the January caucus, and later denounced it as undue interference in the Executive branch by the Legislative branch—an argument picked up by newspapers favoring Clinton.

FlashFocus: James Madison

4th President, 1809–1817

Born: March 16, 1751, Port Conway, Virginia
Died: June 28, 1836, Montpelier, Virginia
Family: Son of James Madison, a planter, and Eleanor Conway; married Dolley Payne Todd
Education: College of New Jersey (Princeton University)

Political career: James Madison is known as the "Father of the Constitution." He left an indelible stamp on American government, notably a belief in limited government held in check by competing interests.

Madison was a delegate to Virginia's constitutional convention of 1776 and wrote a draft of the state constitution. He served in the Virginia legislature (1776–77) and the Continental Congress (1780–83). Convinced the new country needed a stronger central government, Madison came to the Constitutional Convention in 1787 with a complete written plan for a national government. Although the Constitution reflected comprises needed to assure passage, its basic form was Madison's. Later Madison campaigned for public acceptance as author (alongside Alexander Hamilton and John Jay) of the Federalist Papers, critical in winning popular support.

Madison served in the House of Representatives from 1789–97, then as President Thomas Jefferson's secretary of state from 1801–09. In Congress, Madison drafted the first ten amendments to the Constitution (the Bill of Rights) as well as legislation establishing various departments of government.

Madison aligned himself with Jefferson in opposing Hamilton's economic program as secretary of the treasury, which Madison thought gave too much privilege to commerce. Madison was a founder of the Democratic-Republican faction based on independent farmers.

Madison was easily elected president in 1808 to succeed Jefferson. In the White House, he struggled for most of his two terms to thread the nation's way between France and England, which were embroiled in the Napoleonic Wars. As a result of continued British seizures of American cargoes and "impressment" of sailors (part of its economic war against France), in 1812 Madison asked Congress to declare war against England.

The United States was ill-prepared for war and suffered the humiliation of seeing its enemy march into Washington, setting fire to the White House and the Capitol. Nevertheless, during the war Madison was decisively elected to a second term. The war was ended by treaty in 1814, setting the stage for westward expansion.

Madison, whose health had always been marginal, died in 1836 at Montpelier, Virginia, the last surviving member of the revolutionary generation that founded the United States.

From March until August, competing factions of Democratic-Republicans jockeyed for influence in state legislatures that would end up choosing the electors, who would in turn vote for the president. Anti-Madison Democratic-Republicans tried to assemble a ticket with Clinton for president and Monroe for vice president. Most of the unofficial presidential campaign was conducted via newspaper articles attacking or supporting the three candidates. Madison's supporters pointed out that Clinton had not favored ratification of the Constitution and wondered how he could be trusted as president under a document with which he might disagree. Others attacked Monroe's tenure as ambassador, accusing him of not following instructions from President Jefferson. Attacks on Madison focused on his early support for the Constitution alongside the Federalist leaders John Jay and Alexander Hamilton.

The Federalists had been in decline since Jefferson was first elected in 1800. In 1808, party leaders debated whether to endorse Clinton, adding their support to dissident Democratic-Republican efforts to thwart Madison, or to nominate their own candidate. In the meantime, they maintained a steady stream of attacks on the trade embargo, which Federalists claimed demonstrated Jefferson's tilt towards the French. In August, Federalists from eight states met in New York. They concluded that rather than nominating a Democratic-Republican, they would nominate a candidate outside their main area of strength, which was New England.

Charles Coates Pinckney of South Carolina had been the Federalist candidate running against Jefferson's bid for a second term. He had gained fame during the infamous XYZ Affair under President John Adams, when he refused a French diplomat's demand for a bribe as the price of meeting with an American delegation led by Pinckney. But in 1804 he had lost badly, gaining only 14 electoral votes to 162 for Jefferson. For vice president, the Federalists named Rufus King of New York.

The Issues

There was, in reality, just one issue in the 1808 campaign: Jefferson's embargo on trade with Europe, imposed at the end of 1807. The embargo was the culmination of a long struggle by Jefferson to maintain freedom of U.S. trade with both Britain and France, trade that Britain, being the stronger power on the sea, was determined to cut off. In June, 1807, a British navy ship fired on an American naval vessel, the USS *Chesapeake*, killing three Americans, wounding eighteen, and then kidnapping four others whom the British claimed were deserters. Efforts to negotiate compensation failed, and in October Jefferson asked Congress to pass the Embargo Act, barring all trade with Europe. Jefferson believed that England and France needed American agriculture goods more than America needed manufactured goods from England and France. But as months passed, the embargo seemingly did little to hurt either European power, whereas American merchants seethed while their empty ships sat idle in American harbors; so, too, did unemployed American sailors. American farmers had suddenly lost a lucrative market for their crops, and the country's economy was experiencing what would later be called a severe recession.

From another viewpoint, however, the embargo was the mirror image of British policy. By 1808, the French fleet had been destroyed by Britain, and while France was dominant on land in Europe, Britain controlled the seas. It was the British who were blocking American ships from trading with France, and for many Americans outside the areas most affected by the embargo, Jefferson's policy was popular as a sign of standing up to America's former colonial master.

In March, 1808, near the end of his second term, Jefferson replaced the embargo with the Non-Intercourse Act, which banned trade only with Britain and France. But this act, too, failed to change the course of the war between Britain and France. As it turned out, the United States did not have sufficient economic strength to make a difference to the much larger economies of England and France.

The other issue in 1808 was the record of Thomas Jefferson compared to that of John Adams, his Federalist predecessor. Democratic-Republican newspapers strongly suggested that Pinckney's election would return the country to the Adams era, which included excise taxes, the Alien and Sedition Acts, and government debt. For their part, the Federalists hearkened to an even earlier Federalist president, George Washington (although Washington did not have a party designation).

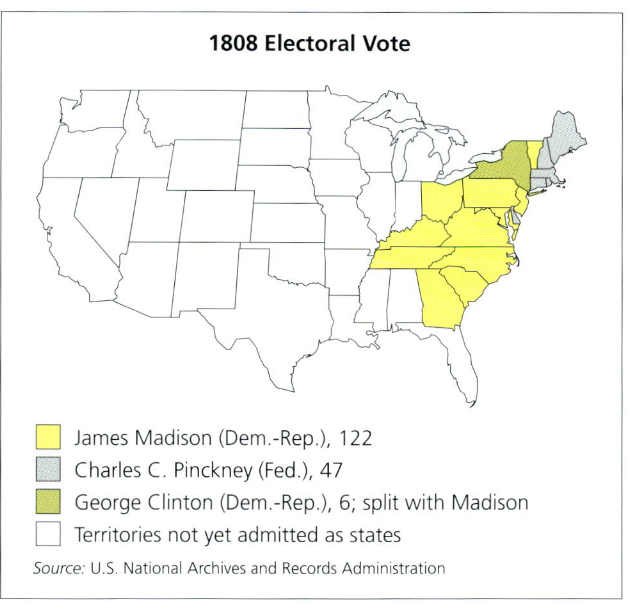

Source: U.S. National Archives and Records Administration

The Outcome

The 1808 campaign bore little resemblance to the contests that developed in later decades. In seven states (Connecticut, Delaware, Georgia, Massachusetts, New York, South Carolina, and Vermont), electors were chosen by the state legislature in 1808. In the other ten states, voters chose the electors, either electing them on a state-wide basis (Ohio, Pennsylvania, Rhode Island, Virginia, New Hampshire, and New Jersey) or in districts (often coinciding with Congressional districts, in Kentucky, Maryland, North Carolina, and Tennessee).

Most of the campaigning had taken place during the spring and summer in newspapers partial to either Madison or Clinton, or to Pinckney. None of the candidates actively campaigned, either for the nomination or for the election that chose the presidential electors committed to each candidate.

The 1808 election was not held on a single day. Rather, each state selected presidential electors separately between November and December; on December 7, the electors in each state cast their ballots, which were then tabulated by the House of Representatives.

Madison won 122 electoral votes out of 176; Pinckney won 47; and Clinton won six. Three states split their electoral votes: New York divided its 19 votes between Madison (13) and Clinton (6); Maryland gave nine votes to Madison and two to Pinckney; and North Carolina divided also its votes between Madison (11) and Pinckney (3).

Pinckney's strength was almost entirely in New England: Connecticut (9 electoral votes), Massachusetts (19), New Hampshire (7), and Rhode Island (4). He also received three votes from Delaware, two from Maryland, and three from North Carolina. Although he came nowhere close to winning, Pinckney's performance was much stronger than it had been in 1804, when he won only 14 electoral votes. Federalists also gained seats in Congress.

George Clinton was reelected vice president, winning 113 votes. His closest competitor was the Federalist candidate, Rufus King, who received 47 votes. James Monroe, once talked about as a Democratic-Republican presidential nominee, received three electoral votes for vice president from New York.

Although the embargo gave way to the more limited Non-Intercourse Act in 1809, the United States continued to be an unwilling participant in the struggle between Britain and France during Madison's first administration, leading eventually to war with Britain in 1812.

More Information

► Koch, Adrienne. *Jefferson and Madison: The Great Collaboration.* Lanham, JD: University Press of America, 1950

► McCoy, Drew R. *The Last of the Fathers: James Madison and the Republican Legacy.* New York: Cambridge University Press, 1989.

► Rakove, Jack N. *James Madison and the Creation of the American Republic.* New York: Longman, 2002.

► Williams, Frances Leigh. *A Founding Family: The Pinckneys of South Carolina.* New York: Harcourt Brance Jovanovich, 1978.

► Wills, Garry. *James Madison.* New York: Times Books, 2002.

On the Web

► Madison, James. "First Inaugural Address, Saturday, March 4, 1809." *Inaugural Addresses of the Presidents of the United States.* Washington, D.C.: U.S. Government Printing Office, 1989; Bartleby.com, 2001. **http://www.bartleby.com/124/pres18.html.**

► "James Madison: His Legacy." James Madison Center, James Madison University. Links to articles related to the fourth president. **http://www.jmu.edu/madison/.**

1812
James Madison (Democratic-Republican) vs. DeWitt Clinton (Federalist)

Two candidates from the same party, the Democratic-Republicans, ran against each other in 1812, marking sharp divisions over the war with Britain that had begun in June, 1812. The main branch of Democratic-Republicans nominated James Madison for a second term, despite the fact that the early war effort was going badly. A splinter group of Democratic-Republicans nominated DeWitt Clinton, mayor of New York City and lieutenant governor of New York State, for president. His uncle, George Clinton, had been Madison's vice president until his death in April, 1812. Clinton was widely backed by the Federalists.

The Context

The United States was unwillingly drawn into the continuing war between Britain and France (the so-called Napoleonic Wars). Britain, trying to cut off shipments to France, harassed neutral shipping, including American shipments bound for France. Britain also stopped American merchant ships and "impressed" (drafted) sailors suspected of being British deserters to work on British warships. Harassment of U.S. merchant ships had been a problem for most of the presidency of Thomas Jefferson (1801–08) and the first term of James Madison. Jefferson and his secretary of state, James Madison, had imposed a trade embargo against Britain in 1807 which ended up hurting American economic interests without significantly changing British behavior. Although Madison replaced the embargo with the Non-Intercourse Act at the start of his first term as president in 1809, tensions with Britain continued and New England merchants in particular felt they were bearing the brunt of an ineffective policy. In other parts of the country, Americans believed that the United States must take a firm stand for freedom of shipping as a matter of national pride.

French Navy ships had pursued a similar policy against neutral shipping, which largely meant the United States, but this attracted less attention from the United States, partly because Britain was the former colonial power in an age when the War of Independence was still fresh in people's minds.

On June 1, 1812 Madison asked Congress to declare war on Britain as it became evident that economic pressures would not change British policy. The House of Representatives voted for war, 79–49, with opposition coming from New England. The Senate agreed by a narrower margin, 19–13. The War of 1812 began just weeks before the presidential election and was the dominant issue.

The Candidates

James Madison was a key architect of the Constitution adopted in 1789 and had served as Jefferson's secretary of state for two terms. The conflict with Britain over the freedom of neutral shipping was not new to Madison when he took office for his first term. Madison had pursued essentially the same policy as Jefferson against British interference, with a similar lack of success. On the one hand, merchants in New England (and to a lesser extent, in New York) were frustrated with the Non-Intercourse Act that followed the embargo; on the other hand, some Americans felt the United States should be taking a stronger position against Britain.

As the Federalists faded, factions within the Democratic-Republican party became harder to control, adding to the frustrations of Madison's first term.

After Madison took the side of the "hawks" and asked for a declaration of war against Britain, the nation remained sharply divided. Some New England governors refused to let their militias take up arms outside their own states.

Despite his long association with what turned out to be a failed policy with regard to Britain, there was never a serious question that Madison would be renominated by the Democratic-Republicans. On May 18, shortly before the declaration of war, a caucus of 82 Democratic-Republican legislators voted unanimously to support Madison. The more interesting question was who would run as Madison's vice president.

The Federalists chose Elbridge Gerry of Massachusetts, a signer of the Declaration of Independence and then governor of Massachusetts. Gerry's nomination addressed two problems of the Democratic-Republicans: his presence on the ticket could help attract support from New England, and he was not from Virginia, suggesting that, as a likely successor to Madison, he might be able to help break the "Virginia Dynasty"—the fact that ever since 1789, when George Washington became president, the White House had been occupied by a Virginian except for the one term of John Adams (1797–1801).

Madison's nomination had not been entirely unanimous, however. At the caucus of Democratic-Republicans nominating Madison for a second term, 51 congressmen had refused to attend, providing an opening for DeWitt Clinton, the well-regarded mayor of New York and nephew of Madison's vice president, George Clinton, who had died in office on April 20, 1812. DeWitt Clinton was also lieutenant governor of New York and a former U.S. senator. While he was officially a Democratic-Republican, he enjoyed widespread support by Federalists.

The obvious unpopularity of the war with Britain, and the apparent split in Federalist ranks, opened the possibility of an alternative to Madison. The Federalist Party, which had been fading from sight ever since Jefferson's election in 1800, saw an opening. Some Federalists wanted to nominate John Marshall of Virginia, the chief justice of the Supreme Court, on grounds he might be able to challenge Madison in the South. Others preferred Rufus King, originally from Massachusetts, a former minister to Britain and senator from New York.

In September, 1812, Federalist delegates from eleven states met in New York to consider an opponent to run against Madison; it was the precursor to later political conventions. King opposed what he considered an opportunistic nomination of Clinton simply on grounds of opposition to the war of 1812; other Federalists argued that backing Clinton offered the most likely chance of defeating Madison.

Rather than formally backing a candidate, the Federalists recommended that voters choose presidential electors who

FlashFocus: DeWitt Clinton

Federalist Candidate for President, 1812

Born: March 2, 1769, Little Britain, New York
Died: February 11, 1828, Albany, New York
Family: Son of James Clinton, a surveyor, farmer, and land speculator, and Mary DeWitt; nephew of George Clinton, former governor of New York; married Maria Franklin (died), Catherine Jones
Education: Kingston Academy; Columbia College; private law studies
Political career: Democrat. New York state assembly, 1798; New York state senate, 1798–1802, 1805–11; U.S. senator from New York, 1802–03; mayor of New York, 1803–07, 1808–10, 1811–15; lieutenant governor of New York, 1811–13; governor of New York, 1817–23, 1825–28

DeWitt Clinton shone in politics as a teenager, writing articles opposing the U.S. Constitution on grounds it made the federal government too powerful. In 1789, at age 20, he became private secretary to his uncle, New York Governor George Clinton.

In 1802 Clinton was appointed to fill an empty U.S. Senate seat. He resigned it the next year to become mayor of New York City.

Shortly after the outbreak of the War of 1812, which was unpopular in New England, Democratic-Republicans in New York nominated Clinton to run against the incumbent, President James Madison. A group of Federalists met in New York in September, 1812, and passed a resolution endorsing Clinton. Technically he was not the Federalist candidate, although the Federalists' meeting faintly resembled future party nominating conventions.

Clinton lost to Madison in the electoral college, 128 to 89. He carried most of the northeastern states; if he had carried Pennsylvania as well, he would have been elected president.

Clinton was the leading advocate of building the Erie Canal to link the Hudson River to Lake Erie. He was elected New York governor four times: in 1818 and 1820, and again in 1824 and 1826. He died on February 11, 1828, while still in office.

See also: James Madison, p. 20.

were committed to vote against Madison, a move designed to subtly support Clinton without making him the official nominee of the Federalists. Nevertheless, Clinton was widely regarded as the Federalist candidate of 1812.

The Campaign

Clinton's strategy in 1812 was to present himself as an alternative to Madison on regional grounds. In New England, his supporters portrayed him as an opponent of the war, as well as someone to end the Virginia Dynasty. In the South and West,

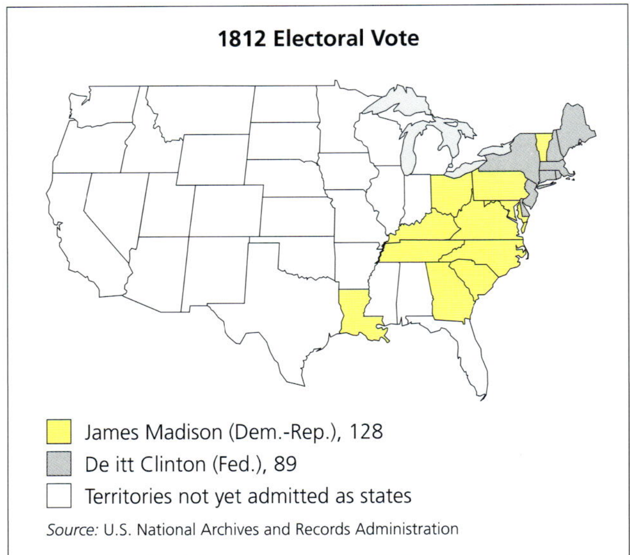

Source: U.S. National Archives and Records Administration

he was presented as being able to conduct the war more efficiently than Madison. It was a strategy that almost worked.

Even before the Federalists had decided to back Clinton, in August a Committee of Correspondence for Clinton, in New York, issued a paper titled "An Address to the People of the United States," outlining the positions that candidate Clinton represented. The paper is widely viewed as the precursor of presidential party platforms formalized many years later. The paper emphasized the influence of Virginia on the presidency, and on Madison's record during his first term. In particular it criticized Madison's failure to build a strong navy in preparation for the war with Britain. The "Address" also denounced the system of choosing presidential nominees through a meeting of Congressmen, on grounds it was prejudiced in favor of larger states at the expense of smaller ones. It argued that states with commercial interests had become alienated from states with agricultural interests, and that the unity of the country was being challenged. The solution: elect someone from New York as the next president.

These sentiments were later echoed by Federalist newspapers in supporting Clinton against Madison. Clinton was portrayed as a less dangerous Democratic-Republican alternative to Madison, and as better able to pursue peace with Britain if possible, or to pursue war more effectively.

Madison's reelection campaign was much lower key than Clinton's. It was notable for two resolutions passed by a convention of Democratic-Republicans in New Jersey and the state assembly in South Carolina, both in support of Madison. The president wrote and published responses to these declarations of support, and in so doing suggested that Clinton supporters lacked loyalty and patriotism. Madison's appreciation for support suggested that Clinton's opposition was making it more difficult for the president to conduct the war against Britain.

In 1812, as had been the case earlier, the bulk of the campaign was conducted in newspapers, with partisan editors attacking the opposing candidate. Since Clinton's candidacy was a fusion of support by some Democratic-Republicans and the Federalists, his organization was not nearly as efficient as Madison's.

The Outcome

The electoral contest in 1812 mirrored many later elections, in which differences between sections made the difference. Going into the election, Madison was assured of widespread support in the South, where the war against Britain was widely supported. The outcome in Virginia was in some doubt, despite the fact that Madison was from Virginia. For Clinton, victory depended on solidly sweeping New England, despite the presence of the governor of Massachusetts on the Democratic-Republican ticket, taking his home state of New York, and also Pennsylvania. In addition he needed to pick up electoral votes from some southern or western states to overcome Madison's built-in advantage. Clinton counted on receiving at least some electoral votes from states, like Massachusetts and Maryland, that chose electors by Congressional district, thereby allowing split votes. In other states, notably Pennsylvania and Ohio, electors were chosen on a statewide popular vote, with the winner receiving all that state's electoral votes.

Despite calculations by both sides about splitting the electoral votes of some states, the result of the election was largely regional. Clinton carried all the electoral votes in New England (Vermont, New Hampshire, Massachusetts, Connecticut, and Rhode island; Maine did not become a separate state until 1820), while Madison carried the South, including Virginia.

There was a real battle for the Middle Atlantic states (New York, New Jersey, Delaware, Maryland, and Pennsylvania) and Ohio. Madison and Clinton divided the electoral votes in Maryland, 6–5. Clinton carried New Jersey (eight electoral votes) and New York (thanks largely to some political maneuvering by a pro-Clinton lawyer named Martin Van Buren [see p. 44]). With the tally of electoral votes nearly even, the final result came down to North Carolina, Ohio, and Pennsylvania.

Although dissatisfaction with the war effort played a role in Ohio, Clinton's strategy of appearing as all things to all people failed and Madison carried all of Ohio's eight votes. In North Carolina rumors (never proven) that Federalists from New York planned to bribe some legislators into choosing pro-Clinton presidential electors caused even Federalists in the state legislature to vote for Madison in order to prove they were not corrupted. Finally, in Pennsylvania, home of Clinton's vice presidential running mate Jared Ingersoll, Madison won all 25 electoral votes. Overall, Madison won 63 percent of the vote for electors. The combination of patriotic unity behind the president during the war, and loyalty by Pennsylvania's Democratic-Republicans, carried the day for Madison.

The final electoral vote was Madison 128, Clinton 89. Had Pennsylvania gone the other way, Clinton would have been elected.

More Information

- Cornog, Evan. *The Birth of Empire: DeWitt Clinton and the American Experience, 1769–1828.* New York: Oxford University Press, 1998.
- Hickey, Donald R. *The War of 1812: A Short History*. Urbana: University of Illinois Press, 1995.
- Rutland, Robert Allen. *The Presidency of James Madiso*n. Lawrence: University Press of Kansas, 1990.

On the Web

- Madison, James. "Second Inaugural Address, Thursday, March 4, 1813." Inaugural Addresses of the Presidents of the United States. Washington, D.C.: U.S. Government Printing Office, 1989; Bartleby.com, 2001. **http://www.bartleby.com/124/pres19.html.**
- "James Madison: His Legacy." James Madison Center, James Madison University. Lliks to many articles related to the fourth president. **http://www.jmu.edu/madison/.**
- Bancroft, Hubert H. (ed.) The Great Republic, Vol. III, War of 1812-Civil War and Reconstruction. Online version of 1902 history includes articles on Madison administration, the War of 1812, and many other subsequent events. **http://www.publicbookshelf.com/public_html/The_Great_Republic_By_the_Master_Historians_Vol_III/.**

<h1 style="text-align:center">1816</h1>

<h1 style="text-align:center">James Monroe (Democratic-Republican)
vs. Rufus King (Federalist)</h1>

FlashFocus: 1816

Candidates

James Monroe & Daniel Tompkins, Democratic-Republican

Rufus King, Jr., Federalist

Issues

War. The War of 1812 had ended in early 181 with Andrew Jackson's victory over the British in New Orleans, helping what had been a political liability for the Democratic-Republicans into an asset. Federalist opposition to the war turned into a liability.

Hartford Convention. A meeting of Federalists in Hartford, Connecticut in 1814 to discuss the war with Britain was exploited by Democratic-Republicans as an act bordering on treason. With an American victory in the war, Federalist opposition was harder to understand in 1816 than it had been in 1814.

Compensation Act of 1816. Congress voted to pay Representatives and Senators salaries, instead of *per diem*. A Federalist newspaper editor in New York succeeded in making the pay of elected representatives an issue, despite the fact that Federalists had also supported the measure in Congress.

Outcome

Electoral College

Madison	183 ✓
Clinton	34

Popular voting results were not kept before 1824.

In 1814 the war with Britain looked like it would derail the election chances of the Democratic-Republicans, especially when British forces invaded Washington in August, 1814, burning half the city and forcing President James Madison and his wife Dolly to flee from the White House. But two years later, with a new peace treaty that ended the war with no concessions to Britain and a fresh victory over British forces in New Oreleans, the future of the Federalists was again in doubt. In the presidential election of 1816, the Democratic-Republicans put forward the last of the Revolutionary War generation, James Monroe, who launched the so-called Era of Good Feeling.

The Context

In August, 1814 British troops invaded Washington and burned much of the city to the ground. The war had been declared by Democratic-Republican President Madison in reaction to the impressment (forced military service) of American sailors into the British Navy during Britain's war against France.

The War of 1812 had been strongly opposed by the Federalists, whose political base was in New England and whose constituents were especially hard hit by cutting trade with England. In congressional and local elections in the autumn of 1814, Federalists dealt serious setbacks to Democratic-Republicans throughout New England and made inroads into Democratic-Republican political strongholds in the South and West.

Less than six months later, what had seemed like impending defeat for the United States had turned into what appeared to be a victory, or at least a draw. The Treaty of Ghent, signed in Belgium, ended hostilities without loss of U.S. territory. Before news of the treaty could reach New Orleans, U.S. General Andrew Jackson defeated a British invasion force outside the city, handing the United States—and the Democratic-Republicans—a clear military victory which ended the war on a positive note.

Also in December, 1814, Federalists in New England met in Connecticut at the so-called Hartford Convention. Although some radical Federalists urged that New England states should secede from the union, more moderate politicians won the day and passed a series of proposals designed to overcome what they viewed as unfair political advantage provided to the Democratic-Republicans by slaves. (Under the Constitution, each slave counted as six-tenths of a person for purposes of calculating representation in Congress, even though slaves had no political rights. In effect, one white vote in a slave state counted for more than one vote in a state without slavery.) Despite the moderate tone of the recommendations from the Federalists' Hartford Convention, the Democratic-Republicans exploited calls at the convention for secession and turned the meeting into a serious political liability for the Federalists.

The Democratic-Republicans

Buoyed by the end of the War of 1812, the Democratic-Republicans in 1816 set about identifying a candidate for the White House. President Madison had already served two terms and was not well. The leading candidate to be nominated for president was the secretary of state, James Monroe, who had also become secretary of war during the conflict with Britain. He had a sterling reputation as an administrator. But Monroe also had a disadvantage: like every president except John Adams, he was from Virginia. Some Democratic-Republican members of congress were eager to end the "Virginia Dynasty," and favored the secretary of the treasury, William H. Crawford of Georgia. In March, 1816 an anonymous invitation proposed a meeting of Democratic-Republican representatives and senators to nominate a candidate for the coming presidential election. Of the 141

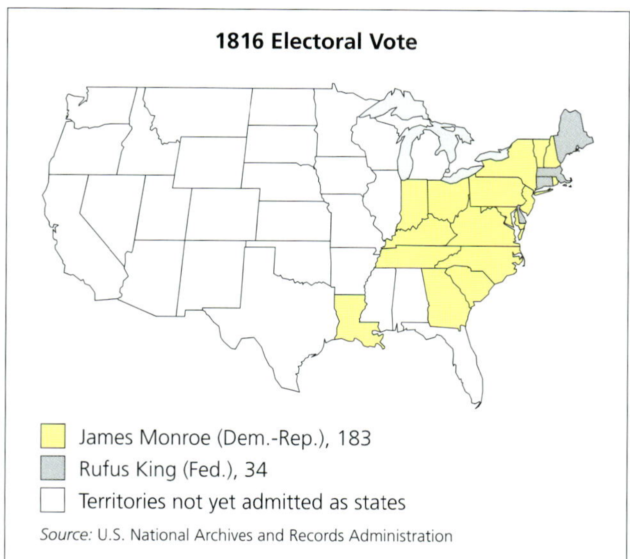

FlashFocus: James Monroe

5th President, 1817–1825

Born: April 28, 1758, Westmoreland County, Virginia

Died: July 4, 1831, New York, New York

Family: Son of Spence Monroe, a planter, and Elizabeth Jones; married Elizabeth Kortright

Education: College of William and Mary; later studied under the guidance of Thomas Jefferson

Political career: U.S. representative from Virginia 1783–86; U.S. senator from Virginia, 1790–94; governor of Virginia, 1811; minister to France and England, secretary of state, 1811–17; secretary of war, 1814–15

Monroe was something of a transitional president. Having fought in the Revolutionary War, he provided a link with that era while also establishing a new, forward-thinking tone for the nation. Personally popular, Monroe presided over the "Era of Good Feelings." He set the tone for his administration by carefully naming both Northerners and Southerners to his cabinet, and by embarking on an extended tour of the states.

During Jefferson's presidency, Monroe had helped to negotiate the Louisiana Purchase from France in 1803. As president himself, Monroe acquired Florida from Spain. The country seemed to be flexing its muscles, growing by great leaps.

Monroe was seen as a rational, balanced leader who insisted on making decisions based on the merits of any case, and leaving his personal opinions aside. This even-handedness was especially crucial, as the issues that would result in the Civil War were already simmering. In 1820, Monroe signed the Missouri Compromise, which admitted Missouri to the Union as a slave state and Maine as a free state.

During these years, many South American countries declared independence from Spain. Wanting the independence movement to succeed, Monroe established the "Monroe Doctrine" in a message to Congress in 1823. It stated the United States' position that European powers should not meddle in the affairs of the Western Hemisphere.

He died on July 4, 1831 in New York City.

Democratic-Republicans invited, only 58 accepted the invitation—all but ten of whom supported Crawford.

Recognizing that the first meeting did not adequately represent the party, a second meeting was held four days later. That session was attended by 119 Democratic-Republican members of Congress. The meeting debated a proposal by Henry Clay of Kentucky and John Taylor of New York condemning the Congressional caucus system of nominating presidential candidates. It was the first time that opposition to a proposed candidate for president had surfaced.

Despite concerns about the Virginia Dynasty, and discomfort with the role of Congressmen and senators in selecting nominees for president, Monroe won the nomination by capturing the support of both the Virginia and New York delegations, the two largest states in the union in 1816.

The Democratic-Republican candidate for vice president was Daniel Tompkins, the governor of New York since 1808, who represented a geographical balance on the ticket with Monroe from the South.

Federalists

The Federalist party was in a much more difficult situation. Their national influence had been waning for years and in 1816 the party had no clear strong candidate for the White House. The Federalists were widely viewed as a party without a program, given that there was peace both at home and abroad. Making matters worse, Democratic-Republican newspaper editors continued to remind their readers of the Hartford Convention two years earlier, which was cast in the light of near treason during the war with Britain.

In state elections for governors and state legislatures in the spring of 1816, the Federalists lost strength even in their strongholds in New England. These elections were broadly viewed as critical to the future of the Federalists, and the results were a near disaster. The Federalist majorities in the state legislatures of Massachusetts and Rhode Island were reduced; the Democratic-Republicans doubled their strength in the legislature of Connecticut, and won control in New Hampshire. In the key state of New York, the number of Federalists in the state assembly dropped from 63 to 36. Only five of New York's 27 congressmen were Federalists, and Federalist Rufus King, the likely Federalist presidential candidate, was overwhelmingly defeated for governor by Democratic-Republican Tompkins, who later ran as his party's vice presidential candidate. Defeat for the Federalists in New York gave the Democratic-Republicans control of the state legislature, and consequently the electoral votes for president later in the year.

In the end, the Federalists did not formally endorse any candidate and made no effort to mount an effective campaign.

The Issues

With the end of the War of 1812, the main issue that the Federalists were counting on to help put a candidate back into the White House had disappeared. Three other issues were raised by Federalists, but to little effect.

The Compensation Act of 1816 had given members of Congress annual salaries, instead of being paid per-day rates. The editor of the New York *Evening Post,* a Federalist, launched a press campaign against the law, which had effectively doubled the pay of federal legislators. The campaign aroused the attention of other editors and some degree of public anger, but it did not directly benefit the Federalists since many of their own members had voted for the change.

Creation of the Second Bank of the United States and the Tariff Act of 1816 might have become potent issues, but the Federalists were not agreed on these issues, and were unable to exploit them in the presidential election.

On the other hand, Federalist opposition to the War of 1812, and particularly the Hartford Convention of 1814 (p. 26), was exploited by Democratic-Republican newspapers as evidence that the Federalists could not be trusted to lead the nation.

Campaign and Outcome

There was no significant presidential campaign in 1816. Of the nineteen states, ten had popular elections for presidential electors and nine chose presidential electors in the state legislature. There was no organized opposition to the Democratic-Republicans in the southern states, or in Vermont, Ohio, or New Jersey. In Massachusetts, the reduced Federalist majority in the state legislature changed the procedure for choosing electors from a popular vote to a legislative decision, and gave the state's twenty-two votes to King of New York. King also received nine electoral votes from Connecticut and three from Delaware, for a total of 34.

The Democratic-Republican candidate, Monroe, received the balance of 183 votes.

In voting for vice president, the Democratic-Republican Tompkins of New York received 183 votes. On the Federalist side, vice presidential votes were divided among former Maryland Senator John Howard (22); former Pennsylvania Senator James Ross (5); Supreme Court Justice John Marshall (4); and Maryland Senator Robert Harper (3). The scattering of Federalist electoral votes for vice president was an indicator of how disorganized and ineffective the party had become.

More Information

▶ Ammon, Harry. *James Monroe, the Quest for National Identity.* Charlottesville: University Press of Virginia, 1990.

▶ Cunningham, Noble E. *The Presidency of James Monroe.* Lawrence: University Press of Kansas, 1996.

▶ Ernst, Robert. *Rufus King, American Federalist.* Chapel Hill: Institute of American History and Culture at Williamsburg. Published by University of North Carolina Press, 1968.

On the Web

▶ Monroe, James. "First Inaugural Address Tuesday, March 4, 1817." *Inaugural Addresses of the Presidents of the United States.* Washington, D.C.: U.S. Government Printing Office, 1989; Bartleby.com, 2001. **http://www.bartleby.com/124/pres20.html.**

▶ James Monroe Museum and Memorial Library. Links to pages about the fifth president. **http://www.mwc.edu/jmmu/.**

1820
James Monroe (Democratic-Republican)

The reelection of President James Monroe in 1820 was perhaps the most apathetic of all presidential elections. The Federalist Party did not designate a candidate to oppose the reelection of President James Monroe, and in the election only a tiny fraction of eligible voters went to the polls. Monroe captured all but one electoral vote. The election seemed to be the epitome of the "Era of Good Feelings," in which political antagonisms largely disappeared during a period of peace after 1816. In some significant ways, though, outer appearances masked regional political divisions that would become apparent in 1824.

The Context

Shortly after his decisive election to the White House in 1816, President Monroe had toured New England, the traditional home of the Federalists. A Boston newspaper, the *Columbian Sentinel,* predicted that Monroe's administration would be marked as an "Era of Good Feelings," the term that has long been used to describe Monroe's two administrations.

There was little in Monroe's first four years in office to challenge the notion of good feelings, or to offer a chance for revival of the Federalists as a national political party. Monroe himself was a living reminder of the generation that had initiated independence from Britain; he wore the familiar costume of the previous century—knee breeches with riding boots under a long black coat—a reminder of the fact that he had been active in the government since the 1790s, when he was the U.S. ambassador to France. During his first term, he had appointed a cabinet reflective of the interests of all three main regions of the country: the North and New England, represented by his secretary of state, John Quincy Adams (son of President John Adams); the South, represented by William Crawford of Georgia as secretary of the treasury; the Mid-Atlantic states, represented by Richard Rush of Pennsylvania as attorney general. For the West, Monroe tried unsuccessfully to recruit Henry Clay of Kentucky as secretary of war, but eventually settled for John C. Calhoun of South Carolina. All of his cabinet secretaries were Democratic-Republicans.

The Issues

Foreign affairs were the principal focus of Monroe's first administration. The end of the long conflict between Britain and France helped ease tensions between the United States and Britain, and a series of negotiated agreements resolved lingering disagreements over the border between the United States and Canada, demilitarization of the Great Lakes, and fishing rights off Labrador and Newfoundland. The United States acquired the territory of Florida from Spain.

FlashFocus: 1820

Candidate

James Monroe & Daniel Tompkins, Democratic-Republican

The other political party in 1820, the Federalists, did not nominate a presidential candidate.

Issues

The Missouri Compromise. Missouri Territory's application to become a state that permitted slavery touched off a debate over the future of slavery. The Missouri Compromise, largely associated with Henry Clay of Kentucky, permitted Missouri's admission as a "slave state" balanced by the admission of Maine as a non-slave state, and barred slavery in the parts of the Louisiana Purchase north of 36°30' latitude (a line roughly corresponding to Missouri's southern border). Monroe eventually signed the compromise, although publicly he disagreed with imposing conditions, such as outlawing slavery, on new states that had not been put on the original thirteen states.

Foreign affairs. The conflict between Britain and France was resolved, and Britain now turned its attention to settlement of various ongoing territorial disputes with the United States. Florida was acquired from Spain as a territory.

"One-party politics." The Federalist Party did not nominate a candidate for president, and the election of 1820 saw some of the lowest voter turnout in history.

Outcome

Electoral College

Monroe	231 ✓
John Quincy Adams	1

One elector, William Plummer of New Hampshire, cast his electoral vote for John Quincy Adams, even though he was not an official candidate. Plummer did so because he favored Adams over Monroe; he had no way of knowing that his vote prevented a unanimous choice of Monroe, preserving that distinction for George Washington.

Popular voting results were not kept until 1824.

See also: James Monroe, p. 27.

In domestic affairs, the principal issue was the looming struggle over slavery. In 1819, the territory of Missouri applied to become a state. New York Senator Rufus King, a Federalist, denounced slavery and proposed that new states, including Missouri, should be required to abolish the institution. President Monroe promised to veto any laws that might force Missouri to renounce slavery on grounds that new states should not have any requirements placed on them that were not put on the original thirteen states. The dispute over slavery in Missouri was eventually settled by the so-called Missouri Compromise, which had three parts: Missouri would be admitted as a state that allowed slavery; Maine, which had been a part of Massachusetts, would be admitted as a non-slave state, thereby maintaining the balance of slave and non-slave states; and slavery would be barred from the part of the Louisiana Purchase north of latitude 36°30" (a line roughly corresponding with the southern border of Missouri). President Monroe did not openly support the compromise, engineered largely by Sen. Henry Clay of Kentucky, but he worked behind the scenes to help persuade southern Democratic-Republicans to support it. The compromise was accepted, and served as a temporary band-aid for a problem that continued to fester and would eventually split apart the country forty years later.

Democratic-Republicans

There was never a serious challenge to Monroe as the Democratic-Republican candidate for reelection in 1820. Disputes over the Missouri Compromise, and in particular the proposal to bar slavery north of 36°30' provided the only semblance of political drama. In Monroe's home state of Virginia, the Democratic-Republicans were led by the so-called Richmond Junto, a group that firmly opposed any limitations on slavery. Virginia's Democratic-Republicans met in a caucus to endorse a presidential candidate in early February, at which time Monroe's son-in-law, George Hay, decided not to let Virginia's Democratic-Republicans know of Monroe's determination to sign the Compromise. Later, after endorsing Monroe as their candidate, members of the Richmond Junto were astounded when Monroe signed the Compromise bill with its limitation of slavery in part of the Louisiana Purchase.

The Federalists

The Federalists did not put forward a candidate for president in 1820, although the party remained a factor in congressional elections and in state legislatures, especially in New England. By the time of the presidential election in 1820, Federalists held just 27 seats in Congress, down from the 65 seats they held in 1814. The Federalist members of Congress did not hold a caucus to endorse a candidate for president in 1820.

Campaign and Outcome

The fact that only one political party, the Democratic-Republicans, actively endorsed a candidate made the election of 1820 a virtual non-event. "One party politics" is the term used by at least one historian to describe the election, which attracted a very small number of voters in states where the popular vote determined the outcome in the electoral college. (The actual number of popular votes has not been preserved. In those states where records are available, the numbers of voters participating in the choice of presidential electors were extremely

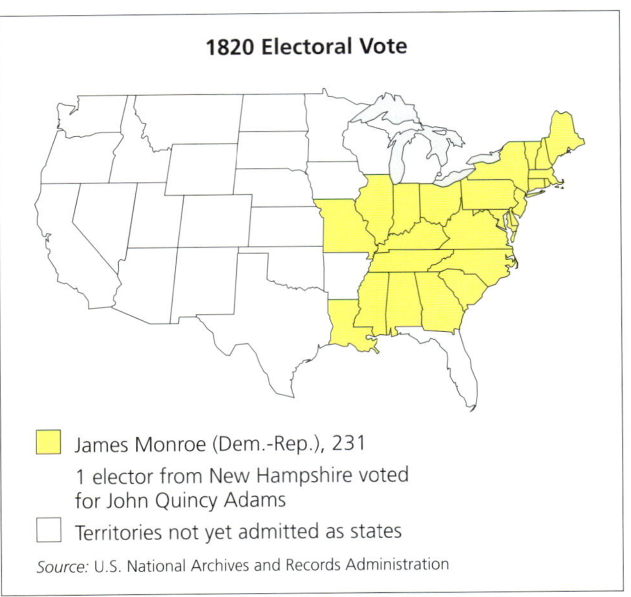

Source: U.S. National Archives and Records Administration

low—only 17 voters in the city of Richmond, Virginia, for example, and just 81 in Providence, Rhode Island.)

In states where the state legislatures chose the electors, there was considerable discontent with President Monroe and his vice president, Daniel Tompkins, the former governor of New York. In Tompkins' home state of New York, for example, more than 40 percent of the legislature opposed the Democratic-Republican ticket.

Despite opposition to Monroe by anti-slavery advocates in northern states, the president won almost unanimous support in the electoral college. The final electoral vote was 231 votes for Monroe to one vote for John Quincy Adams. That single vote was cast by William Plumer of New Hampshire. For many years, it has been a popular myth that Plumer voted for Adams simply in order to preserve for George Washington the distinction of being the only president elected unanimously. In reality, Plumer had no way of knowing how electors in other states were voting. A more likely explanation is that Plumer did not care for Monroe, and thought Adams, the son of the second president, was a more qualified candidate.

What drama existed in the election took place in the vote for vice president. Monroe's running mate Tompkins received only 218 electoral votes, thirteen fewer than Monroe. Four electors in Delaware voted for Daniel Rodney of Delaware; eight votes in Massachusetts were cast for Richard Stockton of New Jersey; and one vote in Maryland went to Robert G. Harper, a Federalist.

The other historical footnote to 1820 involves the total number of electoral votes cast. The legislature of Missouri had cast three electoral votes for Monroe and Tompkins, but there was a question of whether to count them. When the House and Senate assembled to tally the electoral votes on February 14, 1821, Missouri had not formally been admitted as a state and at least one congressman from New Hampshire protested counting Missouri's votes. At this, two Virginia delegates protested loudly. In the end, the Senate's electoral votes were counted both ways, with and without Missouri's three votes. In both cases, Monroe was reelected and was inaugurated for a second term on March 5, 1821.

More Information

- ▶ Cunningham, Noble E. *The Presidency of James Monroe.* Lawrence: The University Press of Kansas, 1996.
- ▶ Hoyt, Edwin P. *James Monroe.* Chicago: Reilly and Lee Co., 1968.
- ▶ May, Ernest R. *The Making of the Monroe Doctrine.* Cambridge: Belknap Press of Harvard University Press, 1975.

On the Web

- ▶ Monroe, James. "Second Inaugural Address, Monday, March 5, 1821." *Inaugural Addresses of the Presidents of the United States.* Washington, D.C.: U.S. Government Printing Office, 1989; Bartleby.com, 2001. **http://www.bartleby.com/ 124/pres21.html.**
- ▶ James Monroe Museum and Memorial Library. Links to pages about the fifth president. **http://www.mwc.edu/jmmu/.**
- ▶ "Era of Good Feeling." Eagleton Institute of Politics, Electronic Government Project at Rutgers University. Contains links related to the second term of James Monroe. **http://www.eagleton.rutgers.edu/e-gov/ e-politicalarchive-goodfeeling.htm.**

1824
John Quincy Adams vs. Andrew Jackson
vs. Henry Clay vs. William Crawford vs. John C. Calhoun

The election of 1824 was decided by the House of Representatives under terms of the Twelfth Amendment. All five leading contenders claimed to be Democratic-Republicans and for the first time, all the candidates came from a generation too young to have participated in the Revolutionary War. Given an apparent lack of ideological differences, the role of sectionalism—loyalty to the different sections of the country and their diverse economic interests—played a prominent role in the election.

The Context and the Candidates

During most of President James Monroe's second term (1821–25), the U.S. economy was mired in slow economic growth. Some voters blamed the policies of the Second Bank of the United States, while others blamed high tariffs for their economic difficulties. Still others believed that national politicians had strayed from the principles of republicanism that had guided the Founders in establishing the United States.

The United States had been at peace during President Monroe's second term, and international relations were not a strong issue in the election of 1824. The famous "Monroe Doctrine" of 1823, declaring that European nations should have no role in the Western Hemisphere, was not an issue in the election.

There was no single obvious candidate for the presidency in 1824. Instead, the campaign featured five ambitious men running for office, each with a unique claim to the White House. All five declared themselves to be Democratic-Republicans. There was no candidate from the rapidly fading Federalist party, and the Whig Party had not yet emerged.

John Quincy Adams of Massachusetts had been secretary of state under President Monroe, and could claim many years of diplomatic experience; he was also the son of the second president, John Adams. He had begun government service as a teenager, while his father represented the United States in France, and he later filled a long string of diplomatic posts in Europe before becoming secretary of state under Monroe. Although his résumé was impressive, Adams' personality was far from that of a typical office-seeker; he was generally reserved and formal, the opposite of a genial, friendly politician. In effect, Adams' candidacy for president was based on his extensive experience as a successful diplomat.

Andrew Jackson of Tennessee was a hero of the War of 1812, in which he had successfully defended New Orleans from British attack in the last days of the war. He later gained fame as a military leader who subdued Native American tribes, and as the man who helped acquire Florida by invading the territory and establishing temporary bases before Spain ceded the area to the United States. Jackson had no experience in office, although his friends and political supporters helped arrange his election as a senator from Tennessee in 1823. Throughout the campaign Jackson avoided taking stands on most specific issues. He was not initially regarded as a likely candidate.

Henry Clay of Kentucky was a prominent member of the House of Representatives and author of the Missouri Compromise of 1820 that admitted Missouri and Maine as states, and barred slavery north of 36°30' latitude (see p. 29). Unlike Adams, Clay had a magnetic personality. He had been elected Speaker of the House of Representatives in his first term, beginning in 1811. He was also strongly associated with the "American System," policies designed to encourage economic expansion, especially in the West.

John C. Calhoun of South Carolina, President Monroe's secretary of war, had been associated with the "hawks" who favored the War of 1812 against Britain. Like Clay, he favored government policies designed to help the national economy grow. It was not until later that Calhoun became closely associated with protecting slavery and a position of promoting the rights of states over the rights of the federal government.

William Crawford of Georgia had been secretary of war under Monroe and later secretary of the treasury. In the midst of the election, Crawford suffered a stroke, from which he never fully recovered and which effectively took him out of the running.

The Issues

In the absence of a unifying foreign conflict, the issues in the 1824 presidential election were related to the sluggish economy and different ideas put forward to stimulate growth. Economic solutions took on a sectional flavor in 1824, with politicians from different regions—notably the Northeast, the South and the West—putting forth differing programs and solutions based on regional economic interests.

The most clear-cut proposal was the "American System" advocated by Clay. This system comprised protective tariffs to help U.S. producers compete effectively with foreign competitors, federal financing of internal improvements, like highways, to encourage settlement and expansion in western territories, and continuation of a national bank that would help finance government projects and establish some central control over the currency.

Protective tariffs in particular emphasized regional differences. In New England and the Middle Atlantic states, tariffs helped protect young industries from competition from Britain, while in the largely agricultural southern states high tariffs represented higher prices for imports with no obvious benefits for the local economy.

The tug-of-war between the relative power and influence of state governments versus the federal government—the "states' rights" issue—also began to emerge in 1824; the issue of slavery, dealt with in the Compromise of 1820, continued to divide the northern states from the southern.

The Campaign and Outcome

The real centerpiece of the 1824 election was the personal ambition of the leading candidates, and their efforts—and the efforts of their supporters—to maneuver their way into the White House. It was recognized early on that the election

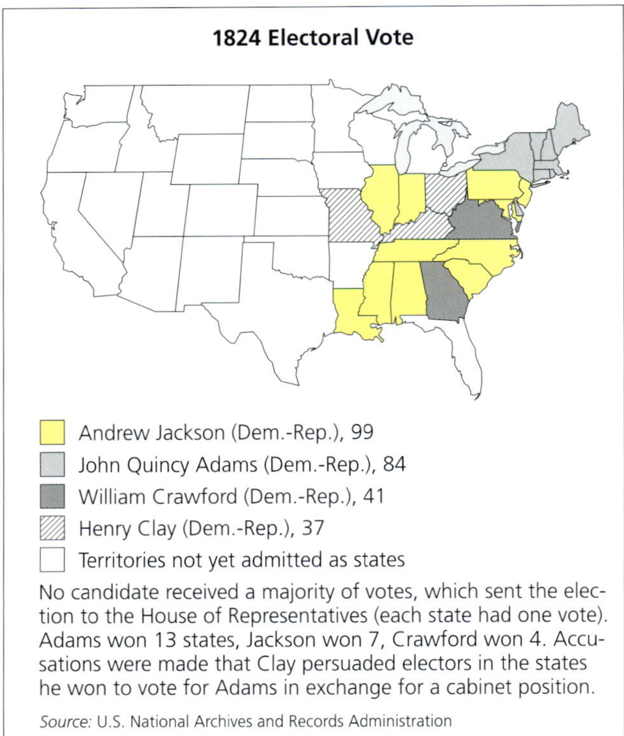

No candidate received a majority of votes, which sent the election to the House of Representatives (each state had one vote). Adams won 13 states, Jackson won 7, Crawford won 4. Accusations were made that Clay persuaded electors in the states he won to vote for Adams in exchange for a cabinet position.

Source: U.S. National Archives and Records Administration

would be likely to be decided by the House of Representatives under terms of the Twelfth Amendment, adopted in 1804 in reaction to the 1800 presidential contest between Thomas Jefferson and his nominal vice presidential running mate, Aaron Burr (see p. 14).

Campaigning began early. In December, 1821, South Carolina's legislators met in a caucus and nominated John C. Calhoun as their preference for the Democratic-Republican candidate. (In fact, there would not be a candidate from any other party, so party designation was largely meaningless in 1824.) Seven months later, a caucus in the Tennessee legislature nominated Andrew Jackson. In November 1822 Missouri's legislative caucus nominated Clay, and Kentucky, Ohio, and Louisiana soon added their support. Partisans of Adams in Maine put forward his name in January, 1823, followed by Massachusetts. The last name entered into the race was Crawford. In February, 1824, New York Representative Martin Van Buren organized a caucus of Democratic-Republican members of Congress with the intention of naming the party's candidate for the White House. Only 68 members of Congress attended the caucus (out of 261 members), and they nominated Crawford. His nomination was effectively cut short in late 1823 when he suffered a stroke from which he recovered slowly and only partially.

The strategies of the five candidates were quite different:

Adams took the public position that the country should request his services, rather than expecting him to request popular support. Although he did not campaign for office, he tried

unsuccessfully to persuade President Monroe to nominate his chief rivals, Jackson, Calhoun, and Clay, for foreign diplomatic posts, which would have removed them from the scene.

Jackson also professed lack of interest in becoming president, although he conceded that he would accept the position if it were offered. But his supporters realized that it was precisely Jackson's lack of political experience that most appealed to voters who distrusted power and suspected political corruption among the other more experienced candidates. The fact that Jackson had never been to Europe and was not part of the political scene in Washington made him seem untainted and more purely "American." During the campaign, Jackson took care not to voice strong positions on the main issues, such as Clay's American System, slavery, or states rights.

Calhoun was the first candidate to recognize that he stood no chance of winning the presidency after he was soundly beaten in a state convention of Democratic-Republicans in March, 1824. He withdrew from the race and announced that he would happily serve as vice president.

Crawford's campaign was rendered largely ineffective by his stroke. Although he was the early starter, he did not wage an effective campaign.

Clay turned out to be the weakest candidate, which was surprising in light of his skill as a politician in Washington. He was highly critical of Monroe's foreign policy, which offended Adams, the secretary of state under Monroe. Clay also attacked Jackson, his fellow Westerner and rival for support from western Congressmen. The Kentuckian also lost support in the South, which did not endorse his American System of economic development but instead was beginning to support the idea of a weaker federal system and stronger rights for the states.

Presidential voting in 1824 did not take place on one day, but was spread over a period of weeks. In six states (Vermont, New York, South Carolina, Louisiana, Delaware, and Georgia), the state legislators chose members of the electoral college. In five other states, electors were chosen by voters on the basis of congressional districts. In the thirteen remaining states, presidential electors were chosen on a statewide basis. The election of 1824 was also the first time that popular vote totals were widely recorded.

At the end of voting by all eighteen states, in December, 1824, it was clear that no candidate had captured a majority of the electoral college. The electoral college totals were:

Jackson	99
Adams	84
Crawford	41
Clay	37

Under the Twelfth Amendment, the election then shifted to the House of Representatives, where each state had one vote. The result was a kind of second presidential campaign that ran from December, 1824 to March, 1825. Clay, whose fourth place finish in the electoral college made him ineligible for the House vote, plunged into a campaign to elect Adams, rather

The presidential contest is presented as a race. Andrew Jackson, shown wearing a sword, is third, just behind John Quincy Adams and William Crawford, while the fourth man in the contest, Henry Clay, is depicted as having given up and putting his right hand on his head. In fact, Jackson won the most popular votes and electoral votes, but eventually lost in the House of Representatives.

than Jackson. The deadline for a vote in the House of Representatives was March 4, 1825; after that, the Twelfth Amendment provided that the vice president would assume the presidency. Calhoun had easily won enough electoral votes to become vice president and stood to benefit if the House failed to select a president.

The House voted on February 9, proceeding from north to south. Adams won the 13 states he needed to be elected. Adams received six votes from the New England states, plus New York, Maryland (where Adams had defeated Jackson in the popular vote), Kentucky, Missouri, Louisiana, Ohio, and Illinois (thanks at least in part to the efforts of Clay). Jackson won seven states. Crawford received four votes.

Although the election had been decided according to the Constitution, a subsequent act by Adams tainted the outcome and raised the charge of a "corrupt bargain." After he had been elected president, Adams nominated Clay to become secretary of state and Clay accepted, suggesting to people at the time that there had been a political deal struck for Clay's support in Congress.

Although Adams and Jackson had admired one another at the beginning of the campaign, after Adams gained the presidency by means of the Twelfth Amendment they soon became bitter political enemies. The campaign of 1828 was already in motion.

More Information

▶ Campbell, James E. *The American Campaign: U.S. Presidential Campaigns and the National Vote.* College Station: Texas A&M University Press, 2000.

▶ Glennon, Michael J. *When No Majority Rules: The Electoral College and Presidential Succession.* Washington, DC: Congressional Quarterly, Inc, 1992.

▶ *Historical Review of Presidential Candidates from 1788 to 1968.* Washington: Congressional Quarterly, Inc., 1969.

▶ Remini, Robert V. *John Quincy Adams.* New York: Times Books, 2002.

▶ Schleslinger, Arthur M., Jr., ed. *History of American Presidential Elections, 1789–1968.* New York: Chelsea House, 1985.

Periodicals

▶ Kolodny, Robin. "The Several Elections of 1824." *Congress and the Presidency,* Fall 1996, page 139.

▶ Gewirtz, Paul. "Jackson's Hole." *The New Republic,* July 27, 1992, p. 40.

On the Web

▶ Adams, John Quincy. "Inaugural Address, Friday, March 4, 1825." *Inaugural Addresses of the Presidents of the United States.* Washington, D.C.: U.S. Government Printing Office, 1989; Bartleby.com, 2001. **http://www.bartleby.com/124/pres22.html.**

▶ *The Adams Papers,* Massachusetts Historical Society. Resources related to the family of John Adams the second president, and his son, John Quincy Adams, the sixth president, including articles, timeline and manuscript reproductions. **http://www.masshist.org/adams_editorial/.**

1828
Andrew Jackson (Democrat)
vs. John Quincy Adams (National Republican)

The battle lines for 1828 were drawn when John Quincy Adams was elected president in the House of Representatives four years earlier, despite the fact that Andrew Jackson had received a third more popular votes than Adams and had won more electoral votes. But while the 1824 election was an anomaly—it was the first time the presidential election was thrown into the House of Representatives under the Twelfth Amendment—the election of 1828 set a precedent for presidential elections for years afterward, making the race for the presidency in part a popularity contest, complete with campaign managers, battles in the press and new lows in personal attacks on the candidates. But while Jackson took an active role in seeking office, Adams refused to make any concessions to electoral politics and as a result became the second Adams limited to one term in the White House (the first was his father John Adams, who lost his bid for a second term to Thomas Jefferson in 1800; see p. 12).

In 1828, political ideology was far from only thing dividing the two candidates. Jackson and Adams could hardly have been more different in their backgrounds, their personalities and their political styles. Compared to earlier presidential contests which had been largely refined contests between similar candidates, the election of 1828 looked much more like the rough-and-tumble politics that would be taken for granted in the twenty-first century.

The Context

The 1828 election was in some respects a continuation of the 1824 election, in which Jackson had won 42 percent of the popular vote and 99 electoral college votes, against 31.9 percent of the popular vote and 84 electoral college votes for Adams. But since Jackson had not won a majority of the 261 electoral votes, the election was thrown into the House of Representatives, where each state had one vote under the Twelfth Amendment. There, Jackson's rival, Henry Clay of Kentucky, had helped Adams win the 13 votes needed for victory. Jackson was furious, and the campaign of 1828 began almost immediately.

Shortly after taking office in 1825, Adams also helped define the next election by laying down an ambitious program for the government in his Annual Message to Congress (which in later years would be named the State of the Union address). Adams proposed, among other things, establishing a new Department of the Interior to govern territories not yet states, a program of building roads and canals to improve transportation, a national bankruptcy law, a national university and new initiatives in geographical and scientific projects, such as a national observatory. In proposing these unprecedented expansions of activity by the federal government, Adams challenged the traditional small-government prejudices of his own party, the Democratic-Republicans. In the South especially, Adams' proposals ran counter to a rising suspicion of growing power in Washington at the expense of state controls. Adams' ambitious proposals quickly led Jeffersonian Democratic-Republicans to conclude that they needed a different leader to protect their vision of limited central government.

The Candidates

In many respects, Adams' proposals were entirely in line with his background. Although his father John Adams (see p. 10) was a key leader in the American revolution, in some respects Adams represented a form of American aristocracy. He had been educated at Harvard University and spent many years as an American diplomat in Europe, starting as a teenager when his father was the U.S. minister to France. He had served as secretary of state under President James Monroe, and in that role had succeeded in acquiring Florida from Spain, extending the U.S. border to the Pacific Ocean, and ending Spain's claims to Oregon Territory. He had also played a major role in formulating the Monroe Doctrine, in which the United States warned European powers against attempting to colonize the Western Hemisphere. Personally, Adams was highly reserved and often ill at ease socially. He once described himself as "reserved, cold, austere and forbidding."

Jackson could hardly have been more different. He had been born in a log cabin in a frontier area near the border of North and South Carolina, the son of a poor farmer from Ireland who died two weeks before Jackson was born. He volunteered to fight in the revolutionary war at age thirteen. He was well known as the Army general who successfully defended New Orleans from a British attack in 1814, giving the U.S. a military victory that ended the inconclusive War of 1812 (a peace treaty had been negotiated days before the battle of New Orleans by a diplomatic team led by John Quincy Adams, but word had not yet reached the combatants). Later, he developed a reputation as an Indian fighter and forceful advocate for removal of Native Americans to make room for European settlers. He had also drawn criticism by some (but praise by others) for a raid on Spain's Florida territory in 1818 chasing runaway slaves and native Americans, during which he oversaw the execution of several Indian leaders and two British citizens. Amidst calls for punishing him for his actions, Jackson had found an ally in Secretary of State Adams.

In addition to his better known military exploits, Jackson had also studied law and was Tennessee's first congressman, as well as judge on the state's supreme court. He was a successful cotton planter and land speculator who owned more than 100 slaves. In 1823, his political allies had helped elect him to the Senate.

The Issues

The election of 1828 was not a clear-cut contest between competing political philosophies or positions on specific issues. Adams and Jackson had admired one another previous to the 1824 election. Nevertheless, by 1828 there were issues that separated them.

The role of the federal government had long been a dividing line in American politics. Although Adams was a

Democratic-Republican, the party associated with a smaller, weaker central government, his proposals for the federal government to take a role in such diverse areas as scientific exploration and building canals and roads reminded some Americans of the old Federalist party. In fact, Adams' proposals were more in line with the American System advocated by Henry Clay of Kentucky, which envisioned government participation in developing Western states by promoting roads and canals, as well as protective tariffs to protect American industry against foreign competition. For his part, Jackson was far more reserved in expanding federal influence at the expense of state government power, a position closer to the traditional limited-government position of the Democratic-Republicans. In time, these differences would emerge as the issue of states' rights versus a strong central government.

The subject of protective tariffs also rose. In general, manufacturing interests in the North favored tariffs (taxes on imports) which helped protect them from foreign competition by making imports more expensive; agricultural interests in the South opposed high tariffs, viewing them as subsidies for other business interests. In Congress, Jackson supporters from the North supported a new tariff act in 1828, while his southern supporters opposed it. But Adams did not raise the tariff issue in the campaign; had he done so, it might have split Jackson's support between North and South.

Slavery was also an issue dividing Adams and Jackson. Although slavery was not as important in 1828 as it would be later, Jackson himself was a slaveholder and Adams was not. The expansion of slavery into new states had been an issue in 1820, when Missouri was admitted as a state that allowed slavery and Maine was admitted as a state that did not. Southern supporters of slavery were aware in 1828 that many anti-slavery Northerners were supporters of Adams.

For the first time, ethnic politics made an appearance in 1828. Jackson's father had emigrated to the United States from Northern Ireland; he was the first candidate whose ancestors were not from England. Moreover, the Jackson campaign in 1828 openly appealed to non-English immigrants (thousands of campaign fliers were printed in German, for example). Adams' reticent personality prevented his participation in asking for votes in any language. For instance, he refused an invitation to speak at the opening of a canal in a German-speaking region of Pennsylvania, a golden opportunity where he could have taken advantage of his fluency in the German language. Instead, Adams allowed himself to be portrayed as representing the traditional New England of the Puritans and propriety, the established political order as opposed to the rising number of non-English immigrants already evident by 1828.

In western New York state in 1826, a man named William Morgan had disappeared after he threatened to reveal details about Freemasonry, a social organization that had included many prominent people including George Washington. A trial of men accused in Morgan's disappearance, and likely murder, ended in acquittal, and later it was revealed that some jurors in the trial were Masons. This incident was seized upon by some editors who perceived a Masonic plot, and the Anti-Masons blossomed into a political party whose influence might have threatened the candidacy of Jackson, who himself was a Mason.

The Campaign

In 1828, the nature of the campaign itself, rather than the qualifications of the candidates or their positions on issues,

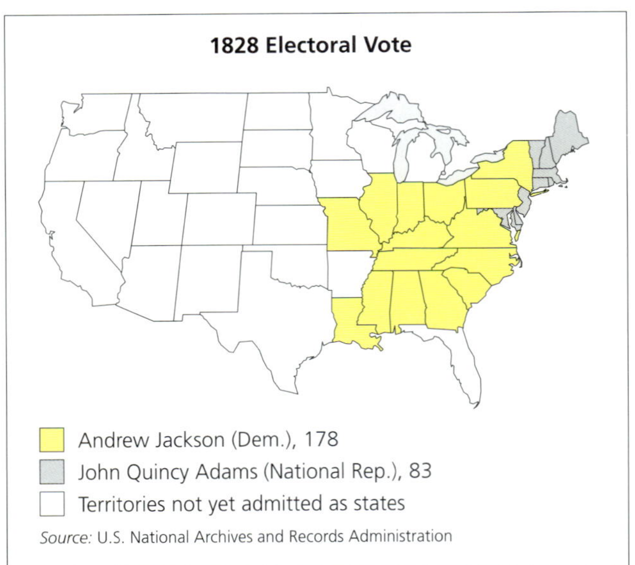

Source: U.S. National Archives and Records Administration

assumed a much greater importance than in previous contests. All but two states (Delaware and South Carolina) selected presidential electors by popular vote, which made an enormous difference in the way the president was chosen. Moreover, earlier restrictions on eligibility to vote (often based on owning a minimum amount of property) were relaxed in most states, making a record number of men eligible to vote, and raising popular interest in the campaign.

The process of choosing candidates also changed in 1828. Both Adams and Jackson were members of the Democratic-Republican party, as the Federalists had finally faded entirely. Consequently, the supporters of Adams called themselves National Republicans, while Jackson's supporters started calling themselves the Democratic Party. The previous role of Congressmen in determining a party's candidate for the presidency in a caucus was replaced by party meetings at the state level, marking the real emergence of political parties independent of congressional delegations.

Neither candidate actively campaigned for office, but Jackson took a participatory role, meeting with advisors and making suggestions. Adams took a hands-off attitude entirely. From early in his administration, Adams left in place appointees that could have been replaced by people more likely to work for his reelection. It was just one of many examples of how Adams passed up opportunities to use the power of the incumbency to promote his candidacy. He usually declined invitations to make speeches as president, even on occasions (such as the sixtieth anniversary of the Battle of Bunker Hill) where the appearance of the president would have been natural and welcome.

In place of active participation by the candidates, party organizers came into their own in 1828 when the popular vote was more important than ever in determining the next president. Skilled organizers arranged popular rallies and parades and used campaign paraphernalia such as buttons, banners and songs to generate enthusiasm.

Newspapers played a key role in the campaign, both in their news coverage and in their editorials. Often the campaigning was far from clean. In Ohio, for example, editor Charles Hammond accused Jackson of being the son of a prostitute who had married a mulatto (a person of mixed race). Jackson's relationship with his wife Rachel was a special target; they had been married in the mistaken belief that Rachel's first husband had been granted a divorce after abandoning her. When they realized their error, after the divorce was actually granted, they quickly were remarried, but this did not stop Jackson's opponents from attacking Jackson as an adulterer and a "home breaker."

Similar false charges were leveled against Adams and his wife, claiming they had entered into marital relations before they had been married and suggesting that Mrs. Adams herself was the child of an unmarried couple.

Since mud-slinging was the order of the day in 1828, the purchase by Adams of a pool table and a chessboard was turned into accusations by Jackson supporters that the president had installed "gambling devices" in the White House. Another report suggested that Adams had procured the sexual favors of a young girl in his household for the Czar while Adams was serving as the U.S. minister to Russia.

In general, the campaign efforts of Jackson supporters were more elaborate and more successful than those launched on behalf of Adams.

The Outcome

Unlike 1824, when Jackson was denied the White House even though he initially had the largest number of both popular and electoral votes, in 1828 the outcome was not ambiguous: in the popular vote, Jackson outpolled Adams 647,286 votes (56 percent) to 508,064 (44 percent). Voter turnout was about twice as great as it had been in 1824, and four times as great as in 1820.

Adams won the electoral votes of Connecticut, Delaware, Massachusetts, New Hampshire, New Jersey, Rhode Island; and split the electoral votes of Vermont, Maine, Maryland, and New York.

Jackson won Alabama, Georgia, Illinois, Indiana, Kentucky, Louisiana, Mississippi, Missouri, North Carolina, Ohio, Pennsylvania, South Carolina, Tennessee, and Virginia, while sharing votes in Vermont, Maine, Maryland, and New York.

The final electoral vote was 178 for Jackson, 83 for Adams. Two states in particular were crucial in Jackson's victory. In Pennsylvania, he received all 28 electoral votes in a state that might have gone to Adams had he made a stronger campaign effort. New York gave 20 electoral votes to Jackson and 16 to Adams. Had Adams won Pennsylvania and captured all of New York's electoral votes, he would have been reelected with 131 electoral votes to 130 for Jackson. Jackson's success in New York was largely due to the efforts of Senator Martin Van Buren, a future vice president during Jackson's second term and president from 1837–41 (see p. 45).

More Information

- Cole, Donald B. *The Presidency of Andrew Jackson.* Lawrence: University Press of Kansas, 1993.
- Hargreaves, Mary W. M. *The Presidency of John Quincy Adams.* Lawrence: University Press of Kansas. 1985.
- Kroll, Steven. *John Quincy Adams: Letters from a Southern Planter's Son.* New York: Winslow Press, 2001.
- Latner, Richard B. *The Presidency of Andrew Jackson: White House Politics, 1829–1837.* Athens: University of Georgia Press, 1979.
- Remini, Robert V. *Andrew Jackson.* Baltimore: Johns Hopkins University Press, 1998.
- Watson, Harry L. *Liberty and Power: The Politics of Jacksonian America.* New York: Hill and Wang, 1990.

On the Web

- Jackson, Andrew. "First Inaugural Address, Wednesday, March 4, 1829." *Inaugural Addresses of the Presidents of the United States.* Washington, D.C.: U.S. Government Printing Office, 1989; Bartleby.com, 2001. **http://www.bartleby.com/124/pres23.html.**
- "Rachael and Andrew Jackson: A Love Story." Nashville Public Television. Links to a variety of articles about Andrew Jackson and his wife, including the presidential campaign of 1828. **http://www.wnpt.net/rachel/index.html.**

1832
Andrew Jackson (Democrat)
vs. Henry Clay (National Republican)

President Andrew Jackson's first term in office following his clear victory over John Quincy Adams had given him an opportunity to enact significant changes in national policy. His administration was marked by further moves to force native Americans to relocate west of the Mississippi, to make room for European settlers. Unlike Adams, his predecessor, Jackson had freely used his powers to appoint sympathizers to political office and to pursue the policies he favored. He had filled his cabinet with politicians representative of the political factions and regions that had supported him, including the West, New York State, and the South (represented by Vice President John C. Calhoun). It was a difficult coalition to hold together, especially after Calhoun resigned from office due in part to his refusal to support high tariffs. In April 1831 Jackson reorganized his cabinet, and in the process eliminated all its original members (including all members of the Southern faction).

The Candidates

When he was elected to his first term as president in 1828, Jackson had represented the "common man" in contrast to Adams who symbolized the more established upper class of the Northeast. Jackson had been born in a log cabin, the son of a Scotch-Irish father who had immigrated from Northern Ireland. Jackson's exploits as a military leader against native Americans made him a hero among the European settlers who continued to migrate to the United States in search of farmland on the western frontier.

Henry Clay, Jackson's strongest opponent, was also a man of the West, having represented Kentucky in the Senate or House of Representatives off and on since 1803. Clay's name was most strongly associated with the American System of government funding for roads and canals. Clay had run last in a field of four candidates in 1824, and had caused controversy over a "corrupt bargain" when he shifted his support to John Quincy Adams over Andrew Jackson when that election was decided in the House of Representatives, then accepted an appointment as Adams' secretary of state.

After Adams' defeat in 1828, Clay had emerged as the new leader of the National Republicans, the party that had unsuccessfully backed Adams. Clay's support for public works projects had won him many friends, not just in the West but also in the East. He was a strong supporter of the Second National Bank, which could help finance development projects on a national, rather than a state, basis, and in turn the leadership of the Second National Bank actively backed Clay in the campaign of 1832.

In New York state, a movement called the Anti-Mason Party had arisen during Jackson's first term and it played a role in the election of 1832. It began with the mysterious disappearance of a man named Captain William Morgan in 1826;

1832 Electoral Vote

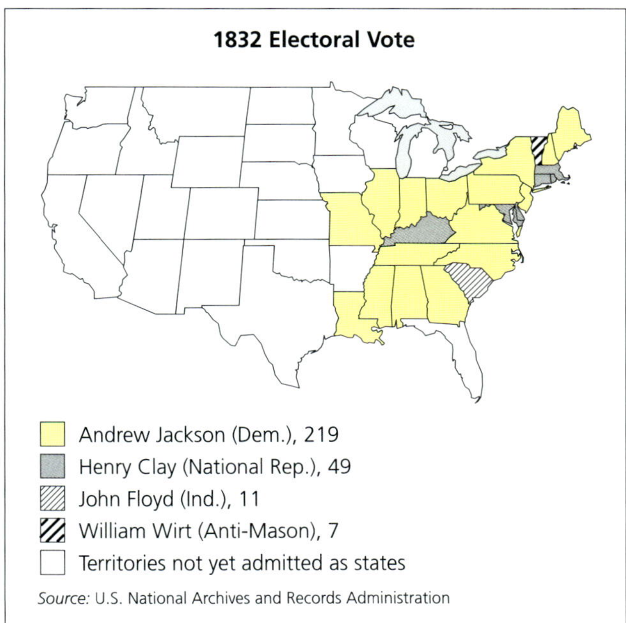

Source: U.S. National Archives and Records Administration

Candidate for President, 1824, 1832, 1844

Born: April 12, 1777, Hanover County, Virginia
Died: June 29, 1852, Washington, D.C.
Education: Little formal education; private law studies; admitted to the bar in 1797
Political career: U.S. representative from Kentucky, 1811–20, 1823–25; secretary of state, 1825–29; U.S. senator from Kentucky, 1831–42, 1849–52

Henry Clay was a perennial presidential candidate and one of the best known politicians for a period of nearly forty years. He was perhaps the most prominent politician who never managed to grab the ultimate prize of the presidency, despite running for the office in 1824, 1832 and 1844.

Clay was directly involved in shaping government policy on most major issues during his career, starting with his advocacy of war with Britain in 1812. Two issues in particular defined Clay's role in history: slavery and development of the nation's infrastructure, such as canals and roads.

Clay formulated and promoted the "American System" program of government support for business, including government financing for improved harbors and new canals, and high tariffs to help domestic manufacturers compete more effectively with foreign goods.

On the issue of slavery—and specifically whether slavery should be permitted in new territories that had not yet become states—Clay authored two key compromises: the Missouri Compromise (1820), and the Compromise of 1850. Both measures temporarily helped balance slave states and non-slave states, but did not solve an issue that eventually led to the Civil War in 1861. Clay said he despised slavery and urged gradual emancipation, even though he himself owned as many as 60 slaves at a time on his Kentucky estate.

Clay was a leader in the Democratic-Republican Party until Andrew Jackson was elected president in 1828, after which Clay helped organize the Whig party in opposition to Jackson's Democrats. He ran for the presidency as a Democrat in 1824, as an anti-Jackson candidate in 1832, and as a Whig in 1844. He tried, but failed, to obtain the Whig nomination in 1848.

Clay died in Washington in 1852, still dreaming of becoming president.

he disappeared shortly after he threatened to reveal the secrets of the Freemasons, a secretive fraternal and social organization that counted many leading politicians, including George Washington, among its members. A newspaper editor, Thurlow Weed, vowed to unveil other members of the Masons and their practices. After the 1828 election, the Anti-Mason movement gained popularity in northern New York State, as well as in Vermont, Massachusetts, Rhode Island, Ohio, and Michigan. The Anti-Masons claimed that special privileges for Masons were negotiated in secret meetings and then carried out by Masons who were in office. Among other Masons holding public office were Andrew Jackson and Henry Clay.

In 1830, Anti-Masons met in Philadelphia to choose a presidential candidate to run against Jackson. The party could not agree on a single man, and waited another year until it nominated General William Wirt, a lawyer and artillery captain in the War of 1812 who had served as attorney general from 1817–1829. His nomination later proved critical in the general election by dividing the anti-Jackson votes between himself and Clay.

The Issues

The principal issue of 1832 was the Second National Bank of the United States. The bank had received a federal charter (license to operate) in 1816; it was scheduled to expire in 1836. The national bank was a unique mixture of public and private interests. The bank depended on the federal government for its authority to operate, and it served as the federal government's banker, but it also had private investors who made profits from its activities, such as issuing currency and making loans.

Henry Clay was a strong proponent of the bank, which he viewed as useful in implementing the "American System," his program promoting federal involvement in infrastructure development, especially in building roads and canals that would provide easier access to eastern markets for farmers in the western states. Clay thought that the involvement of the federal government was necessary, since individual states might not be able to afford such projects; there could also be a lack of interest in projects whose main beneficiaries might live in another state.

Jackson, on the other hand, believed the federal government's activities should be limited to narrow boundaries, such as national defense. There was nothing in the Constitution mentioning establishment of a bank, or even of having the federal government actively participate in economic development. Jackson's belief in a more limited role for the federal government reflected the much older dispute between Thomas Jefferson and Alexander Hamilton in the 1790s, when Jefferson championed the philosophy of limiting powers for the central government as a means of preventing the possible rise of a tyranny. For Jackson, like Jefferson before him, keeping power within the states was the best guarantee that the federal government would not spin out of control.

In 1832, it was Clay and his National Republicans who brought the issue of the Second National Bank to the forefront. The bank's charter was not scheduled to expire until 1836, and there was no pressing need to consider the question of renewing it until then. For Clay, however, it was a convenient symbol of the role the federal government could play in economic development.

The Second National Bank controversy almost overshadowed a dispute between South Carolina and the federal government over imposing high federal tariffs. Manufacturing interests in the North favored high tariffs (taxes on imports) which raised the cost of imports and made it easier for American companies to compete with foreign companies, and especially with the British. In the South, the tariffs were viewed simply as raising the price of imported goods without helping any native industries. Consequently, the legislature of South Carolina defiantly declared that it had the right to "nullify," or cancel, the tariffs and not collect them at South Carolina ports.

The Campaign

In May, 1830, Jackson had vetoed a law that provided federal funds to build a road in Kentucky. Partly in response to the veto, conventions of National Republicans in Kentucky, Delaware, and Connecticut that year nominated Clay to run for president two years later. A meeting in New York in December 1830 called for a national convention of the party to take place in Baltimore in December, 1831. There, 156 delegates from eighteen states and the District of Columbia gathered to consider endorsing individual states' nomination of Clay. The delegates voted unanimously to endorse Clay's nomination for president, and also nominated John Sergeant of Pennsylvania for vice president. Although the convention did not nominate Clay in the strictest sense—it was ratifying his nomination by separate state gatherings earlier—it was nevertheless a precedent for the role of national political conventions in nominating presidential candidates.

Neither Clay nor Sergeant attended the convention, in keeping with the practice by which candidates stayed away from active campaigning in presidential elections. Later, however, Clay sent an acceptance speech to the convention in which he attacked Jackson's opposition to the American System and accused the president of misuse of power.

Jackson's nomination for a second term was never in doubt. In October, 1830, members of the Pennsylvania legislature loyal to Jackson put his name forward as their nominee for reelection, followed by supporters in New York, New Hampshire, and Alabama. At the time, that was all that was required to nominate a candidate for the presidency. But following the lead of the National Republicans and the Anti-Masons, Jackson called for a national convention of his party as well, largely to nominate a vice presidential candidate. At the Democratic convention in May, 1832, the party adopted a rule that required two-thirds of the delegates to agree on a vice presidential nominee, with each state having as many delegates as it had members of the Electoral College. The vice presidential nominee was Martin Van Buren (see p. 45) of New York who had been instrumental in Jackson's election in 1828 and had served both in his cabinet and later as U.S. ambassador to Britain.

In the campaign, Jackson started with a strong advantage. His winning coalition in 1828 was largely intact, except for Calhoun, and Jackson was able to take advantage of a well-organized group of newspaper editors who supported his candidacy. Federal officials appointed by Jackson joined enthusiastically in the election, organizing parades, meetings, and picnics to build popular excitement for the election.

Henry Clay was hampered by the participation of a second anti-Jackson party, the Anti-Masons, whose influence was concentrated in New York, Pennsylvania, and New England. Clay himself was a Mason and refused to denounce the organization, which prevented him from gaining support from a significant portion of those opposed to Jackson.

Clay received active support, including money, from the Second National Bank, which he supported. The bank paid to distribute Clay's speeches, funded newspapers supportive of Clay, and provided coins to distribute as bribes on election day. On the other side, Jackson's supporters also turned the national bank into their own issue, characterizing the institution as a "monster."

The 1832 presidential campaign, unlike the previous election of 1828, included relatively few personal attacks on the candidates. The Democrats focused attention on an issue that had been raised by the National Republicans, the national bank, while the National Republicans emphasized the American System of internal improvements and protective tariffs.

The Outcome

Jackson's reelection was aided greatly by the presence of not one, but two opposing sides, the National Republicans of Clay and the Anti-Masonic Party of Wirt, as well as a southern faction loyal to John C. Calhoun. In some states, Clay's National Republicans traded support with the Anti-Masonic Party, but Clay's membership in the Masons made it impossible for him to capture the enthusiastic support of the Anti-Masons in the key state of New York. In Pennsylvania, another important state in terms of electoral votes, the National Republicans agreed to give up their support for Clay and to back Wirt of the Anti-Masons, but the political agreement was only partial and many National Republicans, especially those with their own ties to the Masons, refused to support the Anti-Masons. In some southern states, Jackson's vice presidential candidate, Martin Van Buren of New York, was highly unpopular, and some Jackson backers shifted their support on the vice presidential side to Philip Barbour, a federal judge, who in turn urged them to back Van Buren.

The election of 1832 actually took place over a period of several months, starting with state elections in August in Kentucky and in October in Pennsylvania; in both states, the National Republican candidate for governor lost, which did not bode well for their presidential candidate.

Eventually, Jackson won a solid victory, winning sixteen states out of twenty-four, good for 219 electoral votes against 49 electoral votes for Clay. Wirt, the Anti-Mason candidate, won seven electoral votes (in Vermont), and a fourth candidate, Governor John Floyd of Virginia (an ally of John C. Calhoun) won eleven electoral votes from South Carolina. In the popular vote, Jackson won 701,780, or 54.2 percent, against 484,205, or 37.4 percent, for Clay.

The share of the popular vote for Jackson was about the same as it had been in 1824. His strength lay in New York (aided, in part, by having Van Buren as a running mate) and Pennsylvania, as well as in the southern states (85 percent of the popular vote in North Carolina, for example). His reputation as an "Indian fighter" also made him popular in Ohio and Indiana.

Clay's strength was concentrated in New England (Connecticut, Rhode Island, and Massachusetts), but was not enough to carry Vermont (which went to the Anti-Mason candidate, Wirt), or Maine and New Hampshire, won by Jackson.

More Information

▶ Baxter, Maurice G. *Henry Clay and the American System.* Lexington: University Press of Kentucky, 1995.

▶ Burstein, Andrew. *The Passions of Andrew Jackson.* New York: Alfred A. Knopf. Distributed by Random House, 2003.

▶ Cole, Donald B. *Martin Van Buren and the American Political System.* Princeton, NJ: Princeton University Press, 1984.

▶ Eaton, Clement. *Henry Clay and the Art of American Politics.* Boston: Little, Brown, 1957.

▶ Gatell, Frank O. *Essays on Jacksonian America.* New York: Holt, Rinehart and Winston, 1970.

▶ Van Buren, Martin. *Inquiry into the Origin and Course of Political Parties in the United States.* New York: Hurd and Houghton, 1867.

▶ Watson, Harry L. *Andrew Jackson vs. Henry Clay: Democracy and Development in Antebellum America.* Boston: Bedford/St. Martin's, 1997.

Periodicals

▶ Weisberger, Bernard A. "The Nullifiers." *American Heritage.* October 1995, p. 20.

▶ ———. "The Lives of the Parties." *American Heritage.* September 1992, p. 43.

On the Web

▶ Jackson, Andrew. "Second Inaugural Address, Monday, March 4, 1833." *Inaugural Addresses of the Presidents of the United States.* Washington, D.C.: U.S. Government Printing Office, 1989; Bartleby.com, 2001. **http://www.bartleby.com/124/pres24.html.**

1836
Martin Van Buren (Democrat) vs. William Henry Harrison, Daniel Webster, Hugh Lawson White (Whigs)

After two terms in office, President Andrew Jackson did not run again, instead endorsing his vice president, Martin Van Buren of New York. Nevertheless, Jackson and his policies remained the central focus of the presidential election campaign of 1836.

The Context

The United States in 1836 was moving toward three separate regional economies. In the North, agriculture was giving way to industrialization, while southern cotton plantations worked by slaves remained dominant. In the West, new immigrants and adventurous Easterners pushed the boundaries of settled territory westward. Regional economic and social differences were reflected in presidential politics.

Jackson's second term had been particularly controversial. At the end of 1832 Jackson had taken a strong stand against the principle that a state—specifically South Carolina—could "nullify," or refuse to observe, a federal law such as tariffs (taxes on imports). Jackson vowed to send troops to collect tariffs after South Carolina threatened to refuse to do so. In 1833, Jackson ordered his treasury secretary to remove federal government money from the Second National Bank, the existence of which he opposed, without consulting Congress. The move was designed to destroy the bank as a viable financial institution, and Jackson's maneuver was regarded by his political enemies as a usurpation of power at the expense of Congress.

Consequently, the election of 1836 became a referendum on Jackson's vision of a strong presidency, as well as a new referendum on Henry Clay's "American System" of federal support for public works, such as roads and canals, and high tariffs to protect domestic industries.

The Candidates

Jackson's vice president, Van Buren, easily obtained the endorsement of the Democratic party—a term that Van Buren himself had started using in 1834 to link supporters of Andrew Jackson with the Democratic-Republicans of Thomas Jefferson. (Previously, many supporters of the president referred to themselves simply as Jacksonians.) Van Buren had the strong endorsement of Jackson himself, which helped overcome opposition to the New Yorker, especially in the South. Van Buren, who had been a senator from New York before becoming vice president, had a reputation as an effective politician and had been instrumental in Jackson's campaigns ever since 1824. But Van Buren lacked the personal charisma of Jackson, or the eloquence of his political rivals, and was often portrayed as a manipulator rather than a political leader.

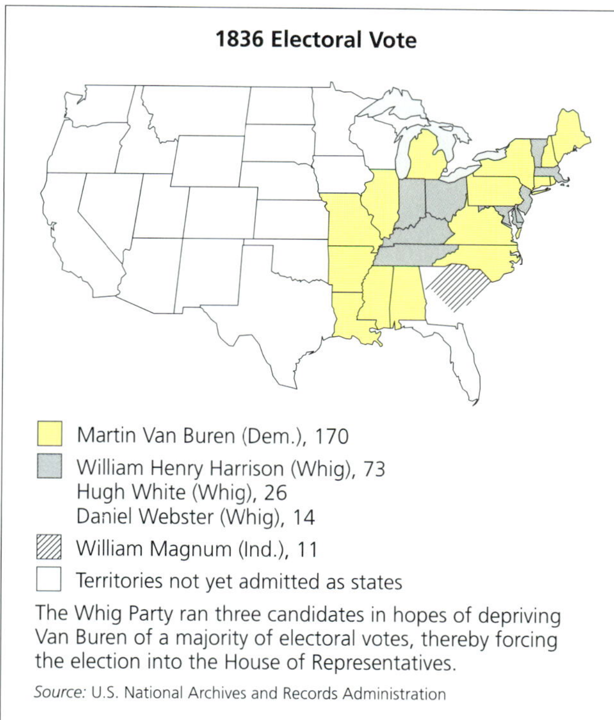

The Whig Party ran three candidates in hopes of depriving Van Buren of a majority of electoral votes, thereby forcing the election into the House of Representatives.

Source: U.S. National Archives and Records Administration

His challenge in 1836 was to hold together the coalition that had elected Jackson twice.

Van Buren was aided by divisions among Jackson's opponents who started calling themselves Whigs. In the 1830s, the name Whig was used to try to unify opposition to Jackson under a single banner that stood for limited presidential powers, an emphasis on law and order, and the principle that no one, including the president, should be above the law. Opposition to Jackson—and then to Van Buren, as Jackson's successor—focused on three politicians in particular in 1836.

Daniel Webster, a senator from Massachusetts, had been associated with the National Republicans of John Quincy Adams and, before that, with the Federalists. He was a strong supporter of Jackson in the controversy over nullification of federal laws. Webster tried in 1833 to build a base of support beyond his home state, travelling to New York, Pennsylvania, and states in the Midwest. But his previous associations with the Federalists and strong ties to the National Bank (he served the bank as a lawyer) made him unacceptable to many other opponents of Jackson. Nevertheless, Webster was nominated and ran for office, although he never picked up significant support outside of Massachusetts.

In the South, Tennessee Senator Hugh Lawson White, who had filled Jackson's Senate seat, had known the president since the War of 1812 and had been political supporter. In 1834 White became the nominee of Whigs who opposed the principle of nullification, but at the same time supported states' rights over the power of the federal government.

The strongest Whig candidate was William Henry Harrison, who like Jackson had fought in the War of 1812 and before that had won a victory over the native American leader

8th President, 1837–1841

Born: December 5, 1782, Kinderhook, New York

Died: July 24, 1862, Kinderhook, New York

Family: Son of Abraham Van Buren, a farmer and tavern keeper descended from Dutch settlers, and Maria Hoes; married Hannah Hoes, a distant relative

Education: Studied law in New York City; admitted to bar 1803

Political career: N.Y. State Senate 1812–20; N.Y.; attorney general 1816–19; U.S. senator from N.Y., 1821–28; secretary of state 1829–31; vice president 1833–37

Van Buren was the first president to have been born an American citizen rather than a British subject. He was an adept politician, with an amiable personality and a sure instinct for winning votes.

Van Buren was Andrew Jackson's most trusted Cabinet member in his first term, and his vice president in his second term. He ran for president in 1836 on the promise of continuing Jackson's policies. But only months after taking office, the Panic of 1837 took hold. Banks suspended the payment of gold for paper money, and the effects of this action rippled into a deep economic depression which lasted three years. The accepted wisdom of the time declared that the government should refrain from interference in the country's economic life, and accordingly Van Buren made no moves to lessen the suffering.

On the slavery issue, Van Buren had pledged to oppose any extension of slavery but to protect it where it already existed. During his term, he opposed the annexation of Texas, since it would have added more slave territory, and opposed a plan to abolish slavery in the District of Columbia.

Van Buren did not win reelection in 1840. He tried for the nomination again in 1844 but ultimately lost to James Polk. In 1848 he ran for president on the Free Soil Party ticket but failed to win any electoral votes.

He died in 1862 in Kinderhook, New York.

Tecumseh at the Battle of Tippecanoe. Harrison had support in Ohio, as well as from Anti-Masons in Pennsylvania. Despite Webster's base in Massachusetts, Harrison emerged as a favorite candidate throughout the Northeast. For the Whigs, Harrison's war record in 1812 served as a counterweight to Jackson's fame, gained during the Battle of New Orleans in 1814. Moreover, he was largely neutral with respect to the Masons and the Anti-Masonic Party.

The Issues

The overriding issue in 1836 was Andrew Jackson, who was not even running. Opposition to Jackson centered on accusations that he had usurped powers rightfully belonging to the Congress in three specific areas:

The National Bank. The charter of the Second National Bank did not expire until 1836, but the question of whether to

Whig Candidate for President, 1836

Born: January 18, 1782, Salisbury, New Hampshire
Died: October 24, 1852, Marshfield, Massachusetts
Family: Son of Ebenezer Webster, a farmer, and Abigail Eastman; married Grace Fletcher (died), Caroline LeRoy
Education: Dartmouth College; private law studies
Political career: U.S. representative from New Hampshire, 1813–17; U.S. representative from Massachusetts, 1823–27; senator from Massachusetts, 1827–41, 1845–50; secretary of state, 1841–43; 1850–52

Daniel Webster was famous as one of the most successful lawyers of his age, and one of the greatest orators. Early in his career he opposed President James Madison's entry into the War of 1812, which he thought ran counter to the interests of his New England constituency. Later, he helped organize the Whig Party, which encouraged high tariffs (helpful to New England manufacturers) and a program of government support for building infrastructure, such as roads. He was a strong ally of fellow Whig Henry Clay of Kentucky.

In 1836, Webster was one of three Whig candidates for president. The Whig strategy was to deprive President Andrew Jackson of a majority in the electoral college and force the election to the House of Representatives, where they hoped they could defeat Jackson. The plan failed, and Webster carried the electoral votes of just his home state of Massachusetts. Later efforts to gain the nomination for president also failed.

Webster was twice secretary of state (under Whig President William Henry Harrison and John Tyler, 1841–43, and under President Millard Fillmore 1850–52. Webster supported the Compromise of 1850, believing that the evil of slavery, which he opposed, was outweighed by threats to national unity.

He died on October 24, 1852, after a riding accident, frustrated in a lifelong ambition to become president.

renew its charter had been an important issue in 1832. Jackson, having been reelected while opposing continuation of the Bank, decided to withdraw U.S. government deposits. Since the law required the treasury secretary to make this move, Jackson moved the pro-Bank treasury secretary, John McLane, to a job in the State Department and appointed a political ally, William Duane, as treasury secretary. But when Duane had second thoughts about moving the government money from the national bank to state banks, Jackson removed Duane and appointed Roger B. Taney as treasury secretary. In January, 1834, Taney began putting federal funds into state banks instead of the National Bank.

In response, Nicholas Biddle, head of the bank, began calling in loans (forcing borrowers to repay loans immediately), on grounds that the Bank was no longer receiving deposits from the government. It was a largely political move designed to combat Jackson's anti-Bank maneuver, and to an extent it worked. The lenders affected were mostly businessmen, who protested loudly in meetings and even marches. The Panic of 1834, although it did not last long, resulted in making new loans hard to obtain, and led to the failure of many businesses, which in turn led to unemployment.

The president's anti-Bank measures raised strong opposition by legislative leaders who felt their prerogatives had been violated by the executive branch. In March, 1834 Henry Clay of Kentucky led a group of senators who passed a censure, or condemnation, of Jackson for exercising "authority and power not conferred by the constitution and laws. . . ." The censure resolution had no practical effect, but it helped make the issue of the Bank the leading issue in the presidential election of 1836.

Nullification also played a role in the election, especially in the South. In November, 1832, a South Carolina convention passed the "Ordinance of Nullification," claiming that the federal tariff acts of 1828 and 1832 (which many southerners thought favored northern manufacturing interests at the expense of southern agricultural interests) were "null" in South Carolina, and urging the state not to collect the taxes. Jackson was quick to respond, threatening to use troops to enforce federal laws, especially collection of the tariffs. In Congress, Clay quickly fashioned the "Compromise of 1833" to defuse the situation. Clay's compromise reduced the tariff, while including the Force Act, giving the president authority to use the armed forces to enforce federal laws. While Clay's compromise ended the immediate crisis, it also reduced support for vice president Van Buren whom Jackson wanted to follow him in the White House. In a larger context, the dispute over tariffs set the stage for the civil war twenty-seven years later over the issues of slavery and state's rights vis à vis the power federal government.

Presidential power. Jackson's handling of the Second National Bank controversy and his threat to use force to collect federal tariffs led to accusations that the president had assumed the powers above and beyond what the Constitution granted. The election of 1836 took on aspects of a referendum on Andrew Jackson.

Masons. The supposed influence of members of the Masonic lodge—a secretive fraternal social organization that aroused the suspicions of non-members—continued to be a factor in 1836 under the flag of the Anti-Masonic Party. Many leading politicians, ranging from George Washington to Andrew Jackson to Henry Clay, were Masons, which made them unacceptable to some voters, especially in New York, Vermont and other parts of New England. Leaders of the Whig movement tried to align themselves with the Anti-Masons, and had limited success, especially in New York state. But other Anti-Masons refused to go along, partly because Whigs in their areas were also Masons.

The Campaign

When it became clear that the Whigs could not unite around a single candidate, three presidential campaigns emerged in

1836—one on behalf of Webster in Massachusetts, one on behalf of White in the South, and one on behalf of Harrison in the Midwest (especially Ohio), New York, and New England. Opponents of Van Buren hoped that each of these candidates could run a strong race in his region, and force the election into the House of Representatives.

Van Buren and the Democrats, on the other hand, managed to create a unified campaign that appealed voters to all sections. After Van Buren's nomination, a committee appointed at the Democratic convention drafted a declaration similar to subsequent party platforms, or statements of principles. The statement was widely reproduced in Democratic newspapers around the country. It warned that Van Buren's opponents were either Federalist sympathizers who wanted to raise taxes to pay for improvements like roads and canals ("the American System"), or that they would fatally weaken the United States by permitting South Carolina's nullification of the federal tariff. To appeal to Southerners disenchanted with Jackson (and by extension, Van Buren) on the tariff issue, the statement recalled that a long succession of Southerners had been elected president, and suggested it was the turn of the North to have one of their own in the White House. The Democratic statement of principles also strongly opposed the abolition of slavery, and suggested that only Democrats could be trusted to protect the institution from attacks by northern abolitionists.

President Jackson played a role in the campaign by giving Van Buren his unqualified support, while helping turn the election into a referendum on Jackson.

The Outcome

The multi-front campaign of the Whigs actually backfired. Instead of having regional candidates who won in their areas to deny the Democrat Van Buren a majority in the Electoral College, the opposite happened: the Whigs largely lost to Van Buren in all regions, giving him an electoral majority.

In the popular vote, Van Buren won 763,291 votes, or 50.8 percent of the total. His closest competitor was Harrison, who won 549,907 votes, or 36.6 percent, followed by White with 146,107 votes (9.7 percent) and Webster with 41,201 votes (2.7 percent).

Van Buren won popular majorities in 15 states which yielded 170 electoral votes out of 294. Harrison won popular vote majorities in seven states, yielding 73 electoral votes. White won majorities in just two states for 26 electoral votes, and Webster on his home state of Massachusetts with 14 electoral votes.

The election of 1836 had one anomaly: none of the candidates for vice president won a majority of electoral votes, and for the first and only time, the choice of vice president was left up to the Senate. Van Buren's running mate, Richard Johnson, won 147 electoral votes, one short of a majority. His candidacy was complicated by the fact that he opened lived with a woman of mixed race, which was regarded as unacceptable in the South. Subsequently, the Senate elected Johnson to serve as Van Buren's vice president.

More Information

▶ Howe, Daniel W. *The American Whigs: An Anthology*. New York: Wiley, 1973.

▶ Niven, John. *Martin Van Burn: The Romantic Age of American Politics*. New York: Oxford University Press, 1983.

▶ Peterson, Merrill D. *The Great Triumvirate: Webster, Clay and Calhoun*. New York: Oxford University Press, 1987.

▶ Remini, Robert V. *Daniel Webster: The Man and His Time*. New York: W. W. Norton, 1997.

▶ Wilson, Major L. *The Presidency of Martin Van Buren*. Lawrence: University Press of Kansas, 1984.

On the Web

▶ Van Buren, Martin. "Inaugural Address Monday, March 4, 1837." *Inaugural Addresses of the Presidents of the United States*. Washington, D.C.: U.S. Government Printing Office, 1989; Bartleby.com, 2001. **http://www.bartleby.com/124/pres25.html.**

▶ Timeline: 1800–1860. National Humanities Center website. **http://www.nhc.rtp.nc.us:8080/pds/triumphnationalism/timeline.pdf.**

1840
William Henry Harrison (Whig)
vs. Martin Van Buren (Democrat)

FlashFocus: 1840

Candidates

William Henry Harrison & John Tyler, Whig
Martin Van Buren & Richard Johnson, L.W. Tazewell,
James K. Polk, Democrat

Issues

The economy. The American economy was in a depression, and President Van Buren was widely criticized for failing to take appropriate action to resolve the situation. The idea of establishing an independent treasury was important during the campaign. Van Buren favored an independent treasury because it would decrease the government's involvement in the country's economy, in keeping with a strict interpretation of the Constitution. Others were against it, arguing that its establishment would prolong and even worsen the depression since it would decrease the number of banknotes that could be printed, therefore taking money out of circulation.

Slavery. Demand for cotton was increasing, both in the United States and in Britain, due to the Industrial Revolution. The economy of the South depended largely on cotton, and southerners relied on slave labor to keep the cotton industry going. Southerners did not trust the more industrialized North to keep southern interests in mind by protecting the institution of slavery. The distrust grew and strengthened as abolitionist groups were formed in the North, and political opposition to slavery became more organized.

Outcome

Popular Vote

Harrison	1,274,624	53.1% ✓
Van Buren	1,127,781	46.9%

Electoral College

Harrison	234 ✓	
Van Buren	60	

The election of 1840 marked the full emergence of political parties as the main vehicle for nominating and promoting candidates for the presidency. The Whigs, a party that had begun to emerge in 1836 as a successor to the National Republicans of John Quincy Adams (see p. 32), took a prominent role in the election of 1840. The election was also marked by an emphasis on campaigning rather than a debate over issues. About eighty percent of eligible voters come to the polls.

The Context

In 1837, two months after Martin Van Buren succeeded Andrew Jackson as president, banks in New York began refusing to exchange paper money they had issued for gold and silver, called "specie." (At the time, private banks issued notes, which were used as currency, that could nominally be exchanged for precious metals. Knowing that not everyone would demand gold or silver for the paper currency, banks were able to print more notes than they had gold or silver; any hint that notes could not be exchanged, however, set off a "panic," in which people rushed to banks demanding specie in exchange for paper currency). Soon, banks outside New York also suspended paying specie for notes. The result of the Panic of 1837 was several years of economic depression, in which money was in short supply, leading to reduced spending or investing in business.

The federal government had played a role in creating the panic. The Democrats opposed the Second National Bank, which had regulated the issuing of private banknotes. After the Bank's charter expired and was not renewed by Andrew Jackson, these regulations also expired. The government under Jackson also began insisting that debts to the government be paid in specie, which had the effect of removing gold and silver from general circulation. As president, Van Buren did nothing to intervene in the crisis, acting from the conviction that the federal government had a limited role to play and intervention in the economy was not authorized by the Constitution.

Consequently, Van Buren and the Democrats lost popular support throughout Van Buren's presidency

The Candidates

When the Whig Party gathered in Harrisburg, Pennsylvania in December, 1839, it had three potential candidates. William Henry Harrison had run second to Van Buren in 1836, carrying seven states, worth 73 electoral votes. Moreover, Harrison had run a very strong second to Van Buren in a number of western and northeastern states. Harrison's chief claim to fame was his military victory over the native American chief Tecumseh at Prophets Town, Indiana, on the Tippecanoe River in 1811 while he was serving as govern of Indiana Territory. That victory led to Harrison's promotion to the rank of general, and he established a successful record during the War of 1812. On the downside, Harrison's political career was undistinguished and he would be 67 years old, the oldest man ever to run for president at the time.

General Winfield Scott was supported by leading Whig politicians in New York, largely as an alternative to Henry Clay of Kentucky. New York accounted for 42 electoral votes, more than a fourth of the number needed to win the White House, or the Whig nomination, which was based on electoral representations. Scott had little to recommend him besides the support of some Whigs in New York: he had no political experience, and in fact had never even been considered for a political office.

The third candidate was Clay, who had run in 1824 and again in 1832 as a National Republican. Clay was well known as an advocate for the "American System" which encouraged the federal government to pay for national improvements, such as roads and bridges, and to protect domestic industries with high tariffs. But Clay had refused to renounce his membership in the Masonic Lodge, which made him suspect among voters in New York, particularly, which had been the home of the Anti-Masonic Party. Moreover, the fact that he owned slaves in his home state made him unpopular with the rising number of abolitionists.

Clay entered the Whig convention with the greatest number of votes, but not enough to win nomination on the first ballot. To thwart Clay, delegates supporting Harrison and Scott pushed through a "unit rule," which required that all the votes of each state should go to the candidate with a majority of votes in the state's delegation. Initially, Clay received votes from the slave states of the South, plus Illinois. Harrison received the votes of Indiana, Ohio, Pennsylvania, Maine, Massachusetts, and New Hampshire, while Scott received the votes of New York and New Jersey.

During the course of the convention, backers of Harrison and Scott agreed that Clay could not win the election, and many of Scott's supporters switched their support to Harrison, at least in part to block Clay from another run for the presidency. For vice president, the Whigs nominated former John Tyler of Virginia, a former senator and governor of Virginia and a Clay supporter.

Harrison was already the Whig nominee when the Democratic Party held its convention in Baltimore in May, 1840. Bands of young Whigs marched through the streets, shouting their support for Harrison while the Democrats met. Van Buren, as the incumbent, had no trouble obtaining the nomination of the Democratic Party for reelection. He had been instrumental in electing Andrew Jackson for the first time, in 1828, and served as Jackson's loyal vice president from 1833 to 1837. Despite his familiarity with the electorate, Van Buren had never attracted the loyal, enthusiastic support that Jackson inspired. Van Buren's greatest burden in the 1840 election was the persistent economic depression than had begun with the Panic of 1837 (see following section). Even members of his own Democratic Party blamed Van Buren for failing to address the economic distress of many voters.

On the other hand, the Democrats could not agree on a vice presidential candidate. Van Buren's vice president, Richard Johnson, had been controversial in 1836 because he lived with a woman of mixed race, which repelled some southern Democrats. No candidate for vice president was able to gather the two-thirds majority needed for the vice presidential nomination, and the Democrats adjourned without a formal vice presidential nominee.

The Issues

The state of the economy was the leading issue in 1840, even if the election campaigns of Van Buren and Harrison did not entirely reflect the fact. The specific political issue was the

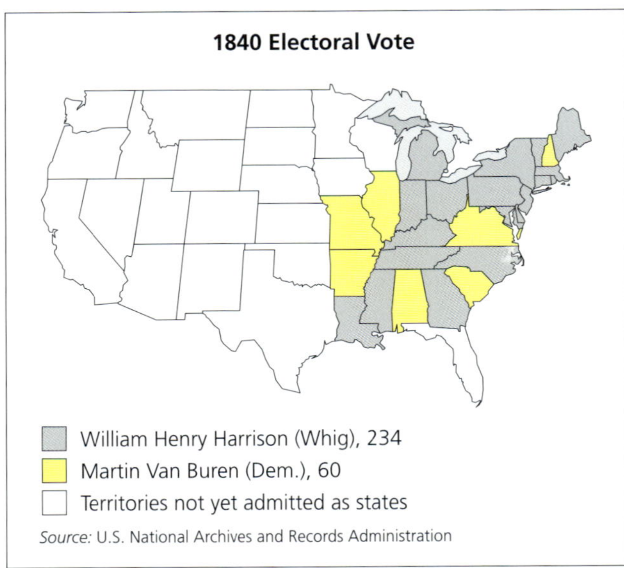

Source: U.S. National Archives and Records Administration

"Independent Treasury" advocated by Van Buren and eventually enacted after a long debate within the ranks of Democratic legislators. In essence Van Buren's plan was to establish an institution responsible for holding the government's gold and silver, which had been previously deposited in state banks following the demise of the Second National Bank (see p. 40). One implication of shifting the government's gold and silver holdings to an independent treasury was that it reduced further the volume of banknotes that state-chartered banks could issue (since banknotes were supposed to be backed up by specie), thereby prolonging the economic downturn. For Van Buren the independent treasury proposal was justified on grounds that it took the federal government out of participating in the banking system, which was not explicitly authorized by the Constitution. But the measure was not popular, even among many Democrats, in part because it did not appear to do anything to relieve the economic depression. Instead, it had the effect of removing more money from circulation, possibly making the depression worse. In state elections held in 1837 and 1838, support for Democrats waned and they lost control of ten state governments.

Slavery also became an explicit issue in 1840, although the subject had long been an undercurrent of presidential politics. In the North, abolitionists (who advocated an immediate and complete end to slavery in the United States) formed the Liberty Party. There was little chance that the party would elect its candidate to the White House, but it was one early example of a third political party devoted to one specific cause that complicated the political maneuvering of the larger parties. It also contributed to the rift between southern slave-holding states and northern states. Southerners had long feared northern politicians could not be trusted to protect an institution that southerners deemed vital to an economy based on large cotton plantations. As the Industrial Revolution was gaining mo-

mentum, both in Britain and the United States, the demand for cotton was also constantly increasing, resulting in renewed dedication in the South to preserving slavery which plantation owners thought was critical to their success.

Although Andrew Jackson had been out of office for nearly four years during the 1840 election campaign, his style of presidential leadership remained an issue, partly because Van Buren had always been closely associated with Jackson. It was a shared opposition to Jackson, in fact, that had led politicians to form the Whig Party, named after the British political party during the eighteenth century that opposed the powers of King George III. The Whigs, many of whom had been National Republicans who backed John Quincy Adams in 1828, felt strongly that Jackson had exceeded the constitutional limits on the power of the presidency. Continuing criticism of "King Andrew" was reflected in the Whig campaign against Jackson's successor.

The Campaign

The election of 1840 saw the introduction of the sort of campaigning that later became familiar: slogans, nicknames, and knickknacks promoting the candidates at the expense of serious discussion of the issues. The Whigs in particular introduced many of the elements that came to characterize successful presidential campaigns later on. The Democrats attempted to emulate the Whigs, but were far less successful.

To overcome the notion that Whigs represented the interests of business owners, Harrison was characterized as the "log cabin" candidate, a man of the people. (In fact, Harrison had been born in a mansion on a plantation in Virginia.) Whig campaign managers emphasized his military experience in Indiana with the slogan, "Tippecanoe and Tyler Too." The Whigs built log cabins in many cities (including one in New York) to emphasize the notion that Harrison was a simple man of the people, and used the cabins as local campaign headquarters. Glass containers shaped like log cabins were filled with liquor supplied by the E. C. Booz distillery in Philadelphia and distributed to potential voters (adding the expression "booze" to American English to describe alcoholic beverages). Whig operatives also organized torchlight parades for their candidate, or games in which men pushed around huge leather balls "to keep the ball rolling," and distributed trinkets or campaign posters.

Whigs also ridiculed Van Buren as someone whose masculinity could not compare with Harrison's. Whigs made fun of Van Buren's distinctive beard (they called him "Sweet Sandy Whiskers") and accused him of wasting public funds on repairing the White House in order to install mirrors "nine feet high and four feet and a half wide" to admire himself.

For the first time in an American presidential contest, the candidate, Harrison, made speeches on his own behalf.

Ironically, it was the Democrats who had first introduced the notion that Harrison was a "log cabin candidate" happiest sitting in the backwoods sipping hard (alcoholic) cider. The Democratic campaign tried to match the Whigs, but their candidate did not generate the same level of enthusiasm. Their campaign was not entirely unsuccessful—Van Buren attracted 350,000 more votes in 1840 than he had in 1836—but the economic depression wore heavily on Van Buren. Vice President Johnson proved to be an effective campaigner, despite the fact that he was not formally nominated for a second term.

The Outcome

The 1840 campaign resulted in a startling increase in voter participation. A total of 2,408,630 votes (about 80 percent of the eligible voters) were cast, up from 1,505,290 (about 57 percent of those eligible) cast in 1836. Even though Van Buren received more votes in 1840 than he received when he was elected president, he lost both the popular vote and the electoral vote to his Whig opponent. The Liberty party candidate, Birney, received only 7,453 votes.

The totals were 1,274,624 (53.1 percent) votes for Harrison, to 1,127,781 (46.9 percent) for Van Buren. In the electoral college, Harrison won with 234 to Van Buren's 60. Harrison won majorities in nineteen states, with strong support in New England and western states. Van Buren carried only six states. South Carolina's electors were chosen by the state legislature rather than by popular vote; they voted for Van Buren.

Whig candidates also fared well in Congressional races; the 27th Congress that convened in 1841 saw both houses controlled by the Whigs: 142–100 in the House of Representatives and 29–22 in the Senate.

Impressive as Harrison's victory was, it was actually quite close in terms of electoral votes. In Pennsylvania, for example, Harrison won by just 334 votes (out of a total of 288,026 cast) to win that state's 30 electoral votes; in Maine, with 10 electoral votes, Harrison won by only 422 votes. On the other hand, Van Buren won Virginia's 23 electoral votes with a margin of just 1,120 votes.

More Information

- Peterson, Norma Lois. *The Presidencies of William Henry Harrison and John Tyler.* Lawrence: University Press of Kansas, 1989.
- Cleaves, Freeman. *Old Tippecanoe: William Henry Harrison and His Time.* Port Washington, NY: Kennikat Press, 1969.

Periodicals

- Simon, Roger. "To the Log Cabin Not Born." *U.S. News & World Report.* August 26, 2002, p. 48.

On the Web

- Harrison, William Henry. "Inaugural Address." Inaugural Addresses of the Presidents of the United States. **http://www. bartleby.com/124/pres26.htm.l.**
- "William Henry Harrison." The White House. **http://www. whitehouse.gov/history/presidents/wh9.html.**
- "Getting the Message Out! National Campaign Materials 1840–1860." Abraham Lincoln Historical Digitization Project at Northern Illinois University Libraries. Links to a variety of articles and primary source materials. **http://dig.lib.niu.edu/ message/about.html.**

1844
James K. Polk (Democrat) vs. Henry Clay (Whig)

The presidential election of 1844 was a mixture of extraordinarily elements. The incumbent president, John Tyler, elected as the Whig's vice presidential nominee in 1840, was repudiated by his party, the Whigs, just as the Democrats repudiated their front-running candidate, former president Martin Van Buren, in favor of a "dark horse," a relatively unknown politician from Tennessee, James K. Polk. The election resulted in a huge turnout and a very narrow victory for Polk, who won just under 50 percent of the votes in a contest in which slavery was an issue of growing concern. The abolitionist James Birney of the Liberty Party won 2.3 percent of the vote.

The Context

On March 4, 1840 William Henry Harrison, the Whig candidate, took the oath of office and delivered an inauguration speech that lasted over two hours in the midst of a freezing rainstorm. Harrison did not wear a coat, and shortly after the speech the president came down with a cold which developed into pneumonia. One month after he became president, Harrison died, on April 4, 1840, the first president to die in office. His vice president, the former Democrat John Tyler, became president.

Tyler had serious reservations about one of the most important planks in the Whig platform: reestablishment of a national bank, which the Whigs had put forward as a way of ending a long economic downturn that had begun with the Panic of 1837. Tyler, like most Democrats, was uncomfortable having the government own a bank, which he viewed as a potentially dangerous expansion of the power of the federal government. In August, 1840 he vetoed a bill passed by the Whig-controlled Congress to reestablish the national bank, which had ceased to exist after its charter expired in 1836. The Congress passed a modified bank bill a month later, which Tyler also vetoed on September 9, infuriating the leadership of the Whig party. The desirability of a national bank to control the issuing of paper currency by state-chartered banks and to help finance government projects, such as roads and canals, had been a favorite project of the Whig party since its formation, and even before that when the bank was supported by the National Republicans in 1832. All but one of Tyler's cabinet members resigned, and four days after his second veto, he was essentially ejected from the Whig party when Whig members of Congress published a statement renouncing Tyler's affiliation with them.

A second issue that swirled in Congress during the presidency of Tyler was statehood for the Republic of Texas, which had won its independence from Mexico in 1837 and almost immediately asked to be admitted to the United States. Texas had been a sparsely populated region of Mexico, and the government of Mexico had invited Americans to settle there; many southerners took Mexico up on the offer. After the revolt which resulted in its freedom, representatives of the new Republic of Texas went to Washington and formally applied for statehood. The request raised a particular problem, however; admitting Texas, where slavery was legal, would upset the balance of slave and non-slave states. At the time the application was first made, President Andrew Jackson asked the Texans to wait until his vice president, Martin Van Buren, could be safely elected without injecting the issue of slavery into the campaign.

The Candidates

As soon as President Tyler's break with his party in September, 1844 opened up the possibility of obtaining the Whig presidential nomination in that year, Senator Henry Clay of Kentucky started laying his plans. He had unsuccessfully run for president twice before, in 1824 in a four-way contest eventually won by John Quincy Adams and in 1832 as a National Republican running against Andrew Jackson. In May, 1842, Clay resigned from the Senate in order to focus all his energy on obtaining the Whig nomination and running for president a third time.

At the Whig convention in Baltimore in May, 1844 Clay came into the convention with the nomination sewed up. The only real question was the choice of a vice presidential candidate. Thomas Frelinghuysen, a former senator from New Jersey, was soon chosen. The convention also passed a very short resolution stating its principles for the campaign: reestablishing a national bank, tariffs to protect American manufacturers against foreign (mostly British) competition, distributing money from the sale of public lands to the states, and "a reform of executive usurpation" a reference to the use of the veto by the president for political, rather than constitutional, reasons.

For the Democrats, former President Martin Van Buren was actively seeking another chance for a second term when the Democratic convention opened in Baltimore on May 27. His leading opponent was Lewis Cass, a senator from Michigan. Although lacking in charisma, Van Buren appeared to have wrapped up the Democratic nomination at the start of the convention. Other rivals included Van Buren's vice present, Richard Johnson of Kentucky, and Senator James Buchanan of Pennsylvania. Several state party conventions that preceded the Baltimore meeting had already endorsed Van Buren, with the result that Buchanan and Senator John C. Calhoun of South Carolina, another perennial presidential hopeful, both announced before the convention that they would not be candidates.

Shortly before the Democratic convention, however, the *Washington Globe* printed a letter from Van Buren indicating that he opposed annexation of Texas on grounds that it could lead to war with Mexico. Whereas a similar sentiment from Henry Clay was welcomed by the Whigs, Van Buren's letter was highly unpopular among the Democrats, especially those from Southern states who strongly favored admitting Texas as a state, at least in part because it would help the cause of slavery. Buchanan and Johnson both reversed course and announced that they would be available as the party's presidential candidate after all. Perhaps more important, Andrew Jackson, in retirement in Tennessee, invited the former Tennessee governor James J. Polk for a visit to the Hermitage, Jackson's home, to discuss the possibility of becoming the party's nominee.

FlashFocus: James K. Polk

11th President, 1845–1849

Born: November 2, 1795, Pineville, North Carolina
Died: June 15, 1849, Nashville, Tennessee
Family: Son of Samuel Polk, a farmer, and Jane Knox; married Sarah Childress
Education: University of North Carolina 1818; studied law, admitted to the bar 1820

Political career: Tennessee state legislature 1823–25; U.S. House of Representatives 1825–39; speaker, 1845–39; governor of Tennessee, 1839–41

James Polk presided over an extraordinarily successful administration during which the land area of the United States grew by about fifty percent. Territory added included Texas and the land now occupied by California, Oregon, Washington, New Mexico, Nevada, Utah, Arizona, and parts of Colorado and Wyoming.

Polk is the only Speaker of the House ever to become president. He left the House in 1839 and served as governor of Tennessee from 1839–41. Polk was not holding any political office in 1844 when the Democratic presidential convention deadlocked between two contenders, former President Martin Van Buren and Senator Lewis Cass of Michigan. Supporters began to mention Polk as a possible compromise candidate, and with the backing of former President Andrew Jackson, he won the Democratic nomination. News of Polk's nomination was telegraphed from the convention at Baltimore, to Washington, D.C., the first official use of Samuel Morse's invention.

In the general election Polk narrowly beat Henry Clay of Kentucky, the Whig candidate who had run against Jackson in 1832.

As president Polk oversaw the addition of Texas as a state, and the addition of Oregon Territory. Negotiations to acquire territory from Mexico failed, and in 1846 the United States declared war with Mexico. By the end of Polk's administration, the northern part of Mexico had become the second largest addition of land to the country after the Louisiana Purchase.

Polk did not run for reelection in 1848, and died of cholera on June 15, 1849, just three months after leaving office.

See also: Henry Clay, p. 41.

When the first vote was taken for the Democratic presidential nominee, Van Buren won 146 votes out of 266, a majority but still 31 votes short of the two-thirds needed to be the candidate. In second place after the first ballot was Cass, with 83 votes. More ballots were taken, and on each succeeding vote, Van Buren lost support and Cass picked up votes. On the seventh ballot, Cass pulled ahead of Van Buren, but both men were far short of the 177 votes needed to win.

The convention was moving towards a deadlock. Even after Van Buren's supporters recognized that their candidate would

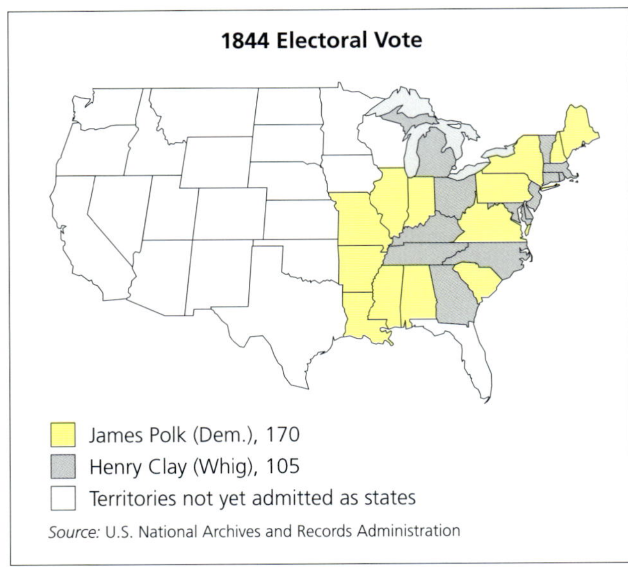

Source: U.S. National Archives and Records Administration

not be nominated, they refused to support the other leading contenders. On the eighth ballot the name of James Polk was put forward as a compromise candidate; he immediately won 114 votes, primarily at the expense of Cass. On the next ballot, the New York delegation accepted that their candidate, Van Buren, would never be nominated. The "dark horse" compromise candidate, Polk, was nominated on the ninth ballot. Shortly afterwards, George M. Dallas, a former senator from Pennsylvania, was chosen as the party's vice presidential nominee.

The two party conventions had left the sitting president, Tyler, without a party. A move among Democrats to endorse Tyler had fallen on deaf ears, and some Democrats had met in a separate convention trying to promote the idea of Tyler as the candidate of a new party. Meeting with little success, Tyler withdrew his name as a candidate in August 1844, clearing the way for a contest between Polk and Clay.

There was one additional candidate in 1844: James Birney of the Liberty Party, which advocated abolishing slavery. Birney was from Alabama, a former slave-holder who had a change of heart and renounced the practice. The Liberty Party had nominated Birney in 1840, primarily as a symbolic gesture, but in 1844 the abolitionists became serious and mounted an enthusiastic campaign.

The Issues

Annexation of Texas. The long-standing application of Texas to join the United States had originally been viewed by both the Whigs and Democrats as dangerous to their causes. Admitting Texas raised the potential of war with Mexico, which still hoped to recover control of its breakaway state, as well as the prospect of upsetting the balance of slave and non-slave states. In late April, 1844 a letter written by Clay was published in the *Washington National Intelligencer,* in which Clay opposed

the immediate admission of Texas on grounds that annexation would be "a measure compromising the national character, involving us certainly in war with Mexico" and would be "dangerous to the integrity of the Union." On the same day, a similar letter written by Van Buren was published in the *Washington Globe,* in which Van Buren declared that Mexico would "regard the fact of annexation [of Texas] as an act of war on the part of the United States." In June, 1844 the Senate, controlled by the Whigs, defeated a bill to admit Texas, and Clay grew worried that the issue could hurt his chances in the South, where admission of another slave state was widely supported. Van Buren's letter led to the intervention of Andrew Jackson, who had suggested that James Polk might make a good compromise candidate.

Slavery was becoming a more important issue by 1844. The debate over admitting Texas was, at its heart, a debate over maintaining the balance of slave and non-slave states. At the same time, the Liberty Party (and the abolitionist movement in general) was gaining support in the North; Birney's pro-abolitionist campaign was much more serious than it had been in 1840. (In the end, Birney won over 62,000 votes, or 2.3 percent of the total, depriving both the Democrats and Whigs from winning a majority of the popular vote.)

The other aspect of admitting Texas, besides the balance of slave and non-slave states, was a popular desire to expand the territory of the United States and to occupy the entire continent from the Atlantic to the Pacific. The phrase "Manifest Destiny" was used in a newspaper article by John L. O'Sullivan in 1845 to capture the spirit of the age, that the United States was a unique nation with a "manifest destiny to overspread the continent allotted by Providence for the free development of our yearly multiplying millions." For this reason, the annexation of Texas was popular, not just in the South where it was viewed as helping to assure the future of slavery, but also in the West where settlers welcomed any policy that served to enhance the legality of their claims on their homesteads. The idea that the United States was meant to stretch its borders "from sea to shining sea" was highly popular throughout the second half of the nineteenth century.

National Bank. The Whigs strongly supported reestablishing a national bank, partly as a means of controlling the printing of paper currency by state-chartered banks, partly as a means of financing public works projects, and partly as a means of exerting a positive influence on the national economy. Democrats continued to oppose such a bank, on grounds that it would give the federal government more power and influence at the expense of the states, and that such a function had not been authorized in the Constitution. The Whigs thought they had won approval of a new bank in 1840, when the Whig-controlled Congress authorized such a bank, only to see the Whig president, Tyler, veto two bills in short succession.

Tariffs. Taxes on imports were another cause of the Whigs, who approved of government actions that would help domestic industry grow by making imports more expensive. Southerners, who were net exporters of agricultural goods, particularly cotton, were disinclined to support tariffs, which they saw as hurting themselves by raising prices, and hurting their customers, especially British textile manufacturers. In 1842, the Congress had passed a new tariff, which posed a political problem for Polk since the tariff was popular in Pennsylvania, a state Polk was counting on to win the election. Polk wrote a letter during the course of the election in which he opposed tariffs just in order to protect domestic industry, but agreed that "moderate discriminating duties" would be acceptable. Both sides of the debate were willing to interpret Polk's letter the way they wanted to see the issue: southerners focused on reducing tariffs, while northerners focused on support for "incidental protection."

The Campaign

Following the example set by the Whigs in 1840, the presidential campaign of 1844 employed a variety of gimmicks and sloganeering at the expense of debate over the issues. Polk's supporters characterized him as "Young Hickory," the natural heir of another Tennessee politician and Polk's initial sponsor, Andrew "Old Hickory" Jackson. The Democrats also supported the annexation of both Texas and Oregon, a territory jointly occupied with Britain. Linking the two proved to be a clever move, since acquiring Oregon along with Texas could maintain the balance of slave and non-slave states while at the same time appealing to the national enthusiasm for acquiring more territory. The Democratic campaign continued to attack long-standing Whig economic ideas (such as protective tariffs) that were especially unpopular in the South. The Democrats asserted that Whig policies were designed to benefit the "rich and powerful" while hurting the working class.

During the campaign, Clay became worried that his position on Texas might be hurting him in the South and West, partly based on his April, 1844 letter opposing immediate annexation. In July, Clay wrote two letters addressed to Whigs in Alabama, first stating that his opposition to the annexation of Texas was based on his fears that northern opponents could threaten the union of the states, and later stating he would be "glad to see" Texas annexed "without war . . . and upon just and fair terms." In his second letter, Clay said slavery should not be an issue in the debate over admitting Texas as a new state. Still later, in September, Clay wrote another letter insisting that he was not an abolitionist. His efforts to shore up support in the South cost Clay support in the North. Sensing this, he wrote yet another letter published in the *National Intelligencer* insisting that he still opposed annexation of Texas. Clay's conflicting messages on the Texas issue raised doubts about his position in both the North and South.

The Outcome

The turnout for the election was nearly as high as it had been four years earlier. In 1844, 79 percent of eligible voters came to the polls, resulting in a very close election. In the popular vote, Polk won 1,338,464, or 49.6 percent, compared to 1,300,097 votes for Clay, or 48.1 percent. Birney of the Liberty Party won 62,300 votes, or 2.3 percent.

In the crucial contest for electoral votes, Polk won 15 states worth 170 electoral votes, to Clay's 11 states worth 105 electoral votes. Polk scored a narrow victory in New York, which provided him with 36 electoral votes and proved critical. Polk won the popular vote in New York by just 5,106 votes out of almost 486,000 cast; a change of just 2,554 votes in New York could have given the election to Clay.

More Information

- ▶ McCormac, Eugene I. *James K. Polk: A Political Biography*. Newton, CT: American Political Biography Press, 1995.
- ▶ McCoy, Charles A. *Polk and the Presidency*. New York: Haskell House, 1973.
- ▶ Bergeron, Paul H. *The Presidency of James K. Polk*. Lawrence: University Press of Kansas, 1987.
- ▶ Remini, Robert V. *Henry Clay: Statesman for the Union*. New York: W. W. Norton, 1991.
- ▶ Eagon, Clement. *Henry Clay and the Art of American Politics*. Boston: Little, Brown, 1957.

Periodicals

- ▶ Volpe, Vernon L. "The Liberty Party and Polk's Election, 1844." *The Historian*. Summer 1991, p. 691.
- ▶ Shattan, Joseph. "One-Term Wonder." *The American Spectator*, October 1996, p. 32.

On the Web

- ▶ "James K. Polk." *North Carolina State Encyclopedia*. State Library of North Carolina. **http://statelibrary.dcr.state.nc.us/ nc/bio/public/polk.htm.**
- ▶ The James K. Polk Ancestral Home. **http://www.jameskpolk. com.**
- ▶ "Henry Clay." University of Louisville Libraries. **http://library.louisville.edu/government/states/kentucky/ kyhistory/hclay.html.**
- ▶ *The Life and Public Services of Henry Clay*. (Author and publisher unknown). 1844. From the Illinois Historical Digitization Projects. **http://lincoln.lib.niu.edu/cgi-bin/navigate?/ lib35/artfl1/databases/sources/IMAGE/.632.**
- ▶ James Knox Polk, Inaugural Address, Tuesday, March 4, 1845. *Inaugural Addresses of the Presidents of the United States*. Washington, D.C.: U.S. Government Printing Office, 1989; Bartleby.com, 2001. **http://www.bartleby.com/124/pres27. html.**
- ▶ "Getting the Message Out! National Campaign Materials 1840–1860." Abraham Lincoln Historical Digitization Project at Northern Illinois University Libraries. Links to a variety of articles and primary source materials. **http://dig.lib.niu.edu/ message/about.html.**

1848
Zachary Taylor (Whig) vs. Lewis Cass (Democrat) vs. Martin Van Buren (Free Soil)

FlashFocus: 1848

Candidates

Zachary Taylor & Millard Fillmore, Whig
Lewis Cass & W. O. Butler, Democrat
Martin Van Buren & Charles Adams, Free Soil
Gerrit Smith & Charles C. Foote, Liberty

Issues

The slavery debate. As the United States continued to expand, the question of whether or not slavery should be allowed in new territories and states became increasingly important. There was a clear divide between the North and the South on the issue of slavery, which led both candidates to adjust their campaigns and positions according to geography. In the North, candidates declared their support for "popular sovereignty," allowing territories to decide for themselves whether or not they wanted to allow slavery. In the South, candidates declared their support for slavery as an important component of the Southern economy. The newly organized Free Soil Party opposed the expansion of slavery into new territories, and the Liberty Party advocated the abolition of slavery altogether.

Tariffs. Taxes imposed on imported goods remained an issue in 1848, with northerners seeing tariffs as a means of protecting their industries from imports, and southerners denouncing tariffs as having a damaging effect on their cotton trade.

Use of the veto. Whigs warned voters that a Democrat would abuse the power of the presidency by using the presidential veto, as Andrew Jackson had done. Taylor, the Whig candidate, declared that he would sign any bill sent to him by Congress, and would not use the veto.

Outcome

Popular Vote

Taylor	1,360,967	47.4% ✓
Cass	1,222,342	42.5%
Van Buren	291,263	10.1%

Electoral College

Taylor	163 ✓
Cass	127

The election of 1848 was held in the midst of rapid change. Expanding slavery to new territories acquired from war with Mexico split both the Democratic and Whig parties. Abolitionists were gaining political strength, and the first women's rights convention was held in the summer of 1848 at Seneca Falls, New York. The Whigs were led by a former general with no political experience and a vague political philosophy. Both Whigs and Democrats went into the election with divided messages—one for the anti-slavery North, another for the pro-slavery South—and opposed by a new group plainly opposed to expanding slavery, the Free Soil Party.

The Context

Northern opposition to the spread of slavery to new territories, and an equally strong insistence in the South that slave owners had every right to transport their property, including slaves, to new American territories, formed the backdrop to the election of 1848. The same issue had also been present in 1844, when it took the form of an argument over whether to admit Texas (a breakaway state of Mexico that had declared independence in 1836) as a new state where slavery was permitted. Both Whigs and Democrats wanted to defer the admission of Texas, which threatened to upset the balance of slave- and non-slave states, until after the election in 1844. Texas was formally admitted as a state on December 29, 1845, and four months later, on April 25, 1846, U.S. troops intervened in a border dispute with Mexico over the southern border of the new state. During the war a Democrat from Pennsylvania, Representative David Wilmot, introduced an amendment to a budget bill that would bar slavery in any territory that the U.S. might acquire from Mexico. The so-called Wilmot Proviso became the main focus of the political debate over the future of slavery after U.S. victory over Mexico in February, 1848. The Treaty of Guadalupe Hidalgo which ended the war also resulted in acquisition by the United States of a broad swath of new territory that comprises the southwestern United States.

The abolitionist movement had been steadily growing in the North ever since William Lloyd Garrison founded *The Liberator* in Boston in 1830, campaigning for the immediate freedom of all slaves. By the late 1840s the movement had gained significant strength, especially in New England. As an outgrowth of the abolitionist cause, a group of 300 men and women led by Elizabeth Cady Stanton and Susan B. Anthony met in Seneca Falls, New York in July, 1848 and adopted a resolution demanding equal political rights for women.

The election was also held in the context of the California gold rush, and growing enthusiasm from all parts of the country to extend control of the United States from the Atlantic to the Pacific Oceans.

The Candidates

Zachary Taylor was an army general who later admitted he had not even bothered to vote prior to 1847. But it turned out that it was precisely Taylor's lack of political experience that

"

made him an attractive candidate to the Whig party, which had lost the election in 1844 when its candidate was Henry Clay, one of the best-known and most experienced politicians in the United States. Clay remained on the sidelines; by 1848 he had already lost three presidential elections (1824, 1832, and 1844) and had tried unsuccefully to gain his party's nomination in 1836 and 1840. Although Clay's name was high on the list of possible candidates, he had taken on the aura of a perpetual loser. Other leading Whig politicians whose names rose included General Winfield Scott, Senator Daniel Webster of Massachusetts, and Supreme Court Justice John McLean, as well as Senators John Clayton of Delaware, Willie Mangum of North Carolina, and John Crittenden of Kentucky.

Taylor, however, with a fresh reputation as a victorious general in the war with Mexico and without a history of political positions taken, was the clear front-runner. His major drawback was that he was not a dedicated Whig, and happily said as much. "If the Whig party desire . . . to cast their votes for me," he declared, "they must do it on their own responsibility without any pledges from me." Taylor's statement of political independence included such traditional Whig positions as support for protective tariffs and public works projects to help stimulate the economy and build up the West, and to limit Presidential vetoes to only those bills thought to be unconstitutional. Seeing Taylor waffle on political principles, Clay tried to breathe new life into his career by emphasizing his strong background on Whig issues. But Clay, long an owner of slaves, refused to endorse the Wilmot Proviso to ban slavery from territory acquired from Mexico, which made him suspect among anti-slavery Whigs in the North.

The American victory over Mexico in early 1848 helped cement support of Whigs for the nomination of Taylor. In April, 1848 Taylor supporters persuaded him to sign a letter declaring that he accepted the principles of the party—he was, he said, "a Whig but not an ultra Whig"—which brought around many supporters. At the Whig convention in June, Taylor had 111 votes on the first ballot; Clay had 97, Scott had 43, and Webster had 22. On the second ballot much of Clay's support vanished, going either to Taylor or to Scott. On the fourth ballot Taylor won the needed votes for nomination. In order to balance the ballot with a vice presidential candidate who did not own slaves, the Whigs turned to Millard Fillmore of New York, a former representative. Concerned that adopting a party platform would underscore the differences between staunch anti-slavery northern Whigs and pro-slavery southern Whigs, the convention adjourned without a statement of principles beyond a vague statement in favor of Taylor as the party's candidate.

On the Democratic side there was for a time lingering hope that President James Polk would ignore his promise in 1844 to run for only a single term. When it became clear that Polk would not again be a candidate, a list of Democratic candidates emerged, including Senator James Buchanan of Pennsylvania, Vice President George Dallas, also of Pennsylvania, Supreme Court Justice Levi Woodbury of New Hampshire, and Senator Lewis Cass of Michigan, who had been secretary

12th President, 1849–1850

Born: November 24, 1784, Orange County, Virginia
Died: July 9, 1850, Washington, D.C.
Family: Son of Richard Taylor, a Revolutionary War officer, and Sarah Dabney Taylor; married Margaret Mackall Smith
Education: Occasional private tutors
Political career: Zachary Taylor had spent his entire career in the Army before entering politics in 1847. He had fought in the War of 1812, then spent years in frontier forts fighting against native Americans. His soldiers nicknamed him "Old Rough 'n' Ready."

Taylor's experience in the war with Mexico made him attractive to the Whig party as a candidate for president in 1848. President James Polk, a Democrat, had criticized Taylor's leniency towards the defeated Mexican Army after the capture of Monterrey, Mexico in September, 1846, and assigned about half of Taylor's forces to the command of Gen. Winfield Scott. Undeterred, Taylor ignored orders to remain in place and instead advanced south to Buena Vista, where he defeated the army of General Antonio López de Santa Ana. The victory won Taylor fame and praise in Congress, but not from Polk.

Taylor returned to the United States in late 1847 and began to campaign for the presidency. The Whig party saw in Taylor a war hero who could help them regain the presidency. Although Taylor's positions often clashed with those of the Whig party, the general was greatly aided by a split in Democratic ranks in 1848 over the expansion of slavery into territories that were not yet states. The official Democratic candidate, Lewis Cass of Michigan, advocated letting the inhabitants of territories decide whether or not to permit slavery. Democrats strongly opposed to slavery formed the Free Soil Party, dedicated to halting slavery in new areas. With the Democratic vote thus split, Taylor was elected president.

In dealing with the new territory acquired from Mexico in the war, Taylor managed to infuriate Southerners by advising residents of California and New Mexico to adopt constitutions as they saw fit and then apply for statehood. Southerners saw little chance of those states choosing to permit slavery, and Southern anger turned to talk of seceding from the United States.

Taylor established a strong policy of protecting and defending the Union above all else, and in this he never wavered. Less than half way through his term, on July 4, 1850, the sixty-five year old fell ill after a long ceremony in the hot sun and died five days later, on July 9, 1850.

of war under Andrew Jackson and an ambassador to France under Martin Van Buren. The Democrats had the same internal party problem as the Whigs: whether to support the extension of slavery to new territories. Many northern Democrats supported the Wilmot Proviso (which had been introduced by a Democrat) barring extension of slavery into territory acquired from Mexico. A middle position, called "popular sovereignty," was advocated by Cass, who wanted to

FlashFocus: Lewis Cass

Democratic Candidate for President, 1848

Born: October 9, 1782, Exeter, New Hampshire
Died: June 17, 1866, Detroit, Michigan
Family: Son of Jonathan Cass, a lawyer, and Mary Gilman Cass; married Elizabeth Spencer
Education: Phillips Exeter Academy; private law studies
Political career: Democrat. Ohio legislature, 1806; governor, Michigan Territory, 1813–1831; secretary of war, 1831–36; minister to France, 1836–42; U.S. senator from Michigan, 1845–48, 1849–57; secretary of state, 1857–60

Lewis Cass fought with valor in the War of 1812; his criticism of his commanding officer's timid approach brought him to the attention of military officials in Washington. At the end of the war he was appointed governor of Michigan Territory.

Cass served as President Andrew Jackson's secretary of war for five years, and then was dispatched as minister to France. In 1848, while serving as U.S. senator from Michigan, Cass was nominated by the Democrats to run against the Whig candidate, Zachary Taylor, for president. The election also saw former President Martin Van Buren running as the candidate of the anti-immigrant, anti-Catholic Free Soil Party.

The leading issue in 1848 was whether to allow slavery in new U.S. territories acquired from Mexico. Cass backed "popular sovereignty"—the notion that the residents of the territories should be left to decide the issue for themselves.

Cass's election chances were hurt by Van Buren, whose party took votes that logically would have gone to the Democrats, thereby helping Taylor to win the election. Cass won fifteen states and 127 electoral votes, compared to Taylor's 15 states and 163 electoral votes.

In 1857, Democratic President James Buchanan appointed Cass as his secretary of state. In these unsettled pre–Civil War years, he was a strong advocate for preserving the Union. Cass died in Detroit, in 1866.

Sea also: Martin Van Buren, see p. 45.

let the inhabitants of the various territories vote on whether or not to allow slavery. Many southern Democrats argued that neither the Wilmot Proviso nor popular sovereignty was acceptable; rather, they said, there was no justification for either the citizens in a territory or for Congress to limit the ability of slave owners to bring their property into a new territory.

During Democratic conventions in the spring of 1848, Cass, Buchanan and Woodbury were initially the leading candidates. Cass and Buchanan both backed "popular sovereignty," while Woodbury, although a northerner, agreed that there was no justificaiton for either the citizens or the Congress barring slavery in new territories. No Democrat appeared to be

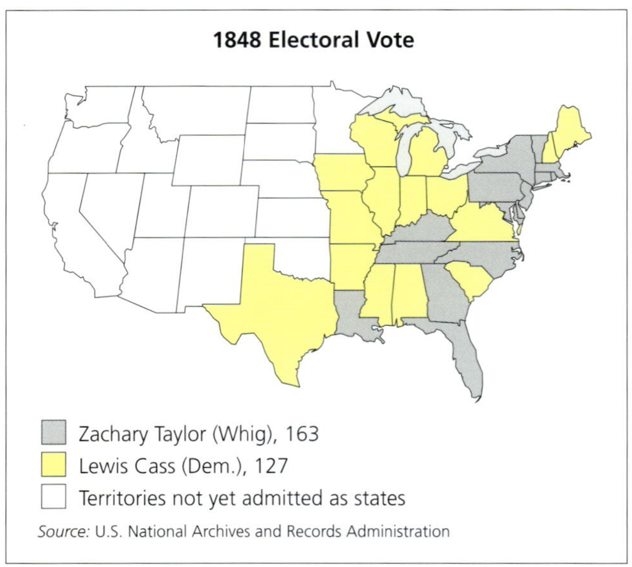

1848 Electoral Vote

Source: U.S. National Archives and Records Administration

sympathetic to the Wilmot Proviso which was backed by many northerners, especially in New York State, where many Democrats, called Radicals, felt their party had fallen under the control of Southern interests.

Among the Radicals in New York, there were two groups, the "Barnburners" and the "Hunkers," originally divided over economic policies. By the time the Democratic convention was held in May, 1848, the Hunkers and Barnburners were so divided that they sent competing delegations; when the convention tried to mollify them by seating both groups, both groups walked out of the convention. In the absence of the New Yorkers, Senator Cass was nominated with support from the western states. His nomination was particularly infuriating to the Barnburners from New York, which felt he had modified his stand on the Wilmot Proviso in order to appeal to southern delegates. For vice president, the Democrats nominated William Butler of Kentucky, a former U.S. Congressman and a major general in the Mexican War.

The Liberty Party, which had steadily gained support for abolishing slavery since it first ran a candidate in 1840, had already nominated John Hale of New Hampshire at its convention in October, 1847. But after the fiasco at the Democratic convention, and a similar but less vociferous argument at the Whig convention, groups from all three parties began discussing forming a new party that would support the Wilmot Proviso and limit the expansion of slavery. Some Liberty Party leaders urged joining like-minded Whigs and Democrats. In June, after the Democratic party's convention, a gathering in Columbus, Ohio expressed dissatisfaction with both Cass and Taylor and called for a national convention to be held in Buffalo, New York six weeks later for the purpose of building opposition to the expansion of slavery.

Gathering in Buffalo, representatives of the Barnburners, the anti-expansion Whigs and the Liberty Party formed a new party, called the Free Soil Party. The Liberty Party candidate,

Hale, yielded to Van Buren as the new party's candidate on a platform that called for "Free Soil, Free Speech, Free Labor and Free Men." The party opposed the expansion of slavery into new territories, but fell short of calling for the abolition of slavery in states where it currently existed. Gerrit Smith of New York was the party's candidate for vice president.

The Campaign

For the first time, the presidential election in 1848 took place on the same day everywhere in the country. The Whigs and Democrats faced the same problem: how to avoid alienating voters over the issue of the Wilmot Proviso. Both parties came up with similar solutions: run two different campaigns, one tailored for the anti-slavery North, the other tailored for the pro-slavery South.

For the Democrats in the North this meant campaigning in favor of "popular sovereignty," letting people living in the new territories decide whether or not to allow slavery. It also meant emphasizing that the Democratic candidate was from Michigan and had never owned slaves, unlike the Whig candidate, Taylor, who did own slaves and who refused to state his position with regard to the Wilmot Proviso. In the South, the Democrats tried to sell Cass as a "northern man with southern principles." The Democrats argued that popular sovereignty was really the best way to protect southern interests, since slavery would be allowed in new territories unless the residents specifically voted to outlaw it.

The Whigs conducted a similar divided approach, trying to appear sympathetic to slavery in the South and antipathetic in the North. In the South, Whigs emphasized the fact that their candidate Taylor was a slave-owner (just as Democrats emphasized the same fact when they campaigned against Taylor in the North) who could be trusted not to betray the interests of his region. On the other hand, the southern Whigs pointed to the Free Soil candidacy of former Democratic President Van Buren as evidence that northern Democrats could not be trusted to protect the rights of slave-owners. Southern Whigs attacked the Democratic candidate Cass on the same grounds—he had never owned slaves and could not be trusted with the interests of Southerners.

Northern Whigs focused their argument on a statement by Taylor that he would sign any constitutional legislation that passed the Congress. The Whigs argued that Taylor could be elected and also relied upon to sign the Wilmot Proviso if and when it passed the Congress. Popular sovereignty, the Democrats' argument in the North, could not be relied upon to block the expansion of slavery.

Neither the Democrats nor the Whigs differed significantly on the question of the expanding slavery into new territories. Their differences were primarily on economic issues: protective tariffs and the government's role in stimulating the economy, and the issue of how the president should use the veto.

In September the Whigs grew concerned that Taylor's lukewarm devotion to Whig principles was doing little to attract Democrats and was leaving regular Whig voters cool to his candidacy. Taylor wrote another letter, widely published in Whig newspapers, vowing his devotion to the Whig's longstanding political principals. The Whigs also attacked the Free Soil candidate, Van Buren, reminding voters that Van Buren had run against the Whigs as a Democrat.

The Outcome

Taylor won the election comfortably, carrying 15 states for a total of 163 electoral votes, compared to 15 states and a total of 127 electoral votes for the Democrat Cass.

In the popular vote, the Whigs also had cause to celebrate. Taylor won 1,360,967 votes, or 47.4 percent, to Cass's 1,222,342, or 42.5 percent, and Free Soiler Van Buren's 291,263, or 10.1 percent.

Even so, there were storm clouds on the Whig's horizon, notably the fact that the Free Soil candidate's share was about four times as much in 1848 as the anti-slavery Liberty Party candidate had received in 1844. The Free Soil candidate received more votes than the Democrats in several key northern states, notably New York, Massachusetts, and Vermont. It was a signal that the slavery issue was of growing importance in the north.

A few months after the election President Taylor declared that he was opposed to extending slavery from new territories, a position that infuriated many voters in the South. That would be reflected in the 1852 elections, the last in which the Whigs would play a meaningful role.

More Information

► Bilotta, James D. *Race and the Rise of the Republican Party, 1848–1865*. New York: P. Lang, 1992.

► Cole, Donald B. *Martin Van Buren and the American Political System*. Princeton, NJ: Princeton University. Press, 1984.

► Dyer, Brainerd. *Zachary Taylor*. New York: Barnes and Noble, 1967.

► McLaughlin, Andrew C. *Lewis Cass*. New York: AMS Press, 1972. (Reprint of volume published in 1899 by Houghton Mifflin.)

► Smith, Elbert B. *The Presidencies of Zachary Taylor and Millard Fillmore*. Lawrence: University Press of Kansas, 1988.

On the Web

► Zachary Taylor, Inaugural Address Monday, March 5, 1849. *Inaugural Addresses of the Presidents of the United States*. Washington, D.C.: U.S. Government Printing Office, 1989; Bartleby.com, 2001. **http://www.bartleby.com/124/ pres28.html.**

► "Getting the Message Out! National Campaign Materials 1840-1860." Abraham Lincoln Historical Digitization Project at Northern Illinois University Libraries. Links to a variety of articles and primary source materials. **http://dig.lib.niu.edu/ message/about.html.**

► "The Politics of Sectionalism." Links to scores of primary documents for the period 1844–1860. **http://www.historyteacher. net/APUSH-Course/Weblinks/Weblinks12.htm.**

1852
Franklin Pierce (Democrat) vs. Winfield Scott (Whig)
vs. John Parker Hale (Free Soil)

FlashFocus: 1852

Candidates

Franklin Pierce & William R. King, Democrat
Winfield Scott & William A. Graham, Whig
John P. Hale & George W. Julian, Free Soil

Issues

Slavery in new territories. As the United States acquired more and more territories, the issue of whether slavery would be allowed in those territories remained at the forefront. Both the Democrats and the Whigs included planks in their platforms stating their support of the Compromise of 1850, but voters were still deeply concerned about the candidates' respective positions regarding slavery. Winfield Scott, the Whig candidate, did not declare a definitive position on the Compromise of 1850, which caused him to lose support among some southern voters, who feared he would not protect their interests. He was also accused of being anti-slavery, which further eroded southern support.

The role of government in the economy. Although overshadowed by the issue of slavery, the question of how much the government should be involved in the economy was still unresolved. The Democrats opposed government intervention and sought to limit the government's role. The Whigs favored government involvement and an increased role for the federal government in the national economy.

Outcome

Popular Vote

Pierce	1,601,117	50.9% ✓
Scott	1,385,453	44.1%
Hale	155,825	5.0%

Electoral College

Pierce	254 ✓
Scott	42

The election of 1852 pitted a virtually unknown candidate from New Hampshire, Franklin Pierce, against the candidate of a badly splintered Whig Party, led by General Winfield Scott, and of the much reduced Free Soil Party, John Parker Hale. The question of whether slavery should be permitted to expand into new western territories—or even whether the federal government had the power to determine the future of slavery—sharply divided both the Democrats and the Whigs. The clearly anti-slavery Free Soil party attracted significantly less support in 1852 than it had four years earlier, and soon after the election it faded from the scene.

The Context

Significant changes were taking place in the United States when voters went to the polls to choose a new president in 1852. Millard Fillmore, the Whig vice presidential candidate in 1848, had become president two years earlier after the unexpected illness and death of Zachary Taylor in July 1850. Taylor, who won fame in the war with Mexico, had taken a strong stand against political leaders in the South who had threatened to secede from the United States over the issue of slavery. In February 1850 Taylor had threatened to hang anyone "taken in rebellion against the Union." His position shocked some Southerners who had expected the slave-owning Taylor to be more sympathetic to the cause of slavery, and specifically the demands of southerners that they be allowed to bring their property—their human slaves—into new territories that were not yet states. A series of laws, collectively known as the Compromise of 1850, had tried to address the issue and put it to rest. Instead, the Compromise of 1850 itself became part of the continuing argument between North and South.

The last four years of the 1840s had seen a major influx of immigrants to the United States. On the East Coast, large numbers of poor Irish farmers arrived, refugees from a devastating failure of the potato crop and consequent famine. Immigrants had also begun arriving in the United States from Germany. In both cases, many of the immigrants were Roman Catholics, arriving in a country that until then had been predominantly Protestant. Many of the immigrants were penniless, having spent their last money on buying tickets to New York or Boston. As they acquired citizenship, these immigrants largely gravitated to the Democratic Party, threatening the power of the Whigs. In California a significant number of Chinese immigrants seeking their fortune in the California Gold Rush had also generated hostility among Americans of European origin, although the Chinese did not generally try to become voting citizens. (Thirty years later, the federal Chinese Exclusion Act of 1882 barred any further immigration by Chinese, a ban that lasted for sixty years.)

The Candidates

Both the Democrats and Whigs entered their nominating conventions in 1852 with no clear choice for a presidential candidate, and both parties required several dozen ballots before settling on someone. The Free Soil Party, which had made a

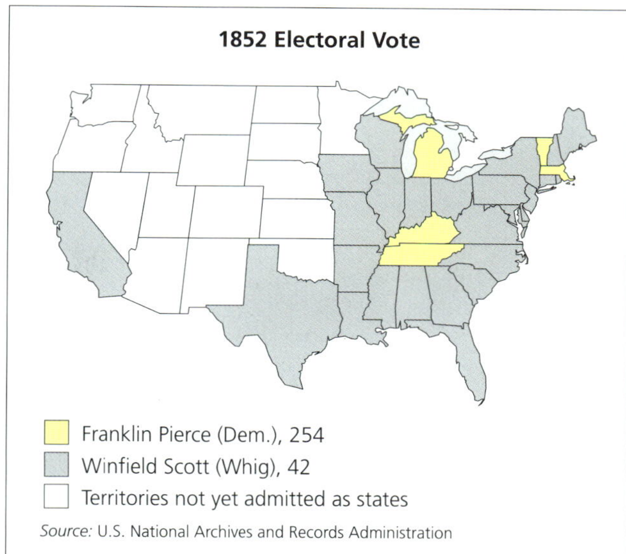

Source: U.S. National Archives and Records Administration

strong showing in 1848 and deprived the Democrats of enough votes to let the Whig candidate win the White House, played a diminished role in 1852.

When the Democratic convention opened in Baltimore on June 1, 1852, there were five leading contenders. Senator Lewis Cass of Michigan, the party's candidate four years earlier, was the early front-runner, but his support was not deep or very enthusiastic. His popularity lay among conservate northern Democrats. James Buchanan of Pennsylvania, a former secretary of state under James Polk, strongly defended southern rights in the ongoing dispute over carrying the rights of slave-owners into new territories. Buchanan had actively sought the nomination for two years, and although he was popular in the South, some interests in his own state were cool towards his candidacy. William Marcy of New York emerged as a possible second choice, partly because he was from the largest state and partly because he did not quarrel with the Compromise of 1850. Finally, Supreme Court justice Levi Woodbury of New Hampshire had the support of many New England Democrats until his death in September, 1851. His place was soon taken by Senator Stephen Douglas of Illinois, nicknamed the "Little Giant" because he had a short, diminutive body and a relatively large head. Douglas was the champion of developing the western states, building railroads, and providing cheap land to settlers, as well as an aggressive foreign policy. As the convention approached, several New England delegates began focusing on Franklin Pierce of New Hampshire, a former senator, representative, and brigadier genreal in the Mexican War. He was not enthusiastic about running, and his wife strongly objected to a campaign, but slowly he allowed himself to be persuaded to cooperate in a New England-led movement to nominate him in Baltimore. His name was put forward on the 35th ballot.

The Democrats voted 48 times, and still no one emerged a winner. One after another, the frontrunners built support, but

FlashFocus: Winfield Scott

Whig Nominee for President 1852

Born: June 13, 1786, Petersburg, Virginia
Died: May 29, 1886, West Point, New York
Family: Son of William Scott, farmer and Revolutionary War officer, and Ann Mason; married Maria D. Mayo
Education: College of William & Mary (one year); private law studies
Political career: Winfield Scott spent fifty-two years in an Army career often marked by controversy. His foray into elective politics, as the Whig candidate for president in 1852, was brief and ineffective. He was soundly defeated by a little-known opponent, Franklin Pierce of New Hampshire.

Scott's military career began in 1808, as a captain in the Army. In the War of 1812, Scott achieved acclaim for leading U.S. troops against the British in Canada. After the U.S. victory, Scott was one of only a handful of senior officers who remained in a shrunken Army. Scott was often in conflict with another hero of the War of 1812, Andrew Jackson. Just as Jackson took a leading role in the Democratic Party, so Scott ran for office, unsuccessfully, affiliated with the Whig Party.

In June, 1841, Scott was named general in chief of the Army by President John Tyler. His biggest victory as a military leader came during the war with Mexico, when he oversaw the capture of Mexico City.

Scott became the Whig presidential candidate in 1852 when the party decided that a military hero with little political history might be able to win the White House, just as General Zachary Taylor had done in 1848. Scott originally supported the Compromise of 1850, but then seemed to change his position, angering voters on both sides of the issue. He lost the election to a little known politician from New Hampshire, Franklin Pierce.

After organizing the defense of the capital early in the Civil War, Scott retired from the Army in 1862.

He died in West Point, New York, on May 29, 1886.

no one could achieve enough votes for the nomination. Finally, on the 49th ballot, Pierce emerged as a compromise candidate, winning 282 votes with only a handful for other possible nominees. In an effort to achieve a geographical balance, the Democrats nominated as vice president William King of Alabama, a planter, former senator and ambassador to France.

The party adopted a platform with the same resolutions that had been adopted at every Democratic party convention since 1840, focusing on the limited role of the federal government and adding one that supported the Compromise of 1850.

The Whig convention opened on June 16, 1852, also in Baltimore. The party was sharply divided between northern and southern members over the issue of slavery. Even though the Whigs had won the presidency four years earlier, the incumbent, Millard Fillmore, did not command a majority of delegates. Southern Whigs, who supported the Compromise of

1850 as a way of permanently settling the slavery issue, supported Fillmore and urged the convention to endorse the Compromise of 1850. Northern Whigs supported General Winfield Scott, a career soldier and hero of the Mexican War, who lacked a history of taking political positions. Their strategy was to repeat the party's success of 1848: choose a military hero without a political history, and thereby to unite the divided party. But the very fact that some northern Whigs, such as William Seward of New York (a so-called Free-Soil Whig, known to oppose the expansion of slavery into new territories) supported Scott made the general unacceptable to many southerners. Scott himself did not make his position on the Compromise of 1850 clear, which deepened southern suspicions. The third contender was Senator Daniel Webster of Massachusetts, long a factor in the Whig party and a supporter of the Compromise of 1850.

Before choosing a candidate, the party adopted a platform which declared its support of the Compromise of 1850—including the Fugitive Slave Act, which was highly unpopular among many northern Whigs—and discouraged any further campaigning on the slavery issue. The party then proceeded to choose a presidential candidate. After 52 ballots none of the leading candidates had achieved the 147 votes needed to be nominated. Finally, on the fifty-third ballot, the party nominated Scott. For vice president, the party nominated William Graham of North Carolina.

The Free Soil party had lost much of its support as anti-slavery Democrats had returned to their party in New York, and anti-slavery Whigs rejoined their party. Unlike the Democrats and Whigs, the Free Soilers opposed the Compromise of 1850, which they felt had not stopped the expansion of slavery. In August 1852 a group of anti-slavery Whigs and abolitionists from the Liberty Party met in Pittsburgh, where they unanimously nominated Senator John Hale Parker of New Hampshire as president and George Julian of Indiana as vice president. The party's platform called for the abolition of slavery, as well as vigorous federal support of economic developments, such as improvements to river navigation and harbors. The party also supported immigration and a policy of giving federal land to settlers at no cost. Before the next election Parker and Julian would abandon the Free Soil party to help found the Republican Party.

The Issues

The question of slavery in new territories in the West was the major issue in the campaign of 1852. Two years earlier, politicians on both sides had tried to resolve the question in a series of laws known collectively as the Compromise of 1850. It had been fashioned by Senator Henry Clay of Kentucky, author of the earlier Missouri Compromise of 1820 which had addressed the same issue. In 1820, the question had been the admission of Missouri to the Union as a state where slavery was permitted; some northern states were concerned that adding another slave-holding state would upset the balance of slave and non-slave states, which in 1820 stood at 11 states each. Clay's compromise was to admit simultaneously Missouri, where slavery would be allowed, and Maine (which had been part of Massachusetts) as a non-slave state. The Compromise of 1820 also held that in the future, slavery would not be allowed in the part of the Louisiana Purchase north of 36°30' latitude (the southern border of Missouri).

In 1850, however, California was applying for admission as a free state, which upset southerners concerned with undoing the delicate balance between free and slave states. Moreover, California occupied territory acquired from Mexico in a war that started as a means of settling a border dispute between the slave state of Texas and Mexico; southerners were furious that territory acquired by the war was about to be admitted as a non-slave state. The compromise engineered by Clay in 1850 had several parts: California would be admitted as a free state; New Mexico and Utah could organize territorial governments with no mention of slavery (meaning in reality that slavery would not be barred); trading of slaves in the District of Columbia was banned; and a new and more stringent federal fugitive slave law that required free states to help apprehend and return fleeing slaves (regarded as the property of their owners). Finally, a part of New Mexico territory claimed by Texas was handed over to the territorial government in exchange for $10 million dollars.

Both Democrats and Whigs hoped desperately that the Compromise of 1850 would put the issue of slavery, and its expansion into new territories, to rest once and for all. It was not to be.

The Campaign

The presidential campaign in many ways reflected the nominating conventions. Both major parties had passed resolutions supporting the Compromise of 1850, primarily as a way of taking the issue of slavery off the table. And although the Democrats held their traditional stand on limited government versus the economic activism favored by the Whigs, the differences in economic policies were much less pronounced than in earlier years.

Without substantive issues dividing them, the parties campaigned on the personalities of their nominees, Scott and Pierce. Whigs belittled Pierce's war experience and alluded to his heavy drinking by declaring he was a veteran of "many a well-fought bottle." He was portrayed as hostile to immigrants—especially Catholics, who were becoming a larger factor as a result of Irish and German immigration during the 1840s. Democrats replied with their own attacks on Scott, calling him a "drunkard" who also was anti-Catholic and against immigrants. In the South, some editors claimed that Scott was really a representative of anti-slavery interests, and several southern Whigs switched parties and supported Pierce on these grounds.

The Outcome

The election was a disaster for the Whigs. Pierce won over 1.6 million votes (50.9 percent) to under 1.4 million for Scott (44.1 percent) and just over 155,000 for Hale (5.0 percent).

In the electoral college, Pierce carried 27 states worth 254 electoral votes, to just four states (42 electoral votes) for Scott.

Scott fared especially poorly in the South, where the Democrat Pierce won lopsided majorities in states like Alabama (60.9 percent to 34.1 percent), Arkansas (62.2 percent to 37.8 percent), Georgia (64.7 percent to 26.6 percent), and Texas (73.1 percent to 26.9 percent).

On the other hand, Pierce was soon to demonstrate that he was no more able to succeed as president than he had in other parts of his career. He was unable to unite the southern and northern wings of his party and his reputation for heavy drinking continued into his presidency.

More Information

► Eisenhower, John S. D. *Agent of Destiny: The Life and Times of General Winfield Scott.* New York: Free Press, 1997.

► Heale, N. J. *The Presidential Quest: Candidates and Images in American Political Culture, 1787–1852.* New York: Longman, 1982.

► Somerville, Barbara. *Franklin Pierce.* Minneapolis: Compass Point Books, 2003.

► Warner, Lee H. *Nathaniel Hawthorne and the Making of the President, 1852.* Concord, NH: New Hampshire Historical Society, 1973.

Periodicals

► Morison, Elting E. "In Praise of Pierce: He Had All the Right Qualities." American Heritage, August–September, 1985, p. 46.

► Taylor, Michael J. C. "Governing the Devil in Hell: 'Bleeding Kansas' and the Destruction of the Franklin Pierce Presidency (1854–1856)." White House Studies. Spring 2001, p. 185.

On the Web

► Franklin Pierce, Inaugural Address Friday, March 4, 1853. *Inaugural Addresses of the Presidents of the United States.* Washington, D.C.: U.S. Government Printing Office, 1989; Bartleby.com, 2001. **http://www.bartleby.com/124/pres29.html.**

► "Getting the Message Out! National Campaign Materials 1840–1860." Abraham Lincoln Historical Digitization Project at Northern Illinois University Libraries. Links to a variety of articles and primary source materials. **http://dig.lib.niu.edu/message/about.html.**

► "The Politics of Sectionalism," Links to scores of primary documents for the period 1844–1860. **http://www.historyteacher.net/APUSH-Course/Weblinks/Weblinks12.htm.**

1856
James Buchanan (Democrat) vs. John Frémont (Republican) vs. Millard Fillmore (American)

FlashFocus: 1856

Candidates

James Buchanan & John C. Breckinridge, Democrat
John C. Frémont & William L. Dayton, Republican
Millard Fillmore & Andrew Donelson, American
  (Know Nothing)

Issues

Slavery in the new territories. As more territories moved toward statehood, the questions of whether to allow slavery in those territories, and whether slave-owners should be allowed to transport their slaves to those territories, were important issues. The Democrats favored allowing the territories to decide for themselves whether to allow slavery; Republicans opposed any expansion of slavery.
Federal government vs. States' rights. Democrats remained firm in their belief that the powers of the federal government should be restricted, leaving more sovereignty to the individual states. Republicans supported a strong federal government, and favored federal involvement in projects such as expansion of railroads in the new territories.
Immigrants. Strong anti-immigrant sentiment began to develop as immigrants, many of them Catholic, entered the United States in greater numbers. Democrats were supportive of immigrants, a majority of whom were consistently Democratic. Several anti-immigrant groups merged to form the American Party (the Know-Nothings) which proposed limits on immigration and immigrant rights.

Outcome

Popular Vote

Buchanan	1,832,955	45.3% ✓
Frémont	1,339,932	33.1%
Fillmore	871,731	21.6%

Electoral College

Buchanan	174 ✓
Frémont	114
Fillmore	8

Four years of prosperity under Democratic president Franklin Pierce were not enough to distract the nation's attention from the issue of slavery in the election of 1856. Large-scale immigration also attracted attention, particularly the large influx of Roman Catholic immigrants from Ireland and Germany. Two new political parties, the Republican Party and the American Party (also known as the Know Nothing Party) ran candidates in 1856, whereas the Whig Party had al-

most completely collapsed and simply endorsed the former Whig, Millard Fillmore, who was already the American Party nominee.

The Context

Fresh from its conquest of Mexico in 1848, the United States during the administration of Franklin Pierce experienced strong economic growth and the beginnings of international power and prestige. In the North, industry was growing rapidly, while continually rising demand for cotton brought affluence to cotton plantation owners in the South. In Asia, Commodore Matthew Perry in 1855 signed a treaty establish trade with Japan, a sign of a growing ability by the United States to project its power abroad.

In the Northeast, a steadily rising number of poor immigrants from Ireland and Germany began to change the face of American society. Virtually all the Irish immigrants and about one third of the Germans were Roman Catholics. The sudden emergence of a large immigrant Catholic community gave rise to anti-immigrant sentiments that melded with a long-standing hostility towards Catholicism dating back to the founding of Maryland as a refuge for Catholics in the 1630s. Anti-immigrant, anti-Catholic feelings took political form as the American Party, a movement that had begun in the 1840s and became known as the Know Nothing Party after the habit of members to answer questions about their activities by saying, "I know nothing."

Settlement of western territories, especially Kansas and Nebraska, had kept alive the argument over whether slavery would be allowed to expand. As settlers continued to move west, federal involvement in financing national transportation systems such as railroads and harbors remained an issue.

The Candidates

As the incumbent, President Pierce should have held a strong advantage to be renominated when the Democrats convened in Cincinnati in June, 1856. But he faced strong challenges from former Senator James Buchanan of Pennsylvania and Senator Stephen Douglas of Illionois. Buchanan had an advantage because he had been in Britian, as the U.S. ambassador, for three years, leaving him out of the contentious debate over slavery. Buchanan led his rivals on the first ballot, and through fifteen more ballots, but fell short of the needed two-thirds majority. Finally, on the seventeenth ballot, Douglas withdrew his name, clearing the way for Buchanan's nomination. For vice president, the Democrats nominated Representative John Breckinridge of Kentucky.

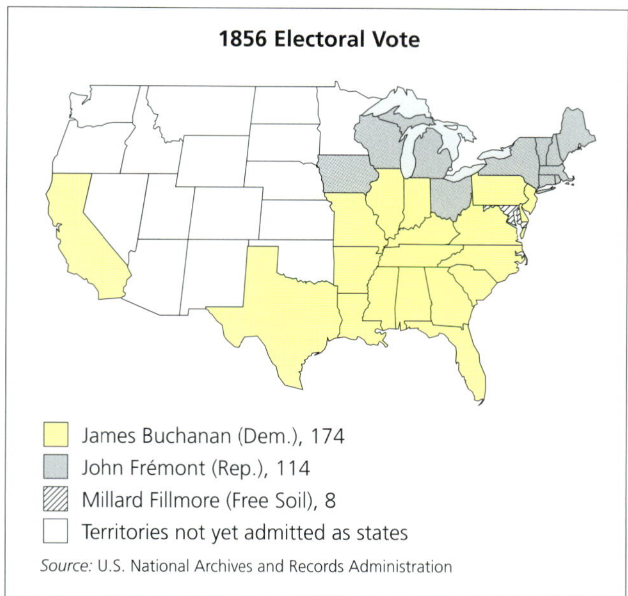

1856 Electoral Vote

Source: U.S. National Archives and Records Administration

Although he was from Pennsylvania, Buchanan generally sympathized with southerners on the question of slavery, preferring to let inhabitants of the territories vote on the issue.

In February 1856 the new Republican Party, formally organized just two years earlier, held its first presidential nominating convention. Notably, there were no delegates from slave-holding states south of Virginia, making the Republicans a sectional party of the North. The popular favorite was John C. Frémont, best known as an explorer of Oregon, California, and Colorado, and briefly a senator from California. His leading rival was Supreme Court Justice John McLean of Ohio, but on the first ballot Frémont won the nomination with 520 votes out of 567. The party adopted a platform which included opposing popular sovereignty, endorsing the traditional Whig position of supporting federal government backing for economic improvements, and opposing a Pierce administration proposal to acquire Cuba from Spain.

Just as the Republican Party was emerging as an alternative and heir-apparent to the Whig Party in the North, the American Party tried to capture the Whig vote, but with an emphasis on immigration. The party held its one and only convention in February 1856 in Philadelphia, and nominated Millard Fillmore of New York, who as a Whig had been elected vice president in 1848 and became president on the death of Zachary Taylor in 1850. Fillmore had been defeated in his bid for the Whig nomination in 1852 by General Winfield Scott. Like the Democrat Buchanan, Fillmore supported the idea of popular sovereignty (popular in the South), and hoped to marry this issue with anti-immigrant and anti-Catholic sentiments that were increasingly popular in the North.

The Whig party also held a convention in 1856, its last. In September Whig delegates gathered in Baltimore and endorsed the American Party candidate, Millard Fillmore.

FlashFocus: James Buchanan

15th President, 1857–1861

Born: April 23, 1791, near Mercersburg, Pennsylvania.

Died: June 1, 1868, Lancaster, Pennsylvania

Family: Son of James Buchanan, a merchant, and Elizabeth Speer. Buchanan was the only president who never married.

Education: Dickinson College; private law studies; passed bar 1812

Political career: U.S. representative from Pennsylvania, 1821–31; U.S. Senate, 1834–45; secretary of state 1845–49; minister to Russia 1832–33; minister to England 1853–56

After he was elected president in 1856, Buchanan tried to defuse the rancorous atmosphere surrounding the slavery issue by making appointments that kept a careful balance of northerners and southerners. The Supreme Court would soon issue a ruling regarding slavery in the territories, and he naively reasoned this would finally put the issue to rest.

This miscalculation doomed his presidency, and he presided over near-chaos. The Supreme Court ruled in the Dred Scott case that Congress did not have power to prohibit slavery in the territories. Northerners were not inclined to accept this as the final word. Buchanan next decided to back the admission of Kansas to the Union as a slave state. This plan was unsuccessful and only solidified northern opposition to him. Buchanan avoided decision-making for the rest of his term.

John Brown's raid on Harper's Ferry, intended to spark a slave rebellion, promoted talk of secession by the Southern states. Seeing Buchanan's indecisiveness and lack of resolve, the South grew bolder, and on December 20, 1860, South Carolina seceded from the Union. Six more states followed before Buchanan left office.

In the election campaign of 1860 the Democratic Party split into northern and southern factions and neither chose Buchanan to run. This split helped assure the election of the Republican candidate, Abraham Lincoln. Buchanan retreated to his estate, Wheatland, in Lancaster, Pennsylvania, where he died in 1868.

The Issues

The debate over slavery continued to focus on the territories, lightly settled western land that had not yet gained enough citizens to become states. Southerners insisted they had a right to bring their property, i.e., slaves, into new territories. Antislavery Northerners insisted that the federal government should ban slavery in the territories, even as abolitionists pushed for a federal ban on slavery everywhere. In 1856 the Democrats and the Know Nothing party endorsed popular sovereignty—leaving the question of permitting slavery up to the inhabitants of each territory. This was the effect of the Kansas-Nebraska Act of 1854, which repealed the Missouri Compromise of 1820 and left the issue of slavery in the Kansas and Nebraska territories up to the settlers living there. After the act passed, both pro- and anti-slavery forces poured into Kansas hoping to alter the outcome. On May 21, 1856 pro-slavery forces attacked the town of Lawrence, Kansas, burned homes and businesses, and killed one man. Three days later anti-slavery zealot John Brown and four of his sons took revenge in a deadly attack on pro-slavery settlers at Pottawatomie Creek; five settlers died.

As a measure of the passions excited by the issue, at about the same time as the May violence in "Bleeding Kansas" Senator Charles Sumner of Massachusetts delivered a stinging attack in the Senate on slavery in Kansas, and on its supporters, including Senator Andrew Butler of South Carolina. Butler's nephew, Representative Preston Brooks, then entered the Senate chamber and started beating Sumner with a cane. Sumner was badly hurt, and the violence on the floor of the Senate enraged many anti-slavery men and women in the North.

Largely unrelated to the slavery debate, an anti-immigrant movement was growing rapidly, especially in the Northeast. A loose network of anti-immigrant clubs came together in 1856 as the American Party (also known as the Know Nothing Party). The American Party advocated barring immigration by the poor or convicted criminals, forcing immigrants to wait twenty-one years before becoming citizens, and reserving government jobs for people born in the United States. The party's one and only convention also adopted a resolution endorsing popular sovereignty on the slavery issue.

The role of the federal government in economic affairs began fading as an issue. Democrats still believed the federal government should play a limited role, while the newly formed Republican Party advocated a more active federal role in developing railroads and improving water transportation.

The Campaign

In many respects the campaign of 1856 represented a rerun of earlier elections. The Democratic party was closely associated with popular sovereignty as the solution to the debate over expanding slavery. The Republican party took the role of the Free Soil party on the slavery issue, opposing expansion of slavery into the territories, and the role of the Whig platform on government support for expansion of transportation networks. The American party tried to avoid being a sectional party, i.e., too closely connected to either the North or the South, by adopting the southern stance on popular sovereignty and introducing the issue of immigration and Catholicism to appeal to the North.

While Buchanan stayed home in Pennsylvania saying little, Democratic Party workers portrayed him as the only candidate who could preserve the Union and avoid secession by the pro-slavery South. Buchanan gained strength in the South as the campaign of Frémont gained strength in the North. Southern voters concluded that Buchanan stood the best chance of beating the Republican candidate, and consequently support for Fillmore of the American Party declined.

Republicans, the only party firmly opposing expansion of slavery, ran strong in the North and made no effort at all in the South. The American Party tried to portray Frémont as sympathetic to Catholicism (Frémont was an Episcopalian who had married a Catholic). The Republican refused to engage in the debate about religion, on grounds that it was not a legitimate issue. The Know Nothings continued to emphasize religion, which may have cost Frémont some support in the North.

Both the Democrats and the Know Nothings in effect ran two campaigns in 1856: one in the South, another in the North. In the South, both parties emphasized support for popular sovereignty as the means of resolving the slavery issue. In the North, the Democrats emphasized their traditional role as the party of working people and immigrants. There were reports that immigrants in some states, notably in Indiana and Pennsylvania, were granted citizenship and voting rights before their legal waiting period was over as a means of adding Democratic voters to the rolls. For the American Party, the southern campaign also emphasized support for popular sovereignty, while the nothern campaign focused on attacking the religious views of the Republican Frémont, limiting immigration, and special protection for native-born Americans in getting government jobs. Both parties claimed that their candidate was best-positioned to preserve the union.

The Outcome

The election of 1856 established the essence of the two-party system that dominated presidential politics for the next 150 years. The Democrat, Buchanan, won 1,832,955 votes, or 45.3 percent of the total. He won 174 electoral votes, carrying every state in the South, plus Illinois, Indiana, Pennsylvania, and New Jersey.

Frémont won 1,339,932 votes, or 33.1 percent, and 114 electoral votes from the six New England states, plus New York, Ohio, Michigan, Iowa, and Wisconsin.

Fillmore of the American Party won 871,731 (21.6 percent) votes, but only eight electoral votes, from Maryland. However, the official outcome obscures the importance of Fillmore and the American Party in 1856. Buchanan's margin of victory was very low in several states, notably in Kentucky, Tennessee and Louisiana. Had Fillmore won those states, depriving Buchanan of their electoral votes, Frémont could very well have won, or at least the election might have been sent to the House of Representatives, as it had been in 1824.

The fact that Frémont won a third of the total popular vote with no effort in the South indicated the degree to which the themes of the Republican Party appealed to the populous northern states. Fillmore's campaign failed to take off in the North, and the Republicans emerged as the heirs to the Whigs.

More Information

▶ Anbinder, Tyler G. *Nativism and Slavery: The Northern Know Nothings and the Politics of the 1850s.* New York: Oxford University Press, 1992.

▶ Foner, Eric. *Free Soil, Free Labor, Free Men: The Ideology of the Republican Party Before the Civil War.* New York: Oxford University Press, 1995.

▶ Gienapp, William E. *The Origins of the Republican Party, 1852–1856.* New York: Oxford University Press, 1987.

▶ Scarry, Robert J. *Millard Fillmore.* Jefferson, N.C.: McFarland, 2001.

▶ Smith, Elbert B. *The Presidency of James Buchanan.* Lawrence: University Press of Kansas, 1975.

▶ Syme, Ronald. *John Charles Frémont: The Last American Explorer.* New York: Morrow, 1974.

Periodicals

▶ Volpe, Vermon L. "The Frémonts and the Emancipation in Missouri." *The Historian.* Winter 1994, p. 339.

On the Web

▶ James Buchanan, Inaugural Address Wednesday, March 4, 1857. *Inaugural Addresses of the Presidents of the United States.* Washington, D.C.: U.S. Government Printing Office, 1989;

FlashFocus: Millard Fillmore

13th President, 1850–1853; Whig Party Candidate for President, 1852

Born: January 7, 1800, Cayuga County, New York
Died: March 8, 1874, Buffalo, New York
Family: Son of Nathaniel Fillmore, a farmer, and Phoebe Millard Fillmore; married Abigail Powers, his teacher, in 1826

Education: Largely self-educated, with the help of a village schoolteacher, Abigail Powers; at age 19, studied law with a local judge; admitted to the bar in 1823

Political career: New York state legislature, 1828; U.S. House of Representatives from New York, 1833–35; U.S. vice president, 1849–50; president, 1850–53

Fillmore was an admirer and staunch supporter of the Whig leader, Senator Henry Clay of Kentucky. They agreed on the slavery issue, and especially on the need for compromise between North and South over the issue.

At the Whig convention of 1848, Clay lost the presidential nomination to Zachary Taylor, a career military officer and hero of the recent war with Mexico who had never voted before. Taylor was not associated with any controversial positions on slavery (or any other issue), as was Clay, and was regarded as likely to be elected. Fillmore was nominated to be vice president in order to placate Clay supporters. Hoping to duck the slavery controversy, the convention adopted no platform, and Taylor was elected president.

As vice president, Fillmore presided over raucous slavery debates in the Senate with even-tempered dignity. When Taylor died suddenly on July 9, 1850, Fillmore was sworn into office. Taylor had already signed into law the provisions of Clay's Compromise of 1850 bill, including the Fugitive Slave Law, earning himself the enmity of the abolitionists. It became a major issue during Fillmore's presidency as well.

In foreign policy, Fillmore advanced plans to establish trade with Japan, which the world at that time knew only as a "sealed" empire with little contact with the outside world.

Fillmore did not run for reelection in 1852. In 1856, he was the presidential candidate of the American Party (also called the Know Nothing Party) but won only eight electoral votes.

He reentered private life as a lawyer and civic leader in Buffalo, and died in 1874.

Bartleby.com, 2001. **http://www.bartleby.com/124/ pres30.html.**

▶ "Getting the Message Out! National Campaign Materials 1840–1860." Abraham Lincoln Historical Digitization Project at Northern Illinois University Libraries. Links to a variety of articles and primary source materials. **http://dig.lib.niu.edu/ message/about.html.**

▶ "The Politics of Sectionalism," Links to scores of primary documents for the period 1844–1860. **http://www.historyteacher. net/APUSH-Course/Weblinks/Weblinks12.htm.**

1860

Abraham Lincoln (Republican) vs. Stephen Douglas (Democrat)
vs. John Breckinridge (Southern Democrat)
vs. John Bell (Constitutional Union)

Candidates

Abraham Lincoln & Hannibal Hamlin, Republican
Stephen A. Douglas & Herschel V. Johnson, Democrat
John C. Breckinridge & Joseph Lane, Southern Democrat
John Bell & Edward Everett, Constitutional Union

Issues

Slavery. The institution of slavery, both in newly acquired territories and in established states, was the central issue of the election of 1860. There was a clear division between North and South. Northerners opposed slavery on moral grounds, and sought not only to prevent it from expanding into the new territories, but to abolish it altogether throughout the entire country. Southerners saw slavery as crucial to their economy and to their way of life, and believed that they should be able to transport their slaves into new territories and retain rights to those slaves as property. There was a growing fear among Southerners that northern abolitionists were serious about ending the practice of slavery, which would end the economic and social system that had made southern plantation owners so wealthy. Neither party had come out in support of abolition, but it was the main issue in the campaign, and forced candidates to adjust their campaigns based on regional differences in attitudes towards slavery.

Union. Well before the election, politicians in southern states were threatening to withdraw from the United States rather than face a threat to their economic structure, which was partly based on slave labor on huge cotton farms ("plantations"). Both northern candidates, Lincoln and Douglas, vowed to keep the country united. But within two months of the election, South Carolina became the first state to secede.

Outcome

Popular Vote

Lincoln	**1,865,593**	**39.8% ✓**
Douglas	1,382,713	29.5%
Breckinridge	848,356	18.1%
Bell	592,906	12.6%

Electoral College

Lincoln	**180 ✓**
Breckinridge	72
Bell	39
Douglas	12

Decades of disputes over the issues of states' rights and slavery came to a head in 1860. In the North, popular agitation to abolish slavery was a potent force. In the South, the push for abolition seemed like an economic attack on the region's cotton plantations, as well as an unwarranted federal intrusion on the rights of states to decide the issue for themselves. In the North, the Republican Party, which ran its first candidate for president in 1856, had expanded the anti-slavery movement from a small group of dedicated reformers to a much larger segment of society, dedicated to the twin propositions of stopping the spread of slavery to new territories and maintaining the unity of the states. The Republicans were a largely sectional party—they had no supporters in the slave states—which helped set the political stage for the civil war soon to come.

Events in the years leading up to the election served to heighten tensions. In 1857, the Dred Scott decision by the Supreme Court ruled that Congress could not legislate the issue of slavery, thereby enraging many northerners. In October 1859 abolitionist John Brown tried to spark a slave revolt with a raid on the federal arsenal at Harper's Ferry, Virginia (later part of West Virginia). The raid was crushed and Brown was tried and executed, but he became a folk hero and symbol of the moral crusade against slavery.

As the Republicans consolidated their strength in the North, the Democrats split over the issue of slavery. Northern Democrats, led by Senator Stephen Douglas of Illinois, tried to maintain the tradition of Andrew Jackson, regarding slavery as a matter to be resolved locally. Southern Democrats, such as Senator Jefferson Davis of Mississippi, thought slavery should receive federal protection and that slave-holders had a right to transport their "property" into new territories.

The Candidates

At the outset of the camaign in 1860, the Democratic Party was the only political institution that could claim to be national in scope. The Party convened in Charleston, South Carolina on April 23, 1860 in hopes of nominating a candidate to succeed Democrat James Buchanan in the White House.

Democrats from the South had another agenda item as well: reaffirming the right of Southerners to their property, i.e., slaves, including in the Territories. Their tactic was to insist on having the Party endorse a federal "slave code" for the Territories, which would supercede any local preferences on the issue of slavery. Without this code, Southerners agreed with Northerners that occupants of the Territories would vote to enter the Union as free states.

Northern Democrats, led by Senator Stephen Douglas of Illinois, preferred popular sovereignty, effectively keeping the federal government out of the dispute and leaving the decision to residents of the territories. Douglas was the leading candidate for the Democratic nomination. Other hopefuls included Senator Andrew Johnson of Tennessee, Senator Robert Hunter of Virginia and former Treasury Secretary James Gutherie of Kentucky.

Douglas was strongly opposed by Southern politicians who presented the convention with a resolution endorsing a federal slave code for the territories. The convention voted instead for an alternative resolution opposing a slave code, causing many Southern delegates to leave in protest, including the entire state delegations from Alabama, Mississippi, Florida and Texas, as well as many delegates from Georgia, South Carolina, Virginia, Arkansas, and Delaware. Although Civil War was still a year away, the Democratic convention in Charleston was a kind of dress rehearsal.

With the delegates from the South missing, the convention tried to settle on a presidential candidate. Douglas got the most votes, but could not get the required two-thirds and finally the convention decided to adjourn and meet again in Baltimore, on June 18, 1860.

The Constitutional Union Party

A week after the Democrats adjourned, the Constitutional Union Party held its convention in Baltimore. This party comprised elements from the old Whig Party and the anti-immigrant Know Nothing Party. The Constitutional Union Party nominated Senator John Bell of Tennessee as president and Edward Everett of Massachusetts as vice president on the second ballot. The party's platform reflected a hope that the slavery issue would essentially go away, or at least be resolved in a compromise that would avoid tearing the country into two parts. Reflective of Whig platforms of the 1840s, the Constitutional Union platform settled for platitudes about peace, union and compromise. It did not endorse any specific proposals.

Lacking a strong base anywhere, the strategy of the Constitutional Union Party was to deprive any nominee of a majority in the Electoral College, and thereby throw the election into the House of Representatives, where compromise might produce a president acceptable to both halves of the country.

The Republican Party

On May 16, the Republican Party held what was only its second national convention in Chicago. The Republicans were distinctly a party of the North. Leading the Republican pack for the presidential nomination was New York senator and former governor William H. Seward. He had adopted a firm policy opposing expansion of slavery into the territories. He had also opposed the anti-immigration policies of the Know

while arresting about 15,000 people and holding them under military detention.

Lincoln signed the Emancipation Proclamation effective January 1, 1863, freeing slaves in territory controlled by the Confederacy. Lincoln hoped the Proclamation would encourage slave revolts and disrupt the Confederate war effort; it accomplished neither. The Thirteenth Amendment to the Constitution, which ended slavery in the entire United States, was not passed for another two years.

The Civil War did not go well in the beginning, and Lincoln felt was compelled to fire a series of generals until Gen. Ulysses S. Grant became the commander of the Union armies and the Union cause started winning.

In 1864 Lincoln was unanimously nominated by the Republicans for reelection. Running on a National Union ticket, his vice presidential running mate was Senator Andrew Johnson of Tennessee, a Democrat. Lincoln's opponent was Gen. George B. McClellan, one of the generals whom Lincoln had fired. The Democrats demanded an immediate cease-fire and negotiated peace. But McClellan did not support his own party's position, and insisted he would continue the war effort more effectively than Lincoln could.

Lincoln won 55 percent of the popular votes in the states still in the Union, and 212 votes in the Electoral College compared to McClellan's twenty-one.

By the time of Lincoln's second inauguration on March,4, 1865, the war was rapidly drawing to a close; a month later Confederate General Robert E. Lee surrendered to Grant at Appomattox Courthouse, Virginia, on April 9, 1865. Five days later, on April 14, a Southern sympathizer, John Wilkes Booth, shot Lincoln while the president watched a play at Ford Theatre in Washington. Lincoln died the next day.

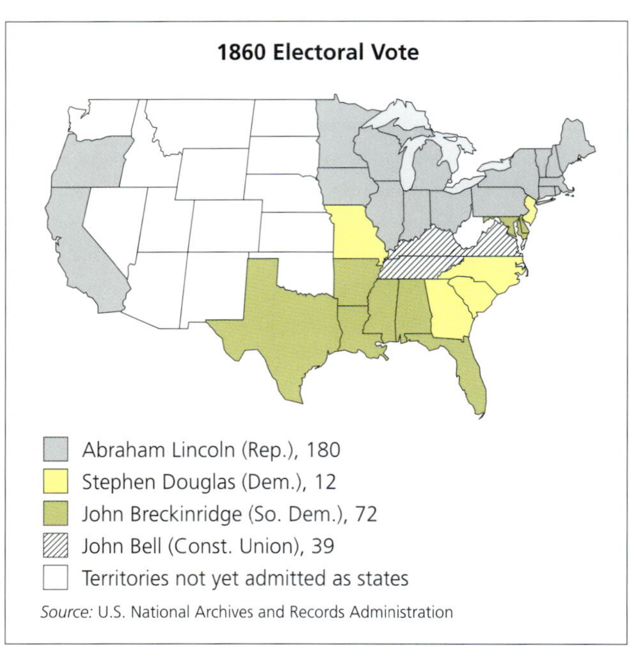

Source: U.S. National Archives and Records Administration

Nothing Party, which retained a following in border states like Kentucky and Tennessee.

Republican politicians worried that Seward would not be able to carry states like Pennsylvania, Indiana, and Illinois, where slavery took second place to economic concerns like protective tariffs, granting of free land to settlers in the West, and expansion of railroads to the West Coast.

Waiting in the wings as alternatives to Seward were Senator Simon Cameron of Pennsylvania, Governor Salmon Chase of Ohio, John Frémont of California, Representative Cassius Clay of Kentucky, Senator Benjamin Wade of Ohio, and Abraham Lincoln of Illinois, who was not currently an office-holder but had gained a national reputation during his losing Senate contest against Stephen Douglas in 1858.

Lincoln had the backing of the Illinois Republican delegation, plus a "home town" advantage since the convention was being held in Illinois. On the first ballot, Seward received 173½ votes to Lincoln's 102, with much smaller numbers for other contenders. A movement towards Lincoln partly sparked by opposition to Seward started on the second ballot (Seward 184½, Lincoln 181). Lincoln was nominated on the third ballot, winning 364 votes out of 466. Sen. Hannibal Hamlin of Maine was nominated for vice president.

On the key issue of slavery, the Republican platform advocated passing laws to prevent its expansion, while remaining silent on the issue of abolition. The party did, however, condemn the Dred Scott decision, which would have interfered with barring slavery in territories or new states.

There was to be one more moment of drama at the Republican convention. Rep. Joshua Giddings of Massachusetts proposed that the Republicans endorse the line from the Declaration that "all men are created equal." Initially the party voted his proposal down. But as the elderly abolitionist slowly made his way out of the chamber, another delegate, journalist George W. Curtis, jumped up and delivered a passionate speech in favor of the idea. As a result, the convention voted again and endorsed the proposition that the Declaration of Independence had declared to be "self-evident."

(Three and a half years later, on November 19, 1863, Lincoln returned to Thomas Jefferson's phrase in a short speech dedicating a memorial to the 45,000 casualties of the Battle of Gettysburg. "Four score and seven years ago," Abraham Lincoln said, "our forefathers brought forth on this continent a new nation, conceived in liberty and dedicated to the proposition that all men are created equal.")

The Democrats Reconvene

On June 18 the Democrats reconvened in Baltimore, but the party was irrevocably divided into northern and southern halves. The convention quickly nominated Stephen Douglas of Illinois to be president. Herschel Johnson of Georgia accepted the nomination to be vice president.

Southerners joined with delegates who had left the Charleston convention a month earlier and met at another hall in

Baltimore. They nominated Vice President John Breckinridge of Kentucky for president, with Sen. Joseph Lane of Oregon for vice president. They called themselves the National Democrats.

Thus at the end of a long nominating period, there were four candidates, none of whom could really claim to be the nominee of a united national party. Lincoln the Republican and Douglas the Democrat represented the North and some Midwestern states; Breckinridge the Southern Democrat represented the Southern states, and Bell represented the middle states, like his home state of Tennessee.

The Issues

Long before 1860 the question of slavery had divided the United States. In the Southern states, where slaves worked on large cotton plantations, slavery was part of the culture and the economy. Attacks on slavery were viewed as attacks on a way of life. In the North, slavery was widely viewed as immoral. The Northern economy was based on "free labor," workers who were paid wages for their work but were otherwise free and equal to any other citizen. Slavery was widely regarded as morally indefensible.

Until the election of 1860 these two views of slavery had been able to coexist. Northern abolitionists agitated for the emancipation of the slaves in the South, but the real debate had been over the territories, land in the West that was sparsely settled but which everyone agreed would someday be populated and turned into states. Would slavery take hold in these areas? Or would it be banned, as it was in the North?

At the start of the election in 1860, many northerners advocated a policy of "popular sovereignty," which would allow the people living in the territories to decide whether slavery should be allowed. Although this seemed like a neutral stance, in fact most Northerners were confident that a majority of settlers would vote against slavery in the territories simply because most settlers came from Northern states. Southerners saw this issue quite differently. They viewed slaves as property and asked why they should not be allowed to take their property westward and keep it. If slaves were in the same category as, say, horses and wagons, how could a migrating Southerner face having some of his property taken away simply because he moved? Thus, for Southerners, "popular sovereignty" was a thinly disguised threat to their property rights, their economic viability and their way of life.

Two events in the years preceding the election of 1860 threw this long-running debate into sharp perspective.

Dred Scott. In 1857, the U.S. Supreme Court issued its decision in *Dred Scott v. Sandford*. It involved a slave, Dred Scott, who had been transported to Illinois, a free state, and back to Missouri, a slave state. Scott brought a lawsuit claiming that when he entered Illinois, he had become a free man. The Supreme Court's decision denied Scott his freedom. The decision said, in effect, that Scott was a piece of property; he was therefore not a citizen and had no right to sue for his freedom; and that the Constitution barred the taking of property, including slaves. The implication of the decision was that the

federal government could not pass laws barring slavery, much less freeing slaves, since such laws would violate the Constitution's ban on taking property. The decision effectively ruled out "popular sovereignty" as a means of preventing the spread of slavery into the territories.

John Brown's Raid. In 1859 a radical abolitionist, John Brown, raided the federal armory at Harper's Ferry, Virginia (located in what would become West Virginia). Brown's aim was to use the arms he seized to free slaves and inspire a slave revolt. Brown's party was soon subdued by troops commanded by Robert E. Lee, and Brown was tried and hanged. His raid did not inspire a slave revolt, but it did have an enormous impact on slave-holders. Memories of earlier slave revolts were

dredged up, inflaming southern fears that the North really had in mind to abolish slavery in the South, possibly by inspiring revolts that would result in widespread terror.

Taken together, these two events set the stage for a confrontation over the issue of slavery. On the one hand, the Supreme Court seemed to block a legislative solution to limiting the expansion of slavery to new states; on the other, John Brown's raid, which received widespread support in the North, was viewed in the South as a forerunner of things to come.

Although slavery was the overriding issue in 1860, more traditional issues were also part of the election. Protective tariffs to protect manufacturers in the north were especially important in the battle for the electoral votes of Pennsylvania. Free land for settlers in the western territories was a potent issue, as was public works (mainly government-financed improvements in transportation systems) in the states of the Great Lakes region.

The Campaign

No major party had endorsed the abolition of slavery. Yet this had become the issue around which the election of 1860 revolved, symbolized by the Republican endorsement of the phrase "all men are created equal."

There were two separate campaigns and, in effect, two separate elections in 1860. Republicans were firmly united behind Lincoln in the North, whereas Lincoln's name did not even appear on the ballot in most southern states. The Republicans employed the most innovative campaign tactics in 1860. They organized clubs whose members wore uniforms and marched in torch-light parades, lending a sort of military atmosphere to political campaigning. These "Wide Awake" clubs turned the election into a social crusade which was especially appealing to young people. By supporting free land for settlers in the West and public workers projects in the Great Lakes region, the Republicans appealed to voters on more than just the issue of slavery.

Douglas, the Democrat, abandoned the tradition of candidates not actively campaigning and tried to capture Lincoln's base in New York and New England. Douglas also campaigned in the southern states, where he argued that secession from the United States would spark a civil war.

Breckinridge, the Southern Democrat, supported the unfettered right of southerners to hold slaves, including the right to take slaves westward into the Territories. Since his position on the issue was only viable in the South, he limited his campaign.

Bell focused his efforts on his home state and on Kentucky, hoping victories there would keep the evident overall winner, Lincoln, from capturing a majority in the Electoral College.

Some Democrats foresaw that their only hope of victory lay in combining (or "fusing") their candidate, Douglas, with the Constitutional Union Party.

State elections held independently of the presidential election in September and October accurately forecast the outcome of the presidential contest in November. In Pennsylvania, Illinois, Indiana, and Maine, Republicans were swept into office. The result was that politicians in the South renewed threats of seceding, or leaving the United States. Republicans largely dismissed these threats as repeats of past efforts to intimidate the North, and Lincoln did not try to broaden his appeal to the South.

Supporters of Douglas, Breckinridge, and Bell tried to arrange an alliance of their supporters in key northern states, notably New York and Pennsylvania, in a last-ditch effort to forestall a Republican victory, possibly by coming up with an entirely new candidate. But they were not successful. Douglas shifted his emphasis to protecting the Union, suggesting that secession and abolition should be put aside in the interests of national unity.

The Outcome

The federal election was held on November 6, 1860. Turnout was huge—over 80 percent of the eligible voters participated. No one captured a majority of the popular votes:

Lincoln (R)	1,865,593	39.8%
Douglas (D)	1,382,713	29.5%
Breckinridge (SD)	848,356	18.1%
Bell (CU)	592,906	12.6%

The popular vote totals did not tell the entire story. Lincoln received only 26,388 votes in the slave states; he did not even appear on the ballot in some states. The great majority of Douglas's votes also came from free states, whereas Breckinridge received only 99,381 votes from free states, mostly from states that bordered on the slave-holding states. The Constitutional Union candidate, Bell, received most of his votes in the slave states and in fact trailed Breckinridge in those states by just over 70,000 votes.

The results in the Electoral College were quite different, however:

Lincoln	180
Breckinridge	72
Bell	39
Douglas	12

On December 20, six weeks after the election, South Carolina seceded from the union. By the time Lincoln took office in March, 1861, six more states had seceded. Just a month after Lincoln's inauguration, Confederates fired on Fort Sumter in Charleston, South Carolina harbor. Four more states seceded and the Civil War had begun.

More Information

▶ Davis, William C. *Breckinridge: Statesman, Soldier, Symbol.* Baton Rouge: Louisiana State University Press, 1974.

▶ Dirck, Brian R. *Lincoln and Davis: Imaginging America, 1809–1865.* Lawrence: University Press of Kansas, 2001.

▶ Jaffa, Harry V. *A New Birth of Freedom: Abraham Lincoln and the Coming of the Civil War.* Lanham, MD: Roman and Littlefield Publishers, 2000.

▶ Johannsen, Robert W. *The Frontier, the Union, and Stephen A. Douglas.* Urbana: University of Illinois Press, 1989.

▶ Johnson, Michael P. *Abraham Lincoln, Slavery, and the Civil War: Selected Writings and Speeches.* Boston: Bedford/St. Martin's, 2001.

On the Web

▶ Latner, Richard B. "The Crisis at Fort Sumter." Tulane University. **http://www.tulane.edu/~latner/.**

▶ "The Election of 1860." *America in Caricature 1865–1865.* The Lilly Library, Indiana University. **http://www.indiana.edu/~liblilly/cartoon/devision.html.**

▶ Abraham Lincoln, First Inaugural Address Monday, March 4, 1861. *Inaugural Addresses of the Presidents of the United States.* Washington, D.C.: U.S. Government Printing Office, 1989; Bartleby.com, 2001. **http://www.bartleby.com/124/pres31. html.**

▶ Abraham Lincoln Historical Digitization Project. Links to articles and primary sources relating to Lincoln. **http://lincoln. lib.niu.edu/aboutinfo.html.**

▶ "Getting the Message Out! National Campaign Materials 1840–1860." Abraham Lincoln Historical Digitization Project. Links to a variety of articles and primary sources. **http://dig. lib.niu.edu/message/about.html.**

▶ "The Politics of Sectionalism," Links to scores of primary documents for the period 1844–1860. **http://www.historyteacher. net/APUSH-Course/Weblinks/Weblinks12.htm.**

Constitutional Union Candidate for President, 1860

Born: February 15, 1797, Nashville, Tennessee
Died: September 10, 1869, Bear Spring Furnace, Tennessee
Family: Son of Samuel Bell, a farmer, and Margaret Edmiston; married Sally Dickinson (died), Jane Yeatman

Education: Cumberland College
Political career: Whig. Tennessee state senate, 1817; U.S. representative from Tennessee, 1827–41; U.S. secretary of war, 1841; Tennessee state house of representatives, 1847; U.S. senator from Tennessee, 1847–59

John Bell graduated from Cumberland College (later the University of Nashville), and established his own law office in Franklin, Tennessee. He served one term in the state senate, but decided not to seek reelection.

In 1827, Bell was elected to the U.S. House of Representatives from Tennessee, where he would serve for 14 years, becoming Speaker of the House in 1834. He was appointed secretary of war by President William Henry Harrison in 1841, but resigned upon Harrison's death a few weeks later.

Bell was elected to the Senate in 1847, where he served until 1859. He showed little tolerance for extremists in the gathering storm of slavery, and pursued moderate policies. The Whig party had disappeared, and Bell considered joining several parties before being nominated as the Constitutional Union party's candidate for president in 1860. He favored preservation of the Union, but his reluctance to take a strong stance on slavery did not resonate with voters.

When Abraham Lincoln was elected president in 1860, Bell spoke out against secession by southern states and worked to prevent civil war. When it became clear that war was inevitable, he advised Tennessee to secede from the Union, which it did. This marked the end of his political career.

After the Civil War, Bell returned to Tennessee, where he remained until his death on September 10, 1869.

1864
Abraham Lincoln (Republican) vs. George McClellan (Democrat)

The centerpiece issues of presidential elections since 1824—the relative balance of power between the federal and state governments, and the future of slavery—were suddenly absent in 1864. Their resolution in the political arena had given way to civil war, with eleven southern states split off from the union and forming the Confederate States of America. In the North, the progress of the war and its possible resolution—either by military victory or negotiated peace—were the only two issues that seemed to matter. The fact that the war did not interrupt the normal schedule of presidential elections provided evidence of how solid constitutional law was in the North.

The Context

The North was steadily gaining the upper hand in the Civil War, although the end was not clearly in sight by the summer of 1864. The Union army had repulsed two Confederate advances into northern territory—in the Battle of Antietam (Maryland) in September, 1862, and the Battle of Gettysburg (Pennsylvania) in July, 1863. The North had also gained control of the Mississippi River, cutting off three Confederate states (Arkansas, Louisiana, and Texas) from the others after the Battle of Vicksburg (Mississippi) in July, 1863. Nevertheless the North had implemented a compulsory military draft in March 1864, which caused rioting in several cities, especially New York, in the summer. President Abraham Lincoln's conduct of the war was questioned on both sides—by those who favored a more aggressive effort, and by those who were pushing for a negotiated settlement.

Politically the Emancipation Proclamation of January 1863 brought a mixed response in the North. The Proclamation only applied to slaves in Confederate territory not controlled by Union forces. It did not satisfy abolitionists in the North, and had no practical effect on slaves in territory controlled by the North. Although the end of the war was not clear, Lincoln had announced plans for "reconstructing" the South after the war—plans that became controversial over terms of black participation in politics and punishment of the Confederate states for having broken away from the union.

The Candidates

No president had been reelected since Andrew Jackson in 1832, leaving ample precedent for a challenge to Lincoln's reelection effort in 1864. His treasury secretary, Salmon Chase of Ohio, was a leader of the Radical Republicans who criticized Lincoln's conduct of the war and his announced plans for governing the Confederate states after the war. Chase, who had long harbored ambitions to become president, was joined by Ohio Senator John Sherman, Representative James Garfield (himself a future presidential candidate in 1880), and Senator Samuel Pomeroy of Kansas in an effort to gain the 1864 Republican nomination instead of Lincoln. Supporters of Chase circulated two pamphlets in February 1864, one of which called for a new president and the other which suggested Chase for the job. Coming in the midst of war, however, the so-called Pomeroy Circular resulted in a backlash against Chase, and the treasury secretary's declaration, on March 5, that he would not be a candidate. In late June Chase offered to resign his cabinet post, and Lincoln accepted.

By the time the Republicans gathered for their convention at Baltimore in June, 1864, Lincoln's nomination was a fore-

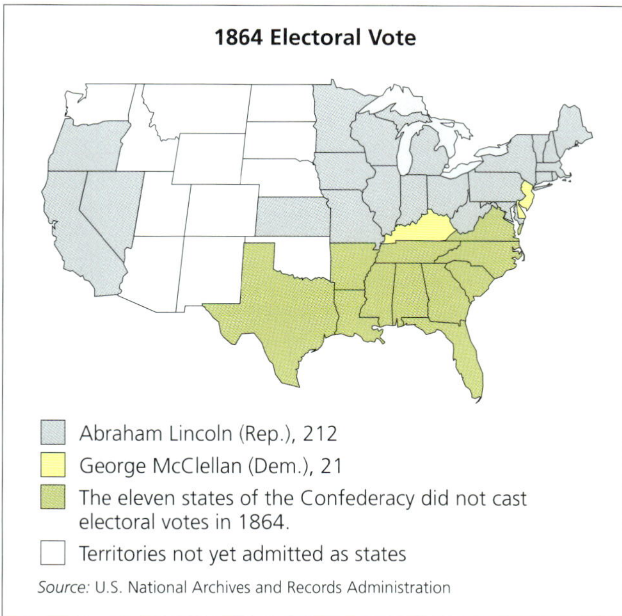

Source: U.S. National Archives and Records Administration

FlashFocus: Andrew Johnson

17th President, 1865–1869

Born: December 29, 1808, Raleigh, North Carolina

Died: July 31, 1875, Carter Station, Tennessee

Family: Son of Jacob Johnson, a laborer, and Mary McDonough Johnson, a washerwoman; married Eliza McCardle

Education: No formal schooling; apprenticed to a tailor at age 14

Political life: Democrat. Tennessee House of Representatives, 1835–37; Tennessee Senate 1841–43; U.S. representative from Tennessee, 1843–53; governor of Tennessee, 1853–57; U.S. senator from Tennessee, 1857–62; military governor of Tennessee 1862–64; vice president, 1865; president, 1865–69; U.S. senator from Tennessee, 1875.

As senator from Tennessee when the Civil Was broke out, Andrew Johnson was against secession and therefore considered a hero in the North and a traitor in the South. Johnson became the military governor of Tennessee in 1862 until 1864, when the Republicans nominated him for vice president in an effort to present a unified front in the face of the Civil War. When President Abraham Lincoln was assassinated in April, 1865, Johnson was sworn in as president, uniquely complicating the political picture.

Radical Republicans insisted on severe measures to reform the defeated Confederate states and were unhappy with Johnson's moderate post-war policies. As Johnson implemented measures, Congress countermanded them. Johnson wanted to welcome Southern states back into full participation in the federal government, but Radical Republicans in Congress instead wanted to impose military governments. The deadlock continued throughout Johnson's term, culminating in the House of Representatives voting on articles of impeachment against Johnson on February 21, 1868. The charge was that by dismissing Secretary of War Edwin Stanton, Johnson had violated the 1867 Tenure of Office Act, which prohibited the president from removing any federal official who had been appointed with the approval of the Senate. (The Supreme Court later ruled the act unconstitutional.) Johnson escaped impeachment by one vote.

Johnson left office in 1869. He was elected to the Senate from Tennessee in 1874, but died shortly after taking office.

gone conclusion. The Republicans began calling themselves the Union Party, and invited Democrats who supported Lincoln's policies to join them. At the convention, the delegates agreed to seat delegates from six states of the Confederacy and allowed delegates from three of them to vote. Delegates from Florida and Virginia were allowed to attend but not to vote, and a delegation from South Carolina was not allowed to attend at all.

Lincoln was nominated on the first ballot, receiving all but Missouri's twenty-two votes, which were cast for General Ulysses S. Grant; afterwards, Missouri moved to make the nomination of Lincoln unanimous.

Lincoln expressed no preference for a vice presidential running mate. His existing vice president, Hannibal Hamlin, wanted the nomination but did not generate enthusiasm among the delegates. Instead, they chose the military governor of Tennessee, Andrew Johnson. Johnson had two advantages: he was a Democrat, and he was a Southerner who had opposed secession. The hope was that he could attract like-minded people to the Union Party ticket. On the first ballot, Johnson led the voting with 200 votes, followed by Hamlin with 150, and former Senator Daniel Dickinson of New York with 108. On the second ballot, the delegation from Kentucky swung their votes to Johnson, which sparked a consensus, leaving Johnson with 492 votes and the nomination.

A week before the Republican (Union) convention, a dissident group of Radical Republicans who were not satisfied either with Lincoln's conduct of the war or with his announced plans for dealing with the South after the war, had met in Cleveland. There, they adopted the name Radical Democracy, and nominated General John C. Frémont for president. Frémont had been the Republicans' first presidential candidate, in 1856, but had clashed with Lincoln early in the civil war. Lincoln had rescinded an emancipation order by Frémont in Missouri in 1861, and relieved him of his military command on two occasions. Frémont was supported by abolitionists in Missouri and some New England abolitionists such as Elizabeth Cady Stanton. The breakaway Republicans endorsed continuation of the war until final victory over the Confederacy, a Constitutional amendment banning slavery, and support for civil liberties, reflecting their opposition to the Lincoln Administration's suspension of the writ of habeas corpus, the Constitutional requirement that the government file charges against people placed under arrest.

While the Republicans found it relatively easy to unite around President Lincoln, the Democratic Party was split into three factions: War Democrats, who supported Lincoln and eventually defected to the "Union Party;" a second pro-war faction that challenged Lincoln's handling of the war; and the Copperheads, or "peace Democrats," who favored a negotiated peace and lenient terms for readmission of the southern states. The Democrats delayed their convention until August, 1864, waiting to see how the war might affect their position.

Gathered in Chicago, the delegates first accepted resolutions of the Copperhead (peace) faction calling for a cease-fire and negotiated settlement. These resolutions were incorporated into the Democratic platform.

However, delegates also voted overwhelmingly to nominate General George B. McClellan as their candidate. McClellan was a War Democrat, and in fact had led the Union army until he was dismissed by Lincoln on grounds of being too cautious on the battlefield. After the Battle of Antietam McClellan had failed to pursue the retreating Confederate Army led by General Robert E. Lee, thereby missing a possible chance to end the war shortly after it had begun. McClellan as a candidate rejected the Democratic peace platform, and resolved to pursue the war to victory. As vice president, the Democrats nominated Representative George Pendleton of Ohio, a peace Democrat.

The Issues

The Civil War had replaced the long-standing debate over the relative powers of the federal government and the future of slavery in the territories. Instead, the 1864 election focused on the conduct of the war and plans for the post-war period.

Conduct of the war. Lincoln's pursuit of the Civil War had long roused controversy. On one end of the spectrum, Radical Democracy, the dissident Republicans supporting Frémont, felt that Lincoln had not been sufficiently aggressive in pursuing war, and completely rejected the idea of a negotiated settlement. At the other end of the spectrum, the Copperheads, or peace Democrats, advocated a quick end to fighting and negotiations between North and South to end the war, with lenient treatment for the breakaway Confederate states. In the middle were the Republicans led by Lincoln, who was in charge of the military effort and who had published a preliminary plan for the post-war period. The Democratic candidate, General McClellan, also fell in the middle. He had rejected the peace platform of the Democratic convention and instead based his campaign on a promise to be more effective than Lincoln in pursuing the war.

Abolition of slavery. On January 1, 1863, the Emancipation Proclamation declared that all slaves in Confederate territory were free. The Proclamation earned Lincoln the nickname Great Emancipator, but in reality did not free a single slave since it only applied to Confederate territory not occupied by Union troops. The earlier debate over expansion of slavery into territories which were not yet states had been addressed by the Republican-controlled Congress in June, 1862 with a law that freed slaves in the territories without compensating their owners for loss of their "property." The Republican (Union) Party platform endorsed the abolition of slavery everywhere in the United States; the Democratic platform was silent on the issue, limiting itself to the conduct of the war and a call for a negotiated peace.

Civil liberties. During the war, the Lincoln administration had suspended some civil liberties, most notably the writ of *habeas corpus,* the provision in the Constitution that required the government to file charges against anyone who was arrested. The platform of Radical Democracy (i.e., dissident Republicans) specifically denounced the administration's move and called for restoration of civil liberties. The Democratic platform also criticized use of martial law and suspension of civil liberties in the process of calling for a negotiated peace.

There were also faint echoes of earlier campaigns in the platform of the Republican (Union) Party in 1864, such as its call for a transcontinental railroad, support for the Monroe Doctrine, and encouragement of immigration. The latter in particular might have seemed odd, since the Democrats had long been the principal beneficiaries of immigration. Support for the transcontinental railroad was a reflection of the philosophy of the defunct Whig party, many of whose supporters had come over to the Republicans in 1856.

The Campaign

Just days after the Democratic convention, Union general William Tecumseh Sherman captured Atlanta and began his infamous "March to the Sea" in which he destroyed property in a broad swath of Confederate territory and split the southern half of the Confederacy from the northern half. Union success on the battlefield almost instantly cut into support for the Democrat, General McClellan, and his contention that he would be more effective than Lincoln in pursuing the war.

The Republican campaign tried to cast the Democrats, and their official peace platform, as virtual traitors, claiming among other things that the Democrats had a secret arrangement with the Confederacy to end the war. The Republicans also seized on an Army report on secret groups of Confederate sympathizers in the North, strongly suggesting that the Democrats were secret Confederates in the heart of the Union.

The Republican campaign also focused on Union soldiers as a source of support. Lincoln's secretary of war, Edwin Stanton, arranged for many Union troops to go on leave in order to return home and vote, presumably for Lincoln. The president himself asked some of his generals to let soldiers from Indiana, Pennsylvania, New York and Missouri—states that Lincoln regarded as critical to his victory—go home in order to vote.

In October, the Radical Democracy candidate, Frémont, began fretting that his campaign could cut into support for Lincoln and cause the election to go to the Democrats. Although the Democratic candidate, General McClellan, supported pursuit of the war, Frémont feared that support for total emancipation of slaves was weak among Democrats. Consequently, Frémont was open to a suggestion by Senator Zachariah Chandler of Michigan, to drop out of the race in exchange for arranging for Lincoln to dismiss a political rival, Montgomery Blair, the postmaster general. In late September Frémont and his vice presidential running mate issued public letters withdrawing from the contest; a month later, Lincoln asked for Blair's resignation, which he received, although there was no explicit deal reached with Frémont.

The Outcome

Lincoln was reelected with 2,206,938 votes, or 55 percent, to McClellan's 1,803,787, or 45 percent. In the electoral college, Lincoln won all but three states (New Jersey, Delaware, and Kentucky), gaining 212 electoral votes to 21 for McClellan. Republicans also gained seats in both houses of Congress, and regained majorities in several state legislatures.

Although the Democratic candidate had supported pursuing the war, the Democratic party was long associated with its peace platform, and would not be able to elect a president for twenty years. On the other hand, the association between the Republicans and the war put the southern states into the Democratic fold for over a century.

More Information

▶ Fletcher, George P. *Our Secret Constitution: How Lincoln Redefined American Democracy*. New York: Oxford University Press, 2001.

▶ Golay, Michael. *A Ruined Land: The End of the Civil War*. New York: Wiley, 1999.

▶ Hassler, Warren W. *General George B. McClellan: Shield of the Union*. Baton Rouge: Louisiana State University Press, 1957.

▶ Hesseltine, William B. *Lincoln's Plan of Reconstruction*. Chicago: Quadrangle Books, 1967.

▶ Klingaman, William. K. *Abraham Lincoln and the Road to Emancipation, 1861–1865*. New York: Viking, 2001.

▶ Vorenberg, Michael. *Final Freedom: The Civil War, the Abolition of Slavery, and the Thirteenth Amendment*. New York: Cambridge University Press, 2001.

▶ Waugh, John C. *Reflecting Lincoln: The Battle for the 1864 Presidency*. New York: Crown Publishers, 1997.

▶ White, Ronald C. *Lincoln's Greatest Speech: The Second Inaugural*. New York: Simon & Schuster, 2002.

Periodicals

▶ Harris, William. "Conservative Unionists and the Presidential Election of 1864." *Civil War History,* December 1992, p. 298.

▶ Vorenberg, Michael. "'The Deformed Child': Slavery and the Election of 1864." *Civil War History,* September 2001, p. 240.

On the Web

▶ Lincoln, Abraham. "Second Inaugural Address," March 4, 1865. **http://www.bartleby.com/124/pres32.html.**

▶ National Park Service "Lincoln, Grant and the 1864 Election." Lincoln Home, National Historic Site. **http://www.nps.gov/liho/1864/1864a.htm.**

▶ Abraham Lincoln, Second Inaugural Address Saturday, March 4, 1865. *Inaugural Addresses of the Presidents of the United States.* Washington, D.C.: U.S. Government Printing Office, 1989; Bartleby.com, 2001. **http://www.bartleby.com/124/pres32.html.**

1868

Ulysses S. Grant (Republican) vs. Horatio Seymour (Democrat)

Candidates

Ulysses S. Grant & Schuyler Colfax, Republican
Horatio Seymour & Francis P. Blair, Jr., Democrat

Issues

Reconstruction. Republicans argued that the former Confederate states needed to institute significant changes and write entirely new state Constitutions before they could be readmitted to the Union. Their demands for the "reconstruction" of these states included the extension of voting rights to black males and ratification of the Fourteenth Amendment, which gave equal rights to all citizens. They painted the Democrats as the party that had supported the expansion of slavery and opposed the war effort. Democrats supported a more lenient attitude towards the former Confederate states, focusing on reconciliation and reunification. They claimed to be the only party that was national rather than regional, and accused the Republicans of taking an oppressive and tyrannical stance towards the southern states. They also pointed out that Republicans were in favor of racial equality, a concept that was distasteful to many voters in both the South and in the North.

"Soft money." The issue of "soft money"—currency not backed by the gold standard—emerged for the first time during this campaign. The idea, popular in the West but unpopular in the East, was to remain an issue for the next several elections.

Outcome

Popular Vote

Grant	3,013,421	52.7% ✓
Seymour	2,706,829	47.3%

Electoral College

Grant	214 ✓
Seymour	80

The interval between the election of 1864 and 1868 was as dramatic as any comparable period in American history. The North and South had fought a bitter civil war over the dual questions of whether slavery should extend beyond its traditional confines in the Southeast, and what should be the relative roles of the federal and state governments. Just a month after fighting ended, President Abraham Lincoln was assassinated, leaving his vice president, Democrat Andrew Johnson of Tennessee, as president. In 1868 the struggle over the future of the nation, and specifically over the future of the vanquished states of the Confederacy, remained up in the air.

The Context

The four years after the election of 1864 proved to be nearly as traumatic for the United States as the war itself. In December 1864 Radical Republicans and some Democrats forced Lincoln supporters to drop a bill that would have readmitted Louisiana as a state; the Radicals wanted a wholesale reformation, or "reconstruction," of the political structure in the former Confederate states. Lincoln and his vice president, the former military governor of Tennessee, Andrew Johnson, favored a more lenient stance towards the rebels. On March 4, 1864 Lincoln took the oath of office for the second time, the first president to be reelected since Andrew Jackson in 1832. In his second inaugural speech, Lincoln ended with words of conciliation for the South, which was by then on the verge of defeat: "With malice toward none, with charity for all, with firmness in the right as God gives us to see the right, let us strive on to finish the work we are in, to bind up the nation's wounds, to care for him who shall have borne the battle and for his widow and his orphan, to do all which may achieve and cherish a just and lasting peace among ourselves and with all nations." Less than a month later, on April 9, Confederate General Robert E. Lee surrendered to Union General Ulysses S. Grant at Appomattox, Virginia, ending the Civil War. And just five days after that, Lincoln was shot while attending a play at Ford's Theatre in Washington on the evening of April 14, 1865; he died the next morning.

In December, 1865, the Thirteenth Amendment was ratified and became law, ending slavery in the United States. Republicans in Congress promptly moved to assure newly emancipated slaves of political rights by means such as the Civil Rights Act, passed in April 1866, and the Fourteenth Amendment (ratified in June) that made all persons born or naturalized in the United States citizens with equal protection under the law. The Amendment also changed the original Constitutional formula for calculating representation in Congress; black people, no longer slaves, counted as whole people rather than six-tenths of a person as in the original Constitution. (The Fifteenth Amendment, which explicitly gave all male citizens, including freed slaves, the right to vote, was not ratified until two years later, in 1870.) Republicans were rewarded for their post–Civil War policies in the congressional elections of 1866 with a two-third majority in Congress, making impossible the efforts by President Andrew Johnson to moderate the Radical Republican reconstruction program.

Continued political fights between the Congress and Johnson resulted in the impeachment of Johnson in March, 1868 by the Republican-controlled House of Representatives. On

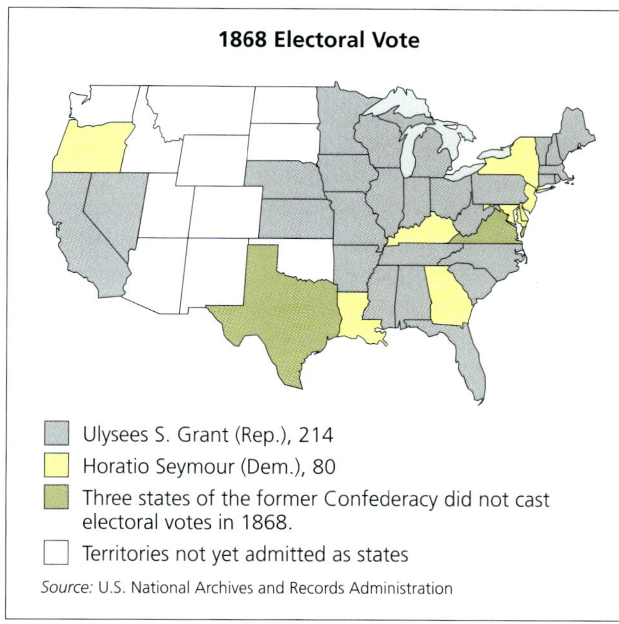

Source: U.S. National Archives and Records Administration

May 16, the Senate, by a single vote, refused to convict Johnson on the first count (accusation) of his impeachment before adjourning in order to allow the Republican members to attend their presidential nominating convention in Chicago.

The Candidates

Although the Republicans had won the presidential election of 1864 with the reelection of Lincoln, the incumbent in 1868, Johnson, was a Democrat and in any case was unacceptable to the Republican Party whose congressional delegation had tried to remove him from office. Meeting in Chicago in May, 1868, the party that now called itself the National Union Republican Party nominated General Ulysses S. Grant unanimously on the first ballot. Grant was a war hero and a moderate. The fact that Republicans had lost political influence in state elections held the previous year in New York, Pennsylvania, and Ohio, convinced even Radical Republicans that a moderate was needed to retain the White House. (About a week later, the Senate reconvened and voted not to convict Johnson on two other counts in the impeachment bill, then decided to drop the case altogether.) For vice president, the Republicans chose Schuyler Colfax of Indiana, Speaker of the House of Representatives.

The Democratic convention opened on July 4, 1968 in New York. It included delegates from the Southern states, who were allowed to vote. At the outset, the two leading candidates for the presidential nomination were President Johnson (who had been a Democrat even though he was elected vice president on a Republican ticket in 1864), and George Pendleton of Ohio, who had run for vice president as a Democrat in 1864. Pendleton was popular in the West, but not in the East, because he advocated so-called "soft money"—printed currency that was not backed by deposits of gold. Politically, the position was popular since it was likely to result in inflation (rising prices)

18th President, 1869–1877

Born: April 27, 1822, Point Pleasant, Ohio
Died: July 23, 1885, Mount McGregor, New York
Family: Son of Jesse Grant, a farmer and Hannah Simpson Grant; married Julia Dent
Education: One-room schoolhouses; U.S. Military Academy, West Point, 1839–43

Political career: Republican. Ulysses Grant was a military officer who never held an elected office before becoming president in 1869. After serving in the war with Mexico (1846–48) Grant left the Army for a series of undistinguished jobs, ending as a clerk working in his brother's store. When the Civil War began in 1861, Grant responded to President Abraham Lincoln's call for volunteers and was appointed a colonel; he was soon promoted to brigadier general.

By the end of the conflict, Grant had been put in charge of the entire Union war effort. In April 1865 he accepted the surrender of Confederate General Robert E. Lee at Appomattox, Virginia.

In 1867, President Andrew Johnson named Grant his secretary of war to oversee Union occupation of the former Confederacy. The following year, Radical Republicans nominated Grant to run for president. As the victorious general of the Civil War, Grant easily defeated Horatio Seymour, a little-known judge from New York.

Once in office, Grant's lack of political sophistication led almost immediately to problems. By following the lead of Radical Republicans in a program of penalties against the South, he alienated more moderate Republicans. In his second term, a series of corruption scandals undermined Grant's reputation and he declined to run for a third term in 1876.

In retirement, Grant was swindled out of his life savings. Disillusioned and suffering from cancer, he feverishly wrote his memoirs in the hope of leaving his family provided for. He died soon after completing them, on July 23, 1885.

and therefore help debtors buy reducing the value of money needed to pay off debts. It was a controversy that was destined to rage for the next four decades.

Pendleton led after the first ballot, followed by Johnson. But neither man was close to the two-thirds majority needed for nomination. After eight ballots, Pendleton still had just 156½ votes out of 212 needed for the nomination. General Winfield Scott, a Civil War general, picked up support over the next ten ballots, rising to 144½ votes on the eighteenth ballot before his support, too, began to dwindle. Senator Thomas Hendricks of Indiana looked like a possible candidate over the next four ballots, gaining 132 votes on the twenty-first ballot. But on the twenty-second ballot, Ohio cast its votes for Horatio Seymour, a former governor of New York and chairman of the convention. From the podium, Seymour declared that he

FlashFocus: Horatio Seymour

Democratic Candidate for President 1868

Born: May 31, 1810, Pompey Hill, New York

Died: February 12, 1886, Utica, New York

Family: Son of Henry Seymour, a wealthy businessman, and Mary Ledyard; married Mary Bleecker; no children

Education: Private academies; studied law and was admitted to the bar in 1832

Political career: Democrat. New York state representative (1842, 1844–46); mayor of Utica, N.Y. (1843); speaker, New York Assembly, 1845; governor of New York 1853–55; 1863–65; Democratic presidential nominee, 1868

Horatio Seymour spent most of his life in politics, starting as the military secretary to New York Governor William Marcy, who remained a political mentor for most of Seymour's career. He was elected to the New York Assembly, where his deft management of legislation led to his election as speaker. He was defeated in a bid to become New York governor in 1850, but won the office in 1852 for one term. He was defeated in 1854, but was elected again in 1863.

Seymour had a long career as a conservative Democrat in what was, at the time, the nation's largest state. He was a life-long supporter of the Erie canal and other public improvements. During the Civil War, he opposed abolitionism (he thought competition with free labor would eventually doom slavery) and the Emancipation Proclamation.

While serving as chairman of the 1868 Democratic convention, Seymour was nominated to run against Civil War hero General Ulysses S. Grant. He lost the popular vote, 52.7 percent for Grant to 47.3 percent for Seymour, and in the electoral college, 214 to 80.

Seymour retired from active politics, but was a mentor to younger Democrats including Grover Cleveland. He died in Utica, New York in 1886, shortly after his protégé, Cleveland, became the first Democrat elected president since 1856 (see p. 94).

black men. The Republicans also required the "reconstructed" southern states to ratify the Fourteenth Amendment (equal rights for all citizens) before they could be freed from the Reconstruction Acts that divided the Confederacy into five military districts, each governed by a Union general backed by federal troops. To regain civilian control, the former Confederate states were required to adopt new constitutions before being readmitted to the Union.

With both houses of Congress firmly in Republican hands, Republicans argued that a Democratic president would simply result in a stalemate.

The Democrats favored a more lenient attitude towards the breakaway states of the South, and they sought to cast reconstruction in terms of racial equality and national reconciliation. Since the Democrats had opposed the war in the first place, they were able to position themselves as the only national party and the one that stood the best chance of reuniting the nation after four years of war and a further four years of military occupation of the South by the victorious Union army. The Democrats denounced the Republicans as the cause of what the Democratic platform called a "disregard of right and the unparalleled oppression and tyranny" of the post-war occupation of the Confederate states. The Democratic platform also accused the Republicans of promoting "military despotism" and "negro supremacy."

The Campaign

Following a long tradition, Grant did not actively campaign for office. Instead, he spent most of his time at home in Galena, Illinois. He took one trip, by rail, to Denver accompanied by two other Union generals, William Sherman and Philip Sheridan, but even then refused to give any speeches. Instead, the Republicans sent hundreds of speakers to deliver speeches, circulate pamphlets, and organize parades. The Republicans lost no opportunity to remind voters that Democrats had supported expansion of slavery and had opposed the war effort. As proof that the South needed to be reconstructed, Republican newspapers emphasized stories of violence against blacks and Republicans in the South. Republicans also claimed that the Democratic candidate, Seymour, while governor of New York in 1863, had referred to anti-draft rioters as "my friends" and linked Seymour to the Copperheads, who favored a peace treaty with the Confederacy, which Republicans viewed as close to treason against the North.

Republicans were given another target in the person of Frank Blair, the Democratic vice presidential nominee and a vocal critic of Radical Republicans. He urged that the Reconstruction Acts punishing the South should be nullified, and claimed that Grant would turn into a military dictator if elected. Republicans cast Blair as an extremist—the New York *Tribune* called him a "revolutionist."

The Democratic campaign focused on claims that the Republicans advocated racial equality, a point not popular either in the South or among many immigrant voters in the North.

was not interested in becoming a candidate, but this did not cause Ohio to change its vote. Backers of Seymour took him out of the convention hall, and after several states switched their votes on the twenty-third ballot, Seymour was the Democratic nominee. For vice president the Democrats chose General Francis Blair of Missouri, a former Republican; he was nominated unanimously on the first ballot.

The Issues

Reconstruction, or the reform of former Confederate states before they would be allowed readmission to the Union, was the leading issue in an election which, like the one in 1864, was largely decided in the North since most southern states had not yet been readmitted to the Union. In 1867 Congress had passed, over Johnson's veto, the law that gave voting rights to

In addition to presenting themselves as the only party representing all parts of the country, the Democrats also tried to portray Grant as a drunk. They seized upon the brief membership of the Republican vice presidential nominee, Colfax, in the Know Nothing movement in the mid-1850s as evidence that he was anti-Catholic.

Most dramatic, however, was a move by some Democrats to dump their candidate after Republicans triumphed in several state elections in September and October, which were held in advance of the presidential polling. Seymour, never keen on running in the first place, did not object to stepping down, but was dissuaded by other Democrats who blamed the Republican gains on vote fraud. Instead, they convinced Seymour to become more involved in the campaign and to go on a tour to deliver speeches. His tour began on October 21, in Syracuse, New York, and went west to Buffalo, Philadelphia, Pittsburgh, Cleveland, Columbus, Detroit, Indianapolis and Chicago.

The Outcome

Seymour's last minute campaign trip did little to reverse the fortunes of the Democrats. The Republican Grant won 3,013,421 votes, or nearly 53 percent of the total, to 2,706,820 votes, or just over 47 percent for Seymour.

In the electoral college vote, Grant won 214 votes to 80 for Seymour. Predictably, Sesmour won a majority in the South, but gained electoral votes only from Georgia and Louisiana. He also won electoral votes in Kentucky, Maryland, Delaware, New Jersey, New York, and Oregon. He lost California by 500 votes. Although the Republicans accused Democrats of vote fraud in New York, and of participating in terrorism against blacks and white Republicans in former Confederate states, where the Ku Klux Klan was active, there was less violence in the South than once feared.

In some respects, the election of 1868 marked the end of the Civil War. Although Reconstruction continued with passage of the Enforcement Acts in 1870 and 1871, and the Ku Klux Klan Act in 1871, all intended to protect the voting rights of freed slaves in the South, Reconstruction gradually lost its clout as an election issue during the first administration of Ulysses Grant.

More Information

- Clark, Judith Freeman. *America's Gilded Age: An Eyewitness History*. New York: Facts on File, 1992.
- King, David C. *Ulysses S. Grant*. Woodbridge, Connecticut: Blackbirch Press, 2001.
- Kirchberger, Joe H. *The Civil War and Reconstruction: An Eyewitness* History. New York: Facts on File, 1991.
- Mantell, Martin E. *Johnson, Grant, and the Politics of Reconstruction*. New York: Columbia University Press, 1973.
- Perret, Geoffrey. *Ulysses S. Grant: Soldier and President*. New York: Random House, 1997.

On the Web

- "The Trial of Andrew Johnson, 1868." *Eyewitness.* **http://www.ibiscom.com/john.htm.**
- "Harper's Weekly Documents," *The Ku Klux Klan Hearings.* **http://education.harpweek.com/ KKKHearings/ ItemsListOf.htm.**
- Grant, Ulysses S. "First Inaugural Address, Mar. 4, 1869." **http://www.bartleby.com/124/pres33.html.**
- Grant, Ulysses S. "First Inaugural Address Thursday, March 4, 1869." *Inaugural Addresses of the Presidents of the United States.* Washington, D.C.: U.S. Government Printing Office, 1989; Bartleby.com, 2001. **http://www.bartleby.com/124/ pres33.html.**
- "Reconstruction and the New South." Links to articles and primary sources for the period 1865–1915. **http://www. historyteacher.net/APUSH-Course/Weblinks/Weblinks14. htm.**

1872

Ulysses S. Grant (Republican)
vs. Horace Greeley (Liberal Republican and Democrat)

The story of the election of 1872 was one of a popular sitting president, Ulysses S. Grant, coasting to victory over a disorganized and dispirited opposition whose candidate died after the election but before the Electoral College could vote. A group of Republicans split from their party to form the Liberal Republican Party; they nominated an eccentric newspaper publisher, Horace Greeley, who also ran as the nominee of the Democratic Party. The Democrats and the Liberal Republicans ran an ineffective campaign that did little to challenge Republican domination of the federal government. The scandals that would mark Grant's second term were not yet widely known. Voters in the northern states were generally satisfied with Grant's enforcement of Reconstruction legislation in the former Confederacy.

After losing the popular vote to Grant, 55.5 percent to 44 percent, Greeley died in November, 1872, before the Electoral College convened. Consequently, his running-mate on the Liberal Republican ticket, Benjamin Gratz Brown, received 18 electoral votes. Thomas Hendricks of Indiana received 42 electoral votes. Three electors from Georgia voted for Greeley posthumously; the House of Representatives did not certify those votes and they were not officially counted.

The Context

Grant's first term (1869–1873) had largely been taken up with implementing the post–Civil War Reconstruction Acts passed by the Republican-dominated Congress. These included the Fifteenth Amendment (ratified March 1870) guaranteeing that "the right of citizens of the United States to vote shall not be denied or abridged by the United States or by any State on account of race, color, or previous condition of servitude," as well as other acts designed to combat Southern white resistance to equality for former slaves. Grant, a Civil War general who had helped conquer the Confederacy, had moved effectively to implement the will of Congress.

The state governments of the former Confederate states had been reorganized, and their representatives readmitted to Congress. By 1872, the nation seemed ready to turn its attention elsewhere.

President Grant had also implemented the first civil service reforms—filling government jobs with people who qualified by taking special exams, rather than with political cronies. Despite this, and although no major scandals had been uncovered before the election, the Grant administration was criticized by many, including many Republicans, for filling jobs based on political favors.

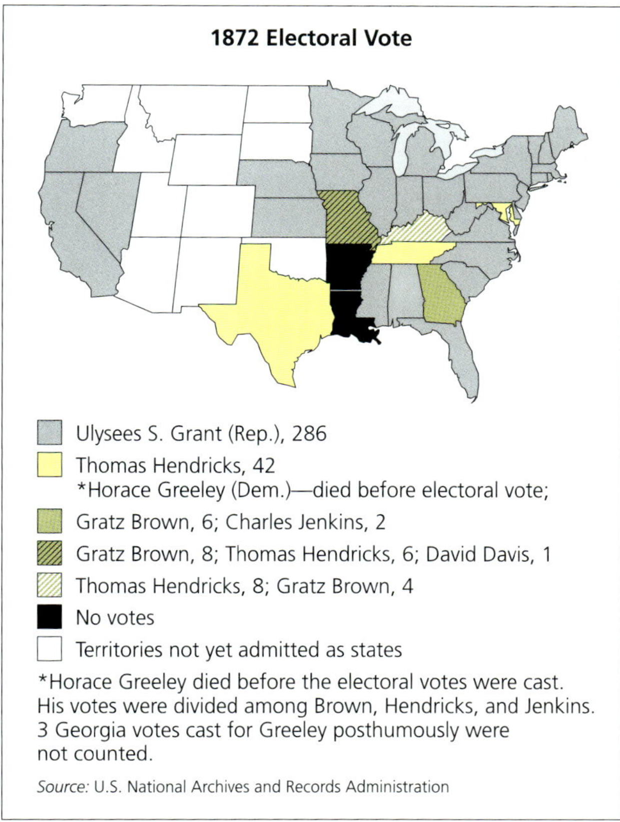

In foreign affairs Grant favored a strong, even aggressive, policy. He considered annexing the Caribbean island nation of Santo Domingo (now the Dominican Republic), and thought about supporting rebels in Cuba, then controlled by Spain. Liberal Republicans firmly opposed both these initiatives.

On the other hand Grant had succeeded in resolving two disputes with Britain, including U.S. claims against the British government for its role in financing and outfitting naval ships of the Confederacy. These claims were settled during the presidential campaign, resulting in a payment of $15.5 million by Britain to the United States.

Industrialization was spreading rapidly throughout the North, and the West was becoming rapidly populated. Expanding railroads helped unite the East Coast with the West Coast, and immigrants were flowing into the United States from Europe, bringing rapid growth in both population and the economy.

The Republicans

In some ways, 1872 was the last referendum on the Civil War. Most of the issues left from the Civil War, notably emancipation of African-Americans and reintegration of the former Confederate states into the Union, had been resolved during Grant's first term.

The president was familiar to voters, and there was no doubt that when Grant made it known he wanted to run for a second term, the nomination would be his. And so it was when the Republicans met in Philadelphia on June 5–6, 1872. Grant was nominated by acclamation.

The only hint of drama lay in the choice of vice president. Schuyler Colfax, vice president during Grant's first term, had hinted that he was receptive to the nomination if Grant decided not to run again. This conveyed a hint of disloyalty, and Colfax was dumped in favor of Senator Henry Wilson of Massachusetts. On the first ballot, Wilson received 364½ votes to 321½ for Colfax. On the second ballot, Wilson picked up the votes from the Virginia delegation, giving him the nomination.

Nevertheless, there was dissatisfaction with Grant among some members of his party—enough to encourage some of them to split off and form a new party altogether.

The Liberal Republicans

The most interesting aspect of the 1872 presidential election was the Liberal Republican Party, initially organized by Republican politicians in Missouri led by Senator Carl Schurz. What started as a wing of the Republicans turned into a separate party in 1872 after Schurz called for like-minded Republicans—including many influential newspaper editors—to unite behind someone besides Ulysses S. Grant.

The main source of discontent was the "spoils" system of staffing the government with political supporters of the winning candidate. Liberal Republicans also favored free trade, currency backed by gold, and public education—but not funding for religious schools, primarily meaning Catholic schools. The Liberal Republicans took a moderate attitude towards the former Confederacy, advocating withdrawal of Army troops from the South and a general amnesty for officials of the Confederacy. They also opposed what they regarded as Grant's aggressive foreign policy.

Responding to Schurz's call, the Liberal Republicans convened in Cincinnati, Ohio on May 1, 1872. Although disillusioned with Grant, they were far from settled on a suitable candidate. Schurz, a native of Germany, was ineligible. Charles Francis Adams, son of John Quincy Adams and grandson of John Adams, was interested but unwilling to participate in rough-and-tumble politics. The Missouri Liberal Republicans, who had started the movement, backed their governor, Gratz Brown. Supreme Court justice David Davis of Illinois actively sought the nomination, but was opposed by some leading editors who wondered whether he was really a Democrat posing as a Liberal Republican. Acting together, the editors of the Springfield (MA) *Republican,* the Chicago *Tribune* and the Louisville (KY) *Courier-Journal* attacked Davis, ruining his chances for nomination. Horace Greeley, the somewhat eccentric editor of the New York *Herald Tribune* was considered a possible vice presidential candidate. At the convention, Adams received the most votes on the first ballot, but not enough to be nominated. Greeley was second, followed by Senator Lyman Trumbull of Illinois, and Governor Brown of Missouri. Partly to block Adams, Brown supported Greeley on the second ballot. Finally, on the sixth ballot, southern and western forces also lined up behind Greeley, giving him the nomination. Brown was nominated to run with him as the vice presidential candidate.

It was an odd choice, notably because the Liberal Republicans were on record as supporting free trade, whereas Greeley was a well-known supporter of tariffs to protect domestic industry.

The Democrats

Two months after the Liberal Republican convention, the Democratic Party met in Baltimore. They were dispirited and lacked a clearly viable candidate. They nominated Greeley for president and Missouri Governor Brown as vice president, calculating that a joint approach stood the best chance of beating Grant and hoping Democrats might be able to "capture" the Liberal Republicans. (The Liberal Republicans had a similar idea of "capturing" the Democrats.) Greeley's nomination by the Democrats was especially surprising since he had been a co-founder of the Republican Party twenty years earlier.

The Campaign

As was nearly always the case in the nineteenth century, President Grant relied almost entirely on federal government officials who owed their jobs to the Republican Party to get out and work for his reelection.

Horace Greeley, on the other hand, barnstormed across the country on a grueling schedule. In one 10-day period in September Greeley delivered almost 200 speeches on a tour that took him through New Jersey, Pennsylvania, Ohio, Kentucky and Indiana.

Greeley's approach was not altogether successful. He sometimes delivered messages thought inappropriate for a would-be president. His running mate, Governor Brown, delivered a well-publicized speech at Yale University while drunk; later he fainted in front of a meeting in New York.

Political cartoonists had a field day adding to the vicious attacks leveled by both sides against their opponents.

Susan B. Anthony, the leading advocate of women's right to vote, provided an unusual historical footnote. She attended the

The Liberal Republican candidate in 1872, Horace Greeley, is depicted as a clown's head at the end of a stick offered by Carl Schurz, a leader of the breakaway Liberal Republicans. The American voters are depicted as a woman in a robe.

conventions of all three parties—the Liberal Republicans, the regular Republicans and the Democrats. After the regular Republicans included a statement in their platform promising to treat women's rights "with respectful consideration"—the first time a major party had included such a statement—Anthony began campaigning for Grant. In November Anthony tried to vote on grounds that the 14th Amendment's reference to "all persons" (*"All persons born or naturalized in the United States and subject to the jurisdiction thereof, are citizens of the United States and of the State wherein they reside. No State shall make or enforce any law which shall abridge the privileges or immunities of citizens of the United States; nor shall any State deprive any person of life, liberty, or property, without due process of law; nor deny to any person within its jurisdiction the equal protection of the laws."*) included women alongside former slaves. But she was arrested and fined $100; it would be 48 years before women were given the right to vote under the 19th Amendment.

There was one cloud over Grant's campaign. In September 1872 *The New York Sun* published a story revealing how the corporate officers of Crédit Mobilier, a corporation formed to hold stock in the Union Pacific Railroad (built with significant federal government funding), had enriched themselves at the expense of the company. The story also said that the executives had bribed members of Congress in an effort to cover up the scandal, and/or to gain leniency. The report came too late to affect the outcome of the election, although it foreshadowed more scandals during Grant's second administration.

The Outcome

In the popular vote, Grant received 3,596,745 votes (55.5 percent) to Greeley's 2,843,446 (44 percent). Grant won 286 electoral votes to Greeley's 66. It was the biggest margin of any president since Andrew Jackson in 1828 and until Theodore Roosevelt's election in 1904.

By the end of the campaign, Horace Greeley seemed like a broken man. In October, 1872, his wife fell ill and died. It was a grave blow to Greeley, who himself was exhausted by the campaign. He died on November 29, 1872, before the Electoral College met to cast its votes. His funeral was held on the same day the Electoral College voted, December 4, 1872.

With Greeley deceased, the result was an oddity in the history of the Electoral College. The Constitution barred voting for a dead man, so Greeley's electoral votes were divided between Thomas Hendricks of Indiana, who had run for vice president as an Independent Democrat (42 electoral votes) and Gratz Brown of Missouri, Greeley's official vice presidential nominee (18 electoral votes). Three electors from from Georgia voted for Greeley after his death, but the House of Representatives decided not to count their votes.

Two other men received three electoral votes. Disputes over the popular vote in Louisiana and Arkansas resulted in those electoral votes not being counted at all, but it made no difference. Grant won decisively with 286 electoral votes.

More Information

- Boothe, F. Norton. *Ulysses S. Grant*. Stamford, Connecticut: Longmeadow Press, 1992.
- Isely, Jeter Allen. *Horace Greeley and the Republican Party, 1853–1861: A Study of the New York Tribune*. New York: Octagon Books, 1965
- O'Brien, Steven. *Ulysses S. Grant*. New York: Chelsea House, 1991.
- Parton, James. *The Life of Horace Greeley*. New York: Arno Press, 1970.

On the Web

- Grant, Ulysses S. *Second Inaugural Address*. **http://www. bartleby.com/124/pres34.html.**
- "Ulysses S. Grant" (biography). *The White House.* **http://www.whitehouse.gov/history/presidents/ug18.html.**
- Grant, Ulysses S. "Second Inaugural Address, Tuesday, March 4, 1873." *Inaugural Addresses of the Presidents of the United States.* Washington, D.C.: U.S. Government Printing Office, 1989; Bartleby.com, 2001. **http://www.bartleby.com/124/pres34.html.**
- "Reconstruction and the New South," Links to articles and primary sources for the period 1865–1915. **http://www. historyteacher.net/APUSH-Course/Weblinks/Weblinks14. htm.**

1876
Rutherford B. Hayes (Republican)
vs. Samuel J. Tilden (Democrat)

FlashFocus: 1876

Candidates

Rutherford B. Hayes & William Wheeler, Republican
Samuel Tilden & Thomas Hendricks, Democrat

Issues

Corruption. Democrats tried to label all Republicans as crooked in the wake of scandals that rocked the incumbent Republican administration of Ulysses Grant. Despite the scandals, Grant remained popular and considered running for a third term.

Immigration. Both parties took a dim view of immigration by Chinese laborers into California who were recruited to work on the western end of the transcontinental railroad.

Education: Republicans urged a constitutional amendment barring government aid to religious schools, which was aimed at Roman Catholic institutions. Democrats generally favored aid to religious schools.

Reconstruction. The Civil War and Reconstruction were fading as issues, but Republicans continued to label Democrats as pro-Confederate. Democrats in the South continued to chafe under post–Civil War laws imposed by the North.

"Hard money." Republicans favored backing currency with gold. Democrats favored issuing paper currency not necessarily backed by gold or silver.

Outcome

Popular vote

Tilden	4,284,020	51.0% ✓
Hayes	4,036,572	48.0%

Electoral College

Hayes	185 ✓
Tilden	184

The popular vote in three states—Louisiana, South Carolina and Florida—was disputed, as was one elector from Oregon—20 electoral votes in all.

Congress named a commission—five senators, five representatives and five Supreme Court justices—to decide the outcome in the four states. The commission voted along party lines and awarded all 20 electoral votes to Hayes. Historians have long debated whether Democrats negotiated a deal to give the election to Hayes in exchange for ending Reconstruction in the South.

The outcome of the 1876 election was complicated and controversial. The eventual winner, Republican Rutherford B. Hayes, was installed by a special committee of senators, representatives and Supreme Court justices after months of wrangling over who won the popular vote.

The Context

The 1876 centennial of America's Declaration of Independence evoked widespread celebrations, highlighted in Philadelphia by the first World's Fair held in the United States. But celebrations were subdued by an economic depression that had started three years earlier in the Panic of 1873.

Hard economic times, plus the fading of the Civil War as an issue, had enabled the Democrats to gain a majority in the House of Representatives in 1874 for the first time since before the Civil War. White voters put Democrats in control of most Southern states as Northern enthusiasm for Reconstruction waned.

Scandals involving senior officials of the administration of President Ulysses S. Grant also gave Democrats powerful ammunition. Aside from the Grant administration scandals, the issues that put the Republicans into power in the first place—abolitionism, the Union and Reconstruction—were fading in 1876. Moreover, the party was splintering into warring factions, just as the Democrats gained control of the House of Representatives.

The Candidates

For a while President Grant hinted he might run for an unprecedented third term. But a resolution passed in Congress expressed a strong sentiment for limiting presidents to two terms, and Grant acquiesced.

The Republican nomination was sharply disputed. At first the favorite was House Minority Leader James G. Blaine of Maine, who had been Speaker of the House from 1869 to 1875 and who was associated with the "Half Breeds," Republicans who took a moderate stance on Reconstruction. But in early 1876 Blaine was tainted by a scandal fanned by his Republican rivals. Another leading contender, Benjamin Bristow of Kentucky, had been Grant's treasury secretary. He had a reputation as an enthusiastic reformer and enemy of corruption. Also in the running was Senator Roscoe Conkling of New York, who was preferred by President Grant. Conkling had a reputation as a "machine politician" in New York, and he was anathema to the party's reform wing. The fourth contender was Rutherford B. Hayes, a former Ohio governor with a reputation as a reformer.

Also in the race was Senator Oliver Morton of Indiana, considered a crucial state that could go either way. But Morton was considered too close to the scandal-tainted Grant administration, and too close to the Radical Reconstructionist wing of the party.

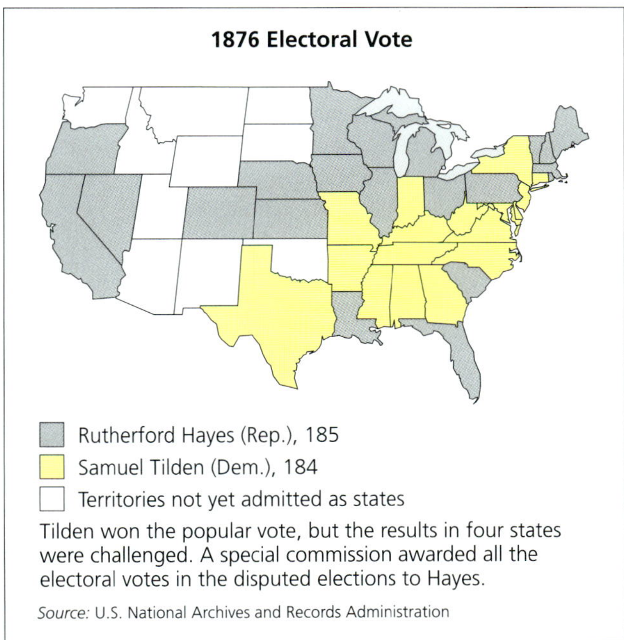

Tilden won the popular vote, but the results in four states were challenged. A special commission awarded all the electoral votes in the disputed elections to Hayes.

Source: U.S. National Archives and Records Administration

The Republican convention took place in Cincinnati in June 1876. For the first time since 1860 the outcome was in dispute. Despite the issue of corruption, a stirring nominating speech for Blaine created excitement on the convention floor that might have won him the nomination had not the vote been delayed by a day. Overnight, backers of Hayes campaigned for support from Bristow's and Morton's delegates.

On the first ballot Blaine got 285 votes, well short of the 378 needed for nomination. Hayes had only 61 votes. Delegates took three more votes with few changes, but on the fifth ballot, Hayes got 384 ballots, six more than needed for the nomination. Representative William Wheeler of New York was nominated as vice president.

The Democrats thought 1876 offered their best chance of winning the White House in twenty years. Two years earlier they won a majority in the House of Representatives, the country was in economic recession, and their likely candidate, Governor Samuel J. Tilden of New York, had a strong reputation as a reformer.

As chairman of the Democratic party in New York, Tilden had helped end the reign of William "Boss" Tweed, a notoriously corrupt New York City politician. Tilden had solidified his reputation as a reformer while governor of New York, the most populous state in 1876.

Tilden easily won the nomination with 535 votes on the first ballot of the Democratic convention held in St. Louis at the end of June. In second place was Gov. Thomas Hendricks of Indiana, with 140½ votes, who became the vice presidential nominee.

The Democratic platform endorsed "soft money" (currency not backed by gold desposits held by the government), condemned the Grant administration for corruption, and en-

FlashFocus: Rutherford B. Hayes

19th President, 1877–1881

Born: October 1, 1822, Delaware, Ohio
Died: January 17, 1893, Fremont, Ohio
Family: Son of Rutherford Hayes Jr., farmer, and Sophia Birchard; married Lucy Webb, a college graduate (unusual in her day) who favored women's suffrage and prohibition of alcohol
Education: Kenyon College (1842); Harvard Law School (1845)
Military: Union major general in the Civil War
Political career: Republican. Elected to Congress, 1865; elected governor of Ohio, 1867, for first of three terms

Rutherford Hayes was a member of the Radical Republicans who favored impeaching President Andrew Johnson and punishing the South after the Civil War. He resigned from Congress to run for governor of Ohio in 1867 and was reelected in 1869. In 1872 he lost a bid for Congress, but he regained the governorship in 1875.

In 1876 Hayes was the Republican presidential nominee. He lost the popular vote to Democrat Samuel Tilden by a margin of 49 percent for Hayes to 51 percent for Tilden, but won the presidency in the Electoral College by a single vote. The outcome was the result of a special commission that ruled on the electoral votes of four states where elections were disputed: South Carolina, Louisiana, Florida, and Oregon. At the time, it appeared that Republicans had deprived Democrats of the White House by manipulating the outcome in the South.

The circumstances of his election clouded the legitimacy of his presidency, especially when he ended Reconstruction by withdrawing the last federal troops occupying the South. Some critics thought a deal had been struck whereby some members of the special commission voted for Hayes in exchange for his promise to end Reconstruction in the South.

Hayes declined to run for reelection as part of his dedication to political reform.

Hayes died on January 17, 1893 in Fremont, Ohio.

dorsed the Reconstruction Constitutional amendments, while simultaneously condemning Reconstruction policies as corrupt and overly harsh. The Democrats also endorsed civil service reform, conservation of public lands, and a tariff to raise revenue.

There were two new single-issue parties offering candidates in 1875. The National Prohibition Reform Party nominated General Green Clay Smith of Kentucky for president and G. T. Stewart of Ohio for vice president on a platform of barring alcoholic beverages. The National Greenback Party nominated Peter Cooper of New York, at age 85, for president and Senator Newton Booth for vice president. The Greenback Party favored issuing currency not linked to the gold reserves. It won few votes.

FlashFocus: Samuel Tilden

Democratic Presidential Nominee 1876

Born: February 9, 1814, Lebanon, New York
Died: August 4, 1886
Family: Son of Elam Tilden, a farmer and storekeeper, and Polly Jones
Education: Yale University; University of the City of New York law school (1841)

Political career: After becoming wealthy as a lawyer for railroads, Tilden followed his father into the Democratic Party. Tilden ardently opposed slavery and joined the anti-slavery "Barn Burners" faction of the Democratic party. He was elected to the New York State legislature in 1846, but two years later Tilden joined the anti-slavery Free Soil Party of Martin Van Buren. He rejoined the Democrats in 1850.

Tilden cautiously supported the Union effort in the Civil War, but strongly criticized the Lincoln Administration's policies on emancipation, paper currency, and the draft. He opposed Radical Reconstruction, favoring President Andrew Johnson's more modest Reconstruction program.

Tilden gained a national reputation for his role in rooting out the corrupt "Boss" Tweed organization in New York City, which helped him gain election to the state legislature in 1872. He was elected governor of New York, then the most populous state, in 1874.

In 1876, Tilden's reputation as a reformer helped him win the Democratic presidential nomination on the first ballot. He won 51 percent of the popular vote, but fell one vote short of a majority in the electoral college.

A Republican-dominated special commission awarded the votes of all four disputed states (Oregon, Louisiana, South Carolina and Florida) to the Republican Rutherford B. Hayes, costing Tilden the election. Tilden retired from political life after the election of 1876, despite some sentiment by Democrats in favor of renominating him in the two following elections.

He died in 1886. Most of his estate went to funding what is now the New York City Public Library.

The Issues

The Republicans fell back on a proven issue—the Civil War—and emphasized the Democrats' supposed ties to the Confederate cause. Violence against African-Americans in the South played into the Republicans hands. Republicans also accused Tilden of cheating on his taxes and of being "a drunkard, a liar, a cheat, a counterfeiter, a perjurer, and a swindler." The Republicans questioned whether Tilden was in good health, his early ties to "Boss" Tweed, and the fact that his hard-money stance conflicted with the soft-money position of his running mate. The party's platform opposed public funding of religious schools (usually meaning Roman Catholic schools), supported equal rights under the law, pensions for Union veterans, a protective tariff and the conservation of public land.

Democrats focused their attention on winning New York's 35 electoral votes for their favorite son candidate. They also launched an unrelenting campaign linking the Republicans to the corruption scandals in the Grant administration. During the campaign, the Democrats succeeded in passing a bill granting statehood to Colorado—which proved to be a mistake, since Colorado eventually gave its three electoral votes to Republican Hayes in an extremely close election.

The Campaign

The election was forecast to be extremely close. The federal government spent almost $300,000 for marshals to help supervise the election, especially in New York City and the South.

Early results pointed to a victory for the Democrats, but as votes were counted in the Western states, the outcome became unclear. Eventually, the Democrat Tilden won 51 percent of the popular vote, Republican Hayes 48 percent, and minor parties one percent.

Based on the popular vote, Tilden had 184 electoral votes, one short of the number needed for election. Hayes' popular vote entitled him to 165 Electoral College votes, twenty short of the number required to win. Twenty votes were in dispute. Of the disputed votes, one was from Oregon and 19 were from three southern states—South Carolina, Louisiana, and Florida. The dispute in Oregon was technical—the Democrats challenged a Republican elector—but in the South, both parties claimed victory and accused the other of vote fraud.

The situation had no precedent. Unlike the elections in 1800 and 1824, in which no candidate had an electoral majority, there was no obvious Constitutional solution to disputed outcomes in the four states. The country faced months of uncertainty and dispute.

Many solutions were proposed. Some Republicans wanted the president of the Senate, Thomas Ferry of Michigan, a Republican, to decide the issue of disputed votes. Other Republicans thought the Supreme Court should resolve the election.

Democrats wanted the House of Representatives (which they controlled) to decide, while also arguing that Tilden had won outright in Louisiana and Florida. Some Democrats from Southern states tried to negotiate a deal with the Republicans: let Hayes become president in exchange for concessions on altering Reconstruction.

The Outcome

In January, 1877 Congress created a special commission to resolve the dispute. The commission had 15 members—five senators, five representatives, and five Supreme Court justices. The commission's findings on the disputed votes would be binding unless both the Senate and House overrode it. The commission members from the House and Senate were evenly split between Republicans and Democrats. The five Supreme Court justices included two Republicans, two Democrats and one Independent, David Davis of Illinois.

No sooner was this even-handed solution agreed than Justice Davis was appointed to the Senate by a coalition of Democrats and Greenbackers from Illinois, hoping to induce him to vote for Tilden.

But the deal backfired. Instead of voting for Tilden, as planned, Davis instead resigned from the Commission without voting, thereby making room for another Supreme Court justice. That turned out to be a Republican, Joseph Bradley, who promptly voted for Hayes and gave the presidential election to the Republicans.

In all four states, the commission voted 8–7 in favor of the Republicans. Incensed, the Democratic House voted to reject the commission's findings, but the Republican Senate voted to approve them. Under the rules establishing the commission, the commission's findings were accepted.

The twenty electoral votes went to Hayes on March 2, 1877 and he won the Electoral College 185–184. Three days later he was inaugurated as the nineteenth president.

More Information

▶ Hoogenboom, Ari Arthur. *The Presidency of Rutherford B. Hayes*. Lawrence: University Press of Kansas, 1988.

▶ Morris, Roy. *Fraud of the Century: Rutherford B. Hayes, Samuel Tilden and the Stolen Election of 1876*. New York: Simon & Schuster, 2003.

▶ Severn, Bill. *Samuel J. Tilden and the Stolen Election*. New York: I. Washburn, 1968.

▶ Trefousse, Hans Louis. *Rutherford B. Hayes*. New York: Times Books, 2002.

On the Web

▶ Hayes, Rutherford B. "Inaugural Address, Monday, March 5, 1877." *Inaugural Addresses of the Presidents of the United States*. Washington, D.C.: U.S. Government Printing Office, 1989; Bartleby.com, 2001. **http://www.bartleby.com/124/pres35.html.**

▶ "Reconstruction and the New South," Links to articles and primary sources for the period 1865–1915. **http://www.historyteacher.net/APUSH-Course/Weblinks/Weblinks14.htm.**

▶ "Finding Precedent: Hayes vs. Tilden. The Electoral College Controversy of 1876–77." *HarpWeek*. Links to articles from *Harper's Weekly* magazine. **http://elections.harpweek.com/controversy.htm.**

1880

James A. Garfield (Republican) vs. Winfield Hancock (Democrat)

FlashFocus: 1880

Candidates

> **James B. Garfield** & Chester Arthur, Republican
> **Winfield Hancock** & William English, Democrat
> **James Weaver** & Benjamin Chambers, Greenback-Labor

Issues

Tariffs. Democrats opposed protective tariffs that raised the price of foreign goods as a means of protecting U.S. manufacturers during a period of rapid industrial growth in the North. Republicans generally supported tariffs, along with other pro-business legislation.

Hard money. Republicans supported "hard money," paper currency backed by gold deposits held by the government. Democrats supported issuing currency not necessarily backed by gold, or "soft money."

Civil service reform. Democrats demanded that federal offices be filled on the basis of merit, shown by tests. Republicans hesitated to change a system that allowed them to offer federal jobs to political supporters.

Reconstruction. Although the Civil War had been over for fifteen years, Republicans continued to back enforcement of Reconstruction laws to protect the rights of emancipated slaves. Liberal Republicans favored a more moderate policy, and Democrats favored relaxing Reconstruction rules.

Polygamy. Republicans attacked the administration of Utah Territory (the Mormon Church) for allowing men to take multiple wives in accordance with the church's teaching.

Outcome

Popular vote

Garfield	4,453,295	48.5% ✓
Scott	4,414,082	48.1%
Weaver	308,578	3.4%

Electoral College

Garfield	214 ✓
Scott	155

Garfield was assassinated four months after taking office; he was succeeded by vice president Chester Arthur.

By 1880, the nation had largely settled down to a period of rapid industrial growth. There were no compelling issues driving voters—the economy was relatively prosperous, and the passions of the Civil War and Reconstruction had largely cooled. The outcome of the presidential election was one of the closest ever, with less than 40,000 votes separating the winner, Republican James Garfield, from the loser, Democrat Winfield Hancock.

The Republicans

The greatest political drama of 1880 occurred during the Republican convention in Chicago starting June 2, 1880. It took 36 ballots to finally settle on a nominee.

The incumbent president, Rutherford B. Hayes, had promised not to seek a second term, which opened the battle for the Republican nomination. The divisions that had split the party eight years earlier still remained.

The conservative wing of the party, called the Stalwarts (for their continued devotion to the issues of Reconstruction) favored former President Ulysses S. Grant, who aspired to a third term. Despite the corruption scandals that marked Grant's second term (1873–1877), the former Union general remained popular and well respected. In addition to championing the principles of Reconstruction, the Stalwarts opposed civil service reform (partly because they relied on handing out federal jobs to political allies as a means of retaining a political foothold in the South) and supported tariffs to protect U.S. manufacturers from foreign competition. The Stalwart faction was led by Senators Roscoe Conkling of New York and John Logan of Illinois.

At the opposite end of the Republican spectrum were the Reformers (sometimes called the Liberals), led by Secretary of State Carl Schurz, a former senator from Missouri. Schurz had been instrumental in creating the Liberal Republican movement of 1872 which split with the Republicans and ran its own candidate, Horace Greeley against Republican incumbent Grant. The Liberals supported a more moderate policy in the former Confederate states, as well as free trade, and civil service reform, i.e., opposition to the "spoils system" under which federal offices were filled with political appointees.

In the middle were the "Half-Breeds," who adopted the middle ground. Their preferred candidate at the convention was Senator James Blaine of Maine, who in most respects was sympathetic to the policies of the Stalwarts. Blaine was a charismatic leader and accomplished politician who might well have succeeded in obtaining the nomination but for his reputation for corruption, which alienated the Reform wing.

During the Republican convention, several other politicians also emerged as presidential hopefuls. Among them were Representative James Garfield of Ohio, associated with the moderates; Treasury Secretary John Sherman of Ohio, also a moderate; Senator George Edmunds of Vermont; Senator William Windom of Minnesota; former Congressman Elihu Washburne of Illinois; and former Secretary of State Hamilton Fish of New York.

When the convention opened, Grant and Blaine between them had two-thirds of the delegates committed to one or the

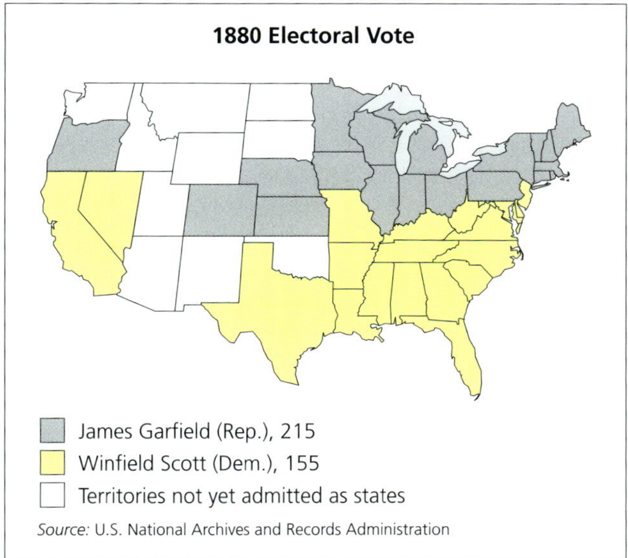

Source: U.S. National Archives and Records Administration

FlashFocus: James A. Garfield

20th President, 1881

Born: November 19, 1831, Cuyahoga County, Ohio (near Cleveland)
Died: September 19, 1881, Elberon, N.J. (assassinated)
Family: Son of Abram Garfield, a farmer, and Eliza Ballou; married Lucretia Randolph
Education: Williams College, 1856
Political career: Garfield was born in a log cabin (the last president who was) to a poor family. After college, he started teaching but abandoned it because of low pay. Intensely religious, he was a lay preacher for the Disciples of Christ.

Garfield launched his political career in the Ohio Senate in 1859 as a Republican. In the Civil War he helped recruit an infantry brigade and rose to major general.

In 1862 he was elected to the House of Representatives, where he stayed for the next 17 years. He was a moderate, backing Radical Republicans on Reconstruction and protective tariffs, while opposing "soft money" not backed by gold.

At the 1880 Republican convention, Garfield managed the campaign of Ohio senator John Sherman, but emerged as a compromise candidate as the convention deadlocked. Thought to be a "jolly good fellow," he was nominated on the thirty-sixth ballot.

Garfield conducted an armchair campaign at his farmhouse in Mentor, Ohio. Rather than hitting the campaign trail he remained at home so as not to seem overly eager for office. He won the election by fewer than 10,000 votes.

In his inaugural speech Garfield promised to end the practice of polygamy in Utah Territory (then run by the Mormon Church) and to implement civil service reform by cutting the number of federal office holders appointed as political favors.

On July 2, 1881, four months after he took office, a disappointed and possibly deranged office seeker, Charles Guiteau, shot Garfield as he boarded a train in Washington. Garfield lived for 11 weeks, and died in Elberon, New Jersey, on September 19, 1881.

---

other, but neither one had a majority (350). On the first ballot, Grant received 304 votes to Blaine's 284. In the meantime, Garfield was working behind the scenes in hopes of emerging as the compromise choice. His campaign manager orchestrated loud ovations when Garfield arrived at the convention, and any other time his name was mentioned, or when he spoke. Garfield delivered an emotional nominating speech for Sherman, the treasury secretary, in which he barely mentioned the candidate but focused on party unity.

The convention proceeded to vote repeatedly. Over the course of 33 ballots, the balance between Grant and Blaine barely changed. But eventually the Sherman delegates, angered by a perceived double-cross by Blaine in maneuvering for the Ohio delegation, switched to Garfield. Soon Indiana and Wisconsin delegates also supported Garfield. Finally, on the 36th ballot, Garfield received 399 votes, 49 more than the required 350, and became the Republican nominee.

The Democrats

The Democrats came to the election of 1880 optimistic that they might regain the White House for the first time since 1856. They had won majorities in both the Senate and House just two years earlier in 1878, and thought this boded well for capturing the White House in 1880.

But the party had no obvious presidential nominee. Samuel Tilden, who had won the popular vote in 1876 but lost in the electoral college after a highly controversial procedure, was physically ailing and unenthusiastic about running again. Moreover, Tilden was opposed by the leader of New York City's Tammany Hall (the political "machine" that generated huge numbers of Democratic votes), which he had fought against earlier in his career.

Another potential candidate was Senator Thomas Bayard of Delaware, although his record included a number of downsides, including his initial agreement to let Southern states secede in 1861. Speaker of the House Samuel Randall of Pennsylvania aspired to the nomination, but his support of protective tariffs contradicted the Democratic platform favoring free trade. Thomas Hendricks of Indiana, who ran for vice president in 1876, wanted the nomination but lacked widespread support.

Eventually Civil War general Winfield Scott Hancock, nicknamed "Superb" for his Civil War exploits as a hero of the battles of Antietam and Gettysburg, became the compromise choice, less because of what he represented than because he had no outstanding negatives and was not objectionable to

FlashFocus: Winfield Scott Hancock

Democratic Presidential nominee, 1880

Born: February 14, 1824, Montgomery Square, Pennsylvania
Died: February 9, 1886
Family: Son of Benjamin Franklin Hancock, a lawer, and Elizabeth Hoxworth; married Almira Russell
Education: Norristown Academy; U.S. Military Academy, West Point.
Military career: After graduating from West Point in 1844, Winfield Hancock began a distinguished military career that included a role in the war with Mexico (1846–48) under General Winfield Scott, after whom Hancock had been named, the violent conflict over extension of slavery into Kansas Territory and the so-called Mormon War in Utah territory. Hancock also participated in fighting against the Seminole native American tribe in Florida in the years preceding the Civil War.

Hancock's real reputation came during the Civil War. Starting as the commander of volunteers, Scott won distinction in a key Union victory at Antietam, Maryland, and in the battles of Fredericksburg, Virginia (1862) and Chancellorsville, Virginia (1863). The highlight of his career was the Battle of Gettysburg, where the Union blocked a Confederate thrust into Pennsylvania. Though wounded, Hancock stood firm against the last-ditch Confederate assault called Pickett's Charge (named after the Confederate general who had been Hancock's classmate at West Point).

Appointed military governor of Louisiana and Texas after the war, Hancock took a moderate view of Reconstruction and allowed civilian courts to resume authority over all non-military matters, in line with President Andrew Johnson's views on Reconstruction. However, General Ulysses S. Grant transferred Hancock to the Dakota Territory, and later to New York City.

Political Career: Hancock had no political experience, but he received votes as a possible Democratic presidential nominee in 1868. He was eventually the Democratic nominee in 1880, but lack of political experience proved costly, especially in one famous incident in which he declared that the debate over protective tariffs was a "local question." Hancock lost the election to Republican James Garfield by a narrow margin.

Hancock died at the military post on Governor's Island, in New York harbor, in 1886 and was buried near his childhood home in Norristown, Pennsylvania.

any of the Democratic factions. Hancock's biggest drawback was that he had never before held any elective office, a fact that was targeted by the Republicans in the election campaign.

The Democrats nominated a former Indiana Congressman, William English, for vice president in hopes he could swing his home state to the Democratic column.

Minor Parties

Two other parties also mounted campaigns. The National Prohibition Party had one basic plank—the abolition of alcoholic beverages. Their nominee was Neal Dow of Maine, who had long campaigned on this issue. He made little impact.

The other party was the Greenback-Labor Party, which eventually garnered more than three percent of the popular vote. This party had sent 15 people to Congress in 1878 during an economic downturn. Their platform supported an eight-hour workday, a graduated income tax, the right of women to vote, and federal regulation of industrial health and safety, as well as enforcement of the rights of African-Americans to vote. Like the Republicans and Democrats, the Greenback-Labor Party nominated a former Civil War general, James Weaver of Iowa, for president and Benjamin Chambers of Texas for vice president.

Although the Greenback-Labor Party did not play a decisive role in 1880, it was a forerunner of left-wing third parties that emerged to play a decisive role in contests between the Republicans and Democrats.

The Campaign

The two main presidential nominees continued to observe the tradition of not being seen to be too eager for office. Given the relative lack of substantive differences between the two parties, both parties turned to personal attacks on their opponent.

The Republicans targeted Hancock's lack of experience in office. The party published a pamphlet titled "A Record of the Statesmanship and Political Achievements of General Winfield Scott Hancock." Inside, the pages were blank. Rumors were rife that Hancock had conspired to overthrow President Abraham Lincoln and had engaged in corrupt practices while stationed in Louisiana after the Civil War. Neither rumor was substantiated. The Republicans also emphasized the Civil War exploits of their presidential and vice presidential nominees, both of whom were former Army generals (as was the Democrat Hancock) as a way of trying to associate the Democrats with the Confederacy.

Two months before the federal election, Maine elected a Democrat as governor (state elections did not usually coincide with federal elections in the era). This prompted Maine's Sen. Blaine to persuade Republicans to begin emphasizing support for tariffs protecting U.S. business from foreign competition.

The Democrats focused on Garfield's ethics, trying to link him to the Credit Mobilier scandal of the Grant administration. They also attacked Garfield's personal business practices, accusing him of failing to pay people who worked for him and refusing to give a veteran spare change.

The Democrats produced a letter (it later turned out to be a forgery) accusing Garfield of supporting the Burlingame Treaty of 1868 that allowed free immigration of Chinese workers to help build the transcontinental railroad. The issue angered many in California who opposed Chinese immigration, and may have been instrumental in putting California and Nevada into the Democratic column in November.

Both parties also fought hard for Indiana's 15 electoral votes and New York's 35. Democrats had carried Indiana for the past decade and had nominated a Hoosier, William English, as vice president. But in the end, the Republicans won the state by a small margin.

New York was a different story. The Republican vice presidential nominee, Chester Arthur, was from New York, and organized campaign rallies and made sure that federal employees appointed to office contributed part of their salary (three percent) to the Republican cause. The Democrats, on the other hand, counted on Samuel Tilden help to carry the state. That turned out to be an error, since Tilden had long ago alienated the influential Tammany Hall organization. In the end, New York's 35 votes went to Garfield. Had it gone the other way, Hancock would have won the election.

The Outcome

The outcome in 1880 was one of the closest of any presidential election. In the total popular vote, Garfield won 4,453,295 votes to Hancock's 4,414,082. Republican Garfield's total represented 48.5 percent of the popular vote, compared to Hancock's 48.1 percent.

James Weaver of the Greenback-Labor Party, won 308,578 votes, or 3.4 percent, not enough to make a difference nationally, although the outcome in three key states—California, Indiana, and New Jersey—might have been different if not for Greenback-Labor.

Garfield won the electoral college vote with 214 votes compared to 155 for Hancock. Both men won 19 states. The Democrats won most of the old Confederate states, plus California, Nevada, and New Jersey. The Republicans won the industrial Northern states, and the more heavily populated states of the West.

Winning the White House without support of the former Confederate states changed the calculus for the Republican Party for over a century. Since the post–Civil War Reconstruction period, they had counted on African-American votes to help carry the South and claim the White House; after 1880, having won the presidency without the South, the Republicans largely conceded the former Confederate states to the Democrats until the election of 1968.

More Information

- Doenecke, Justus D. *The Presidencies of James A. Garfield and Chester A. Arthur.* Lawrence: Regents Press of Kansas, 1981.
- Hancock, Almira Russell. *Reminiscences of Winfield Scott Hancock, By His Wife.* New York: C. L. Webster & Co., 1887.
- Peskin, Allan. *Garfield: A Biography.* Kent, Ohio: Kent State University Press, 1978.
- Reeves, Thomas C. *Gentleman Boss: The Life of Chester Alan Arthur.* New York: Knopf, 1975.

FlashFocus: Chester A. Arthur

21st President, 1881–1885

Born: October 5, 1829, Fairfield, Vermont
Died: November 18, 1886, New York City
Family: Son of William Arthur, a teacher and Baptist minister, and Malvina Stone Arthur; married Ellen Lewis Herndon
Education: Union College, 1848; private law studies; passed bar 1853
Political life: A Stalwart Republican.

Chester Arthur never ran for any elected office except as James Garfield's vice presidential running mate in 1880. He became president after Garfield was assassinated in 1881, but he was not nominated by the Republicans in 1884.

Arthur was as an abolitionist lawyer when he attended the first convention of the New York Republican party in 1856. He found a niche building the party's organization behind the scenes. His efforts put him under the wing of Senator Roscoe Conkling, and although Arthur was never accused of using his power for personal gain, he had no scruples against doling out jobs and favors to benefit Republican interests. He was removed from his job as federal Collector of the Port of New York, where he controlled more than a thousand jobs, by President Rutherford Hayes as part of a government reform campaign.

When he became president on the death of Garfield in 1881, Arthur also became a reformer. He signed the Pendleton Act in 1883 establishing the Civil Service Commission and making many government jobs subject to competitive examinations. The act also protected government workers from removal from their jobs for political reasons.

Arthur's signing of the 1883 Tariff Act enraged some Southerners and Westerners and the tariff issue began to dominate political differences. Arthur was not nominated to run in his own right in 1884. One of Arthur's last ceremonial appearances as president was at the dedication of the Washington Monument on February 21, 1885.

He died on November 18, 1886.

- Smith, Theodore Clarke. *The Life and Letters of James Abram Garfield.* Hamden, Connecticut: Archon Books, 1968.

On the Web

- Garfield, James. "Inaugural Address." **http://www.bartleby.com/124/pres36.html.**
- "Reconstruction and the New South,." Links to articles and primary sources for the period 1865–1915. **http://www.historyteacher.net/APUSH-Course/Weblinks/Weblinks14.htm.**
- "The Presidential Election of Grover Cleveland," from The Great Republic by the Master Historians, Vol. III, Hubert Bancroft, ed. (published 1902). **http://www.publicbookshelf.com/public_html/The_Great_Republic_By_the_Master_Historians_Vol_III/grovercle_ib.html.**

1884
Grover Cleveland (Democrat) vs. James Blaine (Republican)

FlashFocus: 1884

Candidates

Grover Cleveland & Thomas A. Hendricks, Democrat
James G. Blaine & John A. Logan, Republican
Benjamin F. Butler & Absolom M. West, Greenback-Labor
John P. St. John & William Daniel, Prohibition

Issues

Third parties. Two factional parties presented candidates in 1884: the Prohibition Party and the Greenback-Labor Party. Prohibitionists advocated a complete ban of alcoholic beverages. They drew their support from Republicans, and Democrats helped to finance the Prohibitionist campaign in order to draw more votes away from Blaine, the Republican candidate. The Greenback-Labor Party supported reforms in working conditions for laborers, an important issue as the Industrial Revolution brought change to the economy, especially in the North. Butler, the Greenback-Labor candidate, drew his support from Democrats, and the Republicans contributed to his campaign in order to draw votes away from Cleveland, as the Democrats had done for St. John in order to undermine support for Blaine.

Scandals. Grover Cleveland, James Blaine, and John St. John were all involved in sex scandals that surfaced during the campaign. Blaine's handling of the situation served to undermine his credibility and integrity. Cleveland was able to gain support through his explanation of his situation.

Outcome

Popular Vote

Cleveland	4,879,507	48.5% ✓
Blaine	4,850,293	48.2%
Butler	175,370	1.8%
St. John	150,369	1.5%

Electoral College

Cleveland	219 ✓
Blaine	182

The election of 1884 promised to be a rerun of 1880: Democrats, again in control of Congress, had won governorships in several Republican states (including Kansas and Massachusetts), and were determined to regain the White House for the first time since before the Civil War. Republicans campaigned to maintain their unbroken string of successes.

The campaign became lively after both candidates were accused of sex scandals, resulting in another close contest in which the winner was separated form the loser by fewer than 30,000 votes. In 1884 there was good evidence that a third party, this time the Prohibition Party, made a crucial difference.

The Context

There was a general air of contentment in the country going into the election of 1884 and a lack of major compelling issues separating the two major parties. Reconstruction in the South had virtually disappeared as an issue (although the Republican candidate tried to keep the question alive) and there was no pressing foreign policy issue. A persistent economic recession in the north may have hurt the Republicans but their incumbent president, Chester Arthur, was not running for reelection.

As in 1880 smaller parties carried the torch for their particular issues: the abolition of alcoholic beverages, in the case of the Prohibition Party, and improvement of working conditions for laborers in the case of the Greenback-Labor Party. This time however, the Prohibition Party siphoned off votes from the Republican candidate, and may well have made the difference in throwing New York's 35 electoral votes to Democrat Grover Cleveland.

The Candidates

Indeed it would have been strange had Cleveland not won the largest state. He was, after all, governor of New York, elected in 1882. But when the Democrats convened in Chicago on July 8, 1884, the nomination was not a foregone conclusion. Like the Republicans, the Democrats had a variety of factions and no shortage of presidential aspirants.

Senator Thomas Bayard of Delaware was a respected proponent of civil service reform, hard money and free trade. Former Speaker of the House Samuel J. Randall of Pennsylvania wanted to run but was hobbled by the unlikelihood of carrying his own state in the general election.

Despite the number of potential candidates Cleveland entered the convention with a large lead. He had demonstrated his ability to carry the big electoral prize—the prize that put a Republican into the White House four years earlier—by being elected governor. He had instituted civil service reform in his own state, and on the divisive question of tariffs, his stand was ambiguous. Most important, Cleveland seemed like a candidate who could beat the Republicans for the first time in almost 30 years.

On the first nominating ballot Cleveland received 392 votes to 170 for Bayard. Impressively, Cleveland won votes from 38 of the 47 states. The second ballot was not taken until the next day. Overnight, Cleveland's campaign managers worked to make sure delegates did not coalesce behind another candidate, and in fact managed to persuade delegates who voted for other con-

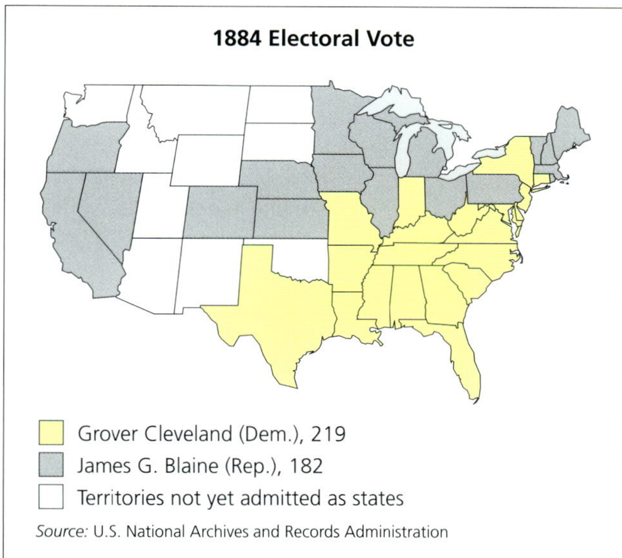

FlashFocus: Grover Cleveland

22nd President, 1885–1889

24th President, 1893–1897

Born: March 18, 1837 in Caldwell, New Jersey

Died: June 24, 1908 in Princeton, New Jersey

Family: Son of Richard Falley Cleveland, a Presbyterian minister, and Ann Neal; married Frances Folsom

Education: Poorly educated; private law studies; passed bar in 1859

Political career: Democrat. Mayor of Buffalo, New York, 1882; governor of New York, 1883–85; defeated in reelection bid 1888; elected to second term, 1892

Cleveland practiced law in Buffalo, N.Y. and became part of the local Democratic Party's inner circle. Elected mayor of Buffalo in 1881, he gained a reputation for attacking local corruption, which led to his nomination and election as governor of New York in 1882.

Cleveland won the 1884 Democratic presidential nomination on the second ballot. Cleveland won the general election by a tiny majority; fewer than 30,000 votes separated him from Republican candidate James Blaine in an election in which the Prohibition Party candidate gained enough votes in New York to throw the state's electoral college votes, and the election, to Cleveland.

In office Cleveland exercised over 300 vetoes against what he viewed as special-interest legislation. "What is the use of being elected," he asked, "unless you stand for something?" Faced by a wave of railroad strikes by the newly-formed Knights of Labor, Cleveland proposed the creation of a commission to settle labor-management disputes, leading to the creation of the Department of Labor.

Cleveland narrowly won the popular vote in his bid for reelection in 1888 but lost the electoral college vote to Benjamin Harrison, the Republican. Four years later Cleveland ran against Harrison again, winning both the popular and electoral vote. He died in Princeton, New Jersey in 1908.

tenders to come over to Cleveland's side. On the second ballot, taken the next morning, Cleveland won the nomination with 683 votes. Later that day Thomas Hendricks of Indiana was nominated as vice president (for the second time).

As they had been for the last three elections, the Republicans in 1884 were sharply divided between the conservative "Stalwart" wing and the reform-minded Liberals, with the middle-of-the road "Half Breeds" in between.

The sitting president was Chester Arthur of New York, who had assumed the presidency in 1881 after the assassination of James Garfield just 100 days into his administration. Arthur wanted to run in his own right but during his term in the White House he had alienated the conservative Stalwarts without gaining the support of the liberal Reform wing. Despite having been diagnosed with a kidney disease (from which he would die in 1886) Arthur chose to fight for the nomination.

Set against him was James Blaine of Maine, a former Speaker of the House and senator who had been named secretary of state by Garfield but resigned shortly after Garfield's assassination. He then began working to undermine support for Chester Arthur, who was a Stalwart leader. Blaine was widely popular with Republican voters and well-respected as a visionary and skilled speaker. Tempering enthusiasm for Blaine was his aggressive foreign policy and a reputation for corruption— an issue that had bedeviled the Republicans since the second Grant administration.

Also against Arthur were the Liberals, led by the irrepressible Carl Schurz of Missouri and including a rising politician from New York, Theodore Roosevelt. They had no clear frontrunner of their own; most of them backed Senator George Edmunds of Vermont, an unlikely candidate, however, because of a cold and argumentative personality. Some midwestern delegates backed Senator John Logan of Illinois, closely associated with Reconstruction.

The Republican convention opened in Chicago on June 3. Despite widespread objections to Blaine his opponents could not agree on a single candidate to oppose him. On the first ballot Blaine received 334½ votes, well ahead of Arthur's 278, Edmunds' 93, and Logan's 63½. (John Sherman, brother of Civil War general William Tecumseh Sherman, got 30 votes.) On the next two ballots Blaine's total kept rising while Arthur's was steady. Finally on the fourth ballot Blaine picked up support from Ohio and Illinois and won the nomination with 541 votes. John Logan of Illinois was then chosen to run for vice president.

Members of the Liberal wing of the Republican Party could not reconcile themselves to the party's nominee. Instead, some members of the faction broke off and campaigned for the

FlashFocus: James G. Blaine

Republican Candidate for President, 1884

Born: January 31, 1830, Westbrownsville, Pennsylvania
Died: January 27, 1893, Washington, D.C.
Family: Son of Ephraim L. Blaine and Maria Louise Gillespie; married Harriet Stanwood, a teacher
Education: Washington College; studied law but did not become a lawyer
Political career: Republican. Delegate to the first Republican national convention, 1856; member and speaker of the Maine state House of Representatives; U.S. congressman; Speaker of the House of Representatives 1869–75; U.S. senator from Maine, 1876–81; secretary of state 1881 and 1889–92

James Blaine was a major force in the Republican Party, the popular leader of the "Half Breeds," a faction of the party so named because they advocated a middle ground between the radical "Stalwarts" and the liberal "Mugwumps."

Blaine began his career as a newspaper editor in Maine, then became a state legislator and later a U.S. Congressman. He was elected Speaker of the House of Representatives three times. Blaine was the leading candidate for the Republican presidential nomination in 1876 but lost to a compromise candidate, Rutherford Hayes.

Blaine was appointed to the Senate in 1876 to fill an unexpired term, then was elected in his own right. In 1880 Blaine was again a leading candidate for the nomination but was blocked by Senator Roscoe Conkling of New York. The convention nominated James Garfield who later rewarded Blaine for his loyalty by naming him secretary of state.

In 1884 Blaine was yet again the leading candidate for nomination, and on the fourth ballot he defeated the incumbent president, Chester Arthur, only to lose the general election to Grover Cleveland.

In 1892 Blaine tried to obtain the presidential nomination, but was defeated by Harrison. Blaine died three months after the election, on January 27, 1893.

Democrat, Cleveland. They became known as the Mugwumps (supposedly a word in the Algonquin language meaning "chief"). Led again by Carl Shurz of Missouri, the Mugwumps focused on three issues: Blaine's reputation for dishonesty; his foreign policy, which supported expansion of American power abroad; and civil service reform (which Blaine opposed).

Alternative parties also ran candidates in 1884. Generally they were ineffectual but this time the Prohibition Party made a difference. Their candidate was former Kansas governor John St. John. The Prohibitionists, who advocated a complete ban on alcoholic beverages, drew much of their support from Republicans, and during the campaign the Republicans took St. Johns' challenge seriously.

The Greenback-Labor Party, which had polled 3.4 percent of the vote four years earlier, nominated Benjamin Butler who had a long list of "formers" to his name: former Democrat, former Republican, former Greenback, former governor of Massachusetts. He advocated "soft" money (currency not backed by gold) as well as a long list of labor reforms in the burgeoning Industrial Revolution. He was thought to draw support from Democratic voters, just as the Prohibitionists drew support from Republicans.

During the campaign that followed the Democrats hoped to hurt the Republicans by financing the campaign of the Prohibitionists, while the Republicans tried the same strategy by contributing to the Greenback-Labor Party.

The Campaign

The 1884 campaign saw three sex scandals—and this in the height of the culturally conservative time known as the Victorian Era (named after Queen Victoria of England).

The least of the scandals affected John St. John of the Prohibitionists. During the campaign it was revealed that he had married at age 19 and fathered a child, only to be divorced—at his wife's request, a most unusual situation in 1884. Shortly afterwards St. John had married someone else, although he had continued to support his son by his first marriage, including getting a political appointment for him.

More embarrassing was a report that showed the Republican, John Blaine, had married just three months before his first child was born. This story might not have been so serious, but Blaine's attempt to explain it reinforced doubts about his integrity. Blaine claimed that he had really been married earlier— privately, without a license, without a clergyman, without the customary public notice. Later, Blaine explained, there had been the public ceremony, held shortly before his son's birth. The explanation had a number of holes and instead of helping explain Blaine's background it reinforced his reputation for dishonesty.

Blaine was also hurt by what came to be known as the Mulligan Letters. He was accused of using his influence as Speaker of the House to enrich himself through sales of railroad bonds, used to finance the rapid expansion of railroads. He was said to have pushed legislation that helped the Texas & Pacific Railroad, owned by a businessman, Tom Scott, who had saved Blaine from serious financial losses on bonds in another railroad company. As with the sex scandal Blaine denied the allegations, until letters made available by a clerk named James Mulligan provided evidence of his misdeeds. On one letter Blaine had written the notation, "Burn this letter!" which became a chant by Democrats at Blaine rallies.

But 1884's most dramatic scandal involved Grover Cleveland. Shortly after he was nominated, a newspaper reported that he had had a son out of wedlock with a widow named Maria Helpin. The story claimed that Cleveland had then arranged for Halpin to be committed to an asylum, and for their son to be placed in an orphanage.

Cleveland's reaction to the story might have held a lesson for politicians much later in American history. Instead of denying the story or making up an explanation that would not hold water, Cleveland insisted that his supporters "tell the truth." He admitted the indiscretion but said that Halpin had been committed to care for alcoholism, not an insane asylum, and that their son had been adopted by a wealthy couple. Cleveland also said he had provided financial support for both the child and the mother.

Cleveland's explanation was widely accepted and in the end the story seemed like one of youthful indiscretion which was handled honorably by Cleveland. The story actually enhanced Cleveland's reputation as an upstanding character whereas Blaine's contradictory and confusing denial hurt him further.

The Outcome

The election was held on November 3, 1884 and attracted a large turnout of voters. Again the results were extremely close, especially in New York, where the final outcome was not known for several days.

In the end the Democrat Cleveland won the popular vote with 4,879,507 to Blain's 4,850,293. The Greenback-Labor party won 1.8 percent of the vote, and the Prohibitionists won 1.5 percent. In upstate New York Prohibitionist votes in particular were thought to have hurt Blaine to cost him the state's critical electoral votes and thus the presidency

Thanks in part to New York's 35 elector votes Cleveland won the Electoral College vote 219–182 and became the first Democrat in the White House since 1861. Cleveland won the South solidly as well as the border states. He also won Connecticut, New Jersey, and Indiana.

More Information

▶ Brodsky, Alyn. *Grover Cleveland: A Study in Character*. New York: St. Martin's Press, 2000.

▶ Crapol, Edward P. *James G. Blaine: Architect of Empire*. Wilmington, Delaware: SR Books, 2000.

▶ Graff, Henry F. *Grover Cleveland*. New York: Times Books, 2002.

▶ Muzzey, David Saville. *James G. Blaine*. Port Washington, New York: Kennikat Press, 1963.

On the Web

▶ Cooper, John S. "Rum, Romanism and Rebellion: The Election of 1884." Suite101.com. **http://www.suite101.com/ article.cfm/presidents_and_first_ladies/34661.**

▶ "The Gilded Age." Gilder Lehrman Institute of American History. **http://www.gliah.uh.edu/resource_guides/content. cfm?tpc=17.**

FlashFocus: John P. St. John

Prohibition Party Presidential Candidate, 1884

Born: February 25, 1833, Brookville, Indiana
Died: August 31, 1916, Olathe, Kansas
Family: Son of an alcoholic farmer; married twice, Mary Jane Brewer (divorced), and Susan Parker
Education: Little formal education; studied law and admitted to the Illinois bar
Political career: Republican and later, Prohibition Party. Kansas state senate (1874–74); governor of Kansas 1878–82; Prohibition Party presidential candidate, 1884

John St. John made his political reputation in Kansas where as Republican governor from 1879–1881 he successfully campaigned for a state constitutional amendment barring the sale of alcoholic beverages. St. John had personally experienced the destruction that alcohol can bring to a family. His father was an alcoholic and St. John had to support himself from age 12.

He was reelected governor as a Republican 1880 and concentrated on enforcing prohibition, but lost his bid for a third term. He was nominated for the presidency in 1884 by the National Prohibition Party. Although never contemplating victory he concentrated his campaign in upstate New York, where the Democrat, former New York governor Grover Cleveland, was locked in a close contest against Republican James Blaine in which New York's electoral votes were critical.

St. John won over 25,000 votes in New York, most of which were thought to have come from Republicans who might otherwise have voted for Blaine. The Democrat, Cleveland, won New York's electoral votes, and the election.

St. John ended his association with the Prohibition Party in 1896, although he spent much of the rest of his life delivering speeches in favor of banning alcohol. He died in Olathe, Kansas, in 1916.

▶ Cleveland, Grover. "First Inaugural Address, Wednesday, March 4, 1885." *Inaugural Addresses of the Presidents of the United States*. Washington, D.C.: U.S. Government Printing Office, 1989; Bartleby.com, 2001. **http://www.bartleby.com/ 124/pres37.html.**

▶ "Reconstruction and the New South," A.P. U.S. History, Historyteacher.net. Links to articles and primary sources for the period 1865–1915. **http://www.historyteacher.net/ APUSH-Course/Weblinks/Weblinks14.htm.**

1888
Benjamin Harrison (Republican)
vs. Grover Cleveland (Democrat)

FlashFocus: 1888

Candidates

Benjamin Harrison & Levi P. Morton, Republican
Grover Cleveland & Allen G. Thurman, Democrat
Clinton B. Fisk & John A. Brooks, Prohibition
Anson J. Streeter & Charles E. Cunningham, Union Labor

Issues

Tariffs. President Cleveland pushed for reducing tariffs (taxes on imported goods) which supplied most of the government's revenue. The tariffs protected northern manufacturing industries from foreign competition, and northerners favored them. The South, having little manufacturing, opposed tariffs. Cleveland proposed reducing the size of the government by reducing its income (largely from the tariffs), which far outstripped its expenses. Republicans argued that the surplus income could be used to fund federal programs or could be redistributed to the states.

Veterans benefits. Cleveland vetoed special pensions for Union Army veterans and blocked a bill that would have granted benefits to disabled veterans. Therefore, Republicans argued, the Democrats must be pro-South, and pro-slavery.

Government appointments. After being elected to his first term Cleveland did not replace Republican political appointees with Democrats, but rather allowed the Republicans to remain in their positions, angering Democratic supporters who had been hoping for those placements. One year into his presidency, he replaced the Republicans with Democrats, which then angered Republicans.

Outcome

Popular Vote

Cleveland	5,537,857	48.6% ✓
Harrison	5,477,129	47.9%
Fisk	249,506	2.2%
Streeter	146,935	1.3%

Electoral College

Harrison	233 ✓
Cleveland	168

The Republicans faced a unique situation in 1888: for the first time they were challenging an incumbent Democrat, having lost the White House four years earlier in a very close contest. The incumbent, Grover Cleveland, had taken enough political missteps to make the Republicans eager for the contest.

The Context

Cleveland had become the first Democrat to occupy the White House since James Buchanan's victory nearly forty years earlier, but Cleveland's election in 1884 had been one of the closest of any election yet conducted. Despite his razor-thin margin of victory in his home state of New York, whose electoral votes were critical in putting him into the White House, Cleveland had not used any of the traditional methods to build support. In particular he had left many officeholders appointed by his Republican predecessor in place for a year, annoying Democrats who had expected to receive federal appointments after his election. Trying to correct the situation a year into office Cleveland proceeded to dismiss many Republican appointees and to replace them with Democrats. In so doing he lost the goodwill of the Republicans, while leaving many Democrats still discontented, and further alienating advocates of civil service reform.

Although the Civil War had been over for more than twenty years, it was still a sensitive political issue. Cleveland managed to offend many Union veterans of the war by first vetoing special disability pensions to many veterans, and then blocking a bill that would have granted veterans general pensions without having to apply for special relief in the form of disability pensions. These acts, plus a decision to return captured Confederate battle flags to their original states (a decision he reversed nine days later), helped renew old charges that the Democratic Party had been disloyal during the Civil War and had secretly backed the South (where the Democrats continued to enjoy solid support among white voters).

Eager to find an issue on which he could build a winning reelection campaign, Cleveland focused on reducing protective tariffs (taxes on imports), a measure popular in the South but far less popular in the North, where domestic industries enjoyed the protection against foreign competition afforded by the tariffs.

The Candidates

Cleveland easily won renomination but not without some opposition. In particular, David B. Hill, the governor of Cleveland's home state of New York, remained annoyed over Cleveland's failure to dismiss Republican political appointees in favor of Democrats early in his administration. Although Hill had little chance of blocking Cleveland's renomination, the president nevertheless arranged for Hill not to be seated at the

"

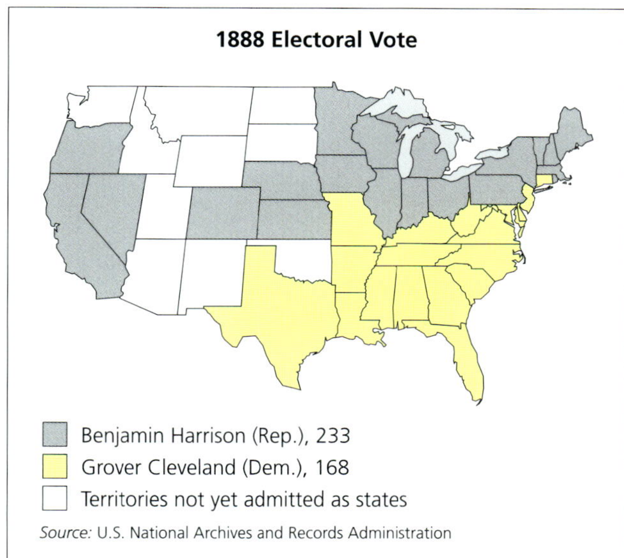

Source: U.S. National Archives and Records Administration

Democratic convention when it opened in St. Louis in June, 1888, thereby deepening Hill's dislike. In a close election New York's electoral votes would prove critical in the general election. Cleveland's nomination passed easily. The death of Cleveland's first vice president, Thomas Hendricks, three years earlier did leave open the number two spot on the ticket, which went to a former senator from Ohio, Allen Thurman, age 75. It was a fateful choice. Thurman was both elderly and ailing, and in an era when vice presidential nominees were expected to shoulder much of the burden of campaigning, Thurman was not up to the job.

For the Republicans, whose convention met in Chicago in late June, the nomination was far from clear. The party favorite, James Blaine, had declared he would not be a candidate. Consequently fourteen possible candidates were competing for the nomination on the party's first ballot. The leading candidate at first was John Sherman, a senator from Ohio. Sherman was well ahead, with 244 votes, on the third ballot; his nearest rival was Judge Walter Gresham of Indiana was 123 votes and Governor Russell Alger of Michigan, who had 122. After adjourning overnight Indiana's former Senator Benjamin Harrison emerged on the second day with 216 votes, up from just 94 the previous evening. After another delay in voting over a weekend Harrison rivaled Sherman, with 231 votes to Sherman's 244. On the next ballot, the seventh of the convention, Harrison pulled ahead and on the eighth roll call Harrison won the nomination with 544 votes. For vice president the Republicans chose Levi P. Morton of New York, a former congressman, on the first ballot.

Harrison was the grandson of former President William Henry Harrison (see 49). He had served in the Senate for one term, was a successful lawyer and widely respected speaker, renowned for his ability to put forward the party's position

with great clarity. He was also popular with supporters of Blaine, thanks in part to his decision at the previous Republican convention four years earlier to throw his political support for the nomination to Blaine. Harrison was strongly opposed, however, by supporters of Gresham, who had been a judge in Indiana but later moved to Illinois where he was also a federal judge; Gresham's supporters wanted Indiana, as well as Illinois, to support their "favorite son."

The Issues

Tariffs. Cleveland, the incumbent, seized upon reducing high tariffs as an issue he thought would help propel him to reelection. Tariffs were the main source of income to the federal government in the era before the individual income tax and income from tariffs far exceeded government expenses. Tariffs drove up the price of imported goods which helped domestic manufacturers but also was blamed, by Cleveland, for driving up the prices of domestic goods as well, to the disadvantage of working people. The chief beneficiaries of tariffs were U.S. manufacturing companies in the North; in the South, where the economy depended on exports of agricultural goods, such as cotton, there were no obvious benefits from high tariffs. For Cleveland reducing tariffs would therefore appeal to his principal sources of political strength: the South, working people in the North, and New York-based traders and merchants. Lowering government income was also in line with the Democratic Party's traditional support for a smaller central government.

The Republicans viewed the issue differently. James Blaine, the unsuccessful Republican candidate in 1884, denounced lower tariffs as chiefly a benefit to British manufacturers at the expense of American companies. The Republicans also pointed out that if federal revenues were more than enough to meet expenses, the surplus could be used to fund new public works or be distributed to state governments in order to reduce property taxes (popular with farmers, especially) or to reduce or even eliminate taxes on tobacco.

Veterans' benefits. Cleveland had angered Civil War veterans by vetoing special pensions for veterans of the Union Army. The pensions, for disabilities, had become standard in the years after the Civil War, when Republicans controlled the federal government. Cleveland also blocked a bill in 1887 that would have automatically granted disabled veterans benefits without having to ask the Congress for help. Finally Cleveland approved a measure that returned captured Confederate war flags to their respective states. It was a symbolic gesture appreciated in the South, an important source of support for the Democrats, but unpopular in the North, where Republicans continued to try to brand Democrats as the pro-slavery, pro-South party.

Civil Service reform. Cleveland, contrary to custom, did not immediately replace Republican political appointees with Democrats. Instead, acceding to the desires of the liberal Republicans known as Mugwumps, he left many appointees in place, resulting in howls of disappointment from his Democratic supporters. Finally, a year after his inauguration, Cleveland switched courses and made way for Democratic appointees, in turn disappointing reform-minded Republicans.

High tariffs on imported goods were the main issue in 1888. In this cartoon, the Democrats are shown offering a working man a knife, labeled "Free Trade, English made" to kill the goose ("Protection") that laid the golden eggs of good wages, good home, good living, prosperity, and clothes. The caption summarizes the Republicans position against free trade: "Free trade would make goods cheaper. But it would lower the American Woman's wages so much that he would be unable to purchase them."

Campaign financing. The Republicans succeeded in raising substantially more money for their campaign than the Democrats. Aided by wealthy businessmen, Republicans raised over three million dollars to pay for rallies, speakers, and masses of campaign literature. Sympathetic business groups also conducted their own campaigns on behalf of the Republicans and the protective tariff.

The Campaign

The Republicans were more than happy to take on Cleveland over the issue of protective tariffs. In the months before the election the chairman of the House Ways and Means Committee, Roger Mills of Texas, proposed a tariff reduction act that would sharply lower duties that helped protect manufacturing and wool producers. Mills had a reputation as a "free trader," someone opposed to high tariffs, and this helped Republicans pin the label of free trader onto Cleveland, despite the president's frantic efforts to tone down the proposed tariff reduction bill. The bill was especially unpopular in New York where Cleveland already faced problems with Governor Hill, whom he refused to endorse for reelection.

The Cleveland-Hill quarrel took on an odd twist. In 1888 voters used ballots distributed by the parties; in order to "split" a vote, voters used stickers (called "pasters"), also supplied by the parties. Governor Hill requested 200,000 pasters for his campaign, intended for use by voters casting Republican ballots for Harrison who wanted to vote for a Democrat, Hill, as governor. In the end Hill was reelected but Cleveland failed to carry New York, suggesting to some observers that Hill had taken his revenge by secretly working with Republicans to help Harrison and at the same time generate "split" tickets for himself as governor.

While the Republicans used their large campaign fund to conduct an efficient and expensive campaign, the Democrats suffered from poor campaign leadership. It was still not considered acceptable for presidential candidates to actively campaign, and Cleveland's vice presidential nominee was too old and too ill to contribute. The man named chairman of the Democratic campaign committee, William Barnum, fell ill and never recovered. The Democratic chairman of the party's executive committee, Calvin Brice, established an organization, then did little to oversee its operations, possibly because he was a wealthy businessman who was not enthusiastic about Cleveland's tariff reduction plans.

The campaign of 1888 saw maneuvers that might be classed as "dirty tricks." In opposing reduced tariffs Republicans accused Cleveland of catering to the interests of British manufacturers, thereby hoping to attract votes from Irish workers who vehemently disliked anything British. A Republican (not acting as part of the official campaign) wrote a letter to the British minister in Washington, asking which candidate would better serve British interests; the minister replied, naming Cleveland. Although President Cleveland expelled the minister for interfering with internal politics some damage may have been done, as intended.

On the other side Republicans were embarrassed at the end of October by a letter supposedly from the Republicans' national treasurer, urging Indiana Republicans to accompany blocks of voters "with necessary funds" and make sure the voters "all vote our ticket." The supposed author of the letter denied writing it and sued the newspaper that published it for libel. Whether the accusation that Republicans were buying votes swayed any voters was never clear.

The Outcome

Compared with 1884, when Cleveland had been first elected, only two states switched sides in 1888: New York and Indiana. But it was enough to swing the electoral college vote to Harrison, who won 233 electoral votes to Cleveland's 168. A change of New York's 36 votes would have resulted in Cleveland's reelection. Out of about 1.2 million votes cast in New York, Cleveland lost the state by just 16,000. In Indiana, with sixteen electoral votes, Harrison won by just two thousand out of 537,000 cast.

Cleveland won the national popular vote by a margin of about 60,000, but this outcome reflected Cleveland's very large margins of victory in Southern states.

More Information

- Jeffers, H. Paul. *An Honest President: The Life and Presidencies of Grover Cleveland.* New York: W. Morrow, 2000.
- Sievers, Harry Joseph. *Benjamin Harrison, Hoosier President: The White House and After.* Indianapolis: Bobbs-Merrill Co., 1968.
- Socolofsky, Homer Edward. *The Presidency of Benjamin Harrison.* Lawrence: University Press of Kansas, 1987.
- Welch, Richard E. *The Presidencies of Grover Cleveland.* Lawrence: University Press of Kansas, 1988.

On the Web

- "The Gilded Age." Gilder Lehrman Institute of American History. **http://www.gliah.uh.edu/resource_guides/content.cfm?tpc=17.**
- "Election of 1888: Electoral College Defeats the Sitting President." C-Span.org. **http://www.c-span.org/classroom/govt/1888.asp.**
- Harrison, Benjamin. "Inaugural Address, Monday, March 4, 1889." Inaugural Addresses of the Presidents of the United States. Washington, D.C.: U.S. Government Printing Office, 1989; Bartleby.com, 2001. **http://www.bartleby.com/124/pres38.html.**
- "Reconstruction and the New South,." A.P. U.S. History, Historyteacher.net. Links to articles and primary sources for the period 1865–1915. **http://www.historyteacher.net/APUSH-Course/Weblinks/Weblinks14.htm.**

1892
Grover Cleveland (Democrat)
vs. Benjamin Harrison (Republican)

FlashFocus: 1892

Candidates

Grover Cleveland & Adlai E. Stevenson, Democrat
Benjamin Harrison & Whitelaw Reid, Republican
James B. Weaver & James G. Field, Peoples Party
John Bidwell & James B. Cranfill, Prohibition Party

Issues

Government spending. Tariff collections had created a budget surplus, which Congressional Republicans used for public works projects. One tariff was introduced and then modified to serve special interests, which made the Republicans seem to be promoting business interests over the public's welfare.

The Force Act. At the polls African-Americans were often discouraged from voting, in clear violation of their rights. Republicans introduced the Force Act which allowed federal investigations of these incidents. Democrats deplored it as another instance of federal interference in state matters, and accused the Republicans of trying to impose more Reconstruction measures on the South.

The Homestead strike. Steelworkers went on strike at the Homestead factory, owned by Andrew Carnegie, who was closely associated with the Republican party. Fighting broke out between the strikers and private guards hired by the company, and the federal government sent in troops. The incident led the Democrats to criticize the Republicans as the party of the wealthy and of business interests, and to portray themselves as the party of working people.

Outcome

Popular Vote

Cleveland	5,555,426	46.1% ✓
Harrison	5,182,690	43.0%
Weaver	1,029,846	8.5%
Bidwell	264,133	2.2%

Electoral College

Cleveland	277 ✓
Harrison	145
Weaver	22

Benjamin Harrison's victory over Grover Cleveland in 1888 had been narrow and based on the electoral college (Cleveland had actually won more popular votes than Harrison). This had not caused the Republicans to show restraint in adopting their programs in Congress, however. There was widespread discontent with the flood of public works projects authorized by Congress in 1890, the result of a large revenue stream from high tariffs passed by the Republicans. In the Congressional elections of 1890 the Republicans lost control of the House of Representatives, an outcome that indicated to most observers that the presidential ticket would face trouble in 1892.

The Candidates

Incumbent Republican president Harrison was not popular among Republican politicians in early 1892, when plans were laid for that year's election. Harrison had a reputation of being personally unfriendly and curt with his colleagues. His performance in the White House was that of a busy executive rather than a politician. Furthermore, his attention was diverted by the illness of his wife, who eventually died during the campaign. Republican Senator Mathew Quay of Pennsylvania tried to generate support for James Blaine of Maine, the secretary of state and previous Republican presidential nominee, but Quay's efforts redoubled the resolve of Harrison to run for reelection.

Blaine had the added disadvantages of being ill and elderly. Another possible challenger was William McKinley of Ohio, who had lost his seat in Congress in 1890, but was then elected governor of Ohio the following year. McKinley, however, preferred not to challenge Harrison. The result was that the Republicans nominated Harrison for a second term with only token opposition by supporters of Blaine and McKinley. On the vice presidential ticket the incumbent vice president, Levi Morton, was replaced with Whitelaw Reid, the owner of Horace Greeley's old newspaper, the New York *Tribune,* and a recent ambassador to Britain. Leaders of the party felt that Reid and his newspaper could help carry New York which was Cleveland's home state and which had the largest number of electoral votes of any state.

When the Democratic convention opened in Chicago Grover Cleveland was favored to win nomination for a third time (he had been elected president in 1884, then lost to Harrison in 1888). Cleveland was widely popular with most state delegations and his assistants calculated that they had nearly enough votes to win on the first ballot. An exception to Cleveland's support was the delegation from his home state of New York. New York's Democratic governor, David Hill, brought hundreds of campaign workers to the convention to try to shout-down popular support for Cleveland. Dressed as Native American warriors, the New Yorkers carried a large tiger into the convention hall that growled whenever Cleveland's name

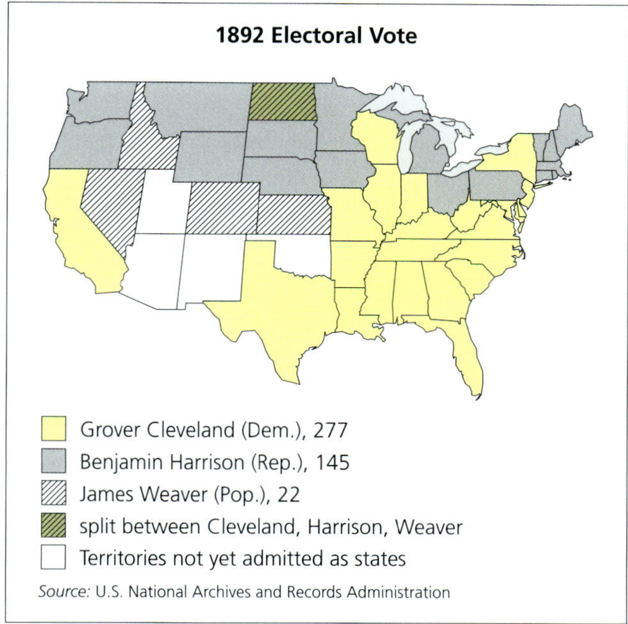

was mentioned. The New York delegation represented the interests of the Democratic organization in New York, commonly called Tammany Hall (their headquarters in New York City). The local party leaders were disenchanted with Cleveland's failure as president after the 1884 election to distribute as many government jobs as they expected.

Despite opposition from the New York delegation the Democrats nominated Cleveland on the first ballot. For vice president, they chose a former Congressman from Illinois, Adlai Stevenson, in hopes he could help the ticket among farmers in the Midwest.

The new Peoples Party, usually called the Populists, also nominated a candidate in 1892—General James B. Weaver of Iowa, a Civil War hero and former Republican and former candidate of the Greenback Party in 1880. The new party attracted farmers dissatisfied with low prices (see following section) as well as interests from organized labor.

The Prohibition Party in 1892 nominated John Bidwell for president and James Cranfill for vice president on a platform opposing the sale of alcoholic beverages, as well as support for women's right to vote, distribution of currency not based on precious metals, and government ownership of railroads and telegraph companies.

The Issues

Government spending. In 1890 the Republican-controlled Congress had adopted an enormous budget to fund public works, partly as a result of having collected a significant surplus from high tariffs. Protective tariffs, which raised the price of imported goods and enabled domestic manufacturers to charge more, had long been an area of dispute between Democrats (anti-tariff) and Republicans (pro-tariff). Cleveland

See also: Grover Cleveland, p. 95; Benjamin Harrison, p. 99.

had made it an issue in his losing 1888 campaign. Although the Republicans did not enjoy a large majority they acted as if they did. Representative William McKinley of Ohio, a future president, had introduced a tariff which was then modified in response to demands by a variety of special interests. Months spent wrangling over special concessions to various industries made the Republicans appear to be dedicated to favoring business interests over consumers. Moreover, higher tariffs were accompanied by approval of "pork barrel" projects, as well as expensive pensions for Union veterans of the Civil War. The 1892 Republican platform declared its support for "the American doctrine of protection" which it claimed was responsible for the nation's prosperity. The Democratic platform, under Cleveland's influence, denounced protective tariffs as "a fraud, a robbery of the great majority of the American people for the benefit of the few." The Democrats insisted that tariffs should be imposed for the sole purpose of raising revenue.

The Force Act. For years African-American citizens in the South had been intimidated and discouraged from voting, a process which not only violated their rights but also frustrated Republican hopes of achieving political inroads in the South on the strength of black voters. In response Republicans in Congress introduced the Force Act to allow federal authorities to investigate voter intimidation and monitor elections, an area traditionally under the authority of state governments. Although there was little doubt that black citizens were denied their rights, the Force Act was portrayed as a new round of Reconstruction and federal interference in state matters, possibly with the ulterior motive of helping Republican fortunes in the South.

Homestead Strike. In the summer of 1892 steelworkers went on strike at the Homestead factory owned by Andrew Carnegie. The company hired private guards and fighting broke out between the strikers and guards from the Pinkerton detective agency on July 6. At least ten people were killed and many more injured. After the initial skirmish the company refused to let the striking workers resume work, and troops were dispatched to maintain peace. Partly because Carnegie had close ties to the Republican Party the strike became an issue in the campaign. Democrats portrayed the Republican Party as the tool of wealthy factory owners like Carnegie, while portraying themselves as champions of working people.

Currency and Populism. In the grain-growing states of the Midwest farmers in 1892 were suffering from the long decline in the price of wheat and corn, and many farmers were unable to pay their debts. The decline in farm prices was probably caused by excess production but that was not how the farmers saw it. They blamed railroad companies, accusing them of over-charging to ship grain to markets in the East, owners of grain elevators, who actually bought the grain and stored it, and bankers in the East who limited the amount of money in circulation. In 1892 discontent among farmers resulted in the formation of the Peoples Party (usually called the Populists), which was especially strong in traditional Republican strongholds like Nebraska and Kansas.

The Campaign

The election campaign of 1892 was relatively subdued. Neither Cleveland nor Harrison actively campaigned, which was still typical of presidential candidates. The closest thing to a campaign appearance was Cleveland's attendance at a rally in Madison Square Garden in New York where he publicly accepted his party's nomination in front of 20,000 supporters. With one important exception Cleveland spent the rest of the campaign at house on Cape Cod. The exception was a meeting held in early September with Democratic Party leaders in New York. The party leaders demanded a promise from Cleveland to reward them with patronage after the election in exchange for their active campaign support. Cleveland refused the demand but the meeting eventually ended amicably when Cleveland said he would "consider" the request from the party organization.

Such trade-offs were not limited to Democrats. A similar meeting took place between the Republican vice presidential nominee, Reid, and the Republican party leader in New York, Thomas Platt, after which Harrison sent Platt a letter agreeing to cooperate with the party organization if he won in New York. (In the end, Cleveland carried New York.)

To keep the South inside the Democratic fold vice presidential candidate Stevenson warned southerners that a Republican victory would result in a new round of Reconstruction. Officials did little to control violence that intimidated African-Americans from voting.

James Field of the Populist Party added what little sparks there were in the campaign, traveling constantly to deliver speeches and collect donations from friendly crowds in order to get to the next stop. His campaign pitches were a mixture of the party's platform and religious fervor—"Read your Bibles every Sunday," he advised his audiences, "and the (Populist Party's) Omaha Platform every day in the week."

In the North the Homestead Strike (see Issues above) was exploited by the Democrats, who sought to tie the strike to Republican support for high tariffs, which were said to have benefited businessmen like Carnegie at the expense of workers forced to pay higher prices for imported goods.

The Outcome

Cleveland won 5,555,426 votes, or 46.1 percent, compared to 5,182,690, or 43.0 percent, for Harrison. The electoral vote more lopsided with 277 for Cleveland and 145 for Harrison. The Populist Party candidate, Weaver, won 1,029,846, or 8.5 percent of the total, and garnered 22 electoral votes from Colorado, Kansas, Idaho and Nevada, plus one vote from North Dakota. It was the strongest showing for a third party since the splintered election of 1860.

Cleveland won all the Southern states plus his home state of New York. He also won Illinois (his vice presidential running mate's home state), Indiana, New Jersey and Connecticut. The victorious Democrats also maintained a majority in the House of Representatives and won a majority in the Senate.

The fact that the Republicans made no inroads in the South was to have a strong impact on African-Americans. Republican efforts to enforce constitutional guarantees of equality were greatly reduced after 1892, to be taken up more than half a century later by the Democratic Party.

More Information

► Krause, Paul. *The Battle for Homestead, 1880–1892: Politics, Culture and Steel.* Pittsburgh: University of Pittsburgh Press, 1992.

► Myers, Elisabeth P. *Benjamin Harrison.* Chicago: Reilly & Lee Books, 1969.

► Tugwell, Rexford G. *Grover Cleveland.* New York: Macmillan, 1968.

On the Web

► Cleveland, Grover. "Second Inaugural Address, Saturday, March 4, 1893." *Inaugural Addresses of the Presidents of the United States.* Washington, D.C.: U.S. Government Printing Office, 1989; Bartleby.com, 2001. **http://www.bartleby.com/124/pres39.html.**

► "Reconstruction and the New South,." A.P. U.S. History, Historyteacher.net. Links to articles and primary sources for the period 1865–1915. **http://www.historyteacher.net/APUSH-Course/Weblinks/Weblinks14.htm.**

► "Grover Cleveland." Internet Public Library Presidents of the United States (multiple links to articles and documents related to Grover Cleveland). **http://www.potus.com/gcleveland.html.**

1896
William McKinley (Republican) vs. William J. Bryan (Democrat)

The election of 1896 was as wild as the election of 1892 had been sedate. Seldom has any campaign witnessed the excesses of 1896. The Republicans hammered on the notion that the Democratic candidate was a madman, and the Democrats accused the Republicans of "crucifying" the common people for the benefit of the wealthy. Businesses actively participated in the campaign, threatening to close their doors the next morning if the Democrats won, revealing a deep sense of dread over passions generated by the Democratic candidate and a fear of possible revolution by millions of unemployed workers. Widespread labor strife added to the sense of impending doom by business owners, most of whom supported the Republicans.

The Context

The overwhelming fact of the 1896 election was a deep and serious economic depression. Ten days before Cleveland was inaugurated for his second term, the Reading Railroad declared bankruptcy. The result was a "panic," the sudden demand by bank depositors to retrieve their deposits in gold. Banks that could not comply shut their doors. The price of stocks also collapsed in May. By the end of 1897 one bank in ten had failed, and the number of unemployed workers ballooned from three million in 1893 to over four million in 1894, to over six million by 1894, when 18 percent of workers were out of a job. This figure understated the depth of the crisis in some areas of the economy, notably in manufacturing.

The causes of the depression were hotly debated. Some Democrats blamed high tariffs enacted by the Republicans in 1890. Many other critics focused on the question of the "gold standard," which maintained that all currency had to be backed up by gold deposits. Many Populists from western states and some Democrats insisted that the solution to the crisis was to put more money in circulation by issuing currency based on silver as well as gold. One Democrat who disagreed was President Cleveland, who supported the gold standard and tried to protect the government's gold holdings, which had fallen precipitously from nearly $200 million in 1889 to about $103 million in 1893, at the start of the depression. The decline was based partly on many investors converting their bonds into gold; it was also based partly on the Sherman Silver Purchase Act of 1890 which required the federal government to purchase silver, to be turned into coins, in exchange for gold. Many Republicans and some Democrats from eastern states wanted to repeal the Sherman Act on grounds that the large quantities of silver, turned into coins, could result in inflation—the reduction in value of existing currency. Democrats in the West, as well as Populists, wanted even more silver to be turned into money in order to put more money into the hands of people and also to make it easier for debtors to pay off their debts.

Candidates

William McKinley & Garret A. Hobart, Republican
William J. Bryan & Arthur Sewall, Democrat-Populist

Issues

The gold standard. The question of keeping to the gold standard or minting silver coins was an important issue in the campaign. William Jennings Bryan, the Democratic candidate, campaigned passionately for silver coinage, which would put more money into circulation and ease the country's economic depression. Republicans opposed abandoning the gold standard, which they argued would lead to inflation and decrease the value of repayments on debts.

Tariffs. The issue of taxes on imports was still hotly debated. McKinley and the Republicans supported tariffs, which protected manufacturing industries, especially in the North, from competition from foreign industries. Democrats opposed the tariffs, claiming that they made imported goods too expensive, and that they contributed to big government by increasing government revenue.

Railroad strikes. The American Railway Union, led by Eugene Debs, initiated union actions in support of workers who were striking at the Pullman Company, which manufactured and operated railroad cars. The Railway Union strikes threatened to shut down railroad travel across the country, leading the attorney general to ban the strike, and President Cleveland to bring in federal troops. The incident and the reaction of President Cleveland hurt the Democrats in the election.

Outcome

Popular Vote

McKinley	7,102,246	51.1% ✓
Bryan	6,492,559	47.7%

Electoral College

McKinley	271 ✓	
Bryan	176	

Alongside the debate over currency was a rising tide of popular discontent with the economic depression. In January, 1894, an Ohio Populist named Jacob Coxey organized a mass march on Washington to protest government economic policies and demand that unemployed workers be hired by the government. Unemployed workers from around the country gathered in Massillon, Ohio to begin a march on the capitol. When they arrived in Washington, however, Coxey was arrested for trespassing and the crowd dispersed. It was, nevertheless, a sobering sight to many politicians who had heard of popular revolutionary uprisings by workers in Europe.

FlashFocus: William McKinley

25th President, 1897–1901

Born: January 29, 1843, Niles, Ohio
Died: September 14, 1901, Buffalo, New York
Family: Son of William McKinley, iron foundry owner, and Nancy Allison; married Ida Saxton
Education: Allegheny College; law school in Albany, N.Y.; passed bar 1867
Political life: Republican. U.S. representative, 1877–1891; governor of Ohio, 1892–1896. McKinley joined the Union Army at the beginning of the Civil War and rose to the rank of major. After the war he opened a private law practice in Canton, Ohio.

In 1877 McKinley was elected to the U.S. House of Representatives, where he supported high tariffs to protect domestic manufacturers from foreign competition. When he took office as president in 1897 he pushed Congress to raise tariffs as a means of bringing the country out of economic depression. He also supported the Gold Standard Act, requiring that currency be backed by gold deposits in banks.

Two years later, in 1898, McKinley guided the country through the one hundred day long Spanish-American War, which resulted in the annexation of Puerto Rico, Guam, and the Philippines. McKinley also sent U.S. troops to join an international effort responding to the Boxer Rebellion in China.

McKinley was renominated unanimously in 1900, with Theodore Roosevelt as his running mate. His campaign theme was "a full dinner pail" for all, while his opponent, Democrat William Jennings Bryan, stumped against imperialism and accused McKinley of being the tool of big business. On election day McKinley was the popular vote winner by more than a million votes, and his electoral vote total was 292 to Bryan's 155.

On September 6, 1901, while greeting well-wishers at the Pan-American Exposition in Buffalo, New York, McKinley was shot by a deranged man, Leon Czolgosz, who styled himself an anarchist. The president died a week later, on September 14, 1901.

The Candidates

The Republican convention opened on June 16 in St. Louis. William McKinley of Ohio was the leading contender for the nomination. He was well known for the so-called McKinley Tariff of 1890, when McKinley was a Congressman, which identified him with the idea of high tariffs to protect U.S. manufacturing companies from foreign competition. On the critical issue of whether silver should join gold as the basis of currency, McKinley supported the gold standard. The Republicans were divided on the issue between "Goldbugs," who favored limiting currency to gold, and "Silverbugs" who supported the free coinage of silver at a fixed rate. (Silver was readily available, and the Silverbugs reasoned that if it were converted into coins at a fixed rate, there would be signifi-

cantly more money in circulation, which would make it easier for people to repay debts.) A group of pro-silver delegates from the West, led by Senator Henry Teller of Colorado, stalked out of the convention during the debate, which opened the way to McKinley's nomination. Teller and other Silverbugs promptly formed the National Silver Party, which supported the Democratic candidate in the presidential election. Thus, the Republican candidate McKinley ran on a traditional Republican platform of supporting relatively high protective tariffs, and the gold standard.

The fact that the economic depression had coincided with Cleveland's term made it unfeasible for him to run again, even if there were not a long-standing tradition of limiting a president to two terms. When the Democratic Party gathered for its nominating convention in St. Louis on July 7, 1892, the party was already split between Gold Democrats, who favored sticking with the gold standard, and Democrats from the West and South, who favored free minting of silver.

The leader of the western and southern Democrats was William Jennings Bryan, a former Congressman from Nebraska and a highly talented orator. At the Democratic convention, Bryan delivered one of the most famous political speeches in American history in defense of minting silver coins.

"Having behind us the producing masses of this nation and the world, supported by the commercial interests, the laboring interests, and the toilers everywhere," Bryan declared, "we will answer their demand for a gold standard by saying to them: You shall not press down upon the brow of labor this crown of thorns, you shall not crucify mankind upon a cross of gold!"

The convention erupted into a wildly enthusiastic demonstration of support by shouting, cheering, weeping delegates who carried Bryan around the hall on their shoulders.

The Issues

Economic depression. The economic depression that had started in 1893 continued through the beginning of the campaign of 1896, one of the worst economic downturns in the nation's history, with nearly one out of every five workers thrown out of work. In some manufacturing communities the unemployment rate was even higher. Among farmers, low grain prices represented a continuation of economic suffering that predated the Panic of 1893.

Silver vs. gold coinage. Opinions differed about the cause of the long-lasting depression and how to go about stimulating the economy. In the campaign of 1896, however, most attention was paid to the question of currency and specifically whether the United States mint should turn silver into coins. Bankers, manufacturers and other business interests in the East strongly felt that only gold should be turned into coins, and that paper currency should be able to be exchanged for gold coins. This meant that large quantities of silver being mined in the West could not be used as coins, which would have greatly increased the amount of money in circulation. Many farmers and workers believed that using both gold and silver as currency would increase the amount of money in the

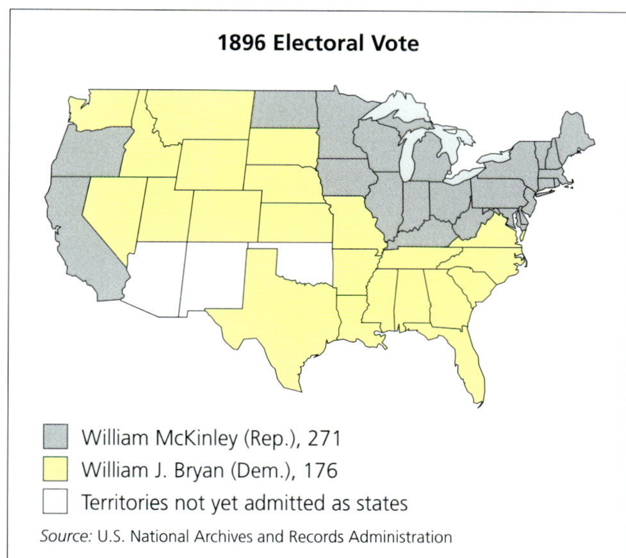

economy and therefore help ease the economic depression, as well as make it easier to pay debts. The Goldbugs believed using silver would make all currency worth less, and in particular it would diminish the value of debt repayments. The Silverbugs argued that more money in circulation would encourage people to spend more and thereby boost economic activity.

Protective tariffs. Some people believed that high tariffs, favored by Republicans, made goods too expensive; others thought high tariffs enabled American manufacturers to charge more, and therefore to pay higher wages. The Republican candidate, McKinley, firmly identified himself as "a tariff man" which was in keeping not only with Republican political theory, but also with the Whig Party that, in some respects, preceded the Republicans between about 1832 and 1856.

Labor strife. In 1894 members of the American Railway Union had agreed to refuse to work on trains that pulled sleeping cars manufactured and operated by the Pullman Company, whose workers were on strike. The association of twenty-four railroads that went in and out of Chicago, in turn, decreed that any worker refusing to work on a train pulling Pullman cars would be fired. The resulting strike, starting in June, 1894 backed up trains as far away as California and New York. Sensing a virtual national shutdown of railroads the U.S. attorney general got a court to ban the strike, and President Cleveland agreed to use federal troops and U.S. marshals to guard trains operated by strike-breakers. The leader of the American Railway Union, Eugene Debs, was jailed for failing to call off the strike. The effect of the strike and Cleveland's actions to stop it alienated Debs and other labor leaders from the Democratic Party in the Congressional elections of 1894, resulting in serious Democratic losses in Congress and in some gubernatorial contests.

Monopolies. Business monopolies in industries like oil (Standard Oil) and steel (Carnegie Steel), called "trusts" in the 1890s, were beginning to emerge as an issue. When President

Democratic Candidate for President, 1896, 1900, 1908

Born: March 18. 1860, Salem, Illinois
Died: July 26, 1925, Dayton, Ohio
Family: Son of Silas Bryan, a Democratic politician, and Mariah Elizabeth Jennings
Education: Illinois College, 1881; Union College of Law (Chicago) 1883
Career: William Jennings Bryan dominated the Democratic party from the mid-1890s until 1912, running as the Democratic candidate three times (1896, 1900 and 1912). He was a renowned orator who unabashedly mixed his Christian religious beliefs with politics in representing the interests of farmers in the West and South and urban industrial workers.

Bryan settled in Lincoln, Nebraska as a young lawyer. He was elected to Congress in 1890 and 1892. Running for a Senate seat Bryan campaigned for "free silver," the unlimited use of silver in coins at a fixed ratio—sixteen ounces of silver equals one ounce of gold. At the 1896 Democratic presidential nomination Bryan delivered a rousing speech in which he declared to eastern banking interests, who wanted only gold to be used as currency, that "you shall not press down upon the brow of labor this crown of thorns, you shall not crucify mankind upon a cross of gold!" The delegates to the convention cheered wildly for half an hour and nominated Bryan, just 36 years old, to become president.

Bryan launched a grueling campaign train tour, abandoning the tradition of presidential candidates not stumping for themselves. He gave hundreds of speeches but lost to Republican William McKinley. In 1900 Bryan and McKinley faced each other again, and Bryan lost again by a slightly larger margin.

Bryan was the Democratic nominee a third time in 1908 but lost to Republican Howard Taft. He was named secretary of state by President Woodrow Wilson in 1913.

In 1925 Bryan helped prosecute schoolteacher John Scopes for teaching Darwin's theory of evolution. Bryan's reputation was later colored by the stage play and film based on the trial, Inherit the Wind, which portrayed Bryan as a religious fanatic unable to cope with the ideas of modern science.

The trial exhausted him and he died on July 26, 1925, five days after the verdict was announced.

Cleveland went to banker J. P. Morgan to help replenish the government's holdings of gold (some people feared that the government might run out of money to pay its bills and obligations), Cleveland was strongly criticized for turning to a leading symbol of Wall Street banking and monopolies to bail out the government.

The Campaign

The symbol of a "cross of gold" became the rallying point for Bryan throughout the campaign; and the religious connotation of "crucify(ing) mankind upon a cross of gold" was reflective of the almost evangelical flavor that Bryan brought to the campaign. By the same token, reactions against Bryan were equally strong. The issue resulted in one of the most dramatic political campaigns up to that time and a far cry from the subdued tone of the previous election in 1892.

Bryan's "cross of gold" speech was a reflection of the Nebraska politician's oratorical powers. After he was nominated he abandoned the previous practice by which nominees let others campaign for him. Bryan was actually the official candidate of three parties: the Democrats, the Silver Party (dissident Republicans who believed in using silver coins), and the Peoples Party (Populists). The latter two parties had nominated Bryan in hopes that the combination of the three groups could overcome the strength of the Republicans backing McKinley. Bryan traveled almost 20,000 miles by train, delivering hundreds of speeches in over 250 cities in twenty-six states. An estimated five million people turned out to hear his renowned oratory, which focused on the importance of using silver to increase the currency supply.

Bryan often used religious imagery to cast his campaign as a kind of holy crusade on behalf of working people and against greedy business interests. Church hymns were sung with words modified to fit the political campaign. One Republican journalist from Kansas claimed that Bryan's backers displayed "something of the same mad faith that inspired the martyrs going to the stake."

The Republicans conducted a different sort of campaign, leaning heavily on companies to contribute money. Altogether, the Republicans raised between $10 and $16 million, roughly thirty times as much as the Democrats. The money was used to print and distribute thousands of fliers and pamphlets, as well as campaign buttons and other paraphernalia. Republican Theodore Roosevelt scoffed that the Republicans promoted McKinley "as if he were a patent medicine."

More telling, the Republicans enlisted sympathetic newspapers to attack Bryan, accusing him of being a "wretched, rattle-pated boy . . . mouthing resounding rottenness" (New York *Tribune*), "an irresponsible, unregulated, ignorant, prejudiced, pathetically honest and enthusiastic crank" (New York *Times*), or resorting to labels like socialist. Psychologists (called "alienists" at the time) issued opinions that Bryan must be insane, although they could not agree on a diagnosis. Among the terms suggested were paranoid, mattoid, megalomania, delirious, querulent logorrhea, graphomania, and reformatia. One alienist was of the opinion that Bryan was not smart enough "to think clearly and consecutively" or even to be paranoid. Republican businessmen warned their employees not to bother coming to work if Bryan were elected, while banks threatened farmers with foreclosure on their mortgages if the Democrats won.

McKinley conducted his campaign from the front porch of his home in Canton, Ohio. The Republican party arranged for thousands of "delegates" to come to Canton (often on special reduced fares offered by railroads to encourage trips to Canton) to hear brief speeches by McKinley. An estimated 750,000 people visited McKinley's home over three months. They took "souvenirs," such as splinters of wood from the front fence and the porch, even blades of grass from the front lawn. By the end of the campaign the fence was destroyed and the front porch needed serious repair.

The Outcome

Despite the money and effort expended on both sides it was an economic recovery that eventually mattered. The crop of 1896 was especially large and foreign demand brought high prices for American grain. Gold mines in South Africa were beginning to pump fresh supplies of gold into the world economy and there were unmistakable signs of new economic activity by the late fall of 1896.

A record number of voters cast ballots. In the end McKinley won with 7.1 million votes, or 51.1 percent of the total, to 6.5 million votes, or 47.7 percent, for Bryan.

In the electoral college McKinley won with 271 votes to 176 for Bryan. McKinley and the Republicans carried the states of the Northeast, the Upper Midwest (Minnesota, Wisconsin, Michigan, Iowa, Illinois, Indiana, and Ohio), and the border states of Kentucky, West Virginia, Maryland, and Delaware. The Democrats carried the Southern states and the Western states (except for California, Oregon, and North Dakota), plus New Jersey.

More Information

- ▶ Durden, Robert Franklin. *The Climax of Populism: The Election of 1896.* Lexington: University of Kentucky Press, 1965.
- ▶ Glad, Paul W. *McKinley, Bryan and the People.* Philadelphia: Lippincott, 1964.
- ▶ Gould, Lewis L. *The Presidency of William McKinley.* Lawrence: Regents Press of Kansas, 1980.
- ▶ Jones, Stanley Llewellyn. *The Presidential Election of 1896.* Madison: University of Wisconsin Press, 1964.
- ▶ Koenig, Louis William. *Bryan: A Political Biography of William Jennings Bryan.* New York: Putnam, 1971.
- ▶ Whicher, George Frisbie. *William Jennings Bryan and the Campaign of 1896.* Boston: Heath, 1953.

On the Web

- ▶ McKinley, William. "First Inaugural Address, Thursday, March 4, 1897." *Inaugural Addresses of the Presidents of the United States.* Washington, D.C.: U.S. Government Printing Office, 1989; Bartleby.com, 2001. **http://www.bartleby.com/ 124/pres40.html.**
- ▶ "Links for First Modern Election: 1896. GOP Victorious." PoliticalFest 2000. Links to articles and primary sources related to the presidential election of 1896. **http://www.beyondbooks. com/gop00/1a_link.asp.**

1900
William McKinley (Republican) vs. William J. Bryan (Democrat)

When Republican President William McKinley met William Jennings Bryan for a rematch of their 1896 contest, a new set of economic circumstances faced the candidates. Four years of prosperity had replaced years of economic depression. The Spanish-American war of 1898 had made the United States into a colonial power for the first time. Finally, a new character had entered the national political stage: Theodore Roosevelt of New York.

The Context

The first election of the twentieth century seemed like a rerun of the last election of the nineteenth century: William McKinley versus William Jennings Bryan. But changed circumstances made an enormous difference: the campaign took place in the midst of relative prosperity instead of at the end of nearly four years of economic depression. The United States had fought a brief war with Spain, and acquired lands outside the continent of North America which it intended to govern as colonies, with no plans for making them part of the United States.

The Spanish-American war had garnered widespread support. William Jennings Bryan had volunteered to join the Army as a private until the governor of Nebraska, a Populist, appointed him a colonel for a regiment of Nebraska volunteers. The war was positioned as support for an independence movement in Cuba. When an American battleship, the *Maine*, exploded and sank in Havana harbor (the reason was never established), the incident was seized upon by advocates of intervention in Cuba who demanded that Americans must "Remember the *Maine*." Two months later, Congress passed a resolution demanding that Spain withdraw from Cuba at once. In response, Spain declared war. In a period of just four months, the United States had invaded Cuba; driven the Spanish fleet out of its Cuban port and sunk every ship; destroyed the Spanish fleet in Manila Bay, in the Philippines; and occupied the Caribbean island of Puerto Rico. In the midst of the war, the United States annexed Hawaii, an independent republic run by American and British owners of sugar cane plantations. In December, 1898, the Treaty of Paris forced Spain to surrender its claims to Cuba, to hand over Puerto Rico and the Pacific island of Guam to the United States, and to accept $20 million from the United States for the Philippines.

The economic recovery that began toward the end of the election of 1896 continued throughout the McKinley administration. The power and influence of the "Robber Barons," owners of monopolistic enterprises like John D. Rockefeller (oil) and Andrew Carnegie (steel), grew steadily. Strong demand for U.S. crops helped farmers begin to recover from the hard times of the 1890s and blunted demands for coinage of silver.

Large numbers of immigrants from southern and eastern Europe continued to flow into the United States, providing a steady stream of labor for expanding industries. Urban industrial workers were beginning to outnumber rural farm workers.

The Candidates

There was little doubt about who the candidates of the Republicans and Democrats would be in 1900. McKinley, the incumbent president, was not challenged for the nomination when

Socialist Candidate for President, 1900, 1904, 1908, 1912, 1920

Born: November 5, 1855, Terre Haute, Indiana
Died: October 20, 1926, Elmhurst, Illinois
Family: Son of Daniel Debs and Marguerite Debs, immigrants and grocery store owners; married Kate Metzel
Education: Did not attend college
Political Career: Democrat and Socialist. Indiana House of Representatives, 1885; Socialist candidate for president, 1900, 1904, 1908, 1912, 1920

Eugene Debs was a founder of the U.S. Socialist Party and for two decades was its best-known political candidate.

Debs left school to work as a railroad locomotive fireman. He was local secretary, and later national secretary, of the Brotherhood of Railway Firemen (1875–81). The Brotherhood was a fraternal organization that looked after the welfare of its injured, ill, or unemployed members.

Debs became the leader of the American Railway Union (ARU) in the early 1890s. In 1894 the ARU honored a strike at the Pullman Co., whose luxury passenger cars were used by several railroads. This had the eventual effect of paralyzing east-west commerce. President Grover Cleveland, a Democrat, sent troops to quell strike-related violence, and Debs was arrested for violating a court order banning the strike. Consequently, Debs concluded that the Democrats were not reliable allies for labor and in 1898 he helped organize the Social Democratic Party. The party advocated government ownership of railroads as well as communications companies (telegraph and telephone) and government aid to unemployed or injured workers.

Debs was the Socialist Party candidate in 1900, 1904, 1908, 1912 and 1920. His best showing was in 1912, when he won 900,672 votes, or six percent of the total. He never carried a state or won an electoral vote.

In 1918, Debs was arrested for delivering a speech critical of American involvement in World War I. He was sentenced to ten years in prison, and conducted his 1920 presidential campaign from jail. Debs was pardoned after two years by President Warren Harding, but prison had ruined his health.

He died in a hospital in Illinois on October 20, 1926.

Other biographies from 1900:
William McKinley, p. 106; William Jennings Bryan, p. 107.

the Republicans convened in Philadelphia; McKinley won unanimously on the first roll call. However, there was a dispute over the vice presidential candidate since McKinley's vice president, Garret Hobart, had died in office the previous year. McKinley expressed no preference for any candidate, which helped the chances of the governor of New York, Theodore Roosevelt, age 41. Roosevelt had emerged from the short

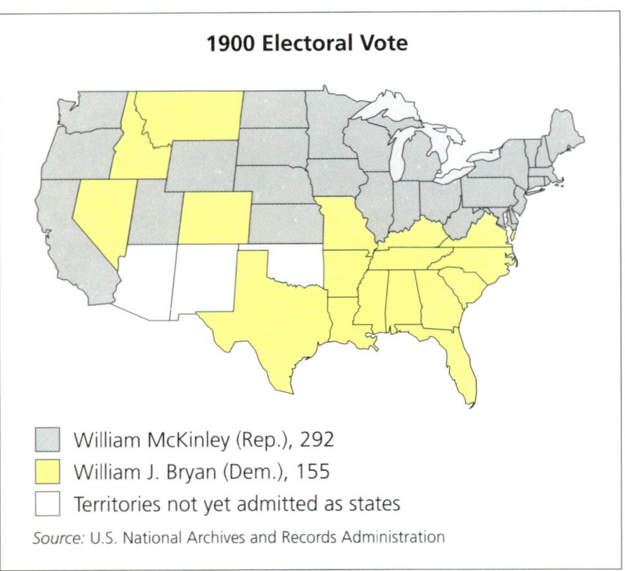

Source: U.S. National Archives and Records Administration

Spanish American war as a hero. He was also the choice of New York State's Republican leader, Thomas Platt, not because Platt particularly liked Roosevelt but because he preferred to see the dynamic young politician leave the state and get into a position that had traditionally led to political obscurity. Although McKinley's campaign manager and advisor, Mark Hanna of Ohio, had grave misgivings about Roosevelt, the New Yorker was nominated with all but one vote on the first ballot; the lone dissenter was from New York.

At the Democratic convention in Kansas City, Missouri, which opened on July 4, 1900, William Jennings Bryan of Nebraska was also nominated unanimously to run against McKinley again. Whereas four years earlier the issue of whether the United States should maintain a "gold standard" (all currency backed by gold) versus accepting the unlimited coinage of silver at a fixed ratio of 16:1 (sixteen ounces of silver would be equal in value to one ounce of gold), there was no dispute over the question in 1900. New York governor David Hill, who had supported the gold standard in 1896, seconded Bryan's nomination. For vice president, the Democrats turned again to Adlai Stevenson of Illinois, who had served as vice president under Grover Cleveland.

The Issues

Gold versus silver. In 1896 the debate over "free silver" (the unlimited use of silver in coins at a fixed ratio to gold of 16:1) had been an emotional and highly contentious issue. Bryan had spoken of "crucifying" farmers and laborers on a "cross of gold." Republicans and some Democrats had forecast economic disaster if anything besides gold were accepted as the basis of the nation's currency. But four years later the issue had lost much of its punch. With the economy having recovered, free silver was not viewed as a panacea for a crippling economic depression as it had been in 1896. The Republican platform supported the party's "allegiance to the principle of the gold standard" and its "opposition to the free and unlimited coinage of silver." For Bryan and the Democrats, free silver remained a cause; the party reaffirmed the 1896 platform call for a bimetallic system (gold *and* silver coins). Although the issue retained its importance and appeal for Bryan, for most of the country the issue had largely faded.

Imperialism. The question of an American "empire" loomed much larger in the minds of many voters. The acquisition of territory from Spain marked the first time the United States had no plans to offer citizenship to the inhabitants. For many Republicans the extension of U.S. control over lands in the Pacific (Philippines and Guam) in particular was a natural extension of the "manifest destiny" of American westward expansion. The United States had grown sufficiently powerful to take its place alongside European nations like England and France, which had extensive colonial holdings. The Republican platform in 1900 declared that "no other course was possible" but to destroy Spanish control over its territories in the Western Hemisphere and the Philippines As for the Philippine independence movement that was launched shortly after the war and the U.S. role in suppressing it, the Republicans claimed the United States had a "responsibility before the world . . . to provide for the maintenance of law and order and for the establishment of good government." For many Democrats, American imperialism violated the very principles of democracy on which the United States had been founded. The Democratic platform declared that "the Constitution follows the flag," and warned that "no nation can long endure half republic and half empire. . . . Imperialism abroad will lead quickly and inevitably to despotism at home."

Anti-trust. The Republican Party continued to enjoy strong support from business interests and did not concentrate on addressing the growing economic power of a few giant corporations. Nevertheless, the Republican platform declared that "we condemn all conspiracies and combinations intended to restrict business, to create monopolies, or limit production, or to control prices," and backed legislation to protect against such practices. The issue of trusts was not a major one during the campaign although it would become key during the next four years. The Republicans were much more keen in 1900 on laying claim to economic prosperity under McKinley and contrasting the previous four years to the economic depression under the last Democratic president, Grover Cleveland.

Panama Canal. Both parties favored construction of a canal to link the Atlantic and the Pacific through Central America. The Republican platform endorsed a plan to build a canal across the isthmus of Panama whereas the Democratic platform backed an alternative route, across Nicaragua.

The Campaign

The campaign of 1900 was a grueling endurance contest between Bryan and Roosevelt. In the last six weeks of the campaign Bryan traveled about 16,000 miles by railroad, delivering over 500 speeches. On the trip, Bryan set a personal record: thirty-two speeches in one day. On most days Bryan's train would stop briefly, the candidate would deliver a short speech to a crowd that had been brought out by local organizers, then depart for the next stop and another speech. On most days Bryan would deliver one longer speech in the afternoon and another in the evening. The pace was exhausting; Bryan often ate six full meals a day to maintain his energy. The Democrats operated their campaign on only about $500,000, roughly one-tenth the amount raised by the Republicans.

Roosevelt proved to be a match for Bryan, and more. The Republican covered even more miles (about 21,000), and delivered more speeches (over 670 in 567 towns spread over 24 states). Typically Roosevelt would have already had breakfast and delivered a speech by 7:30 in the morning and keep going until 11 o'clock at night. In between he got in some reading on topics as diverse as poetry and wildlife. Roosevelt made the hat from his military outfit as a "Rough Rider" (as his unit had been called in the Spanish American war) a trademark and constant reminder of his war exploits, brief though they were.

At first Bryan picked up where he left off in 1896 and concentrated on the issue of the coinage of silver. But he quickly realized that question had lost its appeal and he switched to "imperialism," as he called the acquisition of colonies. He insisted that denying people in the Philippines the right of

This pro-Democrat cartoon by Frederick Opper in 1900 depicts President William McKinley (lower right) as dominated by big business interests ("The Trusts") and Senator Mark Hanna, portrayed as the mother of the family sitting on an immature Republican Vice Presidential candidate, Theodore Roosevelt, whose toy horse and sword are on the floor. The cartoonist suggested that Hanna was the politician really in charge, not McKinley, who was running for reelection in 1900.

self-determination would end up threatening the same rights for Americans. As with the silver issue, Bryan gave a religious tinge to the imperialism question: "It was God himself who placed in every human heart the love of liberty," he declared. The Republicans wrapped themselves in the flag of patriotism, and claimed that Democratic opposition to imperialism was in fact encouraging Filipino rebels and thereby prolonging the conflict. Roosevelt the Rough Rider took pride in his exploits, claiming that he had personally killed a Spanish soldier with a knife.

The big campaign issue for the Republicans, however, was the prosperity that had coincided with the McKinley administration. New supplies of gold had eased the monetary crunch of the 1890s, and steady expansion of American industrialization had made the United States a challenger to Britain for industrial and economic supremacy.

The Outcome

McKinley won the election by an even larger margin than in 1896. He won over 7.2 million votes (51.7 percent) to 6.4 million votes (45.5 percent) for Bryan. In the electoral college McKinley's margin over Bryan was 292 votes to 155.

McKinley won throughout the Midwest, including Bryan's home state of Nebraska, as well as Utah and Wyoming, all three of which had gone to Bryan four years earlier.

The strong economy during McKinley's administration essentially robbed Bryan of his strongest issue, the free coinage of silver, and diminished the impact of other issues such as tariffs. The "patriotism" promoted by McKinley on the strength of the American victory in the Spanish American war proved more persuasive to voters than the message of "anti-imperialism" preached by Bryan. The Populist vote had nearly disappeared by 1900 and other minor parties, such as the Prohibition Party, made no significant impact on the outcome.

The other result of the election, though no one knew it at the moment, was the elevation of Theodore Roosevelt to the office of president. Just six months into his second term, McKinley was assassinated in Buffalo, New York, thereby elevating the young and dynamic Roosevelt into the White House.

More Information

▶ Ashby, LeRoy. *William Jennings Bryan: Champion of Democracy*. Boston: Twayne Publishers, 1987.

▶ Cherney, Robert W. *A Righteous Cause: The Life of William Jennings Bryan*. Boston: Little, Brown, 1985.

▶ Clark, Judith Freeman. *America's Gilded Age: An Eyewitness History*. New York: Facts on File, 1992.

▶ Glad, Paul W. *McKinley, Bryan and the People*. Philadelphia: Lippincott, 1964.

▶ Gould, Lewis L. *The Presidency of William McKinley*. Lawrence, KS: Regents Press of Kansas, 1980.

▶ Leech, Margaret. *In the Days of McKinley*. New York: Harper, 1959.

▶ Trachtenberg, Alan. *The Incorporation of America: Culture and Society in the Gilded Age*. New York: Hill and Wang. 1982.

Periodical

▶ Weisberger, Bernard A. "Election in Silver and Gold." *American Heritage,* October 1996, p. 16.

On the Web

▶ McKinley, William. "Second Inaugural Address, Monday, March 4, 1901." *Inaugural Addresses of the Presidents of the United States.* Washington, D.C.: U.S. Government Printing Office, 1989; Bartleby.com, 2001. **http://www.bartleby.com/124/pres41.html.**

▶ "Elections of 1896 and 1900," A Biography of America. Annenberg/CPB Learner.org. **http://www.learner.org/biographyofamerica/prog17/feature/index.html.**

▶ "The Progressive Age." A.P. U.S. History, Historyteacher.net. Links to articles and primary sources for the period 1865–1915. **http://www.historyteacher.net/APUSH-Course/Weblinks/Weblinks20.htm.**

1904
Theodore Roosevelt (Republican) vs. Alton Parker (Democrat)

President William McKinley had died in September, 1901, barely into his second term. His death left Vice President Theodore Roosevelt, at age 42, the youngest man ever to assume the presidency. Over the balance of McKinley's first term Roosevelt brought his highly energetic style to the White House, pursuing regulation or dissolution of business monopolies (called "trusts" in his era), an unapologetically imperialist foreign policy, and a treaty to build a canal through the isthmus of Panama to link the Atlantic and Pacific Oceans.

Before running for vice president in 1900 Roosevelt had been governor of New York, and before that, Police Commissioner of New York City. While he adhered to his party's long-standing pro-business policies he also responded to the unfettered power and influence of giant corporations that had monopolized some industries. In March, 1904, before the presidential election really got started, the Supreme Court ruled in favor of the government's request to disallow a merger of the two competing railroads that served the northern tier of states. The court ordered that the Northern Securities Company, which owned two competing lines, had been formed simply for the purpose of stifling competition and should be broken up. It was the first case in which the government succeeded in breaking up such a monopoly, and earned Roosevelt the nickname of "trust buster."

Roosevelt took other stands that marked a distinct shift from the nineteenth to the twentieth centuries, as Roosevelt recognized the need for government to modernize as the industrial revolution replaced agriculture as the mainstay of the U.S. economy. He helped mediate in a coal strike, and for the first time a president took the side of labor against the coal mine operators.

It was Roosevelt who first applied the term "muckrakers" to a group of investigative journalists who wrote about horrific working and living conditions of workers in many industries, about local government corruption, and about unsafe consumer products, especially meat. These revelations aroused public indignation and created an atmosphere in which Roosevelt was able to institute reforms that gave the government new powers to regulate business.

The Candidates

Although Roosevelt was widely popular it was not a foregone conclusion that he would be nominated for a full term. None of the other four vice presidents who had succeeded to the presidency on the death of a president had managed to do so. Roosevelt's main rival for the Republican nomination in 1904 was Mark Hanna, the Ohio senator who had been William McKinley's chief political advisor. For Hanna, the death of McKinley and the accession of Roosevelt had been a night-

mare come true; in 1900 he was unenthusiastic about the choice of Roosevelt as the Republican vice presidential nominee, whom he once described as a madman. In early 1904 however, Hanna contracted typhoid fever and died, clearing the way clear for Roosevelt's nomination.

When the Republicans met in Chicago from June 21–23, 1904, there was little drama or excitement. The nomination of Roosevelt was assured, and for vice president the Republicans nominated Senator Charles Fairbanks of Indiana, widely viewed as a conservative who would help "balance" the Republican ticket.

FlashFocus: Theodore Roosevelt

President, 1901–1909; Progressive Party Candidate for President, 1912

Born: October 27, 1858, New York, New York
Died: January 6, 1919, Oyster Bay, Long Island, New York
Family: Son of Theodore Roosevelt and Martha Bulloch; married Alice Lee (died), Edith Carow
Education: Harvard University
Political career: New York state assembly, 1882–84; colonel in U.S. Army during Spanish-American War; governor of New York, 1899–1901; vice president, 1901; Nobel Peace Prize, 1906; candidate for Republican nomination for president, 1916

Theodore Roosevelt grew up in Manhattan as a sickly child who devoted considerable time and effort to rebuilding his body and learning to physically defend himself—early evidence of his extraordinary will and force of personality.

Roosevelt attended Harvard, then studied law. He abandoned his studies to enter the New York State Assembly in 1881 where he quickly developed a reputation as a reformer. He served on the Civil Service Commission, then was Commissioner of the New York City police force, and from there was appointed assistant secretary of the Navy. At the outbreak of the Spanish-American War in 1898 he resigned his Navy position to organize the First U.S. Volunteer Cavalry, or the "Rough Riders," which gained fame for its charge up Kettle Hill in Cuba.

In 1898 Roosevelt was elected governor of New York, which led to his nomination as vice president under President William McKinley in 1900. The ticket won decisively. When McKinley was assassinated in 1901 Roosevelt became president. It was the era of robber barons and "muckrakers," journalists who exposed abuses in government and unregulated private industry. Roosevelt was an energetic, active president, tackling a wide range of issues ranging from attacking business monopolies and instituting federal regulations on business to bringing about the construction of the Panama Canal and mediating an end to the Russian-Japanese War, for which Roosevelt won the Nobel Peace Prize in 1906.

Roosevelt ran as president in 1904 and easily defeated Alton Parker, an obscure judge from New York. Upon being elected Roosevelt pledged not to run again, but later regretted this statement, and challenged his designated successor, President William Howard Taft, for the 1912 Republican nomination. When Taft won the nomination Roosevelt left the Republican Party to form the Progressive, or "Bull Moose," Party. In a three-way contest against Taft and Democrat Woodrow Wilson, Roosevelt ran far ahead of Taft but lost the election to Wilson. Roosevelt refused the Progressives' nomination in 1916 and returned to the Republican Party.

He died January 6, 1919 at Oyster Bay on Long Island Sound, New York.

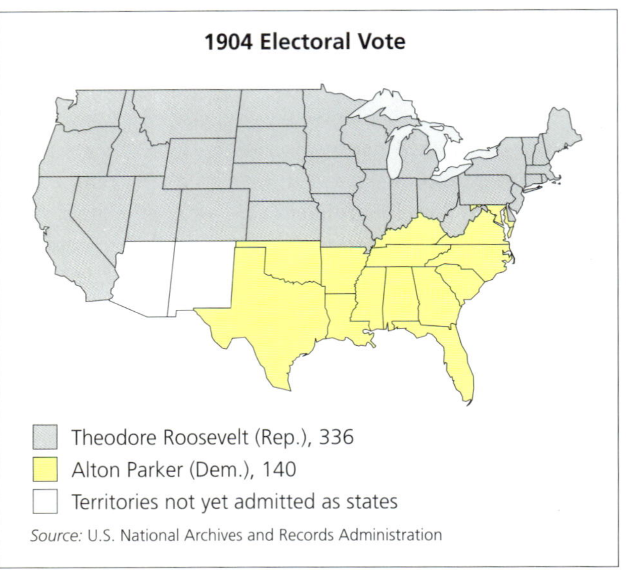

Source: U.S. National Archives and Records Administration

The Democrats had lost two elections in a row and they had no governorships in a broad swath of the country between Connecticut and Illinois. On the other hand, the Democrats could count on their candidate receiving 150 electoral votes from states of the former Confederacy in the so-called "solid South," leaving them in need of just 89 more electoral votes to win the White House. They needed to identify which of the remaining states were most likely to give their candidate their electoral votes.

It was this calculation that led some Democrats in the North to reach out to members of labor unions in addition to Midwestern farmers—whom William Jennings Bryan had championed as the Democrat candidate in 1896 and 1900—as a means of breaking the Republican grip on northern states. Other Democrats were more inclined to stay with the conservative approach of the last successful Democratic presidential candidate, Grover Cleveland, who had upheld the "gold standard" (all money was backed by gold, to the exclusion of silver). This debate was fundamental to the future of the Democratic party: whether to be the party of urban workers and poor farmers, or whether to stick with the century-old Democratic Party philosophy of a strictly limited role for the federal government.

William Jennings Bryan was not running in 1904 but he and his followers nevertheless exerted a strong influence. They backed William Randolph Hearst, a newspaper publisher from California with a reputation for promoting reform in government, but also as having an troublesome personal life and being an ineffective legislator during a term in the House of Representatives.

More conservative Democrats backed Alton B. Parker of New York, chief judge of the state's highest court, the Court of Appeals, and one of the few Democrats to hold a state-wide elective office in the East. His backers promoted him as a "safe" candidate in contrast to Hearst. The prospect that Parker could help put New York's electoral votes in the Democratic column greatly enhanced Parker's appeal. By the time the Democrats met for their convention in St. Louis in early July, Parker had obtained endorsements from most state parties and his nomination was a certainty. Parker was nominated on the first ballot. For vice president the Democrats chose Henry G. Davis, a former governor of West Virginia who was most notable for his age. At seventy-nine, he was the oldest candidate for political office yet nominated.

There was a third candidate in 1904, Eugene V. Debs, who ran as the candidate of the small Socialist Party offshoot, the Social Democrats. Debs, a former labor union organizer, had also represented the Socialists in 1900 on a platform that shared some planks with the Peoples Party, or Progressives.

The Issues

With Roosevelt firmly in control of his party the Republican platform of 1904 largely reflected his views. The platform reaffirmed the party's support for the gold standard, protective tariffs, and imperialism. On the subject of dealing with business monopolies the Republican platform declared: "Combinations of capital and of labor are the results of the economic movement of the age, but neither must be permitted to infringe upon the rights and interests of the people. Such combinations, when lawfully formed for lawful purposes, are alike entitled to the protection of the laws, but both are subject to the laws and neither can be permitted to break them." It was an extraordinarily mild presentation of the idea that the Roosevelt administration might take aggressive legal action to control business abuses and to "bust" the dominant trusts of the era.

For the Democrats the old issue of the gold standard again rose to the fore, even though the issue was far from the minds of the public. Bryan, although not a candidate, was unwilling to see the party abandon the principles he had campaigned on in 1896 and 1900, especially the unlimited coinage of silver at a fixed ratio to gold. Bryan succeeded in removing a statement from the platform to the effect that the gold standard was no longer a political issue; he also pushed for a resolution opposing trusts. But shortly after he was chosen as the Democratic candidate for president Judge Parker sent a telegram to the convention declaring that he favored the gold standard, and offering to quit as the party's candidate if his position on gold was objectionable. Parker's telegram was widely viewed as a direct repudiation of Bryan. Eventually the convention decided that its platform did not specifically ban a gold-standard advocate, and concluded that the gold standard would not be an issue in the campaign anyway. But the incident did drive a wedge between the Bryan progressive wing and Parker's more conservative supporters which in part benefited the Socialists.

Theodore Roosevelt himself became an issue, with the Democratic platform denouncing his administration as having

been "spasmodic, erratic, sensational, sensational, spectacular and arbitrary."

The Campaign

The 1904 campaign was a prelude to the campaigns to follow in the twentieth century. Republicans had a well-organized, well-financed campaign that included speeches, rallies, and parades, as well as advertising. The Democrats targeted mini-campaigns to specific ethnic groups, such as Irish Catholics, German-Americans, or immigrants from the Austrian-Hungarian empire.

The Republican party received contributions from prominent business figures such as J. P. Morgan, who had been targets of Roosevelt's reform efforts during his first three years in office. Altogether the party raised about $2 million, of which

A NAUSEATING JOB, BUT IT MUST BE DONE

(President Roosevelt takes hold of the investigating muck-rake himself in the packing-house scandal.)

President Theodore Roosevelt is shown holding a "muck rake," investigating unsanitary practices in the meat packing industry uncovered by novelist Upton Sinclair's book *The Jungle* published in 1906. Although the meat packing scandal came after the 1904 election, Roosevelt's desire to implement government regulations on business was a campaign issue in 1904.

around three-fourths came from corporate supporters. Near the end of the campaign a single contribution of $100,000 from the Standard Oil Company, a future target of Roosevelt's anti-trust reform, was uncovered by newspapers; Roosevelt insisted that the contribution be returned.

Judge Parker was a relatively colorless campaigner. Worse, while many people in the country favored federal action to regulate and control huge business monopolies, Parker declared that "common law" was sufficient to regulate business. The phrase "common law" clearly referred to state laws and seemed to put Parker on record as favoring allowing states to regulate national corporations like Standard Oil. For most of the campaign Parker adopted the "front porch" strategy used in earlier elections by William McKinley. Not until late October did Parker launch on a limited speaking tour of New York, New Jersey and Connecticut, a tour that proved ineffective at best and counter-productive at worst. Parker's attacks on Roosevelt, and his alleged "blackmailing" of corporations, drew attention to the fact that Parker himself received backing from financial houses in New York City.

The Outcome

Theodore Roosevelt's margin of victory in the popular vote, 57.4 percent to 37.6 percent for Parker, was the largest yet recorded, surpassing even that of Andrew Jackson in 1828 (56 percent). In the electoral college Roosevelt won 336 votes to Parker's 140. The Democrat carried only the states of the Confederacy, plus seven electoral votes in the border state of Maryland. Roosevelt carried all the rest.

Most observers blamed the Democrats for returning to policies pursued by Grover Cleveland in 1892, and thereby turning away many urban voters who might otherwise have supported the progressive platform that the Democrats ran on in 1900.

The election of 1904 generated far less voter excitement than the elections just past. Voter participation (limited to men) was the lowest in almost seventy years; the total number of voters in 1904 was 400,000 less than it had been in 1900, despite a rapidly growing population.

More Information

- Auchincloss, Louis. *Theodore Roosevelt*. Waterville, Maine: Thorndike Press, 2002.
- Glad, Paul W. *The Trumpet Soundeth: William Jennings Bryan and His Democracy, 1862–1912*. Lincoln: University of Nebraska Press, 1960.
- Morris, Edmund. *The Rise of Theodore Roosevelt*. New York: Coward, McCann and Geoghegan, 1979.
- Morris, Edmund. *Theodore Rex*. New York: Random House. 2001.
- Roosevelt, Theodore. *Theodore Roosevelt, An Autobiography*. New York: Da Capo Press, 1985 (c. 1913).

On the Web

- Roosevelt, Theodore. "Inaugural Address, Saturday, March 4, 1905." *Inaugural Addresses of the Presidents of the United States*. Washington, D.C.: U.S. Government Printing Office, 1989; Bartleby.com, 2001. **http://www.bartleby.com/124/pres42.html.**
- "Theodore Roosevelt." Internet Public Library Presidents of the United States. **http://ipl.si.umich.edu/div/potus/troosevelt.html.**
- "The Progressive Age." A.P. U.S. History, Historyteacher.net. Links to articles and primary sources for the period 1865–1915. **http://www.historyteacher.net/APUSH-Course/Weblinks/Weblinks20.htm.**

1908
William H. Taft (Republican) vs. William J. Bryan (Democrat) vs. Eugene Debs (Socialist)

The 1908 presidential election had in one sense begun on election night in 1904, when Theodore Roosevelt unexpectedly announced that he would not run for another term. Although he had only been elected once (he became president after the assassination of William McKinley in 1901) Roosevelt was determined not to violate the tradition of no president running for more than two terms. (There was no exact precedent for Roosevelt, since he had become the first president renominated by his party after assuming office from the vice presidency.) For the Democrats, the election represented a return to the efforts of William Jennings Bryan to build a coalition of western farmers and urban workers against the designated political heir of Roosevelt.

The Context

Except for the fact that he had promised not to run for another term President Roosevelt might well have been reelected in 1908. He remained highly popular among Republicans and the public at large, while the Democratic party remained divided between the progressive-minded supporters of Bryan, the party's unsuccessful candidate in 1896 and 1900, and the more conservative, business-oriented wing of the party associated with Alton Parker, the unsuccessful candidate in 1904.

Roosevelt had moved steadily toward the progressive wing of his party during his first full term in office, advocating government regulation of industry in ways designed to protect both consumers and workers from abuse. These reforms were not always pleasing to the so-called Old Guard, which represented the interests of large corporations.

During Roosevelt's administration a string of stories in magazines and newspapers about the dire poverty of workers, unsanitary practices in the meat industry in Chicago (highlighted in the novel *The Jungle* by Upton Sinclair, published in 1906), and other corporate abuses whetted the appetite of the public for government intervention.

One cloud on the horizon was the Panic of 1907. ("Panic" was the term used for a sudden rush on banks to exchange paper currency for gold bullion, resulting in banks demanding immediate repayment of loans and/or going out of business; the result was economic contraction, business failures and unemployment.) Another panic in 1893 had plagued the administration of Democratic president Grover Cleveland and led to an unbroken string of Republican successes, starting with the election of William McKinley in 1896. A panic during a Republican administration raised the question of whether the Grand Old Party could still claim to be the party of prosperity.

FlashFocus: 1908

Candidates

William H. Taft & James S. Sherman, Republican
William J. Bryan & John W. Kern, Democrat
Eugene V. Debs & Benjamin Hanford, Socialist
Eugene W. Chafin & Aaron S. Watkins, Prohibition

Issues

Organized labor strife. Roosevelt and Taft failed to persuade Republicans to support limits on injunctions (temporary prohibitions issued by courts) against labor union strikes, leaving organized labor dissatisfied with the Republican Party. Bryan incorporated pro-union limits on injunctions as part of the Democratic Party platform.

Republican factionalism. Disagreements between the conservative wing and the progressive wing of the Republican Party left moderates alienated. Religious blocs added their social reform agenda to the mix.

The Standard Oil Trust. A letter was released that documented favors that Oklahoma governor and Democratic National Committee treasurer Charles N. Haskell had done for the Standard Oil Trust, a target of the anti-trust efforts of Roosevelt's Republicans. Roosevelt eagerly publicized the incident as evidence that the Democrats could not be trusted to break up the widely despised oil monopoly. William Jennings Bryan publicly defended Haskell. The incident tainted Bryan's reputation as a champion of working people while improving the reputations of Roosevelt and his designated successor, Taft.

Outcome

Popular Vote

Taft	7,675,320	51.6% ✓
Bryan	6,412,294	43.1%
Debs	420,793	2.8%
Chafin	253,840	1.7%

Electoral College

Taft	321 ✓
Bryan	162

The Candidates

While determined to stick by his decision not to run again, Roosevelt wanted the next Republican candidate to reflect his philosophy. Although he himself was sympathetic to social reformers Roosevelt did not seriously consider naming a reformer, such as Senator Robert LaFollette of Wisconsin, to succeed him as the Republican presidential candidate. Nor was he willing to

FlashFocus: William Howard Taft

27th President, 1909–1913

Born: September 15, 1857, Cincinnati, Ohio

Died: March 8, 1930, Washington, D.C.

Family: Son of Alphonso Taft, former attorney general and secretary of war, and Louise Torrey; married Helen Herron

Education: Yale University; Cincinnati Law School

Political career: Republican. Superior Court judge, 1887–90; judge of U.S. Court of Appeals, 1892–1900; governor of Philippine Islands, 1900–04; U.S. secretary of war, 1904–08; chief justice of U.S. Supreme Court, 1921–30

William Howard Taft was the only person to head two of the three branches of government—the executive branch, as president, and the judiciary, as Supreme Court chief justice.

Taft was a federal appeals court judge when President William McKinley appointed him governor of the Philippines, recently acquired after a war with Spain. Taft's job was to administer the islands as a U.S. colony, and to squelch Filipino guerrilla war seeking independence. Taft turned down at least two offers by President Theodore Roosevelt, McKinley's successor, to join the Supreme Court—a long-held dream—out of dedication to completing his job in Manila. Roosevelt then named Taft secretary of war, promising that he would still be in charge of the Philippines in his new job.

Taft, with Roosevelt's support, became the Republican presidential nominee in 1908, and won the presidency over his Democratic opponent William Jennings Bryan.

As president Taft pursued a less progressive program than Roosevelt would have preferred. The former president then challenged Taft for the 1912 Republican nomination. After Roosevelt lost the nomination he ran for president as the candidate of the Progressive Party (Bull Moose Party). The split Republican vote allowed Woodrow Wilson, a Democrat, to win the election; Roosevelt was second, Taft a distant third.

In 1922 Taft realized his long-held dream of serving on the Supreme Court with his appointment as chief justice by President Warren Harding, where he served until his death, on March 8, 1930.

Other biographies from 1908:
William Jennings Bryan, p. 107.

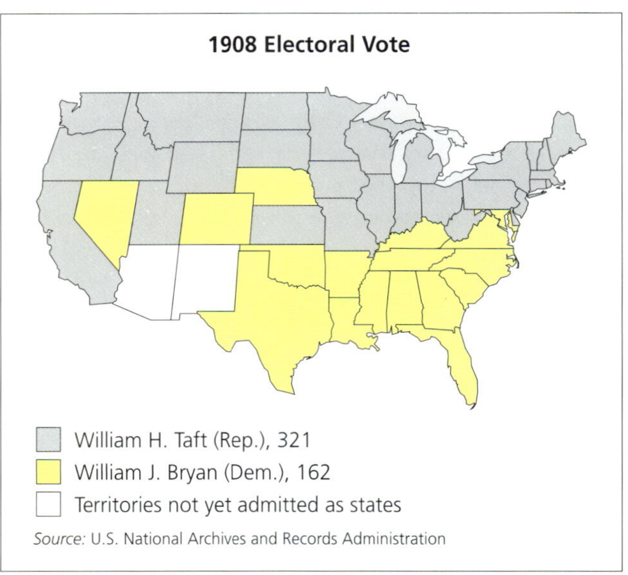

Source: U.S. National Archives and Records Administration

become a Supreme Court justice, but Roosevelt persuaded him to defer that ambition in favor of succeeding Roosevelt as the Republican candidate for president. Taft was far from a "natural" politician—his own mother thought that another man, Roosevelt's secretary of state, Elihu Root, should be the nominee instead—but he reluctantly agreed to go along with the president, partly at the urging of his ambitious wife.

Although Taft was Roosevelt's personal choice as the candidate he was not completely in line with Roosevelt's thinking. Whereas Roosevelt thought that the president should exercise broad powers in order to protect the national interests, Taft took a more lawyerly view that presidents could not act without specific legal authorization.

In the months leading up to the Republican convention Roosevelt shifted political appointments to favor supporters of Taft, as well as making his views well known. Roosevelt also moved to derail movements that favored New York governor Charles Evans Hughes, regarded as a moderate reformer, or his treasury secretary, George Cortelyou, widely praised for taking effective action to counter the panic of October, 1907. By the time the Republicans gathered in Chicago in mid-June Taft had well over half the votes needed for the nomination. In a speech to the convention Senator Henry Cabot Lodge, a confidant of Roosevelt, praised the president, setting off enthusiastic applause and chants of "Four, four, four years more!" But the following night, the convention bowed to Roosevelt's wishes and nominated Taft, who received 702 votes (out of 980) on the first ballot. For vice president the Republicans chose Representative James Sherman of New York, a close associate of Speaker Cannon and a well-known member of the party's anti-reform Old Guard.

For the Democrats the disastrous defeat of 1904 opened the way to a third run by William Jennings Bryan, the Populist from Nebraska and unsuccessful candidate in 1896 and 1900. As Roosevelt began attacking abuses of wealth and privilege,

draw upon the ranks of more conservative, pro-business Republicans such as House of Representatives Speaker Joseph Cannon of Illinois or his vice president, Charles Fairbanks.

Instead, Roosevelt focused on his secretary of war, William Howard Taft of Ohio. Taft had served Roosevelt in the Philippines, where he helped oversee the defeat of an independence movement and the acceptance of U.S. colonial rule by Filipino leaders. Taft had been the U.S. solicitor general (who represents the United States in cases before the Supreme Court) at age 33, and a federal judge at age 36. Taft's ambition was to

Bryan took the president's attacks as proof that he had been right all along. In fact, opposition by the Republican Old Guard meant that Roosevelt needed support from Democrats in Congress to pass many of his programs. More conservative Democrats from the "solid South" agreed to accept Bryan as a means of putting together a coalition of southern Democrats, Western populists, and northern labor interests in order to regain the White House.

In some respects, Bryan was past his time. The issue on which he rode to the nomination in 1896, the free coinage of silver in addition to gold, had long since faded in importance. Bryan himself was older, and balder, than he had been eight years earlier. Always ready to mix religious metaphors with his political views, Bryan took on some aspects of a Protestant preacher as well as a political candidate—an aura that did not always sit well with urban Catholic voters in the Northeast, whom the Democrats counted on to capture New York's huge cache of 39 electoral votes.

Bryan had kept himself in the public spotlight since his last run for the White House by publishing a newspaper, the *Commoner,* from his home in Omaha, Nebraska, which he used to generate a list of subscribers whose support he could probably count on in a future campaign. The Democratic convention was held in Denver from July 8–10. On the first ballot for the presidential nominee, Bryan received 889 votes to a total of just 105 for all his rivals combined. For vice president the Democrats nominated John W. Kern of Indiana, who like Bryan was a progressive.

The Socialist Party also hoped to play a key role in 1908. Greatly encouraged by the showing of its candidate, Eugene V. Debs, in 1904, when the Socialists received over 400,000 votes. The Socialists nominated Debs again in 1908.

The Issues

Competition for the support of votes of working people played a significant role in 1908. The Republicans hoped to hold on to the support of urban workers as well as middle- and upper-class voters, while the Democrats and Socialists both competed to form a coalition of urban workers and poor farmers.

Organized labor. At the Republican convention, which was attended by Samuel Gompers, leader of the American Federation of Labor (a coalition of unions representing skilled workers), Taft and Roosevelt pushed for a party platform endorsing a limit on court injunctions (orders) barring strikes. This was an effort to counter the political effects of an injunction that Taft had granted, as a federal judge, and his jailing of a railroad union official who defied the injunction against boycotting trains that hauled cars owned by the Pullman Co. during a protracted labor strike. But the conservative Old Guard of the party declined to go along, resulting in such a mild statement that Gompers left the meeting and later endorsed Bryan of the Democrats. The incident was a significant move on the road towards support for the Democrats by organized labor.

Prosperity. Despite the economic downturn represented by the Panic of 1907, the Republicans continued to portray themselves as the party of prosperity, an echo of the 1896 campaign in which Bryan was also the Democratic nominee. The Democratic platform denounced the Republicans as the party of "privilege and private monopoly." Bryan tried to capitalize on the issue by reminding voters that the Republicans, too, could preside over a panic. However, the tactic seemed to backfire since it served to remind voters of the Democrats' association with the much worse economic downturn of 1893, when Grover Cleveland was in office.

Rights of labor. The Democrats courted the votes of union members by endorsing creation of a federal Department of Labor, an eight-hour day for all work done for the government, and "rigid impartiality" in court cases involving labor and management. The Republican plank on labor was much weaker while the Socialist platform was much more straightforward. The Socialists in 1908 endorsed a shorter work day and a six-and-a-half day workweek; a ban on employing children under sixteen years old; and a ban on products made by child labor from interstate transportation. The Socialists also endorsed government unemployment, accident and health insurance.

Religion. Since the early 1890s Republicans had been able to count on the support of conservative Protestant factions, especially in the Midwest, but in 1908 some of these factions asserted demands for prohibition of alcoholic beverages and other measures they regarded as morally correct. Bryan, the Democrat, often employed the language of Protestant preachers in urging support for the Democratic platform and in 1908 he occasionally implied, subtly, that Taft was not a proper Christian because he did not believe in the divinity of Jesus (Taft was a Unitarian).

The third party, the Socialists, campaigned on a platform of extensive reform, led by the federal government. The Socialists urged public ownership of some industries—railroads, telegraph and telephones, and steamships—and regulation of others. Among the demands of the Socialist platform were new taxes on estates (inheritance tax) and income. The Socialists also favored letting women vote, abolishing the Senate, and making it easier to adopt constitutional amendments.

The Campaign

In 1908, as in earlier elections, the Democrats counted on about 140 electoral votes from the South and needed 100 more to achieve a majority. Their strategy for getting the necessary electoral votes was to concentrate on states that could go for either party, notably New York (39 electoral votes), Indiana (15), and Illinois (27), as well as a selection of other states in the West and North whose votes would add up to the magic number needed for success.

As it had before and would do later, campaign funding played a major role in the election of 1908. The Republicans had little trouble raising over $1.6 million—more than two-and-a-half times the $620,000 raised by the Democrats. Bryan hurt his chances by promising to publish a list of everyone who contributed more than $100 in an effort to portray the Republicans as the party of the rich. Democrats, encouraged by sympathetic newspapers, urged voters to send in contributions of one dollar but their campaign paled next to that of Taft and the Republicans, even though Taft also promised to publish a list of his contributors. The Socialist candidate, Debs, actually charged people to listen to his speeches as a means of raising money for his campaign.

Bryan again tried to counter the Republicans' superior financial resources by plunging into a whirlwind campaign, delivering as many as twenty-one speeches a day during one four-day tour of his home state of Nebraska.

Taft, on the other hand, relied on William McKinley's old strategy of "front porch" campaigning, largely remaining out of sight while others carried on the campaign for him. However, in September and October, Taft hit the campaign trail and proved to be an effective campaigner. President Roosevelt, while not a candidate, played an active role in the campaign to elect his chosen successor. He was able to do this with good effect when opponents of Taft attacked the Roosevelt administration, giving the popular soon-to-be-ex president an opening to defend his record and by extension to campaign for Taft.

The Outcome

Taft won the popular vote but by a significantly reduced margin compared to Roosevelt's victory four years earlier. Taft won 7,675,320 votes, or 51.6 percent, compared to 6,412,294 votes, or 43.1 percent, for Bryan and 420,793, or 2.8 percent for Debs, the Socialist. A fourth candidate, Eugene Chafin, won 253,840, or 1.7 percent, running on the Prohibition Party ticket.

In the electoral vote Taft won 321 votes to 162 for Bryan. The Democrat gained the electoral votes of Colorado (5), Nebraska (8), Nevada (3), and Oklahoma (7, voting for the first time in 1908), but lost one electoral vote in Maryland. Although the Democrats maintained the solid South they failed to make a significant dent in the additional votes needed to win the White House. Most significantly, the Democrats did not succeed in capturing votes of industrial states by appealing to organized labor. The Republicans maintained their grip on such big cities as New York, Chicago, and Baltimore.

Taft did not have long electoral coattails. In five states where he carried the presidential vote Democrats elected new governors, including in his home state of Ohio. Democrats also gained strength in the House of Representatives and the Senate.

The longest lasting change in 1908 was bringing Democrats more firmly in line with the party's progressive wing, backing taxes on income, reform of protective tariffs, laws protecting workers, and other business reforms. For his part, Taft began drifting away from Roosevelt's aggressive populism and towards the more conservative positions of the Republican "Old Guard" almost as soon as the voting booths closed. In some respects, the next contest had already begun.

More Information

- ▶ Anderson, Donald F. *William Howard Taft: A Conservative's Conception of the Presidency*. Ithaca, NY: Cornell University Press. 1973.
- ▶ Ashby, LeRoy. *William Jennings Bryan: Champion of Democracy*. Boston: Twayne Publishers. 1987.
- ▶ Coletta, Paolo E. *The Presidency of William Howard Taft*. Lawrence: University Press of Kansas. 1973.
- ▶ Koenig, Louis W. Bryan. *A Political Biography of William Jennings Bryan*. New York: Putnam. 1971.
- ▶ Manners, William. *TR and Will. A Friendship That Split the Republican Party*. New York: Harcourt, Brace and World. 1969.

On the Web

- ▶ Taft, William Howard. "Inaugural Address, Thursday, March 4, 1909." *Inaugural Addresses of the Presidents of the United States.* Washington, D.C.: U.S. Government Printing Office, 1989; Bartleby.com, 2001. **http://www.bartleby.com/124/ pres43.html.**

1912

Woodrow Wilson (Democrat) vs. William H. Taft (Republican) vs. Theodore Roosevelt (Progressive) vs. Eugene Debs (Socialist)

Three of the four candidates running for president in 1912—Woodrow Wilson, the Democrat, Theodore Roosevelt, the Progressive, and Eugene Debs, the Socialist—agreed on the fundamental notion that the federal government should take an active role in countering and controlling the rising influence and power of large corporations ("trusts" in the vocabulary of 1912). The sole "conservative" in the race, Republican president William Taft, received only about half the popular vote he had received four years earlier, as Roosevelt's chosen successor, and a mere eight electoral votes.

The election of 1912 also demonstrated the continuing importance of political party organizations in determining the outcome of national elections. Roosevelt, who could not gain the Republican nomination over his former protégé Taft, was unable in a short time to assemble the complex organization that might have enabled him to translate his widespread personal popularity into an election victory over the relatively unknown governor of New Jersey, Wilson. Indeed, it had been Taft's control over the party apparatus that enabled him to wrest the nomination away from Roosevelt at the Republican convention, leading Roosevelt to form a third party, the Progressive Party (often called the "Bull Moose" Party), which came in second to the Democrats and performed better than any third party before or since.

The Context

Large corporations were far from new in 1912. Neither was the debate over how government should react to institutions that exercised far more influence and power over peoples' lives than any single family business had done in the early years of the Industrial Revolution. By 1912 the United States had reached a solid national consensus that the federal government should take an active role in regulating corporate behavior and protecting individuals from economic dislocations far beyond their ability to control. It was a debate that would continue into the twenty-first century.

President Taft had been hand-picked by Theodore Roosevelt to run as the Republican nominee in 1908. But even as Taft won he was beginning to edge away from his mentor. Roosevelt had steadily moved towards more government involvement in regulating businesses—a position that made Taft, a former federal judge, uncomfortable. Moreover, the Republican party was split between a "progressive" wing, represented by Roosevelt, and a more conservative, pro-business wing. While Roosevelt was in the White House his out-sized personality had put the conservatives in the shadows. In Taft they found a more sympathetic audience.

FlashFocus: 1912

Candidates

Woodrow Wilson & Thomas R. Marshall, Democrat
Theodore Roosevelt & Hiram W. Johnson, Progressive ("Bull Moose")
William H. Taft & Nicholas M. Butler, Republican
Eugene V. Debs & Emil Seidel, Socialist
Eugene W. Chafin & Aaron S. Watkins, Prohibition

Issues

Role of the government in the new corporate economy. As large economic organizations, which came to be known as corporations, became the dominant force in the economy Americans were uneasy about their effect on the nation. These corporations were profitable and contributed to economic growth but many feared that they would erode the traditional values of American society. Roosevelt, in his "New Nationalism" program praised the corporations, claiming that they were not only necessary but beneficial. He argued for federal government regulation and supervision of corporations to prevent corruption and unethical practices. Wilson, in his "New Freedom" program, spoke out against corporations, asserting that they were impossible to regulate, and that they would ultimately have detrimental effects on society.

Direct democracy. During this election there was a shift away from the existing presidential nominating system, in which presidential nominees were chosen in private, closed-door meetings. Popular primaries, in which nominees were selected by the voters, were gaining acceptance. Building on this concept of "direct democracy," Roosevelt proposed several initiatives that would put more political power in the hands of the voters. Wilson did not directly oppose direct democracy, but was skeptical of its results. Roosevelt also supported women's suffrage, which Wilson opposed.

Outcome

Popular Vote

Wilson	**6,296,547**	**41.9%** ✓
Roosevelt	4,118,571	27.4%
Taft	3,486,720	23.2%
Debs	900,672	6.0%
Chafin	206,275	1.4%

Electoral College

Wilson	**435** ✓
Roosevelt	88
Taft	8

FlashFocus: Thomas Woodrow Wilson

28th President, 1913–1921

Born: December 28, 1856, Staunton, Virginia
Died: February 3, 1924, Washington, D.C.
Family: Son of Joseph Wilson, a minister, and Janet Woodrow; married Ellen Axson (died), Edith Galt
Education: Davison University; Princeton University; Johns Hopkins University
Political Career: Democrat. Governor of New Jersey, 1911–13; Nobel Peace Prize, 1919

Woodrow Wilson entered politics after being president of Princeton University. As governor of New Jersey he gained a reputation as a "progressive," establishing a primary election to select presidential candidates and promoting laws regulating utilities, curbing government corruption, and establishing employers' liabilities for workers' injuries.

Wilson was the Democratic candidate for president in 1912. He won the White House over the Republican incumbent, William Taft, and former President Theodore Roosevelt., candidate of the new Progressive Party.

Wilson promised action to rein in corporations and to protect workers. He reestablished a national bank, called the Federal Reserve System, to help regulate interest rates and currency. The Federal Trade Commission Act established an agency to assure competition and squelch monopolies. Congress passed the Clayton Antitrust Act and an income tax act, as well as establishing federal funding for education.

With the beginning of World War I in the summer of 1914 Wilson's attention turned to foreign affairs. Although he attempted to maintain American neutrality, efforts by Britain to restrict American trade, and attacks by German submarines on U.S. ships made the policy impossible to sustain.

Wilson was elected to a second term in 1916. In April, 1917 Germany spurned an American offer to negotiate peace and decided to conduct an unlimited war at sea. In response, Wilson asked Congress for a declaration of war against Germany.

After victory by the Allied Forces in November, 1918, Wilson's proposals for the post-war period were thwarted. He advocated a peace treaty based on his "Fourteen Points" but Britain and France were unimpressed, being more intent on punishing Germany. His proposal for establishing a League of Nations as a means of avoiding future wars was only a qualified success: the League was formed but the United States never joined. In addition Wilson seemed out of touch with the weary and isolationist mood of the American electorate. His inflexibility on his peace proposals was counter-productive; many observers believed he could have gained his points if he had been willing to make deals. For his troubles, however, Wilson won the Nobel Peace Prize for 1919.

In the summer of 1919 Wilson suffered a major stroke which partially incapacitated him. He left office disappointed that the United States had failed to participate in the League of Nations. He died on February 3, 1924.

See also: Theodore Roosevelt, p. 114.

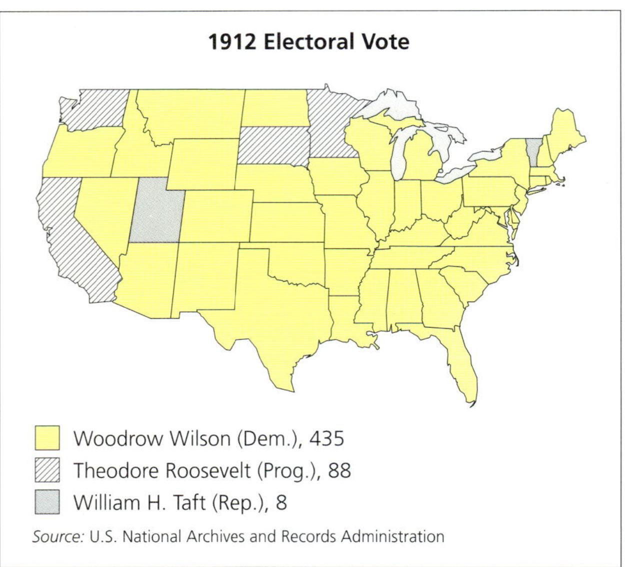

1912 Electoral Vote

Source: U.S. National Archives and Records Administration

Roosevelt had left the country shortly after Taft's election, intentionally staying out of the limelight in order to give his successor a chance to make his own way as president. When Roosevelt returned from an extended big game expedition in Africa he was unhappy with Taft's performance. Roosevelt was not the only Republican to challenge Taft's policies as president; other progressives, like Senator Robert LaFollette of Wisconsin, were also itching to replace Taft. The 1910 Congressional elections saw gains for both Democrats and for progressive Republicans, lending credence to the notion that the progressives of both parties were in touch with the mood of the electorate.

The Candidates

President Taft had never been comfortable with politics and he had not played his political hand very effectively in the White House. Because he was uncomfortable with extending the power of his office in the way Roosevelt might have, Taft disappointed the more progressive members of the Republican Party who favored a more forceful program of corporate regulation and legislation to benefit workers. He also failed as a replacement for the dynamic Roosevelt in the minds of many Republicans who were devoted to the former president. At the same time, however, Taft had learned from Roosevelt something about controlling the Republican Party apparatus through the use of patronage (granting federal jobs as a reward for political favors). It had been a technique Roosevelt used to maneuver Taft, his hand-chosen successor, into the nomination for president in 1908 over other contenders, including LaFollette of Wisconsin.

Watching La Follette's attacks on Taft in 1911, Roosevelt began to waver in his earlier resolve not to run for another term. As Roosevelt had moved more towards the progressive wing of his party, Taft had become more conservative and less eager to extend federal regulation. Finally in early 1912 Roosevelt declared that he would challenge Taft for the nomination.

Roosevelt was undoubtedly the most popular candidate among Republicans, as he demonstrated by succeeding in the handful of popular primary elections held to choose delegates to the Republican convention. But popular primaries were in their infancy in 1912; most delegates were chosen in party meetings, subject to manipulation by party officials. Consequently when the Republican nominating convention opened in Chicago in June, Roosevelt had most of the delegates chosen by popular elections, while Taft controlled delegates chosen by party officials in meetings called caucuses. Roosevelt tried to overcome his weakness by challenging the credentials (the right to attend) of many delegates pledged to Taft. But Taft's forces controlled the convention and virtually all of Roosevelt's challenges were rejected.

After losing his challenges to Taft delegates—which he knew would result in losing the nomination as well—Roosevelt urged his followers to remain in the convention but to refuse to vote. They were marked "present" but not voting. In the end only Taft and La Follette were nominated to be the Republican presidential candidate. Taft easily won the nomination on the first ballot with 556 votes to La Follette's 41. Roosevelt, though not officially a candidate for the nomination, received 107 votes. For vice president Taft's forces renominated Vice President James "Sunny Jim" Sherman, but because of his advanced age they also resolved that the party's national committee might fill any vacancy that might occur. In fact Sherman died on October 30, a week before the election was held.

The day after the Republicans adjourned followers of Roosevelt met in Chicago and laid plans for another convention of a new party—the Progressive Party—which they held in August. There more than 2,000 delegates convened, representing a broad array of causes. Like the Populist crusades of William Jennings Bryan, the Democratic nominee in 1896, 1900 and 1908, the Progressives sang hymns like *Onward Christian Soldiers* and *Battle Hymn of the Republic* and endorsed a range of issues including women's suffrage (Jane Addams of Chicago, the well-known social worker and campaigner for women's rights, delivered a speech seconding Roosevelt's nomination), the direct election of senators (instead of election by state legislatures), and a variety of social welfare programs that eventually became law after 1932. As vice president the Progressives selected Governor Hiram Johnson of California.

For the Democrats the fight for the presidential nomination was much less divisive. The leading contenders were the Speaker of the House of Representatives, Champ Clark of Missouri, and New Jersey governor Woodrow Wilson, former president of Princeton University and a former political science professor. Wilson was a supporter of William Jennings Bryan, the three-time Democratic nominee (1896, 1900, 1908). On the first ballot for the Democratic nomination, Clark won a simple majority of delegates with 440½ votes, but fell short of the two-thirds majority (730) required for nomination. Wilson was second with 324 votes. There followed a marathon of voting in which Clark at first seemed to inch towards victory but then stalled at 556 votes on the tenth ballot.

Thereafter Clark slowly began losing support. During voting on the fourteenth ballot Bryan addressed the convention to announce that he was shifting his vote to Wilson from Clark, but even after this development, the vote on the fourteenth ballot was Clark 553, Wilson 361. A third candidate, Representative Oscar Underwood of Alabama, had 111 votes.

The balloting went on and on. Slowly the trend moved towards Wilson. On the thirtieth ballot Wilson passed Clark by five votes. After an overnight rest Illinois switched to Wilson, giving the New Jersey governor a simple majority of votes, but not yet two-thirds. Finally on the forty-sixth vote Underwood withdrew his name, as did Clark. Wilson received 990 votes, and the Democratic nomination, on the forty-sixth ballot—the longest balloting by a political party since 1860. The choice of vice president took much less time. Wilson preferred Underwood, to shore up the solid South, but Underwood declined. On the second ballot Governor Thomas Marshall of Indiana, a key state in Democratic strategy, won 644½ votes and his only rival, Governor John Burke of North Dakota, withdrew, making Marshall's nomination unanimous.

The Issues

In a sense there was only one issue in 1912: which brand of progressivism would prevail, Roosevelt's or Wilson's? Roosevelt believed that corporations were a natural development in the course of economic growth, and not something to be resisted. Rather, Roosevelt believed that the growth of corporations needed to be matched by the growth of government powers to protect ordinary citizens from potential abuses by monopolies. Roosevelt also advocated what he called "New Nationalism," a program under which the government would assist in economic growth in order to benefit the entire society and to make the United States the wealthiest and most influential nation in the world, while at the same time protecting society from the potential excesses or misbehaviors of private business.

Wilson took a different view largely reflecting the opinions of lawyer and reformer Louis Brandeis. Wilson did not see corporate power as either natural or desirable. Rather, he favored government action to break up huge corporations in order to maintain economic competition between smaller businesses. In Wilson's view, a world of smaller business units competing with one another was the only way to preserve traditional American ideals of freedom and independence. In this way Wilson was able to appeal simultaneously to working people and to owners of small businesses, who were often threatened or overshadowed by giant corporations. Wilson called his approach "New Freedom," in opposition to Roosevelt's "New Nationalism."

Roosevelt also favored a variety of proposals described as direct democracy, such as primary elections to choose party nominees, the direct election of senators, and programs such as the initiative (in which non-office holders could initiate legislation), referendum (popular votes on measures, rather than voting through legislatures); and recall (non-scheduled votes to recall elected officials). Wilson, although a progressive in most other respects, did not favor most of these issues; neither did Taft.

Despite their fundamental difference in outlook Roosevelt and Wilson shared many short-term objectives. Democrats endorsed a graduated income tax (higher rates on higher incomes), direct election of senators, government-regulated prices charged by railroad and communications (telegraph and telephone) companies, as well as an amendment to set a one-term limit on presidents. Echoing Democratic platforms of the nineteenth century, the Democrats endorsed the sovereignty of the individual states.

The Republican platform had endorsed the protective tariff and legislation to bar corporations from contributing to political campaigns as well as reforms in the courts to make them more efficient. The Republicans also endorsed many positions adopted in the Democratic platform and praised the accomplishments of the past three Republican presidents, including Roosevelt.

The Progressives, in addition to regulation of corporations, advocated both a graduated income tax and a graduated inheritance tax (levied on estates), as well as a relatively comprehensive social insurance program that would care for the elderly and workers who became ill or lost their jobs.

The Campaign

The tenor of the campaign in 1912 was rough. It had started out even before the conventions with Roosevelt referring to Taft, the president, as a "fathead." Taft, who owed his office to Roosevelt's efforts, replied that his former mentor was hungry for power and a potential dictator.

As expected, Roosevelt launched into an energetic campaign, counting on his personal popularity to overcome the lack of political organizational support enjoyed by the Republican Taft and the Democrat Wilson. Roosevelt's campaign was cut short in Milwaukee when he was shot in the chest by a would-be assassin. Roosevelt, who reveled in his image as a "Rough Rider," waved his bloody handkerchief to the crowd to show that he had been wounded but kept on talking, reinforcing his image as the tough guy of the campaign. Roosevelt's wound was more serious than he first admitted, however, and after the incident he was unable to continue campaigning.

Wilson, the former college professor, adopted a dignified style more in keeping with his background in academia. For his part, Taft seemed to drop out of the campaign after winning the Republican nomination. It was as if Taft, having maintained his pride in defending his position at the head of the Republican Party, threw in the towel rather than face the dynamic and formidable personality of Roosevelt.

In the end the campaign was a contest between Roosevelt and Wilson, in which party organization played at least as big a part as personality.

The Outcome

The outcome in the electoral college was an overwhelming victory for Wilson. He won 435 electoral votes representing all but seven states. Roosevelt won 88 electoral votes (California, 11; Michigan, 15; Minnesota, 12; Pennsylvania, 38; South Dakota, 5; and Washington, 7). Taft captured only two states, Utah and Vermont, with four electoral votes each.

The popular vote, however, told a different story. Wilson won 6,296,547 votes, or 41.9 percent of the total. Roosevelt won 4,118,571 (27.4 percent) and Taft came in third with 3,486,720 (23.2 percent). Taft's popular vote was less than half the number he had won in 1908. The Socialist candidate, Eugene Debs, won 900,672 votes, or six percent, the most ever received by a candidate of the Socialist party. Wil;son won the electoral votes of many states with under forty percent of the popular vote (e.g., Idaho, 32 percent; Oregon, 34 percent; Illinois, 35 percent; and all six New England states with between 36 and 39 percent).

In some respects the outcome offered some consolation for everyone. The official Republican (Taft) and the former Republican (Roosevelt) together polled 7.6 million votes, well ahead of the Democrat's 6.3 million. The two leading Progressive candidates, Wilson and Roosevelt, together polled over 69 percent of the popular vote (and if the Socialist vote is added to the total for "progressives," the percentage grows to 73 percent). There seemed little doubt at the end of 1912 that an era of progressive politics had begun. There was little consciousness that a war in Europe in less than two years would dramatically change the set of issues for the next election.

More Information

- Auchincloss, Louis. *Woodrow Wilson*. Thorndike, ME: Thorndike Press, 2001.
- Brands, H. W. *Woodrow Wilson*. New York: Times Books, 2003.
- Gable, John A. *The Bull Moose Years: Theodore Roosevelt and the Progressive Party*. Port Washingotn, NY: Kennikat Press, 1978.
- Mowry, George E. *Theodore Roosevelt and the Progressive Movement*. New York: Hill and Wang, 1960. (c. 1946).

Periodicals

- Pavord, Andrew C. "The Gamble for Power: Theodore Roosevelt's Decision to Run for the Presidency in 1912." *Presidential Studies Quarterly,* Summer 1996, p. 633.
- Ponder, Stephen. "Partisan Reporting and Presidential Campaigning: Gilson Gardner and E. W. Scripps in the Election of 1912." *Journalism History,* Spring–Summer 1990, p. 3.

On the Web

- "Woodrow Wilson: A Portrait." American Experience Public Broadcsting System. **http://www.pbs.org/wgbh/amex/wilson/portrait/wp_election.html.**
- Wilson, Woodrow. "First Inaugural Address, Tuesday, March 4, 1913." *Inaugural Addresses of the Presidents of the United States.* Washington, D.C.: U.S. Government Printing Office, 1989; Bartleby.com, 2001. **http://www.bartleby.com/124/pres44.html.**

1916
Woodrow Wilson (Democrat) vs. Charles E. Hughes (Republican)

The enthusiasm for reforms that had marked the 1912 election had given way by 1916 to worries about war. The United States had launched a military expedition into Mexico to punish the revolutionary bandit Pancho Villa for his raid on Columbus, New Mexico, and the Great War in Europe had ground to a stalemate. American ships were being attacked despite official American neutrality and American lives were being lost, giving rise to demands for action.

President Woodrow Wilson had delivered on many of his 1912 promises to enact progressive measures that would protect workers and consumers against abuses by giant corporations, while Theodore Roosevelt had begun to fade from the political scene.

Large numbers of poor immigrants continued to stream into the United States from southern and eastern Europe, challenging American society to accept the new diversity.

The Candidates

The choice of President Wilson as the Democratic candidate was a foregone conclusion by the time the Democrats opened their convention in St. Louis on June 14. William Jennings Bryan, the three-time Democratic presidential candidate, addressed the convention in Wilson's favor and the vote was virtually unanimous at 1,092 to 1. Vice President Thomas Marshall was chosen by acclamation to run for a second term as well.

For the Republicans, choosing a candidate posed a more difficult problem, complicated by the fact that the Progressive Party held a separate, parallel convention in the same city (Chicago). The Progressives, who had broken away from the Republicans in 1912, were considering whether to rejoin the Republican Party; they decided not to nominate a candidate until they could see whom the Republicans chose. For many Republicans, wishing to reunite with the Progressives but still reluctant to nominate Roosevelt, the most attractive choice was Supreme Court Justice Charles Evans Hughes, a former governor of New York who had earned strong progressive credentials with an independent investigation into the insurance industry in 1905. He was doubly attractive because, having been nominated to the Supreme Court in 1910 by former President William Taft, Hughes had not participated in the divisive 1912 campaign.

A total of 17 possible candidates received votes on the first Republican ballot. Hughes was in first place with 253½ votes, followed by Senator John Weeks of Massachusetts (105 votes) and former Senator Elihu Root of New York (103). A second ballot saw Hughes increase his total to 328½, after which the convention adjourned while a delegation of Republicans met with Progressives across town. Roosevelt, at home on Long Island, suggested another compromise: Senator Henry Cabot Lodge of Massachusetts, a well known conservative and friend of Roosevelt's. The Progressives responded by unanimously nominating Roosevelt; in turn, the former president said he would back Hughes if the justice's positions on the major issues proved acceptable. (Hughes, sitting on the Supreme Court, had not been active in the maneuvers leading up to the convention.) The result of Roosevelt's telegram was that

FlashFocus: 1916

Candidates

Woodrow Wilson & Thomas R. Marshall, Democrat
Charles E. Hughes & Charles W. Fairbanks, Republican
A. L. Benson & George R. Kirkpatrick, Socialist
J. Frank Hanly & Ira Landrith, Prohibition

Issues

War in Mexico. Wilson claimed that he did not want to enter a war with Mexico in response to a Mexican revolution that threatened U.S. business interests, but eventually Wilson was forced to intervene to protect those interests. Hughes attacked Wilson's policies as being inconsistent.

War in Europe. Wilson promised to continue his policy of neutrality in World War I despite the sinking of American merchant ships by German submarines. This established Wilson as the antiwar candidate, while the Republicans promised a more aggressive stance towards Germany.

Progressivism and reform. Wilson established himself early on as the more progressive candidate, pointing to initiatives he had pressed for during his first term in favor of social justice and rights of labor unions. Hughes, the Republican candidate, avoided the issue of progressivism except to criticize Wilson for abusing the government's power to regulate the economy.

Women's suffrage. Both Republicans and Democrats supported giving the power to vote to women on a state-by-state basis. Wilson opposed the movement to make an amendment to the Constitution giving women the right to vote; Hughes supported a Constitutional amendment.

Outcome

Popular Vote

Wilson	9,127,695	49.4% ✓
Hughes	8,533,507	46.2%
Benson	585,113	3.2%
Hanly	220,506	1.2%

Electoral College

Wilson	277 ✓
Hughes	254

FlashFocus: Charles Evans Hughes

Republican candidate for president, 1916

Born: April 14, 1862, in Glens Falls, New York

Died: August 27, 1948, in Osterville, Massachusetts

Family: Son of David Charles Hughes, a minister, and Mary Connelly; married Antoinette Carter

Education: Madison University; Brown University; Cornell Law School

Political career: Republican. Governor of New York, 1907–10; Supreme Court justice 1910–16; U.S. secretary of state, 1921–25; chief justice of U.S. Supreme Court, 1930–41

Charles Evans Hughes resigned from the U.S. Supreme Court to run for president and was narrowly defeated by Woodrow Wilson. After serving as secretary of state to both Harding and Coolidge he returned to the Supreme Court as chief justice in 1931.

Hughes spent twenty years as a successful but largely anonymous lawyer. In 1905 Hughes led a New York state investigation into natural gas prices and urged that they be regulated. The next year Hughes investigated the insurance industry and uncovered a pattern of corruption that often involved his fellow Republicans.

Hughes's reputation for honesty led to the Republican nomination to be governor of New York in 1906. Hughes pursued a program of government regulation of some industries, including a Public Service Commission to regulate public utilities.

President William Taft appointed Hughes to the Supreme Court in 1910. Hughes resigned in 1916 to run as the Republican candidate for president against Woodrow Wilson, narrowly losing. In 1921 President Warren Harding appointed Hughes secretary of state, a position he maintained through the administration of Calvin Coolidge. In 1930 Republican president Herbert Hoover named Hughes chief justice of the Supreme Court, where three years later Hughes led the court's largely unsuccessful opposition to many of President Franklin D. Roosevelt's economic recovery proposals under the New Deal.

Hughes retired from the Supreme Court in 1941. He died on August 27, 1948.

See also: Woodrow Wilson, p. 122.

Hughes received 949½ votes (out of 987) on the third ballot. Roosevelt's former vice president, Charles W. Fairbanks of Indiana, was chosen as the Republican vice presidential nominee. Since Roosevelt had declared he would support Hughes the Progressive Party ceased to be a factor in the election, leaving both Republicans and Democrats to compete for the votes of people who identified with the movement.

The Issues

Foreign Relations. American involvement in Mexico began to fade as the election neared. Wilson's decision to blockade the Mexican port of Vera Cruz in 1914, and later to send a military expedition into Mexico in 1916 to chase the revolutionary leader Pancho Villa (in retaliation for murder of sixteen Americans aboard a train in Mexico and the Villa raid on Columbus, New Mexico) had disturbed some Americans who wanted to avoid involvement with foreign countries. Americans with business interests in Mexico favored U.S. involvement. Wilson successfully sidestepped the issue of Mexico by advocating a negotiated settlement with the government of Mexico, rather than pursuing General John Pershing's military campaign.

The issue of World War I was more difficult. German submarines had attacked U.S. merchant and passenger ships, as well as British ships which carried American passengers. Wilson had pursued a policy of neutrality from the time hostilities broke out in August, 1914 and during the campaign he vowed to continue that policy. Wilson had also built up military strength in anticipation of possible U.S. involvement. For Republicans, the war in Europe presented a dilemma. The progressive wing of the Republican party was strongly against war but the "Old Guard" conservative wing favored a strong stance against German attacks on American shipping. Hughes did his best to steer a middle course.

Progressive Reform. In 1912 Roosevelt had broken from the Republican Party and formed the Progressive Party, dedicated to passing legislation that would curb the power of large corporations and protect workers and consumers. Although Roosevelt had decided to rejoin the Republicans in 1916 the issue of progressive reform was ever-present. Three pieces of legislation in particular defined the issue. The Keating-Owen bill outlawed child labor; Wilson, who had run as a progressive candidate in 1912, helped push the bill through the Senate to buttress his claim to the role of progressive candidate in 1916. The Adamson Act, also passed with Wilson's support, imposed an eight-hour workday for railroad workers, much to the dismay of railroad companies. Finally, the Democrats also advocated a bill to provide workers' compensation for federal employees who were hurt on the job or fell ill. The Republican response to these initiatives had the effect of ending the party's flirtation with the progressive movement. Hughes accused Wilson of abusing the government's power by interfering in worker-employer relations. In fact Hughes made opposition to the Adamson Act a centerpiece of his campaign in the final weeks.

Women's Suffrage. By 1916 the debate over women's suffrage centered on whether there should be an amendment to the U.S. Constitution granting women the right to vote; both the Democratic and Republican party platforms advocated voting rights for women but Wilson, pointing to his party's traditional support for states rights, refused to endorse a constitutional amendment, preferring to leave the issue to individual states to decide. The Republicans also had declined to endorse a Constitutional amendment, but in August Hughes attempted to seize the issue for himself and declared that he supported an amendment. (Many prominent suffragettes also favored other progressive causes and identified more closely with the Democrats. Consequently they were not swayed by Hughes.)

The Campaign

In the campaign the Democrats enjoyed two advantages: the incumbency of their candidate, Wilson, and the awkward speaking style of Hughes, their opponent. To run his campaign Hughes had chosen an old friend who had little practical experience in electoral politics. The men had great difficulty in defining the Hughes candidacy in a positive way. The chosen campaign theme was "Americanism," but Hughes had difficulty in precisely defining what this meant. Although he performed well in face-to-face encounters with voters his speeches tended to sound dry and legalistic, as might be expected of a candidate fresh from the Supreme Court. His style was also ineffective with the great number of voters who read his speeches in newspapers.

As in previous campaigns the Republicans were able to raise far more money than the Democrats, and for the first time brought in professional advertising executives to run a coordinated campaign using techniques learned in selling soap and other packaged goods. Both campaigns produced short films—in 1916, a relatively new technology—to promote their candidates.

The Republicans had the advantage of strong support from business interests, which flocked to Hughes's side after passage of the Adamson Act. On the other side labor unions, notably railway workers' unions and the American Federation of Labor, supported Wilson. Support of the railway workers was generally enthusiastic but labor unions were not able to deliver a unified show of support for Wilson. Partly this reflected the hesitation of some local unions, which were dominated by German- or Irish-American workers distrustful of earlier pro-British statements by Wilson. These local unions were not enthusiastic about Hughes either, but their wariness of Wilson precluded them from playing an active role in the campaign.

The Outcome

The results in 1916 were much closer than they had been four years earlier. In the popular vote Wilson won 9.1 million votes, or 49.4 percent, to 8.5 million, or 46.2 percent, for Hughes. The Socialist, A. L. Benson, won 585,113 votres (3.2 percent) and Prohibition Party candidate J. Frank Hanley won 220,506, or 1.2 percent.

Wilson won 277 electoral votes to 254 for Hughes. In general Hughes did not attract progressive votes, and after 1916 the Republican Party was no longer associated with progressive reforms. The irony of the election was that while Wilson ran as the candidate dedicated to keeping the United States out of the war in Europe, it was Wilson who led the United States into the war in 1917.

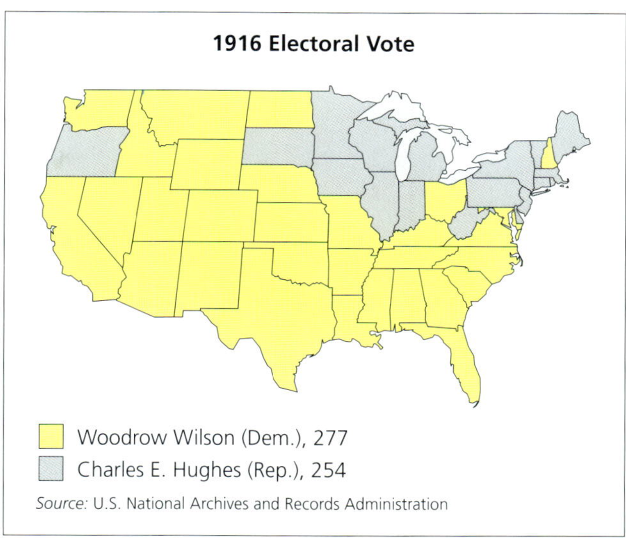

Source: U.S. National Archives and Records Administration

More Information

▶ Anderson, Donald F. *William Howard Taft: a Conservative's Conception of the Presidency*. Ithaca, NY: Cornell University Press, 1973.

▶ Blum, John M. *Woodrow Wilson and the Politics of Morality*. New York: HarperCollins, 1990.

▶ Gable, John. *The Bull Moose Years: Theodore Roosevelt and the Progressive Party*. Port Washington, NY: Kennikat Press, 1978.

▶ Knock, Thomas J. *To End All Wars: Woodrow Wilson and the Quest for a New World Order*. New York: Oxford University Press, 1992.

▶ Ninkovich, Frank A. *The Wilsonian Century: U.S. Foreign Policy Since 1900*. Chicago: University of Chicago Press, 1999.

▶ Pinchot, Amost R.E. *History of the Progressive Party, 1912–1916*. New York: New York University Press, 1958.

Periodicals

▶ Brookhiser, Richard. "How Smart Should a President Be?" *American Heritage,* Sep. 1999, p. 59.

▶ Yarbrough, Jean M. "The Forgotten T.R." Public Interest, Summer 2002, p. 49.

On the Web

▶ "Woodrow Wilson—Biography." Nobel Museum. **http://www.nobel.se/peace/laureates/1919/wilson-bio.html.** (Also contains Wilson's Nobel Peace Prize acceptance speech.)

▶ Wilson, Woodrow. "Second Inaugural Address, Monday, March 4, 1916. *Inaugural Addresses of the Presidents of the United States.* Washington, D.C.: U.S. Government Printing Office, 1989; Bartleby.com, 2001. **http://www.bartleby.com/124/pres45.html.**

▶ Woodrow Wilson." Web site of American Experience. **http://www.pbs.org/wgbh/amex/wilson/index.html.**

1920
Warren Harding (Republican) vs. James Cox (Democrat)

Americans were confronted with a complex and confusing set of circumstances by the time the election of 1920 finally arrived in November. President Woodrow Wilson had suffered a serious stroke in September 1919, which had left him largely incapacitated. Nevertheless he continued to push for U.S. membership in the League of Nations and held out the possibility of running for a third term. Also in 1919 Wilson's attorney general, A. Mitchell Palmer, and his assistant, J. Edgar Hoover, had arrested about 10,000 Socialists and Communists. Palmer warned that Communists planned to launch a violent revolution on May 1, 1920. There were two dozen race riots in 1919 including a major incident in Chicago.

At the end of January 1919, the Eighteenth Amendment to the Constitution was ratified, banning the manufacture, transport, or sale of alcoholic beverages, launching the era of Prohibition despite widespread distaste for the law in most urban centers, and giving rise to the "speakeasies" of the 1920s.

The disturbances in the summer of 1919 came after two decades of changes engineered by the Progressive movement. State and federal governments had assumed responsibility for controlling the conduct of large corporations on a variety of issues ranging from regulating the prices charged for utilities, such as natural gas, to limiting the length of the workday for railway workers and prohibiting the use of child labor.

The Candidates

The Democrats future was unclear at the end of Woodrow Wilson's second term. The president was unwell after suffering a stroke but he did not clearly say whether or not he would run for an unprecedented third term. Wilson's reluctance to rule out another campaign made it difficult for one leading Democrat in particular to campaign for the nomination—William McAdoo, Wilson's son-in-law. McAdoo had served as secretary of the treasury, chairman of the new Federal Reserve Board (central bank), and chairman of the Federal Farm Loan Board under Wilson and was well-known to the public. Another possible contender was Palmer, the attorney general, who declared himself a candidate and won the presidential primary in Georgia, but he was weakened after May 1, 1920 passed without the violent political upheaval he had predicted. A third contender was James Cox, governor of Ohio. Cox had an appealing story: he was a poor farm boy who started as a school janitor and became a self-made man and influential newspaper publisher. Moreover, Cox had been elected governor in a state usually controlled by Republicans.

When the Democratic convention opened in San Francisco in late June there was no clear leader. Wilson conceded he would not run again, but did not endorse anyone else. On the first ballot McAdoo led with 266 votes (out of the 729 needed to win nomination), followed by Attorney General Palmer (254 votes), Ohio governor Cox (1134) and New York governor Alfred Smith (109). In all, there were two dozen candidates on the first ballot.

As with many previous Democratic conventions, delegates voted time after time after time with no candidate getting enough votes to win the nomination. Cox gained ground on the second day only to lose his lead to McAdoo on the third day. On the thirty-sixth roll call the count was McAdoo 399,

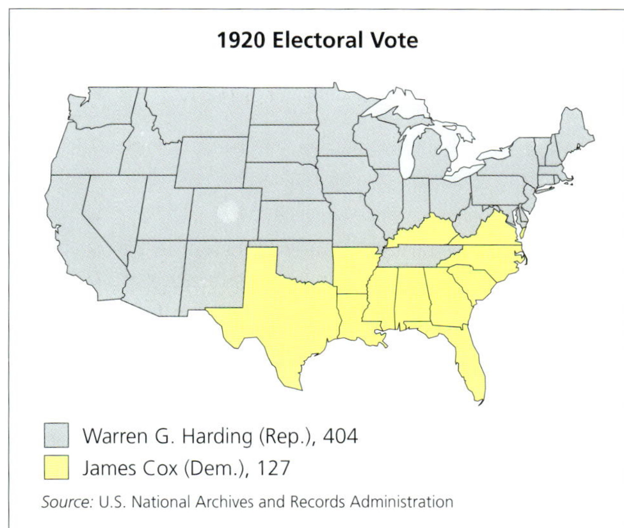

1920 Electoral Vote

Source: U.S. National Archives and Records Administration

FlashFocus: Warren G. Harding

29th President, 1921–1923

Born: November 2, 1865, Blooming Grove, Ohio
Died: August 2, 1923, San Francisco, California
Family: Son of George Harding, a farmer and physician, and Phoebe Dickerson; married Florence DeWolfe
Education: Ohio Central College
Political Career: Republican. Ohio state legislature, 1899–1903; lieutenant governor of Ohio, 1904–06; U.S. senator, 1915–21

Elected after a tumultuous decade that had included World War I, a new federal income tax, the granting of women's suffrage, a Constitutional amendment outlawing alcoholic beverages, urban race riots, and dire warnings of an imminent Communist revolution in the United States, Warren Harding portrayed himself as the man who could restore "normalcy" to American life.

Harding was a newspaper publisher in Marion, Ohio when he won a seat in the Ohio state legislature. He was elected to the U.S. Senate in 1914, where he was an easy-going and well-respected member of the "club," disinclined to rock the boat.

At the Republican presidential nominating convention in 1920 Harding was the compromise choice after the convention deadlocked between two better-known candidates, General Leonard Wood and Governor Frank Lowden of Illinois. After winning the White House Harding surrounded himself with men of stature, such as Secretary of State Charles Evans Hughes, a former (and future) Supreme Court justice. He also had in his cabinet men who would later be convicted of taking bribes in exchange for granting oil leases on federal property.

Harding did not live to witness the series of scandals that consumed his administration. En route home from a trip to Alaska he suffered a heart attack and died on August 2, 1923, leaving his vice president, Calvin Coolidge, to clean up the corruption scandals that subsequently became public.

Harding accomplished little of note in his brief administration, and his reputation was permanently scarred by scandal.

Cox 377, and Palmer 241. On the forty-fourth ballot, taken on the evening of the third day of voting, Cox was tantalizingly close: 699½, just 50½ votes short of the nomination. At last the convention adopted a motion to nominate Cox and shortly thereafter Cox designated the assistant secretary of the Navy, Franklin D. Roosevelt of New York, as his vice presidential running mate; Roosevelt, a cousin of Theodore Roosevelt, was nominated by acclamation.

The Republicans also lacked an obvious nominee at their convention in Chicago. There were three front-runners: Senator Hiram Johnson of California, representing the party's progressive wing; General Leonard Wood, a progressive who had been Theodore Roosevelt's commanding officer in the Spanish-American war, and Governor Frank Lowden of Illinois. Theodore Roosevelt had died of a stroke in January 1919, and the Republican nominee of 1916, Charles Evans Hughes, declined to run again.

Wood, thought to be the natural political heir of Roosevelt, moved to an early lead, followed by Lowden and Johnson. There were other nominees as well, including Senator Warren Harding of Ohio, in sixth place. After four ballots the convention chairman, Senator Henry Cabot Lodge of Massachusetts, called for an adjournment, giving party leaders a chance to meet privately. Legend has it that at two o'clock in the morning, Harding was invited to meet the Republican leaders and asked whether there was anything in his past that might preclude his nomination. Harding went next door to consider his answer, then returned and said, No. Whether such a meeting took place in just those circumstances is questionable. What is clear is that the next day Harding moved up from a distant sixth in the balloting and took the lead, largely thanks to a wholesale shift of Lowden's votes to the amiable senator from Ohio. On the tenth ballot Harding went over the top with 692⅕ votes to Wood's 156, Johnsons's 80⅘, and scattered votes for other candidates. The governor of Massachusetts, Calvin Coolidge, was nominated for vice president by a delegate from Oregon and his nomination sparked a long and enthusiastic demonstration. Coolidge had gained a national reputation by stepping in to crush a strike by Boston policemen in the tumultuous year of 1919. Coolidge was nominated as vice president on the first ballot.

Many politicians regarded Harding as a nearly ideal candidate. Although not yet well known outside Ohio Harding looked and seemed presidential—he was over six feet tall and 200 pounds—which was important in a campaign that used motion pictures extensively to let the country see the candidates.

The Socialist Party for the fifth time nominated Eugene V. Debs, but under odd circumstances. Debs had been arrested and accused of violating the Sedition Act by delivering a

FlashFocus: James Middleton Cox

Democratic candidate for president, 1920

Born: March 31, 1870, Jacksonburg, Ohio.

Died: July 15, 1957, Dayton, Ohio.

Family: Son of Gilbert Cox, a farmer, and Eliza Andrews; married Mayme Harding (divorced), Margaretta Blair

Education: Did not attend college

Political career: Democrat. U.S. representative, 1909–13; governor of Ohio, 1913–15, 1917–21; candidate for president, 1920

James Cox left school at age fifteen and worked as a school janitor before tutoring himself and qualifying as a teacher. Later he became a successful newspaper reporter, then private secretary to U.S. Representative Paul Sorg, a wealthy tobacco manufacturer, who helped Cox purchase the Dayton, Ohio Daily News where Cox made his fortune as publisher.

Cox pursued an aggressive editorial policy of investigating corruption and supporting progressive reforms which helped him win a seat in Congress as a Democrat in 1908 and again in 1910. He served three terms as governor of Ohio, implementing a long list of reforms including a minimum wage, a nine-hour workday for women, and worker's compensation.

At the Democratic convention in 1920 Cox became locked in a contest for the presidential nomination against former treasury secretary William McAdoo, and A. Mitchell Palmer, Woodrow Wilson's attorney general. Finally, after the forty-fourth ballot the convention adopted a resolution naming Cox the candidate. The fact that he had been elected governor in Ohio, a key state for Democrats, had tipped the scales in Cox's favor.

Cox support American membership in the League of Nations, but voters were tired of foreign involvements and Cox lost the presidency to his fellow Ohioan, Warren G. Harding.

Cox never again ran for public office and turned down offers by President Franklin Roosevelt for appointments, preferring to tend to his publishing empire.

He died in 1955 in Dayton, Ohio.

speech protesting American involvement in World War I. Convicted, Debs was sentenced to ten years in prison and was both nominated and ran from his cell in the federal penitentiary in Atlanta.

The Issues

League of Nations. On his return from the Versailles peace conference ending World War I Wilson was hailed as a hero. He won the Nobel Peace Prize in 1919 but he could not win acceptance for his League of Nations in the U.S. Senate without some changes, and he refused to consider any modifications whatsoever. The leader of the opposition to the League was Senator Henry Cabot Lodge of Massachusetts, a Republican, and consequently membership in the League of Nations became a leading campaign issue separating Democrats and Republicans. Ironically, neither presidential candidate held strong feelings on the subject and many prominent Republicans, such as former President Howard Taft, were avid supporters of an international organization designed to prevent another great war.

Women's votes. The Nineteenth Amendment, giving women the right to vote, was ratified on August 26, 1920, making it the first election in which women throughout the nation could vote for president. Both parties courted women without any knowledge of how those women were actually likely to vote. The Republicans made an especially strong case for women's votes while the Democrats seemed to suffer slightly due to Wilson's long opposition to the women's suffrage amendment.

Red Scare. The Bolshevik Revolution in Russia in 1917, helped convince some Americans that a similar violent upheaval could happen in the United States. Certainly Wilson's attorney general, Palmer, thought so; his home had been damaged by a bomb in one of a series of explosions set off in the summer of 1919 and blamed on anarchists. In November 1919, Palmer rounded up 10,000 people he suspected of being Communists, Socialists, or "Reds" in general. A few months later a further 6,000 were arrested. Most were eventually released without charges, although 245 were deported to the Soviet Union. Also in 1919 a series of race riots swept through several cities, notably Chicago, giving rise to feelings on the part of many Americans that things were spinning out of control. Palmer himself predicted that radicals planned to launch a violent revolution on May 1, 1920. When it failed to materialize Palmer lost support and came under criticism for violating the civil liberties of many of those arrested the previous autumn.

The Campaign

Harding set the tone for the campaign, and perhaps captured the mood of the country, in May 1920 when he declared that the United States needed "normalcy, not revolution." Imitating McKinley's successful "front porch" campaign of 1900 Harding seemed the embodiment of "normalcy" during the campaign, while Republican party operatives brought thousands of people to meet the candidate at his home in Marion, Ohio. The party arranged specific groups of people to come and be seen with Harding, such as a large group of women voters who visited on "social justice day" to hear a speech by Harding promising a new federal department to advance public welfare and humanitarian work. The Republican party also arranged visits by celebrities of the day, mostly stage actors and entertainers like singer Al Jolson. Although Harding's campaign was consciously designed to remind voters of McKinley's homey campaign—and of the years of prosperity and social stability under McKinley—the campaign also used modern technology, such as motion pictures and advertising and public relations techniques to maximize the candidate's reach.

Cox's campaign was hampered by the image of Wilson, who had lost most of his popularity and who conveyed an image of being old and sick. The Democrats tried to breathe life into their electioneering by linking Republicans to the interests of large corporations. Cox claimed that the business sector had given up to $15 million to the Republicans, an unheard of sum for an election in 1920, in order to buy influence and control over the federal government.

Woodrow Wilson played a role in the campaign by aggressively pushing the League of Nations. Neither party was clearly in favor of, or opposed to, the League, but the presence of Wilson meant that Cox was forced into defending the idea and Harding was pushed into opposing it. In the case of the Republicans this was especially awkward since former Republican President Howard Taft was firmly in favor of the League, as was the Republican candidate in 1916, Hughes. Nevertheless in early October Harding declared that he would ignore the proposal if elected. Cox backed the idea of joining the League, but not very happily or enthusiastically.

The Outcome

Harding won the popular vote with 16.1 million votes, or 60.4 percent of the total—the highest winning percentage recorded in presidential elections up to that time. Cox won 9.1 million votes, or 34.2 percent, with 919,799 (3.4 percent) going to Socialist Eugene Debs, campaigning from prison.

Harding's electoral victory was almost as overwhelming: 404 electoral votes to 127 for Cox. The Democrats only managed to carry the "solid South," and even then lost Tennessee to Harding and the Republicans. In Ohio, home state of both candidates, Harding won 58.4 percent of the vote to Cox's 38.6 percent.

The Republican victory in 1920 marked the end of the Progressive era and the beginning of a decade of peace and prosperity, marked by a desire on the part of the American public to turn its back on the rest of the world and enjoy the Jazz Age and the Roaring Twenties. It was a decade dominated by the Republicans, despite the surprise of Harding's death in office and the subsequent exposure of a pattern of scandals that was one of the worst ever uncovered.

More Information

▶ Mee, Charles L. *The Ohio Gang: The World of Warren G. Harding.* New York: M. Evans. 1981.

▶ Murray, Robert K. *The Politics of Normalcy: Governmental Theory and Practice in the Harding-Coolidge Era.* New York: Norton. 1973.

▶ Young, Marguerite. *Harp Song for a Radical: The Life and Times of Eugene Victor Debs.* New York: Alfred Knopf. 1999.

▶ Radosh, Ronald. *Debs.* Englewood Cliffs, NJ: Prentice Hall. 1971.

Periodicals

▶ Sferrazza, Anthony. "The Most Scandalous President." *American Heritage,* July–August 1998, p. 53.

▶ Schwarz, Frederic D. "The Teapot Starts To Boil." *American Heritage,* April 1997, p. 105.

On the Web

▶ "The Presidential Election of 1920." *American Leaders Spea: Recordings of World War I and the 1920 Election.* Library of Congress, American Memory Collection. **http://memory.loc. gov/ammem/nfhtml/nfhome.html.** (Includes links to short audio selections.)

▶ Harding, Warren G. "Inaugural Address, Friday, March 4, 1921." *Inaugural Addresses of the Presidents of the United States.* Washington, D.C.: U.S. Government Printing Office, 1989; Bartleby.com, 2001. **http://www.bartleby.com/124/ pres46.html.**

▶ "The Presidential Election of 1920," *American Leaders Speak: Recordings from World War I and the 1920 Election.* Motion Picture, Broadcasting and Recorded Sound Division, Library of Congress. (Links to audio files of presidential candidates, 1920.) **http://memory.loc.gov/ammem/nfhtml/nfhome. html.**

1924
Calvin Coolidge (Republican) vs. John W. Davis (Democrat) vs. Robert LaFollette (Progressive)

On August 2, 1923 President Warren Harding died of a heart attack in San Francisco, elevating Vice President Calvin Coolidge into the presidency. In the months that followed the nation learned of a series of scandals that marked the Harding administration, including the indictment and conviction of his interior secretary, Albert Fall, for accepting enormous bribes in exchange for granting leases to government oil reserves at Teapot Dome, Wyoming, and Elk Hills, California. Fall was sentenced to a year in prison, the first U.S. cabinet minister ever jailed for corruption. The head of the Veterans Bureau, Charles Forbes, left the United States for Europe; Harding's attorney general, Harry Daugherty, refused to provide investigating senators access to justice department files and refused to testify before Congress.

In response to Daugherty's lack of cooperation President Coolidge demanded his resignation. The new president also appointed two special prosecutors to investigate the Harding administration. Coolidge was thus able to control the situation and avoid having Harding's scandals taint his own administration.

Amid the political scandals, despite an economic recession in the early 1920s, most Americans were experiencing a period of prosperity by the time Coolidge took office. The face of the nation was rapidly changing thanks to the Ford Motor Company's Model T, which made it possible for ordinary working people to own automobiles for the first time. Production of cars virtually exploded in 1923, with production exceeding the total number of cars made in the past decade combined. The radio was also rapidly becoming commonplace in households, just as television sets did after World War II and the Internet did in the 1990s. Radio was destined to play a major role in the presidential election for the first time in 1924.

The Candidates

Calvin Coolidge had gained a national reputation as the governor of Massachusetts when he sent the state militia to Boston to put down a strike by the police in 1919, declaring that there could be no right to strike against the public safety. Coolidge had attended cabinet meetings under Harding, which was unusual for vice presidents, and was well briefed on matters when he was suddenly thrust into the presidency. Coolidge's firm handling of the corruption he inherited from Harding not only left Coolidge clean of scandal, but helped cast him in the role of the politician who took steps to clean up the mess.

Consequently Coolidge was easily nominated on the first ballot of the Republican convention in Cleveland in June. Senator Robert La Follette of Wisconsin received just 34 votes (compared to 1,065 for Coolidge) and another Republican progressive, Senator Hiram Johnson of California, received 10. The nomination of a vice president was more complex. De-

"

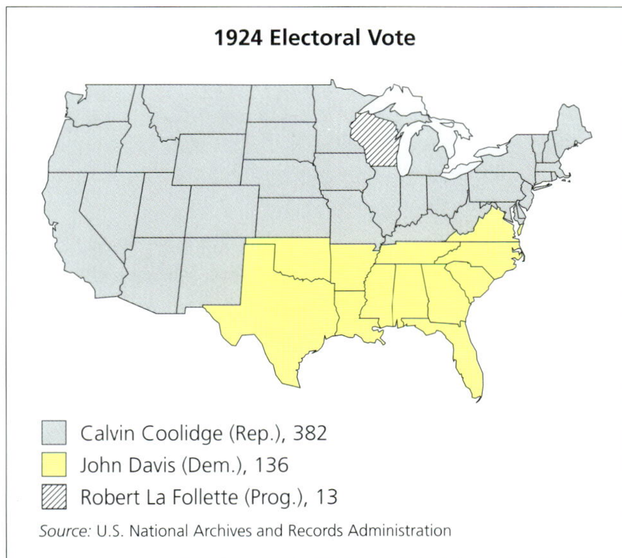

Source: U.S. National Archives and Records Administration

FlashFocus: John Calvin Coolidge

30th President, 1925–1929

Born: July 14, 1872, Plymouth Notch, Vermont

Died: January 5, 1933, Northampton, Massachusetts

Family: Son of John Calvin Coolidge, a farmer and storekeeper, and Victoria Josephine Moor; married Grace Goodhue, a teacher

Education: Amherst College; private law studies

Political career: Republican. Massachusetts House of Representatives, 1907; mayor of Northampton, Mass., 1910; Massachusetts state senate, 1912; lieutenant governor of Massachusetts, 1916–19; governor of Massachusetts, 1919–21; vice president, 1921–23

Calvin Coolidge personified small-town New England—frugal, quiet, hard-working, conservative, pious and honest—traits that inspired confidence in the era of the Roaring Twenties, when those same traits of a bygone America were seemingly in short supply.

In 1919 Coolidge became nationally known after a Boston police strike, when his declaration that "there is no right to strike against the public safety by anybody, anywhere, any time," struck a chord with a public weary of race riots and bombings.

In 1920 Republican Warren G. Harding was elected president, with Coolidge as his vice president. When Harding died of a heart attack in 1923 Coolidge took over just as scandals of the Harding administration were coming to light. Coolidge appointed special prosecutors and fired the attorney general for refusing to testify before the Senate, turning what could have been a political disaster into an advantage by acting the role of an honest politician cleaning up Harding's messy scandals.

In 1924 Coolidge easily won reelection, with more votes than the Democrat, John W. Davis, and Progressive Party candidate, Robert La Follette, combined.

Coolidge viewed the president as an administrator, not a leader, with initiatives residing in Congress. He consistently backed the interests of big business, which he thought would lead the country to prosperity.

He retired to Northampton, Mass., where he died of a heart attack on January 5, 1933.

spite protestations that he would not accept the nomination, Frank Lowden, former governor of Illinois, was nominated on the second ballot—but he stuck to his word and refused to accept the nomination. On the third ballot the convention nominated Charles Dawes, a former director of the federal Bureau of the Budget.

The Democratic convention, which opened in New York on June 24, 1924, turned out to be just the opposite of the orderly Republican meeting. The Democratic convention lasted over a period of seventeen days and required a record 104 ballots before delegates could settle on a candidate. To make matters worse for the Democrats, the convention was broadcast on the radio, treating listeners at home to what seemed to be an endless, almost comical, string of roll calls, each beginning with the same words: "The State of Alabama casts twenty-four votes for Underwood."

The marathon convention marked the sharp division in the Democratic party between the faction representing urban workers in the north and rural white farmers of the South and Midwest. The division between these two groups was as wide as it was profound; it incorporated religious differences as well as social and economic differences. The split in the Democratic party was not new in 1924, but it proved extraordinarily difficult to cover over at the convention.

William McAdoo had the backing of the southern faction. He was a native of Georgia who had moved to Tennessee and eventually became Woodrow Wilson's treasury secretary (and, coincidentally, son-in-law) before settling in California. McAdoo was supported by the Ku Klux Klan, an anti-black, anti-Catholic, anti-Jewish, anti-immigrant organization that had been founded in 1915 using the name of an anti-Reconstruction organization of the 1870s. McAdoo also supported the prohibition of alcohol and restrictions on immigration. His political opposite was the governor of New York,

Alfred ("Al") Smith, the grandson of Irish Catholic immigrants, an opponent of prohibition (as governor, he oversaw repeat of the New York law to enforce prohibition) and champion of northern, urban workers. There were fourteen other contenders, including Senator Oscar W. Underwood of Alabama whose supporters announced his name at the start of the roll call. The fact that the Democrats required a two-third majority to obtain the nomination made it exceedingly difficult for one candidate to overcome the other.

FlashFocus: John William Davis

Democratic candidate for president, 1916

Born: April 13, 1873, Clarksburg, West Virginia
Died: March 24, 1955, Charleston, South Carolina
Family: Son of John Davis, an attorney and former Democratic congressman, and Anna Kennedy; married Julia McDonald
Education: Washington and Lee University
Political career: Democrat. West Virginia House of Delegates, 1899; U.S. representative from Virginia, 1911–13; U.S. ambassador to Great Britain, 1918–21; candidate for Democratic nomination for president, 1920

John Davis was one of the country's best known attorneys when he ran as the Democratic presidential nominee in 1924. After law school Davis practiced law with his father in Clarksburg, WV. He was elected to the state House of Delegates in 1900 and twice elected a U.S. representative in 1910 and 1912. President Woodrow Wilson appointed Davis solicitor general in 1913. As the lawyer who argues the government's cases before the Supreme Court, Davis was widely admired—some Supreme Court justices hoped that he would be appointed to the Court. After five years Wilson named Davis as ambassador to Britain, where he won many British admirers despite diplomatic tensions with the United States. Some critics thought Davis won British friends by inadequately representing U.S. interests.

In 1921 Davis joined a New York law firm representing prominent corporations. Three years later he was the compromise Democratic presidential candidate after 103 ballots (a record). He ran against incumbent Calvin Coolidge and lost decisively.

After the election Davis focused on his law practice. He argued many cases before the Supreme Court, notably in 1952 when he succeeded in overturning the seizure of U.S. Steel by President Harry Truman. In 1954, Davis argued unsuccessfully on behalf of South Carolina to defend the segregation of public schools. It was his last case before the Supreme Court; he died the next year in South Carolina.

After the first week of balloting, which covered 77 ballots, McAdoo led with 513 votes, well short of the 749 needed to win, with Smith in second place with 367 votes. In third place was John Davis of New York. William Jennings Bryan, the party's candidate in 1896, 1900 and 1908, delivered a speech on behalf of McAdoo but was virtually drowned out by boos from Smith supporters. In the second week of balloting the convention agreed to release delegates from any commitments (such as from presidential primaries), which seemed to help Smith, who passed McAdoo on the eighty-sixth vote. Franklin Roosevelt, who had nominated Smith, announced that his candidate would withdraw if McAdoo also withdrew, but McAdoo refused. But after ninety-nine ballots, McAdoo acknowledged that he would not be the winner and released his delegates, many of whom gave their support to Underwood, who moved to second behind Davis. In effect, the contest between McAdoo and Smith was transformed into a fight between Underwood and Davis.

Finally after the one hundred third ballot, the Iowa delegation switched its support to Davis, causing other states to do the same and making Davis the nominee after a record 103 ballots. The vice presidential nomination proved to be considerably easier: a contest between Charles Bryan, governor of Nebraska and younger brother of William Jennings Bryan, and George Berry, a labor leader from Tennessee, ended after the first ballot with Bryan as the nominee.

The ease with which Coolidge won nomination masked a division in the Republican party between those who supported mostly eastern business interests and those who represented western farmers, notably La Follette of Wisconsin. The Republican convention had dismissed, by voice vote, a platform report by Wisconsin Republicans who were still dominated by the old progressive forces that had backed Theodore Roosevelt in 1912. In 1924 representatives of labor and farm groups, along with liberals who supported social causes, met in Cleveland in July to launch a new version of the Progressive Party with La Follette as its presidential candidate and Senator Burton Wheeler of Montana, a Democrat, for vice president. As in earlier elections the Progressive Party focused on the power and influence of major corporations on the government. The Progressives also supported government ownership of railroads (viewed as a resource similar to highways) and water utilities, reduced military spending, and a ban on court injunctions against labor strikes. "The great issue before the American people today," the party's platform declared, "is the control of government and industry by private monopoly."

The Issues

Race. Neither party platform in 1924 mentioned the Ku Klux Klan but the organization was in the forefront of the minds of many people during the election. The first Ku Klux Klan was an organization of Confederate officers formed after the Civil War to restrain the political power of freed slaves. That Klan largely disappeared after Reconstruction, but another organization using the same name was formed in 1915 in Georgia. It eventually gained about four million members, with chapters in virtually every state, especially throughout the South and Midwest. The Klan represented a mix of religious fundamentalism, racism, anti-Catholicism and support for Prohibition. The Klan opposed Catholic schools and advocated restrictions on immigration (which passed the Congress in 1924). In some respects the Klan was the dark side of Harding's 1920 theme of "normalcy;" it represented a southern and Midwestern rural reaction against the growth of the urban, industrial culture of the north, including an influx of Catholic and Jewish immigrants from southern and eastern Europe. The Klan was a hot potato for both the Republicans and Democrats who would be competing for votes of Klan members. The Republicans made no mention of it in their platform. A minority report offered to the Democratic convention proposed a plank denouncing the Klan by name; after a long debate, the Democrats decided by a margin of just ten votes not to denounce the Klan and its opposition to Catholics, Jews, immigrants and African-Americans—the first three of whom were important constituents of the northern, urban wing of the Democratic party.

Progressivism. For over two decades the term "progressive" had stood for efforts to control the activities of large corporations to ensure competition and protect workers and consumers from abuse. The issue had split the Republican party in 1912 when former President Theodore Roosevelt formed the Progressive Party and ran against Republican incumbent Howard Taft. In 1924, Republican senator Robert La Follette became the candidate of a newly organized Progressive Party, which had a similar agenda: government ownership of railroads and water utilities, tax reform (lower taxes on the middle and lower classes, higher taxes on the wealthy), direct election of federal judges, direct popular election of the president, and a national referendum on important questions, such as going to war. The Progressive Party also started to attracted African-Americans, such as W. E. B. Du Bois, a leading civil rights campaigner, after both major parties failed to denounce the Ku Klux Klan.

The Campaign

Radio changed the presidential campaign in 1920 much as television changed campaigning twenty-five years later. Coolidge spent most of the campaign in the White House while his vice presidential running mate, Dawes, covered just 1,500 miles. Davis, the Democrat, and La Follette, the Progressive, made more extensive train tours of the Midwest and West, but these were modest compared to previous years.

By contrast Coolidge's speeches were broadcast by radio from the White House, enabling him to reach far more people than any train tour could hope to do. Democratic rallies were also broadcast.

As in previous elections Republicans vastly outspent Democrats. Coolidge's campaign spent over $3.5 million, compared to under $1 million for the Democrats. For the first time, spending on radio became a factor; the Republicans spent about $50,000 for radio, the Democrats about $40,000.

It was the second election in which women were allowed to vote throughout the country. While both parties made strong efforts to attract women voters, the pattern of voting by women did not appear to differ from the pattern of men.

The Outcome

Only about half the eligible voters went to the polls in 1924, compared to almost 80 percent in 1896. Coolidge won the popular vote with 15.7 million votes, or 54 percent), compared to 8.4 million votes (28.8 percent) for Davis and 4.8 million (16.6 percent) for La Follette. Voting patterns suggested that La Follette, although a Republican before the election, took more votes from Davis than from Coolidge.

In the electoral college Coolidge won 382 votes to 136 for Davis and 13 for La Follette. Davis carried the "solid South" for the Democrats (except for Kentucky), plus Oklahoma. La Follette's electoral votes all came from his home state of Wisconsin. Coolidge carried the Northeast, the Midwest, and the West (except for Arizona and Wisconsin).

More Information

- Unger, Nancy C. *Fighting Bob La Follette: The Righteous Reformer.* Chapel Hill: University of North Carolina Press, 2000.
- Sobel, Robert. *Coolidge: An American Enigma.* Washington, DC: Regnery Pub., 1998.
- Murray, Robert K. *The Politics of Normalcy: Governmental Theory and the Practice in the Harding-Coolidge Era.* New York: Norton, 1973.
- Harbaugh, William H. *Lawyer's Lawyer: The Life of John W. Davis.* New York: Oxford University Press, 1978.
- Kyvig, David E. *Daily Life in the United States, 1920–1939: Decades of Promise and Pain.* Westport, CT: Greenwood Press, 2002.

Periodicals

- Nichol, John. "Portrait of the Founder, Fighting Bob La Follette." *The Progressive,* January 1999, p. 10.

On the Web

- Coolidge, Calvin "Inaugural Address, Wednesday, March 4, 1925." *Inaugural Addresses of the Presidents of the United States.* Washington, D.C.: U.S. Government Printing Office, 1989; Bartleby.com, 2001. **http://www.bartleby.com/124/pres47.html.**
- Calvin Coolidge Library and Museum. **http://www.forbeslibrary.org/coolidge.html.**

1928
Herbert Hoover (Republican) vs. Alfred Smith (Democrat)

FlashFocus: 1928

Candidates

Herbert C. Hoover & Charles Curtis, Republican
Alfred E. Smith & Joseph T. Robinson, Democrat

Issues

Tariffs and farm relief. As in the election of 1924, subsidies for farmers and tariff adjustments continued to be important issues in the campaign. However the two candidates held similar positions on these issues, so neither candidate could gain the upper hand.

Religion, background and personality. Democratic candidate Alfred Smith's background as a Catholic from the streets of New York City both helped and hurt him. He gained support from the growing urban and ethnic populations but was unable to attract moderate voters. Herbert Hoover had a more difficult time identifying with urban, ethnic and working-class voters, but still many voters concluded that he was the better candidate and more fit for the presidency. Religion and social background were inevitably very prominent issues in this campaign, indicating the changes in American society and the growing cultural divide between urban and rural populations.

Outcome

Popular Vote

Hoover	21,391,993	58.2% ✓
Smith	15,016,169	40.9%

Electoral College

Hoover	444 ✓
Smith	87

The Republicans continued their domination of the White House with a victory in 1928, but this would mark the end of their string of successes. The next Republican victory would not come for twenty years.

The Context

For many Americans the era of "normalcy" promised in 1920 by Warren Harding looked comfortable and appealing in 1928. The country was enjoying widespread prosperity in a decade when businessmen like Henry Ford were national heroes. Most segments of the economy were prospering in 1928 and there were no compelling foreign issues to distract most Americans from the "Roaring Twenties." The fact that stock prices were rising, and that many middle class people were participating in the market, was viewed as part of prosperity and not as a darkening cloud.

The Candidates

President Calvin Coolidge was well-liked and probably could have been reelected. But on his summer vacation in August, 1927, Coolidge had summoned reporters and distributed slips of paper with the same typewritten message: "I do not choose to run for president in 1928." Coolidge never explained his decision nor did he ever waver. The Republican party took him at his word and there was no effort to draft Coolidge for a second full term (he had become president in 1923 upon the death of President Warren Harding). Nor was there a stampede among possible candidates for the nomination. The commerce secretary, Herbert Hoover, was widely admired as a millionaire mining engineer who had turned to administering government relief efforts after World War I. Hoover entered presidential primaries and, with the exception of three losses to "favorite son" candidates, had won in California, Oregon, New Jersey, Michigan, Massachusetts and Maryland. By the time the Republican nominating convention opened in Kansas City in mid June, Hoover had a commanding lead. He handily won the nomination on the first ballot with 857 votes. His closest challenger, former Illinois governor Frank Lowden, received 74 votes. The choice of vice president was equally quick: Senator Charles Curtis of Kansas received 1,052 votes on the first ballot.

Hoover was not a talented politician but he was a proven administrator. He had made his fortune as a mining engineer, then gained admiration for his work in distributing food aid to Europe after World War I. Harding appointed him commerce secretary in 1921 and he remained in the same post during the Coolidge administration. His name was prominent in the news in 1927 when he directed relief operations after flooding on the lower Mississippi.

Hoover's political philosophy reflected his training as an engineer. He believed that business should be the engine of prosperity, with government working in a cooperative role. Hoover was neither a progressive, in the tradition of Theodore Roosevelt, nor a strict conservative. He presented an image of a highly competent, if personally unexciting, administrator who could be trusted to keep the good times rolling.

The Democratic party, remembering its long and divisive nominating convention of 1924 and its subsequent landslide defeat at the polls, entered the 1928 election determined not to repeat its earlier mistake. Its leading presidential contender was the governor of New York, Alfred E. Smith, universally known as "Al." Smith clearly represented the urban, working-class faction of the Democratic party. The party's conservative, rural, Southern wing was still led by William McAdoo,

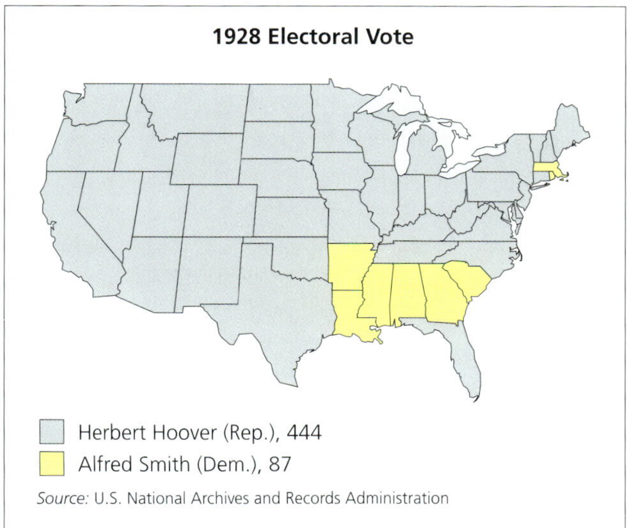

Source: U.S. National Archives and Records Administration

who had participated in the marathon convention of 1924, only to drop out at the last minute. But McAdoo had no taste for a rerun of 1924, which he feared would permanently split the Democratic party. Consequently he decided not to run for the nomination in 1928, opening the way for Smith.

On the first ballot Smith came within ten votes of the two-thirds majority needed for the nomination, a picture of unanimity compared to the 103 ballots required four years earlier. After the first ballot Ohio switched 44 votes to Smith, putting him over the top. To balance the ticket, Democrats then chose Senator Joseph Robinson of Arkansas as vice president on the first ballot, the first southerner to be on the ticket of either party since the Civil War.

Smith was not merely the representative of the northern urban working-class wing of the Democratic party; he was a living example. His mother had immigrated from Ireland; his father drove horse-drawn carriages for a living. He was born on New York's Lower East Side, home of many poor immigrants, and worked his way up through New York City's Democratic organization, or "machine," called Tammany Hall. Smith spoke with a pronounced New York accent, and could usually be seen with a cigar in his mouth. Most important, in the eyes of many, he was Catholic.

The Issues

Religion. Smith's Catholicism was the most compelling issue in the 1928 campaign. It was symbolic of the enormous changes in American society brought about by waves of immigrants, starting with the Irish in the late 1840s. Unlike the earlier immigrants, primarily Protestants from northern Europe who settled on farms, the immigrants of the second half of the nineteenth century were often Catholics from southern or eastern Europe and often settled in cities, where they found jobs in the rapidly growing industrial economy. There was no shortage of evangelical, fundamentalist Protestants who is-

sued dire warnings that a Catholic president would result in control of the United States by the Vatican. At bottom, though, the Catholic issue was a symbol of a much larger cultural divide between the rural South and Midwest and the urban areas of the North.

Prohibition. When he accepted the Democratic nomination Smith had created a flurry by declaring that if he were elected, there would be "fundamental changes" in national Prohibition. The abolition of alcohol was supported in the

ing of their crops in an effort to ease fluctuations in farm prices. The Democrats favored a similar, if somewhat more active, system. Neither party endorsed a proposal to buy surplus crops as a means of propping up prices when harvests were bountiful.

The Campaign

Hoover adopted as his campaign slogan, "A car in every garage and a chicken in every pot." The slogan seemed to fit a period of Republican prosperity, combined with peace abroad. At the outset of campaigning, Hoover declared that the United States was "nearer to the final triumph over poverty than ever before," and promised to maintain policies that would assure continued economic good times. He also promised a shorter workday, expanded public works, and relief for farmers. At a campaign appearance in Iowa, where he had been born, he declared that coming from a small town was "the entry of life which I could wish for every American boy or girl."

A small town in Iowa was clearly the furthest thing from Al Smith's entry of life, which was the bustling immigrant neighborhood of the Lower East Side in Manhattan. Nearly everything about Smith's campaign drew some cultural distinction between himself and Hoover but he neglected to outline where they differed in policy. By focusing on cultural differences, Smith underscored points about himself that made vast numbers of voters uneasy while failing to give them a reason to overlook his religion, his accent and his style.

Both parties made extensive use of the radio in 1928 which seemed to work to Smith's disadvantage. To many ears outside of New York his voice seemed too loud and a bit grating. Hoover was far from an accomplished orator but his voice seemed more familiar to most Americans.

Hoover, whose family were Quakers, never raised the issue of Smith's religion. But he didn't have to; Baptist and Methodist preachers in the South undertook anti-Catholic campaigns of their own. On the few occasions when Smith responded to attacks on his religion, he was criticized for injecting the issue into the campaign.

The Outcome

By most accounts Hoover won the election in a landslide. In the popular vote he won 21.4 million votes, or 58.2 percent, to Smith's 15 million (40.9 percent). Hoover won 444 electoral college votes to Smith's 59. A third candidate, Norman Thomas of the Socialists, won 881,479 popular votes, or 1.9 percent of the total.

As dismal as Smith's showing was, he nevertheless won almost twice as many votes as Democrat John W. Davis had won four years earlier, and as a percentage of the popular vote, Smith did better than either Davis (28.8 percent), or the 1920 candidate, James Cox (34.2 percent).

On the other hand Hoover managed to break the Democrats' hold on the "solid South" for the first time since the Civil War by capturing the electoral votes of Texas, Florida, North

conservative South and Midwest; it was not popular in the cities. Smith himself was a "wet" (against Prohibition), and even though the Democratic vice presidential candidate, Robinson, was a "dry," this issue was, like Smith's Catholicism, a cultural rather than a political challenge to conservative Democrats.

Business. Ignoring a chance to solidify his natural urban base Smith shot himself in the foot by choosing John Raskob as party chairman. Raskob was a Catholic business leader and an opponent of trade unions. Smith's choice tended to blunt the enthusiasm of labor for the Democratic platform. In some respects, Hoover had more impressive "progressive" labor credentials than Smith.

Agriculture. The Republican platform promised support for a Federal Farm Board to help farmers organize the market-

Carolina, Virginia and Tennessee. There was little doubt that anti-Catholic sentiment in those states delivered their electoral votes to the Republicans.

Smith's "northern urban" strategy did not even pay off in his home state of New York, which he lost. Smith carried only eight states in all: Alabama, Arizona, Georgia, Louisiana, Massachusetts, Mississippi, Rhode Island, and South Carolina.

The day after the election it might have seemed to Republicans and Democrats alike that the future of Republican domination of the presidency was virtually assured. In fact Hoover was the last Republican elected president for more than twenty years and his name became permanently associated with the worst economic depression in U.S. history.

More Information

- Finan, Christopher M. *Alfred E. Smith, The Happy Warrior.* New York: Hill and Wang, 2002.
- Moore, Edmund A. *A Catholic Runs for President: The Campaign of 1928.* Gloucester, MA: P. Smith. 1968.
- Nash, George. *The Life of Herbert Hoover.* New York: W. W. Norton, 1988.
- David Burner, *The Politics of Provincialism: The Democratic Party in Transition, 1918–1932.* New York: Knopf, 1970.

Periodicals

- Martin, James. "Anti-Catholicism in the United States: The Last Acceptable Prejudice?" *America,* March 25, 2000, p. 8.

On the Web:

- Hoover, Herbert. "Inaugural Address, Monday, March 4, 1929." *Inaugural Addresses of the Presidents of the United States.* Washington, D.C.: U.S. Government Printing Office, 1989; Bartleby.com, 2001. **http://www.bartleby.com/124/pres48.html.**
- Wooley, John and Gerhard Peters. "The American Presidency Project." University of California, Santa Barbara, Department of Political Science. Links to presidential papers of Herbert Hoover and others. **http://www.presidency.ucsb.edu/site/docs/index_pppus.php.**
- Herbert Hoover Presidential Library and Museum. Links to papers and documents about Herbert Hoover. **http://www.hoover.archives.gov/education/index.html.**

1932

Franklin D. Roosevelt (Democrat) vs. Herbert Hoover (Republican)

A precipitous decline in stock prices in October, 1929 marked the start of the worst economic depression yet experienced by the United States. By 1932 about one in four Americans was out of work. Banks and stock brokerage firms had been ruined; mortgages on homes and farms were being foreclosed; and thousands of business enterprises had gone out of business. Outside many cities unemployed workers who could not afford housing huddled in temporary camps derisively named "Hoovervilles" after President Herbert Hoover.

The root causes of the Great Depression are complex and still debated among historians and economists. Nevertheless the magnitude of the economic disaster was unprecedented.

Making matters much worse, a drought hit agricultural regions of the Midwest, putting added pressure on the farm economy even as the industrial economy was tottering.

Hoover responded to the crisis with several programs designed to relieve suffering and at the same time to shore up failing financial institutions. In 1932 the government created the Reconstruction Finance Corporation to lend money to financial institutions and railroads. The Emergency Relief and Construction Act of 1932 provided federal loans to state governments for payments to the unemployed and loans for construction projects. The Federal Home Loan Bank Act lent money to banks to help homeowners avoid foreclosure on their mortgages. Despite these efforts the Depression continued unabated, and Hoover faced growing criticism in some quarters for excessive borrowing and for failing to balance the federal budget.

The Candidates

Hoover had scored a landslide victory over Democrat Al Smith in 1928 but four years later no one gave the president much chance of being reelected. Whether or not Hoover bore responsibility for the Depression or could have done more to alleviate its effects, he came across as a dull, dour leader who did not seem to care about people who were suffering. Hopeless as his chances were thought to be, there was no meaningful opposition to his nomination for a second term when the Republican convention opened in Chicago on June 14, since no Republican politician relished the task of running for president in 1932. Hoover was nominated on the first ballot with all but about two dozen votes; vice president Charles Curtis was similarly nominated a second time. The atmosphere of the Republican convention seemed to reflect the attitude of the country: depressed and defeatist.

The Democratic convention was more upbeat. For the first time in more than a decade the Democrats sensed that they would elect the next president. The front-runner was New York governor Franklin Delano Roosevelt, a distant cousin of former President Theodore Roosevelt. Franklin Roosevelt had been the Democratic vice presidential candidate in 1920 and a supporter of Al Smith (also a former governor New York) in 1928. Oddly, Smith was Roosevelt's major challenger for the nomination in 1932, along with the Speaker of the House, John Nance Garner of Texas, who was backed by William McAdoo, a contender for the nomination in 1920 and 1924. When the convention opened in Chicago in late June Roosevelt had a majority of votes, but was short of the two-thirds majority needed for the nomination.

The first roll call did not begin until 4:30 A.M. after an all-night session. Roosevelt received 666¼ votes out of 770 needed

FlashFocus: Franklin Delano Roosevelt

32nd President, 1933–1945

Born: January 30, 1882, Hyde Park, New York
Died: April 12, 1945, Warm Springs, Georgia
Family: Son of James Roosevelt, vice president of a railroad company, and Sara Delano; married Anna Eleanor Roosevelt, a cousin
Education: Groton School; Harvard University; Columbia Law School
Political career: Democrat. New York state senate, 1911–13; candidate for vice president, 1920; governor of New York, 1929–33

Franklin Roosevelt was president longer than any other person (he was the only man elected four times) and led the United States during two of the most traumatic crises in the nation's history: the Great Depression in the early 1930s, and the second World War. He was revered by millions of Americans who credited him with saving the country in times of unprecedented hardship. He was reviled by others who blamed him for instituting unprecedented government intervention in the economy and society through programs known as the New Deal. Roosevelt's economic and political policies set the agenda for more than half a century as his contemporaries and successors fought to expand or contract, continue or abandon, programs like social welfare, unemployment insurance, Social Security, and aid to farmers.

Internationally Roosevelt steered the United States into backing Britain in its fight against Nazi Germany, then presided over a two-front war, combating Germany in Europe and North Africa, and Japan in Asia and the Pacific. Roosevelt negotiated arrangements for the post-war world that shaped world politics for half a century.

Roosevelt was a man of extraordinary personal courage and political savvy whose determined optimism was beamed into millions of homes over the radio in his "fireside chats," during which he assured Americans that better times would come, and that he was working hard to hasten the day.

In politics Roosevelt drew on his personal experience of overcoming, at age 39, poliomyelitis (polio), a disease that left him permanently unable to walk without leg braces and a cane. Roosevelt learned to give the appearance of walking by swinging his legs, encased in braces, while using a cane and leaning on the arm of a friend. He faced his own life disability with optimistic determination—a quality he transferred to the country during the great Depression of the 1930s.

Roosevelt was born in Hyde Park, New York, just north of New York City, in 1882. He led the privileged life of an American quasi-aristocrat, graduating from Harvard University and Columbia University's school of law. Roosevelt began working his way up through the Democratic party, starting as a reform-minded state senator. He ran for vice president on losing ticket headed by James Cox in 1920. After a period in private business, Roosevelt was elected governor of New York for two consecutive terms.

Roosevelt ran for the presidency four times—in 1932, 1936, 1940 and 1944—winning each time. Each election was distinctive.

In 1932, Roosevelt ran against incumbent Republican Herbert Hoover, a mining engineer and administrator who was overwhelmed by the economic crisis brought on by the stock market crash of 1929. The extent of unemployment and despair was so great by 1932 that it seemed possible any Democrat could have beaten the Republican candidate.

In 1936 Roosevelt won by an even bigger margin. This time the election was a referendum on Roosevelt's handling of the Depression and on his series of government programs known as the New Deal, instituted in an effort to alleviate the nation's widespread economic suffering. Roosevelt had fought for four years to enact programs that offered government relief to unemployed workers and aid for drought-stricken farmers. Roosevelt's policies were overwhelmingly endorsed in the presidential election; he beat Republican Alfred Landon with 60.8 percent of the vote to Landon's 36.5 percent.

In 1940 a different crisis loomed. The German army had invaded much of western Europe and warplanes were bombarding England in the Battle of Britain. In Asia, Japan had invaded part of China and threatened to extend its empire throughout former European colonies in Asia. Although both Roosevelt and his Republican opponent, Wendell Willkie, said they opposed war, by the autumn of 1940 it was clear that the United States needed an experienced leader to face the crisis. Willkie, a corporate executive, had never held any elective office, although he managed to trim Roosevelt's winning margin to 54.8 percent to 44.8 percent. Roosevelt may have been hurt by concerns that he was breaking a precedent set by George Washington that presidents did not run for more than two terms.

In his final race, in 1944, the United States had successfully invaded German-occupied France, and with Soviet armies advancing from the east it seemed apparent that victory would come soon. Roosevelt had been at the country's helm throughout the war and voters were not inclined to throw out the chief before the course was run. Despite Dewey's claim that the Roosevelt administration—and by implication, Roosevelt himself—was dominated by "tired old men," Roosevelt was elected to a fourth term by a margin of 53.5 percent to 46 percent for Republican Thomas Dewey, recently elected governor of New York.

On April 12, 1945, freshly returned from a conference with British prime minister Winston Churchill and Russian leader Joseph Stalin at which the three men discussed arrangements for the period after World War II, Franklin Roosevelt suffered a cerebral hemorrhage (stroke) and died in Warm Springs, Georgia.

See also: Herbert Hoover, p. 137.

to win the nomination, well ahead of Smith (201¾ votes) and Garner (90¼). At 9:15 the exhausted delegates agreed to adjourn until the evening.

On the fourth ballot McAdoo announced that California's 44 votes would switch to Roosevelt, wishing to avoid a repeat of the 1924 convention, which took over 100 ballots to decide on a nominee. In addition the Texas delegation narrowly voted to back Roosevelt after he offered their favorite son, Garner, the vice presidential slot.

Upon being informed of his nomination, Roosevelt took an unprecedented move: he boarded an airplane in New York and flew to Chicago to accept the nomination. His acceptance speech is largely forgotten except for one phrase: he promised "a New Deal for the American people."

The Issues

The depression was *the* issue in 1932. The surprising aspect of the election is that Roosevelt and the Democrats did not present detailed plans to deal with the crisis; it was enough that the Depression had come on during Hoover's administration and had not eased before the election. Hoover had already taken steps in 1932 to try to alleviate the worst suffering, steps that resembled in many ways the programs Roosevelt and his advisers later instituted. In fact the Democratic platform of 1932 advocated "an immediate and drastic reduction of government expenditure" and a balanced budget. The platform also advocated extending federal loans to the states to provide unemployment relief in cases where states could no longer afford to help those out of work, and an expansion of public works projects to create jobs. The Democrats also urged a reduction in the workweek, as a means of sharing the work among more people.

Hoover's response to the depression had not been politically astute. He had long insisted that the causes for the downturn were rooted in the international economy and that there was little that the president could do to change the situation. The Republican platform, like the Democratic one, also urged a reduction in public spending. On the subject of aid to the unemployed the Republicans declared: "The people themselves, by their own courage, their own patient and resolute effort in the readjustments of their own affairs, can and will work out the cure. . . . The (Hoover) administration has regarded the relief problem as one of state and local responsibility."

Prohibition remained as an issue, although an overshadowed one. The Republicans advocated a national referendum (popular vote) on whether to pass a new Constitutional amendment that would leave the issue of prohibition up to each individual state. The Democrats took a more aggressive stand, urging repeal of the Eighteenth Amendment (which had instituted Prohibition).

The Campaign

In the campaign Hoover proved no match for Roosevelt. Hoover had never been an inspiring speaker and during the campaign of 1932, some critics thought his speeches sounded like dull economics lectures. Roosevelt, on the other hand, had

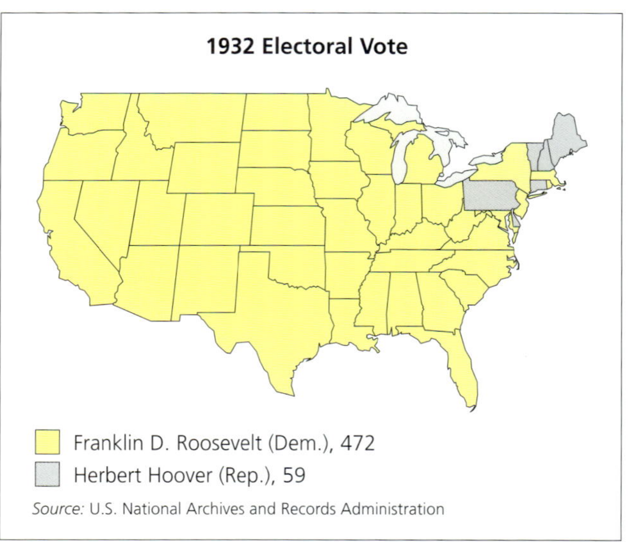

Source: U.S. National Archives and Records Administration

the ability to exude enthusiastic optimism while at the same time conveying the sense that he cared about voters' economic suffering.

As the campaign progressed the differences between Hoover and Roosevelt actually became more pronounced. Roosevelt voiced what seemed to be radical thoughts on some occasions and conservative ideas on others. He attacked Hoover for over-regulating business and for excessive spending, driving up the federal debt. Other times he advocated much greater government involvement in managing the economy and redistributing wealth from the rich to the poor.

For his part Hoover increasingly focused on what he called Roosevelt's "radical" proposals. Hoover's approach was to portray himself as the technical master of economic policy—hence his long, often boring speeches that reminded some of economics lectures. Yet if Hoover were an expert why had he not been able to counter the effects of the Depression? By attacking Roosevelt as a radical, Hoover underscored his own image as a representative of the interests of big business. The incumbent was in a no-win situation.

The Outcome

The 1932 results were almost a mirror image of the 1928 election. Roosevelt won 22.8 million votes, or 57.4 percent, to Hoover's 15.8 million, or 39.7 percent. (In 1928 Hoover had won 58.2 percent of the vote and Democrat Al Smith 40.9 percent). Norman Thomas, the Socialist candidate, won 881,951 votes, or 2.2 percent.

In the electoral college Roosevelt won an overwhelming 472 votes to Hoover's 59. Hoover carried six states: Connecticut, Delaware, Maine, New Hampshire, Vermont and Pennsylvania.

Roosevelt succeeded in putting together a powerful coalition of urban industrial voters and farmers in the South and West. He had done so, however, without any particular policy initiatives. These would come later, during his first administration, and would result in an even more astounding landslide in 1936.

The inauguration of Franklin Roosevelt in 1932 is depicted as a coronation of an emperor or a pope in this painting by Miguel Covarrubias that appeared in *Vanity Fair* magazine in March, 1933. Roosevelt is shown about to be crowned with a wreath, while his wife Eleanor is to his right. The defeated Herbert Hoover is shown holding a top hat, third from the left on the top row, while various other Washington luminaries are caricatured in the crowd below.

More Information

- Freideal, Frank. *Franklin D. Roosevelt: A Rendezvous with Destiny*. Boston: Little Brown, 1990.
- Gerdes, Louis (ed.) *The Crash of 1929*. San Diego: Greenhaven Press, 2002.
- Klein, Maury. *Rainbow's End: The Crash of 1929*. New York: Oxford University Press, 2001.
- Rosen, Elliott. *Hoover, Roosevelt and the Brains Trust: From Depression to New Deal*. New York: Columbia University Press, 1977.
- Rosenman, Samuel I. *Working with Roosevelt*. New York: Harper, 1952.

Periodicals

- Goode, Stephen. "Herbert Hoover: An Uncommon Man Brought Down by the Great Depression." *World and I*, March 2001, p. 282.

On the Web

- Roosevelt, Franklin D. "First Inaugural Address, Saturday, March 4, 1933. *Inaugural Addresses of the Presidents of the United States*. Washington, D.C.: U.S. Government Printing Office, 1989; Bartleby.com, 2001. **http://www.bartleby.com/124/pres49.html.**
- Wooley, John and Gerhard Peters. "The American Presidency Project." University of California, Santa Barbara, Department of Political Science. Links to presidential papers of Franklin Roosevelt and others. **http://www.presidency.ucsb.edu/site/docs/index_pppus.php.**
- Franklin D. Roosevelt Presidential Library and Museum. Digitized documents from the museum's collection. **http://www.fdrlibrary.marist.edu/online14.html.**

1936
Franklin D. Roosevelt (Democrat)
vs. Alfred "Alf" Landon (Republican)

The 1932 presidential election had been a national referendum of the policies of the Herbert Hoover administration; the 1936 election was a referendum on the New Deal policies of President Franklin Roosevelt. Just as Hoover had lost overwhelmingly in 1932 so Roosevelt won overwhelmingly in 1936, collecting the electoral votes of every state except Maine and Vermont and defeating the Republican candidate in his home state of Kansas.

The Candidates

Presented with Roosevelt's widespread popularity in 1936 the Republicans felt desperate to avoid a repeat of the 1932 fiasco,

in which Roosevelt had trounced the incumbent Herbert Hoover in both the popular vote (57 percent to 40 percent) and the Electoral College (472–59). The governor of Kansas, Alfred ("Alf") Landon was one of only seven Republicans elected governor in 1932 and the only one elected to a second consecutive term in 1934. He had a reputation as a progressive, having supported Theodore Roosevelt from 1912 to 1916 and battled monopolies in his home state. Best of all, perhaps, Landon had no close ties to Hoover.

At the Republican nominating convention in Cleveland Landon entered as the clear front-runner. The convention briefly applauded Hoover, then started voting for a presidential nominee. Landon won overwhelmingly on the first ballot, 984 votes to 19. The vote for Landon's running mate, Chicago publisher Frank Knox, was unanimous. Knox had a reputation as a conservative and could point to service in the Rough Riders of Theodore Roosevelt in the Spanish-American war of 1898.

With Knox to hold onto conservative Republican supporters in the banking and business community and Landon representing more moderate Republicans, the party hoped it could overcome the advantages of the Democratic incumbent.

Roosevelt's nomination for a second term was barely contested at the Democratic convention, which opened on June 23, 1936 in Philadelphia. The Democrats also stuck with their 1932 vice presidential nominee, John Nance Garner of Texas. Roosevelt was wildly popular with the electorate in 1936: he was an optimistic upper-crust New Yorker who turned class conflict to his own advantage by linking the Republican Party to the "over-privileged." Roosevelt's attacks on wealth and privilege also attracted more traditional leftists such as American Socialists and Communists, who adopted a so-called "Popular Front" policy of supporting the Democratic candidate.

Although Roosevelt faced little opposition for the nomination he was not the choice of all Democrats. The 1928 Democratic candidate, former New York governor Al Smith, and the 1924 candidate, John W. Davis, both joined the independent Liberty League movement to raise money to combat Roosevelt's reelection.

There was a third party movement in 1936 assembled by activists operating largely outside the arena of elective politics. These leaders included Senator Huey Long of Louisiana, Catholic priest Charles Coughlin of Michigan, and Dr. Francis Townsend of California. Long (who was assassinated in 1935) had organized Share Our Wealth clubs, calling for a straightforward redistribution of income. Townsend was founder of a private pension plan called Old Age Revolving Pensions, Ltd., with almost 3.5 million members. Coughlin, who hosted a

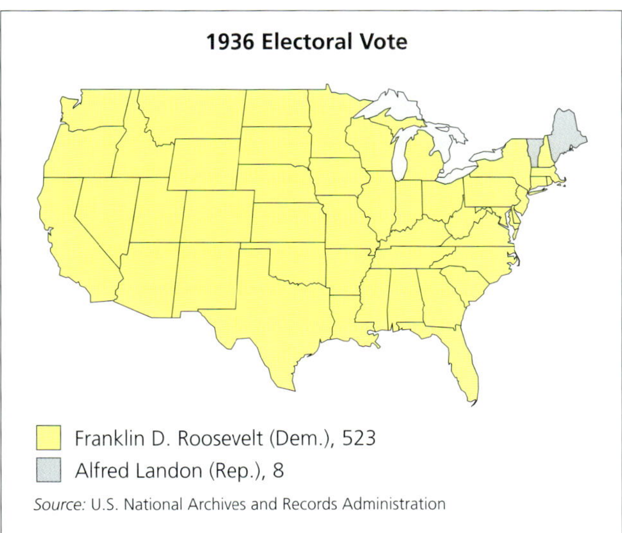

FlashFocus: Alfred "Alf" Landon

Republican Candidate for President, 1936

Born: September 9, 1887, West Middlesex, Pennsylvania
Died: October 12, 1987, Topeka, Kansas
Family: Son of John Manuel Landon, an oil prospector, and Anne Mossman; married Margaret Fleming (died), Theo Cobb

Education: University of Kansas Law School

Political career: In the 1936 election against Franklin Roosevelt, Alf Landon carried only two states, Vermont and Maine—the worst showing since the evolution of the modern two-party system to that time.

Landon followed his father into the oil prospecting business and earned a modest fortune. He enlisted in the army during World War I but fighting stopped before he was sent abroad.

Landon became active in politics during the 1912 Progressive ("Bull Moose") Party campaign of Theodore Roosevelt. In 1924 he worked for newspaper editor William Allen White's independent campaign for governor, which highlighted White's opposition to the Ku Klux Klan.

Landon was popular with most factions of the Republican party and in 1928 was elected Kansas state chairman while managing the gubernatorial campaign of Clyde Reed. In 1932 Landon was elected governor himself, the only Republican candidate for governor elected west of the Mississippi in the year Franklin D. Roosevelt inflicted a crushing defeat for Republicans nationwide.

As governor Landon adopted moderate positions, including some that were opposed by more traditional conservative Republicans, such as a moratorium on foreclosures of farms. Landon was reelected governor in 1934, the only Republican governor reelected that year.

Landon was nominated for president in 1936. He waged a dual campaign: one against Roosevelt and one against conservative Republicans bitterly opposed to the New Deal. Landon campaigned on the basis that government programs could be better administered. Landon's differences with conservative Republicans mattered little: Roosevelt was overwhelmingly reelected.

The 1936 campaign marked the end of Alf Landon's political career; he never ran for office again.

See also: Franklin Roosevelt, p. 141.

popular radio program, also advocated redistributing wealth and criticized Roosevelt for being "soft" on bankers. In June, 1936, between the Republican and Democratic conventions, Coughlin called for a new party, the Union Party, to bring together supporters of these three leaders into a new party. An independent member of Congress, William Lemke of North Dakota, declared his candidacy for the Union Party's nomination and chose a Boston lawyer, Thomas O'Brien, as his vice presidential running mate. The party did not officially endorse Lemke, but Coughlin's organization, the National Union for Social Justice, did endorse him in August. Lemke eventually polled fewer than a million votes (out of about 45 million cast) and won no electoral votes. The Union Party disappeared after the election.

The Issues

The economic depression that had started to take hold after the stock market crash of September, 1929 was the most serious downturn the United States had ever experienced. The issues of the 1936 campaign revolved around Roosevelt's proposals to deal with the crisis, collectively called the New Deal.

Role of the Federal Government. The Democratic platform omitted its standard reference in support of states' rights, a position that had been standard in Democratic platforms since the days of Thomas Jefferson and Andrew Jackson. Instead, it was the Republican platform that warned: "America is in peril"—not from the Depression and the prospect of widespread social unrest rising from massive unemployment, but from the New Deal's efforts. "The powers of Congress have been usurped by the president," the Republican platform declared. "The integrity and authority of the Supreme Court have been flouted. The rights and liberties of American citizens have been violated. . . . The New Deal Administration constantly seeks to usurp the rights reserved to the States and to the people." The Democratic platform, on the other hand, scoffed that the Republicans proposed to "meet many pressing national problems solely by action of the separate States. We know that drought, dust storms, floods, minimum wages, maximum hours, child labor, and working conditions in industry, monopolistic and unfair business practices cannot be adequately handled exclusively by 48 separate State legislatures, 48 separate State administrations, and 48 separate State courts. Transactions and activities which inevitably overflow State boundaries call for both State and Federal treatment."

It was a dramatic switch from the traditional roles of the Democrats and Republicans and helped mark one of the biggest turning points in American political history.

Government spending and taxation. The Republicans called for reducing government spending and not raising taxes as simultaneous measures to balance federal expenses and income. While promising to reduce the expenses of government the Democratic platform predicted that "as the requirements of relief [welfare] decline and national income advances, an increasing percentage of Federal expenditures can and will be met from current revenues, secured from taxes levied in accordance with ability to pay."

Foreign policy. Both Republicans and Democrats promised to avoid becoming enmeshed in the growing turmoil in both Europe and Asia during the second half of the 1930s. The Republicans promised not to join the League of Nations or the World Court; the Democrats promised to "continue to observe a true neutrality in the disputes of others."

The Campaign

Republican Landon had a difficult task. By attacking Roosevelt's New Deal too strongly he risked being linked to business interests and alienating millions of voters. On the other hand, by advocating more moderate versions of New Deal solutions to social problems, he risked appearing as a weak "me too" candidate. In the end Landon tried both tactics, with disastrous results. Early in the campaign Landon claimed to support some New Deal programs. He soon switched tactics and attacked Roosevelt, the Democrats, and the New Deal as threats to freedom. By being sharply critical and yet offering few alternatives, Landon let Roosevelt go on the offensive.

The president delivered a series of rousing speeches in the autumn of 1936 that defended his New Deal and ridiculed the Republicans. Recalling the period from 1921 to 1933, Roosevelt declared: "For twelve years this Nation was afflicted with hear-nothing, see-nothing, do-nothing government. The nation looked to government, but the government looked away. Nine mocking years with the golden calf and three long years of the scourge. Nine crazy years at the [stock] ticker and three long years in the breadlines. Nine mad years of mirage and three long years of despair. Powerful influences strive today to restore that kind of government with its doctrine that the government is best which is most indifferent." The president accused the Republicans as having been a mere tool of the wealthy and business classes during the three prior Republican administrations. These interests, he declared, "had begun to consider the government of the United States as a mere appendage of their own affairs. We know now that government by organized money is just as dangerous as government by organized mob."

The Republican Party was not the only organization combating the Democrats in 1936. A private organization called the Liberty League led by Landon's campaign manager, John Hamilton, helped organize dissident Democrats and wealthy contributors. Among Democrats participating in an anti-

Roosevelt campaign in 1936 were the Democratic Party's two previous candidates, Alfred Smith (1928) and John W. Davis (1924). The League distributed tens of millions of pieces of literature claiming that the Democratic Party gained support with a "free lunch to hoboes, relief clients, underprivileged transients and others who won't work."

The Republican campaign outspent the Democrats, $14 million to $9 million in 1936 although some Republicans efforts, like those launched by the Liberty League, may have helped the Democrats more than they helped the Republicans.

The Outcome

Roosevelt won reelection with no hint of ambiguity. In the popular vote he beat Landon by more than ten million votes: 27.7 million votes (60.8 percent) to 16.7 million (36.5 percent). Lemke of the Union party polled just 882,479 votes, less than two percent. In the electoral college, Landon won two states, Vermont and Maine, for eight electoral votes to 523 electoral votes for Roosevelt.

In the same election Democrats gained seven seats in the Senate and eleven in the House of Representatives. Democrats won 26 of the 33 elections for governors in 1936.

Sixty-one percent of eligible voters went to the polls in 1936, the highest percentage since 1916. The election helped guarantee the entrenchment of programs and policies, such as Social Security, social welfare and the rights of organized labor, that would change the political face of the United States for the rest of the twentieth century.

More Information

▶ Rosen, Elliott. *Hoover, Roosevelt and the Brains Trust: From Depression to New Deal*. New York: Columbia University Press, 1977.

▶ Roosevelt, Franklin D. (Russell Buhite & David Levy, eds.). *FDR's Fireside Chats*. Norman: University of Oklahoma Press, 1992.

On the Web

▶ "Franklin Roosevelt's Fireside Chats." The American Presidency Project, University of California at Santa Barbara. http://www.presidency.ucsb.edu/site/docs/fireside.php.

▶ "Riding the Rails" (teenage hobos in the Depression). American Experience, Public Broadcasting Service. **http://www.pbs.org/wgbh/amex/rails/.**

▶ Roosevelt, Franklin D. "Second Inaugural Address, Wednesday, January 20, 1937. *Inaugural Addresses of the Presidents of the United States*. **http://www.bartleby.com/124/pres50.html.**

▶ Wooley, John and Gerhard Peters. "The American Presidency Project." University of California, Santa Barbara. Links to presidential papers of Franklin Roosevelt and others. **http://www.presidency.ucsb.edu/site/docs/index_pppus.php.**

▶ Franklin D. Roosevelt Presidential Library and Museum. **http://www.fdrlibrary.marist.edu/online14.html.**

1940
Franklin D. Roosevelt (Democrat) vs. Wendell Willkie (Republican)

Although Franklin D. Roosevelt's election to an unprecedented third term in 1940 may appear on the surface to be just one more in a series of four, the circumstances of the election were actually extraordinary. The Republican nominee, for example, had been a Democrat until just a year before the election, and had never held political office. In some respects the two opponents were closer to one another than they were to many members of their own parties.

The Candidates

In 1940 the Republicans made one of the boldest nominating moves in U.S. political history. They chose as their presidential candidate Wendell Willkie, a man who was still a registered Democrat in September, 1939, and who had never before held any political office. He largely agreed with Franklin Roosevelt on the need to resist German Nazi aggression in Europe and he had long cheered many programs of Roosevelt's New Deal. Nevertheless, Willkie, a corporate executive working for a utilities holding company (a company that owns other companies) in New York, became the unlikely Republican nominee in 1940, to the consternation of the party's better known and more likely potential candidates.

Having been decisively crushed by Roosevelt in 1936 the Republicans had no obvious candidate in 1940. Initially Senator Arthur Vandenberg of Michigan appeared possible. He opposed U.S. involvement in the European war and he was a moderate conservative. Unfortunately he also had a dull personality. The district attorney of Manhattan, Thomas Dewey, age 37, launched a campaign for the nomination, partly on the strength of fame he gained for successfully prosecuting organized crime leaders. A third possibility was Senator Robert Taft of Ohio, son of former Republican president William H. Taft and a spokesman for the conservative wing of the Republican Party.

In early 1938 Willkie participated in a radio program on the subject of the government's relations with private industry, especially in the area of developing electric plants using hydropower in the Tennessee River valley. A member of the Republican national committee, Samuel Pryor of Connecticut, heard Willkie and thought he might make a good Republican candidate. Pryor helped arrange for Willkie to meet the editor of *Fortune* magazine, Russell Davenport, who organized a forum for potential presidential candidates in August, 1939.

In some respects, Willkie became the candidate of the media, which in 1940 meant newspapers and magazines. Publishers such as Henry Luce, of Time, and newspaper publishers John and Gardner Cowles began publicizing Willkie as a possible Republican alternative to old-line politicians. In the spring of 1940 *Fortune* published an essay by Willkie titled

"We the People," and the obscure corporate lawyer suddenly became the second-ranked Republican in the weeks before the Republican convention in Philadelphia.

At the convention no candidate had enough votes on the first ballot to gain the nomination. On the second ballot frontrunner Dewey lost votes while Willkie almost jumped into second place over Taft. Pryor, who had "discovered" Willkie on the radio, was in charge of convention arrangements, He was able to let outside people, organized for the purpose, slip into

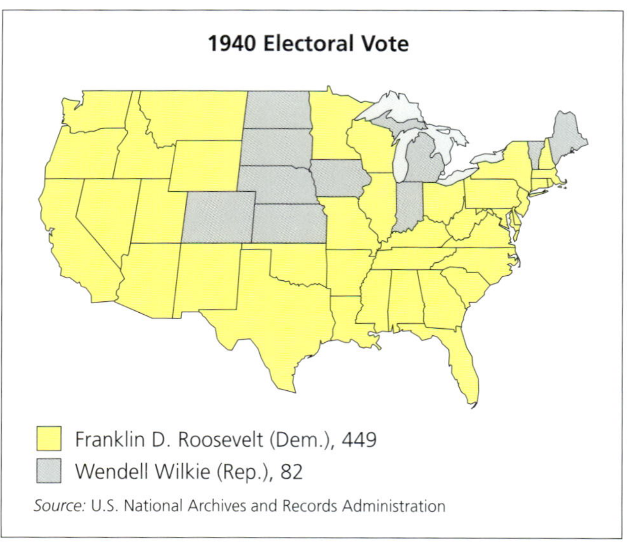

Source: U.S. National Archives and Records Administration

the hall to incite chants of "We want Willkie." On the fifth ballot the 1936 nominee, Alf Landon, released the Kansas delegates to Willkie. Michigan senator Vandenberg did the same thing on the sixth ballot, putting Willkie over the top. For vice president Willkie chose Senator Charles McNary of Oregon, another representative of the Republican Party's "progressive" wing. The stage was set for a political amateur, Willkie, to run against one of the nation's most experienced politicians: President Franklin Roosevelt.

The previously-unbroken but unofficial rule—presidents do not run for a third term—hung over the 1940 presidential election long before the two parties gathered in the summer to choose their candidates. Roosevelt, the overwhelming victor in 1932 and again in 1936, was clearly conscious of the tradition that started with George Washington but he made no public statements in the months running up to the Democratic convention. The idea of running for a third term presented a dilemma to both Roosevelt and the nation. On the one hand was the weight of tradition, reinforced by a distaste for anything that might resemble a life-long rule by a single individual. On the other hand war in Europe, which had broken out in earnest in September, 1939, clearly posed a potential threat to the United States and there was no obvious alternative to Roosevelt waiting in the wings. Roosevelt's vice president, John Nance Garner, was a bitter political foe of the president's and had launched his own campaign for the nomination on the very issue of avoiding a third term. Roosevelt did nothing to ease the suspense; he remained silent right up to the moment of the Democratic convention in July, on the question of whether or not he would seek a third term.

On the opening day of the convention, July 10, chairman Alben Barkley of Kentucky read a statement from the president to the convention stating Roosevelt's wish to retire after two terms. For a moment the delegates sat in stunned silence. Suddenly, over the loudspeakers, came a voice: "We want Roosevelt! Roosevelt! Roosevelt!" Instantly, twenty-thousand people packed into Chicago Stadium took up the chant: "We want Roosevelt! We want Roosevelt!" The next day months of uncertainty ended with the nomination of Roosevelt for an unprecedented third term. For his vice presidential nominee, Roosevelt chose Agriculture Secretary Henry Wallace of Iowa. It was not a popular choice among the convention delegates and the president's wife, Eleanor Roosevelt, was dispatched to the convention to help enforce the president's choice.

Was it just the enthusiasm of the crowd, comprising both delegates and 17,000 spectators from Chicago, that overcame Roosevelt's reluctance to run again? Or was it a complex maneuver by one of the twentieth century's most canny politicians to overcome popular uneasiness over the two term "rule?" The voice over the loudspeaker that started the chant, it was discovered days afterward, belonged to Tom Garry, the Chicago Superintendent of Sewers. He was stationed in the basement of the stadium listening to the proceedings (including Barkley's reading of Roosevelt's message) over the radio. At just the right moment he switched on his own access to the public address system and boomed the words, "We want Roosevelt!" Clearly not a coincidence, or even spontaneous, the plan was never attributed to Roosevelt. Some politicians felt certain that Roosevelt wanted a third term, partly because he saw no politician ready to take over as president in the face of the crisis in Europe, which was worsening even as the U.S. presidential election was unfolding. Certainly the "spontaneous" display of support at the convention helped the president overcome widespread uneasiness over the traditional limit of two terms.

The Issues

War. The United States was at peace in 1940 but war clouds had enveloped both Europe and Asia. Starting in September, 1939, the German Army had over-run most of Poland, then Holland, Belgium and eventually France (Austria and Czechoslovakia had already been annexed by Germany). Britain was holding out against constant German air raids directed at London. In Asia, Japan had seized Manchuria, a part of China and had begun expanding into Southeast Asia. In their 1940 platforms, both U.S. political parties emphasized two points: the need for strong defenses, and a desire to remain out of the war. The Republican platform declared that the party was "firmly opposed to involving this nation in foreign war." At the same time it endorsed "preparedness" and blamed Roosevelt for "our unpreparedness and for the consequent danger of involvement in war." At the same time the Republicans endorsed aid to "all peoples fighting for liberty," by which it meant Britain, so long as such aid did not violate international law. The Democratic platform was not very different, declaring: "We will not participate in foreign wars, and we will not send our army, naval or air forces to fight in foreign lands outside of the Americas, except in case of attack." Like the Republicans the Democrats endorsed preparation for war. "We must be so strong that no possible combination of powers would dare to attack us," the Democratic platform said.

The economy and the New Deal. In 1937 a new economic recession had wiped out much of the recovery that had occurred under the Roosevelt administration. However, by the time of the 1940 election, renewed economic growth seemed well on its way, helped in part by increased military production caused both by aid to Britain and by a buildup of U.S. forces. Nevertheless the Republicans continued to attack the idea of stimulating the economy by government spending, and attacked the New Deal as raising the threat of centralizing "all power in the president" and subjecting "every act of every citizen to regulation by his henchmen." The attack in some ways was misdirected since the last "New Deal" act had been passed two years earlier, in 1938. The Democratic platform

praised the Roosevelt administration over the previous seven years for strengthening democracy by "increasing our economic efficiency and . . . improving the welfare of the people."

Third term. Despite the antics of the Democratic convention, concern over a third presidential term played a role in the election. The Republicans explicitly attacked it in their platform. The Democrats were silent on the issue, relying on voters to be comfortable with a familiar leader in uncertain times.

The Campaign

The 1940 campaign was oddly short. Willkie, although unknown to most of the public, took a prolonged vacation for five weeks after the convention. He opened his campaign in his hometown of Elwood, Indiana on August 17 in 103-degree weather, wearing a coat and tie. Whether from inexperience or the heat Willkie's initial appearance disappointed many political professionals. Although he entered the campaign with no political experience he continued to rely on his own advisors, often ignoring or disregarding the advice of more seasoned Republicans. He initially focused his attacks on the Roosevelt administration's preference for public power projects over private utilities, an issue that failed to engage the popular imagination but did remind voters of Willkie's personal background as a utility company executive. In an era when dictatorships had taken over many governments in Europe (notably Germany, Spain, Italy and Russia), Willkie raised the threat that another term for Roosevelt could cause the United States to fall under a "totalitarian government" as well.

Willkie's campaign, often pitting political professionals against Willkie's amateurs, never succeeded in latching onto

Franklin Roosevelt is shown as the Egyptian sphinx whose smile kept his intentions under wraps. Would he run for an unprecedented third term? Roosevelt was not saying when this cartoon was published, leaving other possible candidates wondering.

an issue that caught fire. Nevertheless in the waning weeks of the campaign, Willkie's standings began to rise.

Roosevelt had largely remained out of the campaign, using as his excuse the need to attend to the unfolding crisis of war in Europe. It was also a way of reminding voters of how serious the international situation could become and perhaps of the need for an experienced president at the helm. Roosevelt made extensive use of appearances over the radio—the equivalent of television in the twenty-first century—where his smooth, familiar delivery was in marked contrast to the somewhat raspy voice of Willkie. If it could be said that Willkie was the candidate of the print media, it might also be said that Roosevelt was the candidate of the electronic media of its day.

In the last weeks of the campaign Willkie increased his attacks, accusing Roosevelt of plotting to drag the United States into war with a secret agreement to send troops to Europe. Roosevelt denied that he had any such arrangement and accused Willkie of playing politics with the security of the United States. Roosevelt assured voters that "your boys are not going to be sent into any foreign wars."

The Outcome

Roosevelt won the popular vote by just under five million votes, versus an eleven million vote margin in 1936. The total was 27.3 million (54.8 percent) for Roosevelt to 22.3 million (44.8 percent) for Willkie, a comfortable margin but much closer than four years earlier. Willkie's showing was perhaps more impressive in light of the fact that he was entirely unknown in the spring before the election and that he had an inexperienced campaign staff matched against Roosevelt's much more capable group.

In the electoral vote Roosevelt won the election with 449 votes to 82 for Willkie. The Republican won ten states: Colorado, Indiana, Iowa, Kansas, Maine, Michigan, Nebraska, North Dakota, South Dakota, and Vermont. However, Roosevelt's winning margin in several states was much thinner than his overall average. In several large states such as Wisconsin and Pennsylvania, the president's victory was within one or two percentage points. In these states, worth 189 electoral votes, a few votes the other way could have changed the outcome of the election.

More Information

▶ Neal, Steve. *Dark Horse: A Biography of Wendell Willkie."* Garden City, NY: Doubleday. 1984.

▶ Moscow, Warren. *Roosevelt and Willkie.* Englewood Cliffs, NJ: Prentice Hall. 1968.

▶ Parmet, Herbert S. *Never Again: A President Runs for a Third Term.* New York: Macmillan. 1968.

Periodicals

▶ Merry, Robert W. he Willkie Analogy and Party Politics." *Ongressioinal Quarterly Weekly Report,* April 27, 1991. p. 1094.

On the Web

▶ "Franklin Roosevelt's Fireside Chats." The American Presidency Project, University of California at Santa Barbara. **http://www.presidency.ucsb.edu/site/docs/fireside.php.**

▶ Willkie, Wendell. "The True Meaning of Liberalism." (speech, May 4, 1948.) **http://www.tpromo.com/gk/files2/wilk-lib.htm.**

▶ Roosevelt, Franklin D. "Third Inaugural Address, Monday, January 20, 1941. *Inaugural Addresses of the Presidents of the United States.* Washington, D.C.: U.S. Government Printing Office, 1989; Bartleby.com, 2001. **http://www.bartleby.com/124/pres51.html.**

▶ Wooley, John and Gerhard Peters. "The American Presidency Project." University of California, Santa Barbara, Department of Political Science. Links to presidential papers of Franklin Roosevelt and others. **http://www.presidency.ucsb.edu/site/docs/index_pppus.php.**

▶ Franklin D. Roosevelt Presidential Library and Museum. Digitized documents from the museum's collection. **http://www.fdrlibrary.marist.edu/online14.html.**

1944
Franklin D. Roosevelt (Democrat) vs. Thomas Dewey (Republican)

The outcome of the election in 1944 was never in doubt. Although the U.S. Army had successfully landed in France in June World War II was far from over. President Franklin Roosevelt had led the United States since 1933, first through the worst economic depression in the nation's history, then through its largest war. Having been elected to a third term in 1940 the issue of whether presidents should run for more than two terms was not as large an issue in 1944.

The Candidates

For the Republicans the question in 1944 was less one of who could get the nomination than one of what credible politician could be persuaded to take the nomination. Only two politicians stepped forward: the governor of New York, Thomas E. Dewey and the 1940 nominee, Wendell Willkie.

Willkie had lost badly to Roosevelt in 1940 although not as badly as Alfred Landon had lost in 1936. But he was not popular with many Republican politicians. Willkie had been a Democrat for most of his life and he did not fundamentally disagree with many of Roosevelt's positions. In his previous campaign he had put together a campaign organization that largely by-passed more experienced Republicans. Moreover, many of Willkie's political positions were at odds with most Republicans views (he had promised to appoint an African-American to the Supreme Court, for example, and was strongly internationalist in his outlook). In January, 1944, public opinion polls showed that Willkie was supported by only a quarter of Republicans. The newly elected governor of New York, on the other hand, seemed more attractive. Dewey had made a stab at the nomination in 1940, when he was just 37 years old and riding on the crest of successful prosecutions of organized crime figures in New York City. He had been elected governor of New York, then the nation's most populous state, in 1942—the first Republican in that office since 1920.

In early 1944 Willkie entered a series of Republican primary elections. He won the first, in New Hampshire, by a thin margin. But an extensive campaign in Wisconsin failed to win a single convention delegate. Dewey, on the other hand, won 17 of Wisconsin's 24 delegates. Willkie dropped out of the race clearing the way for Dewey's nomination. At the Republican convention in Chicago Dewey was nominated by another governor, Earl Warren of California (a future Supreme Court chief justice), and chose yet another governor, John Bricker of Ohio, as his vice presidential running mate.

For the Democrats there was no question who the nominee would be: Franklin Roosevelt. In 1940 when the "no third term" tradition had presented a possible obstacle to his re-

FlashFocus: 1944

Candidates

Franklin D. Roosevelt & Harry S. Truman, Democrat
Thomas E. Dewey & John W. Bricker, Republican

Issues

World War II. As a popular wartime president Roosevelt presented an immense challenge to Dewey, the Republican candidate. Dewey tried to criticize Roosevelt for not having prepared the country properly for the war. He was careful to never mention the attack on Pearl Harbor, which had taken America by surprise, and in general had to tread carefully so as not to be seen as criticizing the war effort.

After the war. With an end to the war in sight people were beginning to look forward to a return to normalcy. Foreign policy in the post-war period was also an important issue. Roosevelt, who had been president for several years, had established a good reputation among world leaders and had considerable experience in foreign affairs. Dewey, on the other hand, was practically unknown outside the United States and could not match Roosevelt in experience or knowledge. Domestically, Dewey pointed out that the end of the war would bring a sharp rise in unemployment when soldiers returned home and could not find jobs. However, Roosevelt's administration had already developed a plan to ensure this would not become a problem.

Communism. Dewey brought the issue of Communism back to the forefront of American politics, attacking the New Deal as a Communist program, and asserting that Communists were using organizations such as the Congress of Industrial Organizations, a labor organization, and the Democratic party to take over the United States.

Outcome

Popular Vote

Roosevelt	25,606,585	53.5%	✓
Dewey	22,014,745	46.0%	

Electoral College

Roosevelt	432	✓
Dewey	99	

nomination, Roosevelt had not made his intentions clear until a seemingly spontaneous demonstration at the Democratic convention demanded that he run again. In 1944, deeply enmeshed in World War II, the only question was who Roosevelt would choose as his running mate.

Whereas in 1940 Roosevelt had threatened to quit the ticket unless the convention approved his choice of Agriculture

"

FlashFocus: Thomas Edmund Dewey

Republican candidate for president, 1944, 1948

Born: March 24, 1902, Owosso, Michigan
Died: March 16, 1971, Bal Harbour, Florida
Family: Son of George M. Dewey Jr., a newspaper editor, and Annie Louise Thomas; married Frances Hutt
Education: University of Michigan; Columbia University Law School
Political career: Republican. U.S. district attorney in New York, 1933; governor of New York, 1943–55

Thomas Dewey was a "wonder boy" of Republican Party politics during the 1940s. He achieved a national reputation as a young federal prosecutor in the 1930s by prosecuting famous organized crime figures such as Salvatore "Lucky" Luciano and Lewis Lepke of "Murder, Inc."

Dewey used his fame to become the Republican candidate for governor of New York in 1938. He lost, then briefly tried for the Republican presidential nomination in 1940, which went to Wendell Willkie. Dewey served three consecutive terms as governor of New York beginning in 1943, during which he assembled an enviable record by seeming to combine financial conservatism with social liberalism. He cut taxes yet ran a budget surplus, while building highways and maintaining high levels of public assistance. Dewey once referred to himself as a "New Deal Republican;" his fiscal policies were moderate while his social policies were liberal. The "secret ingredient" that made it possible was federal aid, but Dewey took much of the credit.

Dewey won the Republican presidential nomination in 1944 but lost the election to Roosevelt. Four years later, Dewey seemed a likely victor over Harry Truman—the Chicago Tribune famously ran a headline declaring him Truman winner—but despite a divided Democratic party, Truman was elected to a full term.

In retirement Dewey advised Republican politicians, including Presidents Dwight Eisenhower and Richard Nixon. He died in 1971, in Florida.

Other biographies from 1944:
Franklin Roosevelt, p. 141.

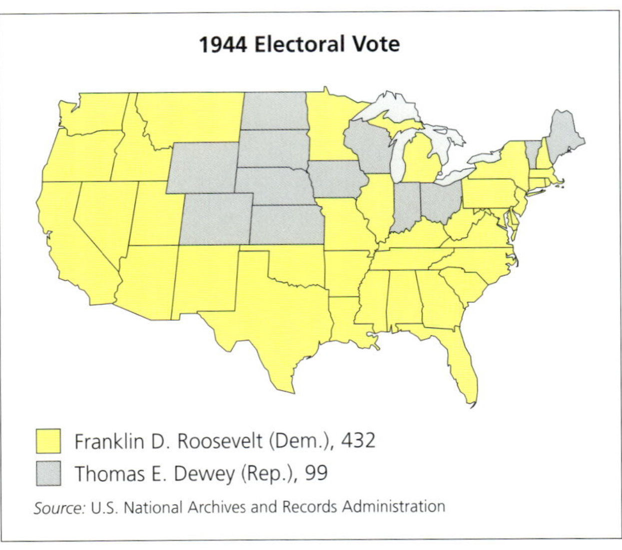

Source: U.S. National Archives and Records Administration

Secretary Henry Wallace to be vice president, four years later Roosevelt did not resist opposition to Wallace inside the Democratic party. In early July, just before the Democratic convention, Roosevelt considered possible choices for the 1944 vice presidential nominee with prominent party leaders. Although Wallace wanted the nomination and was trying to line up support, Roosevelt and the others decided opposition to Wallace in the South was not worth a political fight. Instead they chose a little-known senator from Missouri, Harry Truman, whose main advantage seemed to be that he had no

strong disadvantages. But Roosevelt did not announce his choice until the start of the convention, when party leaders sat down with Truman in a hotel room and asked him to run. In the voting, Wallace was the leader on the first ballot, followed by Truman. But on the second ballot, party leaders of big urban Democratic organizations, allied with more conservative southerners, pushed Truman over the top.

The Issues

The Republican platform in 1944 was largely reduced to the idea that "anything they can do, we can do better." Dewey largely supported existing New Deal programs but promised that a Republican administration could implement government programs more efficiently. Republicans clearly wanted to make Roosevelt's age an issue but the issue posed a dilemma: would a campaign against a popular president on the basis of his age backfire? Dewey himself never mentioned the issue in the campaign but he did go out of his way to remind voters that at age 42, he was highly energetic and athletic. In his acceptance speech (delivered at the convention, in a break with tradition) Dewey described the Roosevelt administration as a group of "stubborn men grown old and tired and quarrelsome in office."

Since Dewey had already declared that the war effort was outside of politics, and therefore not an issue, the Republicans had to search hard for areas in which to attack the Democrats.

The New Deal. Denouncing Roosevelt's programs designed to aid victims of economic depression was standard in Republican platforms after 1932, and it was no different in 1944. The Republican platform warned again that "four more years of New Deal policy would centralize all power in the president, and would daily subject every act of every citizen to regulation by his henchmen; and this country could remain a Republic only in name." The major difference in 1944 was that the Republican candidate, Dewey, in fact endorsed most New

Deal programs, such as Social Security, unemployment insurance, welfare, and the right of workers to organize into unions. Dewey's chief argument was that as president he would be more efficient in administering the programs.

The war. Although Dewey said the war itself was not an issue Republicans accused the Democrats of being unprepared for the Japanese attack against Pearl Harbor on December 7, 1941. Dewey claimed that American lives had been lost needlessly because of poor preparation. This argument did not gain traction in the campaign, as American troops continued to advance in Europe and in Asia.

Post-war international arrangements. By 1944 the outlines of an Allied victory against Germany were becoming clear. The Republican platform, which had long opposed membership in the defunct League of Nations, now endorsed "responsible participation by the United States in post-war cooperative organization among sovereign nations to prevent military aggression and to attain permanent peace with organized justice."

The Campaign

Initially Roosevelt left campaigning to others while Dewey tried to find an issue on which to attack the president. Although Dewey declined to attack Roosevelt personally, some Republican campaign workers distributed photographs of a Roosevelt looking tired and old. For his part Dewey pounded on the theme of "tired old men" who should be replaced by younger, more energetic men such as himself.

Roosevelt realized he needed to respond to the Republican attacks and in late September he delivered a scathing attack on the Republicans. The president scoffed at charges that he was a "tired old man," or that the United States had not prepared for war. Roosevelt seized on Dewey's charge that it was the Democrats, not the Republicans, who were to blame for the depression. The word depression, Roosevelt said, was the last word he would use if he were a Republican.

Republicans had also charged that after Roosevelt had visited U.S. bases in the Aleutian islands, off the southwest coast of Alaska, he had accidentally left behind his dog, named Fala, and had dispatched a Navy destroyer to retrieve his pet at great expense. It was a story that grew and grew, as one destroyer turned into a flotilla of ships, all for Fala. (Evidently there was no truth at all to the Fala story.) In his speech Roosevelt demonstrated why he had dominated the politics of the nation for the past dozen years. Declaring that Fala resented the insinuations ("he has not been the same dog since," Roosevelt declared, tongue in cheek), the president said: "These Republican leaders have not been content with attacks on me, or my wife, or on my sons. No, not content with that, they now include my little dog Fala. . . . I am accustomed to hearing malicious falsehoods about myself . . . But I think I have a right to resent, to object to, libelous statements about my dog."

Suddenly, the Republicans were running not only against Roosevelt, but against his little terrier.

The Outcome

Roosevelt won a fourth term with 25.6 million votes, or 53.5 percent, to 22 million (46 percent) for Dewey. Roosevelt's margin was the lowest in his four elections (1932: 57.4 percent; 1936: 60.8 percent; 1940: 54.8 percent), but the outcome was not in doubt.

In the electoral college vote Roosevelt had 432 electoral votes to 99 for Dewey. Dewey's electoral votes came from the Midwest (North Dakota, South Dakota, Nebraska, Kansas, Wisconsin, Iowa, Ohio, and Indiana), plus Colorado, Wyoming, Maine, and Vermont.

It was clear from the results that most Americans did not want to change leaders in the midst of war, and that they trusted Roosevelt to negotiate arrangements after the war ended. Shortly after his election to a fourth term Roosevelt traveled to Yalta, in the Soviet Union, to meet British prime minister Winston Churchill and Soviet leader Joseph Stalin, to discuss the nature and terms of peace after the defeat of Germany which by early 1945 was imminent. In April Roosevelt took a vacation to Warm Springs, Georgia. There, on April 12, 1945, he suffered a serious cerebral hemorrhage (stroke) and died within minutes.

More Information

▶ Brinkley, Alan. *Liberalism and Its Discontents*. Cambridge, Mass.: Harvard University Press. 1998.

▶ Evans, Hugh E. *The Hidden Campaign: FDR's Health and the 1944 Election*. Armonk, NY: M.E. Sharpe. 2002.

▶ Ferrell, Robert H. *Choosing Truman: The Democratic Convention of 1944*. Columbia: University of Missouri Press.

▶ Fleming, Thomas J. *The New Dealers' War: Frankling D. Roosevelt and the War Within World War II*. New York: Basic Books. 2001.

▶ Smith, Richard N. *Thomas E. Dewey and His Times*. New York: Simon and Schuster, 1982.

▶ Walker, Stanley. *Dewey, an American of This Century*. New York: McGraw-Hill, 1944.

On the Web

▶ Roosevelt, Franklin D. "Fourth Inaugural Address, Saturday, January 20, 1945. *Inaugural Addresses of the Presidents of the United States*. Washington, D.C.: U.S. Government Printing Office, 1989; Bartleby.com, 2001. **http://www.bartleby.com/124/pres52.html.**

▶ Wooley, John and Gerhard Peters. "The American Presidency Project." University of California, Santa Barbara, Department of Political Science. Links to presidential papers of Franklin Roosevelt and others. **http://www.presidency.ucsb.edu/site/docs/index_pppus.php.**

▶ Franklin D. Roosevelt Presidential Library and Museum. Digitized documents from the museum's collection. **http://www.fdrlibrary.marist.edu/online14.html.**

1948
Harry S Truman (Democrat) vs. Thomas Dewey (Republican)

Republicans could practically taste victory in 1948 after four consecutive losses to Franklin Roosevelt. The former President had died in April, 1945, leaving his little-known successor, former Missouri Senator Harry S Truman, to cope with a host of domestic and foreign problems stemming from World War II. Moreover, two traditional pillars of Democratic political strength seemed to be crumbling. The South threatened to split off into the newly formed States' Rights Party ("Dixiecrats" as they were called in the press) and liberals were tempted by the Progressive Party of former Vice President Henry Wallace. So certain did Republican victory seem that *Time* and *Life* magazines prepared special issues marking the victory of Republican Thomas Dewey, and even on the night of the election, an early edition of the *Chicago Daily Tribune* splashed a headline across the front page: "Dewey Defeats Truman."

The *Tribune* headline is famous because the next day, news photographers captured Truman holding up a copy of the paper for all to see. Truman was grinning broadly, as well he might: he had just defeated Dewey and won a full term in his own right. How he managed to do so is a story of political shrewdness by Truman, and political awkwardness by the Republicans.

The Context

Truman had been in office for three-and-a-half years at the time of the 1948 election. He had overseen the final Allied victories over Germany and in Japan (having authorized the dropping of two nuclear bombs on Japan), as well as dealing with dramatic challenges at home and abroad. The Soviet (Russian) Army remained in eastern Europe where they supported newly installed Communist governments. Communist parties in unoccupied countries, including Turkey, Greece, Italy and even France, seemed on the verge of power. Truman had begun implementing the Marshall Plan, large-scale American economic assistance in parts of Europe not occupied by Russian troops, as a means of countering Communist political influence. Truman had dispatched U.S. warships to the eastern Mediterranean to discourage the Soviet Union from occupying northern Iran. These strong measures were part of the Truman Doctrine, which the president described as a policy "to support free people who are resisting attempted subjugation by armed minorities or outside pressure," a reference to the Soviet Union. Although the United States and Russia had been allies in the fight against Nazi Germany, even before fighting ended a new struggle was already evident, and Truman adopted a policy of "containment," intended to limit the geographical areas where the Soviets were the dominating influence. After the worldwide trauma of World War II, a new conflict had begun almost seamlessly: the Cold War, a decades-long period of international tensions between the United States and the Soviet Union in which each side sought to gain influence without resorting to outright warfare.

In the United States the sudden end of fighting in World War II and the return of scores of thousands of soldiers threatened severe disruptions, including housing shortages and an economic downturn caused by the cessation of massive war production. Also, African Americans were inclined to be more vocal in their demands for their civil rights. The diplomatic concerns of the Cold War were beginning to echo in domestic

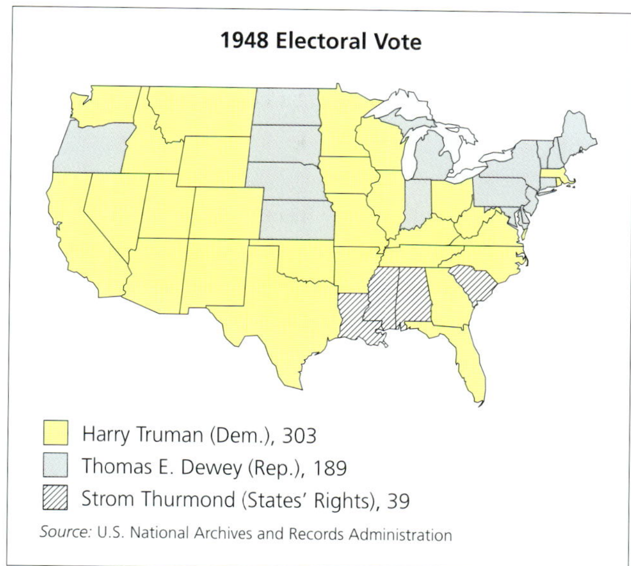

politics, where the loyalty of American members of the Communist Party was questioned, and suspicions were raised about possible undercover influence by people who belonged to the Communist Party or who sympathized with its goals.

The Candidates

The Republican Party had gained control of the Congress in the elections of 1946, which helped give rise to expectations that victory in the presidential election was close at hand. However, the party was not unified. On one side was the conservative senator from Ohio, Robert Taft, son of former President William Howard Taft. He and other Republican conservatives were intent on rolling back the New Deal where possible by reducing spending on welfare and curbing the rights of labor unions. Taft also opposed U.S. involvement in international organizations, such as the United Nations. Taft entered the Republican convention in June, 1948 aiming for the presidential nomination.

Opposed to Taft was New York Governor Thomas Dewey, the Republican nominee in 1944 and a representative of a more moderate wing of the party. Unlike the cold and dour Taft, Dewey was energetic even while maintaining a formal, dignified appearance at all times. Dewey supported many New Deal programs but thought the Republicans could do a better job administering them. In New York State Dewey had achieved an enviable record of success dealing with the economic tensions of converting from a wartime economy to a peacetime one.

In the first political convention in which television coverage reached a significant number of people, the Republicans took three ballots to nominate Dewey over Taft and a third challenger, former Governor Harold Stassen of Minnesota. The convention selected the governor of California, Earl Warren, as Dewey's vice presidential running mate.

The Democrats faced a seemingly more difficult situation when their convention opened. The former vice president,

See also: Thomas Dewey, p. 152.

Henry Wallace, bolted from the Democrats and accepted the nomination of a newly organized Progressive Party. Wallace, with the support of many American Communists, insisted that the United States and Soviet Union could cooperate in world affairs. The Progressives also focused on expanding the civil rights of African Americans, which Wallace felt had been ignored too long by the Democratic Party, still dependent on white Southerners for its electoral majorities. Wallace was often pelted with rotten vegetables when he spoke to racially integrated audiences in the South the attacks did little for his support in the South, but they did a great deal to build up support among liberal Democrats in the North.

Partly in response to Wallace's challenge, some Democrats favored inserting a plank in the 1948 platform endorsing civil rights for African Americans. It was an explosive issue for white Southern Democrats, who insisted that civil rights was an issue left to the individual states. In one of the Democratic convention's most dramatic moments, the Mayor of Minneapolis, Herbert Humphrey, called on the party to "walk forthrightly into the bright sunshine of human rights" by endorsing a strong civil rights plank. In response, delegates from Mississippi and Alabama stalked out of the convention. Dissident southern Democrats met a few days later in Birmingham, Alabama and formed the States' Rights Democratic Party, often called the "Dixiecrats." They nominated the governor of South Carolina, J. Strom Thurmond, for president and Mississippi's Governor Fielding Right for vice president. It appeared that the Dixiecrats would pose a grave challenge to Truman and the rest of the Democratic Party, since Democrats had long depended on the electoral votes of the former Confederate states to win the White House.

Truman's own nomination was not seriously challenged in the remaining parts of the Democratic party, and he chose Senator Alben Barkley of Kentucky as his running mate.

The Issues

Civil Rights. The withdrawal of conservative southern Democrats opposed to civil rights in fact made it possible for the Democratic Party in 1948 to adopt a platform that endorsed "the right of full and equal political participation . . . , the right to equal opportunity of employment . . . , the right of security of person . . . , and the right of equal treatment in the service and defense of our nation" to African Americans. The Republican platform also endorsed civil rights, and included a plank condemning "lynching or any other form of mob violence anywhere (as) a disgrace to any civilized state," as well as abolishing the "poll tax" (a fee for voting, which effectively barred many poor voters from casting ballots). Wallace's Progressive Party took the strongest stand, urging a presidential proclamation to end official racial segregation and all forms of discrimination in the federal government, including the army. Off by themselves on the issue, Thurmond's Dixiecrats declared: "We stand for the segregation of the races and the racial integrity of each race: the constitutional right to choose one's associates . . . and to earn one's living in any lawful way. We favor home rule, local self-government, and a minimum interference with individual rights."

Communism and the Cold War. The Republicans took a much stronger view of the threat that domestic Communists posed than did the Democrats. The Republican platform promised "a vigorous enforcement of existing laws against Communists, and enactment of such new legislation as may be necessary to expose the treasonable activities of Communists and defeat their objective of establishing here a godless dictatorship . . ." The Democrats promised to enforce laws against "subversive activity" while also observing constitutional guarantees of free speech, free press and "honest political activity." The Progressive Party viewed the issue from the opposite end of the spectrum, demanding "negotiation and discussion with the Soviet Union to find areas of agreement to win the peace."

Republicans also endorsed participation by the United States in the newly organized United Nations, despite the isolationist sentiments of the party's conservative wing. The Democrats and Progressives also endorsed using the United Nations as a means to achieve international peace, and questioned the Republican commitment to the organization by reminding voters that the Republican congress had refused Truman's request to grant the United Nations a loan.

The economy. The rights of labor unions were an issue in the election following passage of the Taft-Hartley Act of 1946, over Truman's veto, which severely limited the rights of unions to strike, especially in areas that might impact the larger economy, such as railroads. The act had been a strong reaction to post–World War II unrest among labor, but was widely disliked by union members. The Republicans touted a list of accomplishments by the Congress elected in 1946 in "safeguarding the entire community against those breakdowns in essential industries which endanger the health and livelihood of all" and promised "continuing study to improve labor-management legislation." Democrats vowed to repeal the Taft-Hartley Act and to raise the minimum wage to 75 cents an hour, up from 40 cents.

The Campaign

For the Democrats the key to the 1948 election was to maintain the party's support among labor unions and urban workers in the North, rural conservatives in the South and, increasingly, African Americans, while at the same time limiting the support of dissidents on the left (the Progressive Party) and the right (the Dixiecrats). Truman followed this approach by making separate appeals to the different blocs of voters. For urban workers this meant supporting, or even expanding, the New Deal. For farmers in the Midwest it meant emphasizing Democratic support for federal programs to buy crops so prices did not fall below the cost of production. For unionized workers it meant emphasizing Truman's veto of the Taft-Hartley Act, which restricted the right to vote. For minority voters it meant underscoring Democratic support for civil rights measures.

To underscore the differences between Democrats and Republicans, Truman called the Congress back into session for two weeks for the purpose of acting on legislative proposals that the Republican platform had supported in public. As Truman sensed, the Republican platform positions were considerably more moderate than those held by conservative Republicans in the Senate and House of Representative. The Congress, still controlled by Republicans, met and adjourned without passing any legislation, giving Truman a chance to denounce the "do-nothing Congress," and embarrass the Republican presidential candidate.

Although Dewey had appeared to be facing a seriously splintered Democratic Party, his own party was also divided between a conservative wing, led by Taft, and a more moderate wing represented by both Dewey and Warren. The short special session of the Congress underscored Dewey's problem in convincing voters that he offered a moderate alternative to Truman, rather than a move to turn back the clock to the days before the New Deal.

As a campaigner Dewey left much to be desired. Although he was a young man and vigorous, his personality gave the impression of arrogance and stiffness. One writer compared him to the "little man on a wedding cake."

The Outcome

On election day many Americans woke thinking that Dewey would be elected president. Most leading public opinion polls predicted such an outcome. Two of the nation's largest-circulation magazines, *Life* and *Time* had prepared special election editions focusing on Dewey.

Voter turnout was low but when the votes were counted, Truman had won, 24,179,345 votes (49.6 percent) to Dewey's 21,991,291 (45.1 percent). Thurmond of the States' Rights Party and Wallace of the Progressives each got about the same number of votes, roughly 1.2 million, or 2.4 percent, each.

In the Electoral College Truman easily won the election with 303 votes to Dewey's 189. The Electoral result was slightly misleading, however. Truman won California's bloc of twenty-five electoral votes by less than 18,000, out of over three million cast; he won Illinois's twenty-eight electoral votes by a margin of under 34,000 (out of nearly four million); he won Ohio's twenty-five electoral votes by just 7,107 votes out of nearly 2.9 million. Truman also managed to keep most of the "solid South" in his column, although the Dixiecrats carried 39 electoral votes from four states: Alabama, Louisiana, Mississippi, South Carolina, plus one electoral vote from Tennessee.

More Information

- Culver, John C. *American Dreamer: The Life and Times of Henry A. Wallace.* New York: Norton, 2000.
- Donaldson, Gary. *Truman Defeats Dewey.* Lexington: University Press of Kentucky, 1999.
- Ferrell, Robert H. *Choosing Truman: The Democratic Convention of 1944.* Columbia: University of Missouri Press, 1994.
- Frederickson, Kari A. *The Dixiecrat Revolt and the End of the Solid South, 1932–1968.* Chapel Hill: University of North Carolina Press, 2001.
- Gullan, Harold. *The Upset That Wasn't: Harry S. Truman and the Crucial Election of 1948.* Chicago: Ivan R. Dee, 1998.
- Karabell, Zachary. *The Last Campaign: How Harry Truman Won the 1948 Election.* New York: Knopf, 2000.
- Offner, Arnold A. *Another Such Victory: President Truman and the Cold War, 1945–1953.* Stanford, CA: Stanford University Press, 2002.
- Savage, Sean J. *Truman and the Democratic Party.* Lexington: University Press of Kentucky, 1997.
- White, Graham J. *Henry A. Wallace: His Search for a New World Order.* Chapel Hill: University of North Carolina Press, 1995.

On the Web

- Truman, Harry S. "Inaugural Address, Thursday, January 20, 1949." *Inaugural Addresses of the Presidents of the United States.* Washington, D.C.: U.S. Government Printing Office, 1989; Bartleby.com, 2001. **http://www.bartleby.com/124/pres53.html.**
- Wooley, John and Gerhard Peters. "The American Presidency Project." University of California, Santa Barbara, Department of Political Science. Links to presidential papers of Harry Truman and others. **http://www.presidency.ucsb.edu/site/docs/index_pppus.php.**
- "1948 Truman-Dewey Election." Eagleton Institute of Politics, Rutgers University. **http://www.eagleton.rutgers.edu/e-gov/e-politicalarchive-1948election.htm.**

1952

Dwight Eisenhower (Republican) vs. Adlai Stevenson (Democrat)

After losing five consecutive presidential elections, the Republican Party in 1952 was determined to take advantage of Democratic President Harry Truman's low approval rating in opinion polls in order to regain the White House. Accordingly, they borrowed a page from the Whig Party's textbook in 1840 and 1848 (see pp. 48, 56) and nominated a popular military leader without any well-known political positions that might hurt him with voters. That man was Dwight Eisenhower, who had led U.S. and British forces to victory in World War II and had been asked by Truman to head the North Atlantic Treaty Organization (NATO) forces standing watch against possible Soviet military aggression in Europe.

The election marked the introduction of television advertising techniques into the political process. The Republicans hired a leading New York advertising firm to promote Eisenhower's candidacy under the slogan, "I Like Ike."

The Context

The United States was at war in 1952, fighting to drive back North Korean Communist forces and maintain the division of the Korean peninsula between the Communist North and the non-Communist South. President Harry Truman had fired the U.S. commander, General Douglas MacArthur, for failure to follow a presidential directive and halt an offensive that brought Chinese troops into the conflict. How the war should be pursued was a major foreign policy issue in the election.

After Truman's razor-thin victory in 1948 Republicans felt strongly they could win in 1952, in part because it had been nearly a quarter century since the last Republican presidential victory (in 1928) and in part because Truman's public approval ratings were around 25 percent. In addition to the war in Korea, a series of spy scandals during the Truman administration involving espionage for the Soviet Union had created popular concerns that a Communist conspiracy was at work in the federal government.

There was a national weariness with conflict. Four years of war (1941–45) had been followed by a period of high inflation and labor strife as the country absorbed returning soldiers and made the transition from war-time production to a peacetime economy. Voters were unenthusiastic about involvement in Korea and concern over the Cold War with the Soviet Union was rising.

The Candidates

Ohio's Republican Senator Robert Taft, grandson of former President William Howard Taft (see p. 118), was a leader of conservative Republicans. He and his allies wanted to reverse the Democratic New Deal legislation of Franklin Roosevelt in favor of a much smaller government. Taft also took a dim view of American involvement in international disputes. In 1952 Taft campaigned vigorously for the Republican presidential nomination.

Opposing the conservatives was a more moderate group, primarily from the East, associated with the party's two previous candidates, Thomas Dewey of New York (1948 and 1944) and Wendell Willkie (1940). The Republican moderates accepted an American role in international affairs, and were willing to maintain many New Deal domestic programs. In 1952, sensing the vulnerability of the Democrats, they were intent on identifying a candidate who could be elected without paying undue attention to ideology.

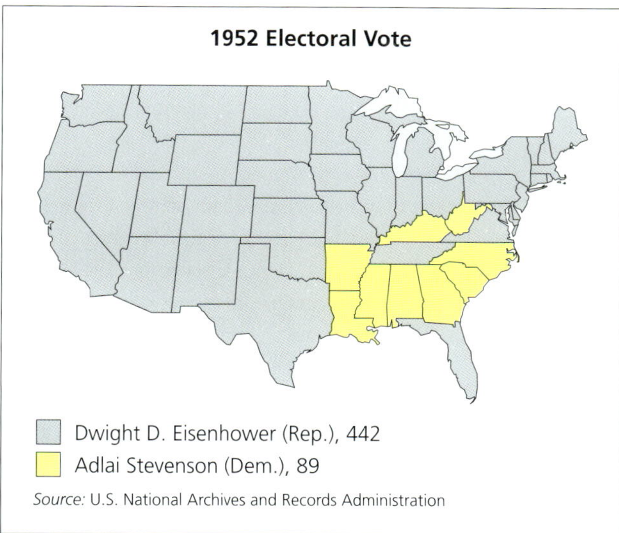

Source: U.S. National Archives and Records Administration

Dwight Eisenhower had been the commander of Allied forces in Europe during the final assault on German occupation of Europe, directing the D-Day invasion of Normandy on June 6, 1944 and the 10-month push to Berlin. He had also been named by President Truman as military commander of the North Atlantic Treaty Organization (NATO), an alliance of anti-Communist governments in Western Europe. Eisenhower had spent his entire career in the military and was not associated with either party. Both parties courted him as a possible candidate, but in October, 1951, Eisenhower agreed to seek the Republican nomination.

The Republican battle for the nomination lasted from January 1952 until the convention in early July. Eisenhower won the primary election in New Hampshire and several other states while Taft showed strength in his native Midwest. Neither man held a majority of votes at the start of the convention, which opened with a heated fight over seating rival groups of delegates, devoted to Eisenhower or Taft, from Texas, Louisiana, and Georgia. Eisenhower won the fight to seat his delegates from Georgia and Texas, giving him 595 votes on the first ballot to Taft's 500. Minnesota then switched its votes to Eisenhower, giving him the nomination. For vice president Eisenhower chose Senator Richard Nixon of California.

On the Democratic side President Truman had already served almost two entire terms. His popularity ratings were around 26 percent in the spring of 1952, with little prospect of improvement. With Truman crippled by low public opinion ratings, Senator Estes Kefauver of Kentucky beat Truman in the early New Hampshire primary, resulting in Truman's announcement that he would not run for reelection. Another possible candidate, Senator Richard Russell of Georgia, was closely associated with conservative Southern interests, especially on the divisive issue of civil rights. A third candidate was the governor of Illinois, Adlai Stevenson, whose grandfather was Grover Cleveland's vice president from 1893–97 (see p. 102). Stevenson established a reputation by attacking corruption in state gov-

34th President, 1953–1961

Born: October 14, 1890, Denison, Texas
Died: March 28, 1969, Washington, D.C.
Education: U.S. Military Academy, West Point, N.Y.
Family: Son of David Eisenhower, a store clerk, and Ida Stover; married Mamie Doud
Political career: Republican. Eisenhower served in the military his entire career until the end of World War II. He was the Supreme Commander of Allied Expeditionary Forces in Europe during World War II and directed the D-Day assault on Normandy. This, and the ensuing battles that forced Germany's surrender, made him an indisputable hero.

After the war, President Harry Truman appointed him Chief of Staff of the U.S. Army. In 1948 he retired from active duty to become president of Columbia University, but in 1948 Truman asked him to become Supreme Commander of the North Atlantic Treaty Organization (NATO).

Eisenhower had never divulged his political leanings and both Democrats and Republicans courted him to run for the presidency. In 1952 he ran for president as a Republican and won based on his war hero popularity and his promise to end the Korean War.

During his two terms Eisenhower supported most of the Fair Deal social welfare initiatives implemented during the Truman years. He approved expansion of the Social Security System and supported development of Interstate Highways. In 1954 when the Supreme Court ruled compulsory segregation in public schools was unconstitutional, he sent federal troops to Little Rock, Arkansas to assure safety to the black students entering the high school there for the first time. He then ordered desegregation of the U.S. Armed Forces.

Cold War issues dominated foreign relations during Eisenhower's administration.

After leaving office he regretted that he could not claim success in the area of global disarmament.

He died on March 28, 1969.

ernment and had a highly credible record of service in the federal government during the Roosevelt administration. In January, 1952, Truman offered to support Stevenson, who was reluctant to run.

The Democratic convention opened in Chicago on July 21. Stevenson, as host Governor, gave a well-received welcoming speech, and decided to try for the nomination. On the first two ballots, Kefauver, Stevenson, and Russell vied for the lead, but after several Midwestern favorite-son candidates switched their support to Stevenson the deadlock was broken and the Illinois governor was nominated. In an effort to placate the South and recapture the region's crucial electoral votes Stevenson chose as his running mate Senator John Sparkman of Alabama, who had been a defender of the New Deal and international involvement even as he defended racial segregation.

FlashFocus: Adlai Ewing Stevenson II

Democratic Candidate for President, 1952, 1956

Born: February 5, 1900, Los Angeles, California
Died: July 14, 1965, London, England
Family: Grandson of Grover Cleveland's second vice president, Adlai E. Stevenson; son of Lewis G. Stevenson, a prominent democrat; married Ellen Borden (divorced), Phyllis Holden (divorced)
Education: Choate Academy, Princeton University, Northwestern University Law School.
Political career: Stevenson began government work in 1932 as special attorney at the Agricultural Adjustment Administration, a New Deal agency established by President Franklin Roosevelt. From 1939 Stevenson was chairman of the Chicago Committee to Defend America, campaigning against U.S. isolation and in favor of aiding Britain. Stevenson later became principal attorney for the secretary of the Navy and worked for the State Department from 1945. He led the U.S. delegation at the conference that founded the United Nations. Stevenson's first bid for office was in 1948 when was elected governor of Illinois. There he doubled spending for public education, reformed the state police, and vetoed a state "anti-subversive" squad designed to root out Communists.

In 1952 President Harry Truman backed Stevenson for the Democratic presidential nomination. Stevenson reluctantly agreed and was nominated to run against Republican General Dwight Eisenhower. He lost the election but began working almost immediately on his run for the 1956 nomination.

Stevenson's 1956 campaign platform included banning nuclear weapons tests and greater efforts to combat poverty. Stevenson was an urbane, witty, sophisticated spokesman for traditional Democratic liberalism but voters were attracted to Eisenhower's aura of safety and security. Eisenhower actually increased his popular margin compared to 1952.

Stevenson was named chief U.S. chief delegate to the United Nations. In the high point of his career Stevenson presented evidence in October, 1962, that the Soviet Union had installed missiles in Cuba.

Stevenson died of a heart attack on July 14, 1965.

The Issues

Korean War. The United States was at war in 1952 on the Korean peninsula, where troops from the Communist government in the north had pushed southwards in June, 1950. Prodded by the U.S., the United Nations sent forces, essentially meaning the U.S. Army, to repel the invaders. Under the command of General Douglas MacArthur, American troops had pushed the North Koreans back close to the Chinese border by November, 1950, at which point Chinese troops entered the battle. After initial successes against the U.S., the Chinese were repelled and U.S. forces were poised to continue their counter-

offensive. In April, 1951, Truman relieved MacArthur of his command for failure to obey Truman's order to halt his northward advance. For the next year there was a military stalemate while the North Koreans and United Nations conducted sporadic, inconclusive armistice talks.

In the presidential election the Korean War was melded with the larger issue of Communist domination of Eastern Europe, where the Soviet Army had installed Communist governments at the end of World War II. The Republican platform deplored Truman's handling of foreign policy in both Europe and Asia. In Korea the Republicans accused Truman of plunging the country into war "without the consent of our citizens" and of carrying on the war "without will to victory." In Europe the Republicans accused Franklin Roosevelt and Truman of making "tragic blunders" in trading "our overwhelming victory [against Germany] for a new enemy and for new oppressions" (the Soviet Union).

Eisenhower was initially reluctant to get involved in the controversy over conduct of the war, but in October he promised that if elected, he would go to Korea and seek to end the conflict—an effective reminder to voters of Eisenhower's role in World War II.

Communism and the Cold War. In 1949 it had been discovered that the Soviet Union had acquired nuclear weapons, and accusations were raised that American spies were responsible. A former State Department official, Alger Hiss, was accused of being a spy for the Soviet Union. He denied the charges, which led to his conviction in 1950 for perjury before a grand jury investigating Communist influence over the government. In March, 1951, Julius and Ethel Rosenberg were convicted of conspiracy to commit espionage for the Soviet Union. These two cases led to charges by Republicans that the Democratic administration had let Communists gain influence in the government. Wisconsin Republican Senator Joseph McCarthy particularly engaged in a dramatic smear campaign without producing concrete evidence.

Civil rights. The Republican Party endorsed a platform that declared "it is the primary responsibility of each State to order and control its own domestic institutions," which the party said was key to preserving the federal system. The party encouraged appointment of qualified people without regard to race, religion or national origin to government positions, and supported federal "action" to eliminate lynching and poll taxes (a fee to vote), and ending segregation in Washington, D.C. The Democrats, conscious of the States' Rights Party revolt in 1948, adopted virtually the same civil rights platform as in the earlier election. It called for federal laws to guarantee equal participation in voting for federal offices, as well as equal rights in employment and "security of persons," a reference to lynching (the murder of African Americans by mobs, usually at night and usually by hanging).

The Campaign

The Republican Party hired a New York City advertising agency, Batten, Barton, Durstine, and Osborne, to outline a campaign plan. It was the first time that sales techniques used for merchandise were applied not only to persuading voters but also to planning the strategy. The plan focused on using television as a key ingredient, and in presenting the Republican candidate as a pleasant grandfather with great experience. "I Like Ike" was the slogan, guaranteed to offend no one.

Eisenhower himself preferred a slightly different theme, referring to his campaign as a "great Crusade" for change after twenty years of Democratic presidents. He ran less as a representative of a set of policies and more as a trustworthy, admired manager. Eisenhower opposed government expansion but promised not to try to "turn back the clock" by eliminating now-familiar New Deal programs such as Social Security and unemployment insurance. "Rights, not issues," he said of programs that many voters took for granted.

Eisenhower's strongest attacks were on Democratic foreign policies, which he said had enabled Communists to gain control of significant parts of Eastern Europe and China. He advocated "liberating" countries from Communist rule, but without saying how, or when, or where.

While Eisenhower presented the calm face of a friendly grandfather his running mate, Nixon, took on the task of launching nasty attacks. He referred to the "dry rot of corruption and Communism" in American politics under Democratic administrations, without ever specifying who might be a Communist. In an attack on Truman's Secretary of State Dean Acheson, Nixon said Stevenson held a "Ph.D. degree from the Acheson's college of cowardly Communist containment."

The most dramatic moment in the campaign came in September, with the discovery of a cash fund made available for Nixon's use by wealthy Republican donors. Was it bribery? Nixon made a sober television presentation explaining that the fund was used only for legitimate purposes relating to his political activities and had not enriched him personally. Nixon offered documentation and audits for proof and laid out his family's modest financial state in detail, pointing out that his wife, Pat, did not own a fur coat, but wore a "respectable, Republican cloth coat." At the end of the speech, Nixon confessed to taking and keeping one gift from a supporter—a cocker spaniel puppy named Checkers. He vowed not to resign from the ticket, and the speech ended rumors that Nixon might be dropped from the ticket well into the campaign.

Stevenson strongly supported the policies of the Truman administration and claimed Democratic credit for the economic prosperity. The Stevenson campaign tried to distance itself from the unpopular incumbent president through measures such as establishing its headquarters in Illinois, far from Washington. Stevenson was a serious speaker who had a dry wit, but also had the reputation of being an overly-intellectual "egghead."

Television played a major role in the campaign. Eisenhower took coaching lessons from an actor and came across well on sets that at that time were black-and-white and relatively small. Stevenson proved to be less adept at using television, sometimes letting speeches run beyond the allocated time and finding himself cut off before he had finished.

The Outcome

Eisenhower scored a convincing victory, winning the popular vote with 33.9 million votes (55.1 percent) to Stevenson's 27.3 million votes (44.4 percent). In the electoral college Eisenhower won 442 votes to Stevenson's 89.

The Democrats carried only nine states: Alabama, Arkansas, Georgia, Kentucky, Louisiana, Mississippi, North Carolina, South Carolina, and West Virginia. Stevenson lost Kentucky by only 700 votes and Tennessee by less than 2,500.

In an election in which voter turnout was 63 percent, the Republicans also regained narrow control of the Senate and House of Representatives.

Many observers agreed that the focus of the election in 1952 was on the personality of Dwight Eisenhower, who was well known and well liked and not tied firmly to any particular political philosophy or program. For such a candidate a strong television campaign linked to the slogan "I Like Ike" proved highly successful.

More Information

▶ Broadwater, Jeff. *Adlai Stevenson and American Politics: The Odyssey of a Cold War Liberal.* New York: Twayne, 1994.

▶ Davis, Kenneth S. *The Politics of Honor: A Biography of Adlai E. Stevenson.* New York: Putnam, 1967.

▶ West, Darrell. *Air Wars: Television Advertising in Election Campaigns, 1952–1996.* Washington: Congressional Quarterly Books, 1997.

▶ Wicker, Tom. *Dwight D. Eisenhower.* New York: Times Books, 2002.

On the Web

▶ "1952: Eisenhower vs. Stevenson." *The Living Room Candidate: A History of Presidential Campaign Commercials. 1952–2000.* American Museum of the Moving Image. **http://www.ammi.org/livingroomcandidate/.**

▶ Eisenhower, Dwight D. "First Inaugural Address, Tuesday, January 20, 1953." Inaugural Addresses of the Presidents of the United States. Washington, D.C.: U.S. Government Printing Office, 1989; Bartleby.com, 2001. **http://www.bartleby.com/124/pres54.html.**

▶ Wooley, John and Gerhard Peters. "The American Presidency Project." University of California, Santa Barbara. Links to presidential papers of Dwight Eisenhower and others. **http://www.presidency.ucsb.edu/site/docs/index_pppus.php.**

1956

Dwight Eisenhower (Republican) vs. Adlai Stevenson (Democrat)

FlashFocus: 1956

Candidates

Dwight D. Eisenhower & Richard M. Nixon, Republican
Adlai Stevenson & Estes Kefauver, Democrat

Issues

Eisenhower's health. Eisenhower had suffered from various health problems during his first term and Democrats questioned his fitness for a second term. Eisenhower assured the country that he was healthy enough to seek reelection.

The new middle class. Eisenhower campaigned on the country's prosperity during his first term. With this prosperity came the emergence of a new middle class, which was to become an important voting bloc.

Nuclear weapons testing. Democratic candidate Adlai Stevenson called for a complete ban on nuclear weapons testing. Eisenhower, while arguing that the issue was too complex to be brought up during the campaign, did point out that a ban was impractical given the Cold War political climate.

International crises. When Eisenhower chose not to help Egypt finance a dam on the Nile River, the Egyptian leader Gamal Abdel Nasser seized and nationalized the dam. Britain and France, ignoring the United States's warning against taking military action, planned an attack on Egypt. Stevenson pointed to the incident as an example of inconsistent foreign policy on the part of Eisenhower. When riots in Hungary threatened to develop into a revolution, Eisenhower again decided not to intervene. His actions on these two issues increased the confidence of the American public in his competence in foreign affairs.

Outcome

Popular Vote

Eisenhower	35,590,472	57.6% ✓
Stevenson	26,022,752	42.1%

Electoral College

Eisenhower	457 ✓	
Stevenson	73	

The 1956 presidential election was essentially a replay of the election of 1952: the calming, confidence-inspiring figure of Dwight Eisenhower running a largely non-ideological campaign against Adlai Stevenson, the former governor of Illinois. It was an election virtually devoid of excitement or serious debates, and Eisenhower easily won by an even larger margin than in 1952.

The Context

The Eisenhower administration had brought the American people the "normalcy" promised thirty years earlier by Warren Harding in the 1920 race. A truce had been negotiated in the Korean war and the economy was growing rapidly; many working people had attained a comfortable middle class existence. Domestic tensions over possible influence of secret Communists in the government had largely dissipated with the Senate's censure of Senator Joseph McCarthy in 1954. McCarthy had been responsible for widely publicized hearings on allegations of Communist influence in the U.S. Army (as in other aspects of American life)—allegations that were never accompanied by any evidence and depended on unsubstantiated rumor and innuendo.

While Cold War tensions between the United States and the Soviet Union continued, Eisenhower had largely defused the two possible causes of conflict, both of which came near the election. At the end of July, 1956, Egypt nationalized (seized control of for its own government) the Suez Canal linking the Mediterranean with the Red Sea, a major short-cut for ocean shipping between Europe and Asia. In the autumn Britain and France, which had controlled the canal, attacked Egypt in an effort to take back control of the canal and overthrow Egypt's leader, Gamal Abdel Nasser. President Eisenhower, conscious of Egypt's close relations with the Soviet Union, acted to defuse the crisis by persuading Britain and France to stop their attacks and accept the change in ownership of the canal.

At about the same time anti-Russian riots broke out in Budapest, capital of Communist-controlled Hungary. The riots represented a challenge not only to the Communist government but also to Soviet influence over Hungary—and potentially, other East European countries. Eisenhower voiced support for the cause of Hungarians and offered asylum for Hungarian "freedom fighters," as they were called, who managed to escape. Eisenhower did not act to challenge Soviet domination of Hungary out of fear that such an action could spark a nuclear conflict with the Russians.

A renewed struggle by African Americans for equal rights was taking hold by 1956. Two years earlier the Supreme Court had ruled that segregated public schools violated the constitutional guarantee of equal treatment under law. A successful black boycott of buses in Montgomery, Alabama had begun in December, 1955, and brought into prominence a local clergyman, Rev. Martin Luther King, Jr.

The Candidates

Eisenhower was a hero of World War II, where he served as the military commander of Allied forces in their victorious assault against Nazi Germany. In 1952 he had run as "Ike," a kindly, grandfather figure who promised to negotiate a truce in the battle against Communist North Koreans and to institute a reliable administration for a country tired of war and economic conflict.

In 1956 the only question mark hanging over Eisenhower's reelection was his health. He had suffered a heart attack during his first term and had taken four months to recover. Early that year he had required surgery for an attack of ileitis, an inflammation of the digestive tract. Newspapers were filled with articles speculating about the health of a president who was then 66 years old. After Eisenhower's own doctors issued statements that he was perfectly healthy and fit to serve another four years, any questions about who the Republican nominee would be in 1956 vanished; the nomination was Eisenhower's.

There were some questions about whether Eisenhower's vice president, Richard Nixon, would be on the ticket a second time. A perennial candidate for the Republican presidential nomination, former Minnesota Governor Harold Stassen, tried to derail Nixon's renomination by promoting the candidacy of Massachusetts Governor Christian Herter. But neither Herter nor Eisenhower would entertain Stassen's challenge and Stassen ended up nominating Nixon for a second term. In his memoirs Nixon recounted a meeting with Eisenhower in late 1955, in which the president urged him to consider not running for vice president again, but rather to accept a cabinet post in a second Eisenhower administration in order to gain more varied experience. Nixon was uncertain whether Eisenhower was trying to discourage a second vice presidential effort but when Nixon sought to run again, Eisenhower never objected.

For Democrats the 1956 nominee was not so clear. In December, 1955, Adlai Stevenson, the former governor of Illinois and Democratic nominee in 1952, announced that he would be a candidate for the nomination in 1956. Although Stevenson had endeared himself to many Democrats, others, notably former President Harry Truman, were unimpressed with Stevenson's campaign style. Senator Estes Kefauver of Tennessee, who had tried unsuccessfully for the 1952 nomination, also indicated interest in the nomination in 1956. Other Democratic contenders included New York's Governor Averell Harriman and Senator Stuart Symington of Missouri.

Kefauver won the New Hampshire primary election by a wide margin over Stevenson (who did not campaign actively and was a write-in candidate, and followed up with wins in the Minnesota primary, where Stevenson did campaign, as well as in Wisconsin. Despite these early setbacks Stevenson was able to round up delegate votes at the convention with the help of powerful local leaders, such as the chairman of the

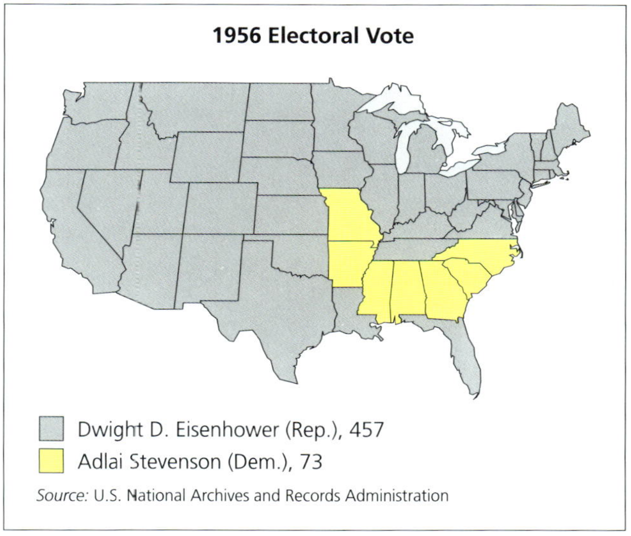

Source: U.S. National Archives and Records Administration

See also: Dwight Eisenhower, p. 159; Adlai Stevenson, p. 160.

Democratic party in Chicago. Stevenson also enjoyed support among southern Democrats, who rejected Kefauver for his failure to fight against civil rights laws in the Senate and his refusal to sign a "Southern Manifesto," a document signed by most southern Democrats attacking the 1954 Supreme Court decision, *Brown v. Board of Education,* which declared racial segregation of public schools to be unconstitutional.

As the convention approached Stevenson campaigned energetically in California and Florida, gaining primary victories that brought him close to clinching the nomination. Harriman's bid for the nomination failed to attract support beyond his own state of New York despite the endorsement of former President Truman. When the Democratic convention opened Stevenson had the endorsement of Eleanor Roosevelt, widow of the former president, to counter any influence Truman may have had and was able to obtain the nomination on the first ballot.

Stevenson decided to let the convention choose a vice presidential running mate rather than picking one himself. This opened an intense contest among Kefauver, Massachusetts Senator John F. Kennedy, (thought to be Stevenson's choice), Senator Hubert Humphrey of Minnesota and Senator Albert Gore, Sr. of Tennessee. After Kennedy came within thirty-nine votes of capturing the nomination on the first ballot, Kefauver was chosen on the second ballot.

The Issues

The 1956 election did not present a set of compelling issues. Stevenson tried to generate concern over some issues, but with little success. In an era of prosperity and peace, the country settled back in a largely self-satisfied mood.

The Suez crisis. During the campaign, Eisenhower was presented with a potential crisis when Britain and France, joined by Israel, tried to reverse the seizure of the Suez Canal by the government of Egypt. Although all three countries were close allies of the United States, Eisenhower was concerned that the action could bring the Soviet Union, an ally of Egypt, into the conflict. Eisenhower put strong pressure on Britain in particular to back away from the conflict, which defused the crisis, leaving Egypt in possession of the canal.

Hungarian revolt. Almost simultaneously with the Suez crisis rioting in Hungary challenged the Communist-led government there. Again Eisenhower adopted a "hands off" policy, while offering political asylum to any Hungarian "freedom fighters" who managed to escape the country. While sympathetic to the anti-Communist rioters, Eisenhower strongly signaled that the United State was not willing to risk war with the Soviet Union. In effect the American policy in Hungary in 1956 locked into place Russian domination of Eastern Europe that lasted another three decades.

Eisenhower's health. While not a political issue in the conventional sense, the health of Eisenhower was a concern throughout the campaign. He had suffered a serious heart attack in his first term and had undergone surgery for ileitis, an inflammation of part of the digestive track, just a few months before the election. Declarations by his physicians that Eisenhower's health would not jeopardize his completing a second term largely put the issue to rest, although the Democratic campaign tried to hint at the issue by referring to Eisenhower as a "part-time president."

Nuclear testing. Stevenson urged that the United States and the Soviet Union should agree to suspend testing of nuclear weapons. Eisenhower declared that the topic was "far too complex and dangerous" to be discussed in a presidential campaign and refused to talk about it further. The issue failed to take hold with the public.

Civil rights. The African American struggle for equal rights had taken a new turn. Encouraged by the 1954 Supreme Court decision declaring that segregated public schools violated the Constitution, African Americans were expanding their struggle to other areas. In Montgomery, Alabama, black citizens started boycotting the city's segregated bus system in December, 1955, led by a young clergyman named Martin Luther King, Jr. Both parties had paid lip service to civil rights in their platforms but neither Eisenhower nor Stevenson was prepared to campaign on the issue in 1956.

The Campaign

For Eisenhower the 1956 election was a referendum on his first term in office, and he was unwilling to campaign vigorously. The president took the attitude that if voters did not appreciate his efforts, he was prepared to retire to his farm near Gettysburg, Pennsylvania. His campaign was leisurely at best, with days separating campaign speeches. The twin crises of Suez and Hungary worked to the president's advantage, allowing him to demonstrate the importance of having an experienced leader at the helm.

Stevenson ran an energetic campaign, delivering 300 speeches and traveling widely. But the Democratic candidate had not fully mastered the art of using television in the campaign. Even when Democrats paid for broadcast time to broadcast his speeches, Stevenson's delivery tended to run either too long or too short. Toward the end of the campaign, Stevenson tried to capitalize on the health issue by warning that a vote for Eisenhower was a vote for Nixon, but this issue failed to make an impact.

The Outcome

Eisenhower increased his margin of victory in the popular vote, winning 35.6 million votes (57.6 percent) to Stevenson's 26 million (42.1 percent). In the electoral vote Eisenhower won 457 votes to 73 for Stevenson. Eisenhower won all but seven states—Alabama, Arkansas, Georgia, Mississippi, Missouri, North Carolina and South Carolina.

Without doubt it was a resounding triumph for Eisenhower. The election was less resounding for the Republican Party, however, since Democrats won majorities in both the Senate and House of Representatives.

More Information

▶ Allen, Craig. *Eisenhower and the Mass Media: Peace, Prosperity, and Prime-Time TV*. Chapel Hill: University of North Carolina Press, 1993.

▶ Beschloss, Michael R. *Mayday: Eisenhowre, Khruschev and the U-2 Affair*. New York: Harper and Row, 1986.

▶ Bowie, Robert R. *Waging Peace: How Eisenhower Shaped an Enduring Cold War Strategy*. New York: Oxford University Press, 1998.

▶ Davis, Kennety S. *The Politics of Honor: a Biography of Adlai E. Stevenson*. New York: Putnam, 1967.

▶ Divine, Robert A. *The Sputnik Challenge*. New York: Oxford University Press, 1993.

▶ Martin, John B. *Adlai Stevenson and the World: The Life of Adlai E. Stevenson*. Garden City, NY: Doubleday, 1977.

▶ McKeever, Porter. *Adlai Stevenson: His Life and Legacy*. New York: Morrow, 1989.

▶ Pach, Chester J. *The Presidency of Dwight D. Eisenhower*. Lawrence: University Press of Kansas, 1991.

On the Web

▶ "1956: Eisenhower vs. Stevenson." *The Living Room Candidate: A History of Presidential Campaign Commercials. 1952–2000*. American Museum of the Moving Image. **http://www.ammi.org/livingroomcandidate/.**

1960
John F. Kennedy (Democrat) vs. Richard Nixon (Republican)

The 1960 election marked the start of the modern era in presidential elections in two ways: Presidential primaries for the first time played a decisive role in determining the nominee of the Democratic party, and television played a deciding role in the outcome of the election. It was the first presidential contest in which the two contenders debated face-to-face. The debates were broadcast to millions of homes on television, and after the first debate the Democrat, Senator John F. Kennedy of Massachusetts, surged ahead of his opponent, Republican Vice President Richard Nixon. Although there were many other factors in the election, there seemed little question that Kennedy made a better impression on voters over television.

The Context

For eight years Republican President Dwight Eisenhower had presided over the nation as a kind of confidence-inspiring grandfather. After Eisenhower negotiated a truce in the Korean war, the country experienced eight years of peace and prosperity, with the exception of an economic recession in 1957. Prosperity had enabled many working class families to join the middle class, and the Eisenhower years saw no dramatic efforts to repeal Democratic social welfare programs initiated during the presidency of Franklin Roosevelt under the New Deal. The fact that the Democrats controlled both the Senate and House of Representatives for Eisenhower's last term helped ensure that these initiatives remained unchallenged, despite the inclinations of the more conservative Republicans. In many respects, the period of Eisenhower's presidency, 1953–61, took on the characteristics of the president himself: conventional, cautious, safe, and dependable.

During Eisenhower's second term America's complacency was challenged. In May 1957 the Soviet Union shocked the world by launching a satellite into orbit around the earth. The technical achievement was viewed in the United States as part of the Cold War competition between Communism and capitalism. It raised the question of whether the United States was falling behind the Soviet Union. Much closer to the election, in May 1960, the Russians shot down a high-altitude U-2 spy plane and captured its pilot. The incident served as a reminder of how dangerous the Cold War could become.

The Candidates

The Republican Vice President, Richard Nixon, was virtually assured of the presidential nomination after his eight years' apprenticeship as vice president. Only one Republican of note, Governor Nelson Rockefeller of New York, considered challenging Nixon. In the spring of 1960 a movement to "draft"

FlashFocus: 1960

Candidates

John F. Kennedy & Lyndon B. Johnson, Democrat
Richard M. Nixon & Henry Cabot Lodge, Republican

Issues

Religion. Democratic candidate John F. Kennedy was a Catholic, which worried many Americans who questioned whether he would maintain separation between church and state. Kennedy pledged that he would indeed honor and maintain the principle of separation, and that he would adhere to the Constitution over any religious authority. Still, a segment of the public refused to be reassured on this point, and the Democratic campaign had to adjust to the fact that many American voters refused to even consider voting for their candidate because of his religious affiliation.

The Cold War. During the campaign, an American U-2 spy plane was shot down while flying over the Soviet Union. The incident emphasized, for candidates and voters alike, how critically important foreign affairs experience could be. Nixon could claim the advantage here, based on his service as vice president to Eisenhower. Kennedy, recognizing the public's preoccupation with the Cold War, countered with a declaration that he would close the "missile gap" that supposedly existed between the United States and the Soviet Union.

Outcome

Popular Vote

Kennedy	**34,226,731**	**49.7% ✓**
Nixon	34,108,157	49.5%

Electoral College

Kennedy	**303 ✓**
Nixon	219

Rockefeller was launched without the New Yorker's involvement. Nixon was not worried that Rockefeller would deprive him of the presidential nomination, but he wanted to avoid a political fight at the convention over the Republican platform. Consequently Nixon requested a secret meeting with Rockefeller in New York City to discuss the issue. Afterwards Rockefeller issued a statement titled the "Fourteen Point Compact of Fifth Avenue," which made it clear that Nixon had agreed to virtually every one of Rockefeller's demands on issues ranging from civil rights to federal involvement in providing health services and education. Although many Republicans were upset with Nixon, his nomination went off without a hitch. After Rockefeller declined Nixon's invitation to be his vice presidential running mate, Nixon chose Henry Cabot Lodge

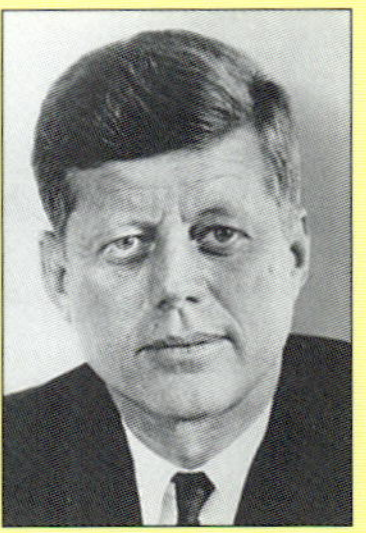

FlashFocus: John Fitzgerald Kennedy

35th President, 1961–1963
Born: May 29, 1917, Brookline, Massachusetts
Died: November 22, 1963, Dallas, Texas
Family: Son of Joseph P. Kennedy, businessman, financier, and ambassador to Britain, and Rose Fitzpatrick; married Jacqueline Bouvier
Education: Choate School; Harvard University
Political career: John F. Kennedy became president at age 43, the youngest man ever to win the office. With a glamorous wife and charming young children, Kennedy symbolized a new generation coming to power.

Kennedy grew up in a large, wealthy family. After Harvard, he served in the Navy on a PT boat in World War II, heroically ensuring the survival and eventual rescue of his crew after their vessel was rammed by a Japanese ship.

Kennedy was elected to the House of Representatives from a Boston district in 1948 and 1950. In 1952, Massachusetts sent him to the U.S. Senate.

Kennedy won the 1960 nomination on the first ballot and chose Senate Majority Leader Lyndon Johnson as his running mate. In the general election, Kennedy edged his Republican opponent, Richard Nixon, by the thinnest of margins, winning the closest election since 1888.

His term was marked by foreign affairs crises such as a failed invasion of Cuba by anti-Communist exiles, a Soviet threat to isolate West Berlin, and a confrontation with the Soviet Union over Russian missiles installed in Cuba.

John F. Kennedy was shot and killed in Dallas, Texas while riding in a motorcade on November 22, 1963. The man arrested for the murder was Lee Harvey Oswald, an ex-Marine who had renounced his U.S. citizenship and had lived for a time in the Soviet Union. Vice President Lyndon Johnson was sworn into office on Air Force One as it flew Kennedy's body back to Washington.

In the decades after the assassination, the Kennedy image took on almost mythical proportions. It was an image carried forward throughout the 1960s and beyond by the 'Baby Boomers," the generation of people born in the decade after World War II.

See also: Richard Nixon, p. 174.

of Massachusetts, also from the party's liberal Northeast wing.

The 1960 Democratic nominating convention held more excitement. The leading contender was Senator John F. Kennedy of Massachusetts, who had been considered for the vice presidential nomination in 1956. Kennedy's strategy was to achieve success in presidential primaries, as a means of demonstrating his appeal to the electorate. His principal rival in this strategy was Senator Hubert Humphrey of Minnesota, who as Mayor of Minneapolis in 1948 had helped push through the strong civil rights platform that led in turn to the formation of the segregationist States' Rights Party (Dixiecrats). Two other senators were also interested in the nomination: Lyndon Johnson of Texas, the majority leader, and Stuart Symington of Missouri. In the background, Adlai Stevenson, the former Illinois governor who was the party's nominee in 1952 and 1956, was known to be interested in a third nomination, but unwilling to openly contest for it.

Kennedy and Humphrey first met head-to-head in the Wisconsin primary in April, 1960. Kennedy came from a large, wealthy family, and he used both his family's wealth and his numerous relatives to help him campaign. Humphrey hoped that people in his neighboring state would give him a boost and help him obtain campaign contributions. Kennedy won the Wisconsin primary decisively with 56 percent of the vote.

The two met next in the West Virginia primary. Since 95 percent of the West Virginia voters were Protestants, the outcome there would serve as a test of whether Kennedy's Catholic religion would be a barrier to his election as president. Kennedy delivered a long television address in which he promised to observe a strict separation of church and state, not to let his religion affect his public policies, and to oppose government funding of religious schools. His approach worked; he won the West Virginia primary with 61 percent of the vote to 39 percent for Humphrey. As a result, Humphrey dropped out of the contest.

Kennedy entered the Democratic convention in July with a majority of the delegates, fearful only that the U-2 spy plane incident could cause some of his delegates to bolt and vote for an older, more experienced candidate. His fears were unfounded; Kennedy won the nomination on the first ballot, with Johnson coming in second. Kennedy then enlisted the Texan to run on the ticket as vice president, hoping to hold on to the "solid South" that had started to show cracks in 1956. In his acceptance speech, Kennedy told delegates that the United States was "on the verge of a new frontier," one that was "not a set of promises—it is a set of challenges."

The Issues

Religion. Kennedy was the first Roman Catholic to run as the candidate of a major party since Al Smith ran, and lost, as the Democratic nominee in 1928. Especially in the Midwest, some Protestant preachers voiced concerns that the Catholic Church could exert undue influence over a Catholic president. Kennedy's West Virginia primary experience helped to ease such concerns, and he repeated the same strategy in the general election. Kennedy repeated his promise to uphold the Constitution over any claims by his religion and repeated his dedication to the separation of church and state. The Republicans never raised the issue of religion, but it was one that hung over the campaign until the end.

Foreign affairs and the "missile gap." Nixon considered foreign relations to be his strong point, and he emphasized his experience during both his acceptance speech at the Republican convention and during the campaign. Nixon had gained notice when he debated the Soviet prime minister, Nikita Khrushchev, during a trade fair in Moscow. Underlying Nixon's emphasis on foreign affairs was the implication that Kennedy lacked experience in this area, and that the nation needed a more experienced man in charge in light of the dangers posed by the Cold War. For his part Kennedy pounced on what he said was a "missile gap" with the Soviet Union, accusing the Eisenhower-Nixon administration of letting the Russians get ahead of the United States in production of nuclear missiles, a charge later found to be false.

Civil Rights. Equal rights for African Americans had gained a permanent place on the Democratic list of key issues. Southern Democrats fought against including a strong civil rights statement in the Democratic platform, but were defeated. The Democrats endorsed the Supreme Court's school desegregation decision *(Brown v. Board of Education)* and said the U.S. attorney general should be empowered to enforce equal rights for African Americans not later than 1962, the centenary of the Emancipation Proclamation. The Republican platform also supported equal rights, but opposed "the pretense of fixing a target date three years from now" for implementing desegregation plans.

The Campaign

Television played a critical role in the 1960 election, as did an accident with a car door. In August Nixon accidentally hit his knee on a car door. A minor incident became important after Nixon developed an infection and had to spend two weeks in the hospital. The Republican candidate had vowed to visit all fifty states, a promise made all the more difficult to fulfill by losing two weeks.

Consequently when Kennedy and Nixon met in the first head-to-head debate, broadcast on television, Nixon looked relatively haggard and exhausted, especially compared to the youthful and handsome Kennedy. The four Nixon-Kennedy debates were unique and attracted widespread attention. The first debate, on September 26, 1960, proved to be the most important one. It was not the substance of what was said as much as the physical appearance of the candidates that seemed ultimately to affect voters.

People who listened to the debate on the radio tended to think that Nixon came out ahead, but television viewers came to the opposite conclusion, and Kennedy's ratings in the polls surged past Nixon's in the days following the first debate. Observers have long debated the impact of that first debate. Whereas Kennedy seemed comfortable, Nixon struck many viewers as nervous and uneasy. The hot lights of the studio made Nixon perspire, and in the glare, it appeared that he was not clean-shaven.

The Outcome

The election of 1960 was one of the closest of any to that date. In the popular vote, Kennedy beat Nixon by a mere 118,574 votes out of more than 68 million votes cast, a margin of 49.7

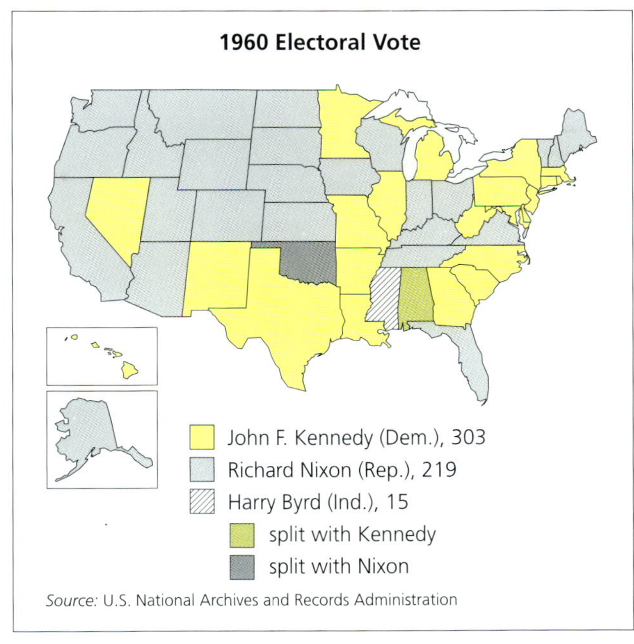

Source: U.S. National Archives and Records Administration

percent to 49.5 percent. The closeness was particularly important in key states, notably Illinois, where the Republicans alleged irregularities in the outcome. Many Republicans were convinced that the Democratic organization in Chicago had arranged for people to vote multiple times, or cast votes under the names of dead people. Nixon, however, declined to challenge the outcome. Kennedy's winning margin in Illinois was just 8,858 votes, out of more than 4.7 million cast. In Hawaii, the margin was just 115 votes for Kennedy, out of about 185,000 cast. The election was so close that Nixon did not concede defeat for eight days.

Kennedy was elected with 303 electoral votes to 219 for Nixon.

Senator Harry Byrd of Virginia also received fifteen electoral votes, eight from Mississippi, six from Alabama and one from Oklahoma. In the case of the Mississippi and Alabama electoral votes, they were cast for Byrd as a Democrat; Strom Thurmond of South Carolina received the same number of votes for vice president—both were an echo of the 1948 Dixiecrat revolt against civil rights. (One Nixon elector from Oklahoma also cast a vote for Byrd, but as a Republican.)

More Information

▶ Fuchs, Lawrence H. *John F. Kennedy and American Catholicism.* New ork: Meredith Press, 1967.

▶ Goldman, Martin S. *John F. Kennedy: Portrait of a President.* New York: Facts on File, 1995.

▶ Jamieson, Kathleen H. and David S. Birdsell. *Presidential Debates: The Challenge of Creating an Informed Electorate.* New York: Oxford University Press, 1988.

▶ Matthews, Christopher. *Kennedy and Nixon: The Rivalry That Shaped Postwar America.* New York: Simon and Schuster, 1997.

▶ Nixon Richard M. *RN: The Memoirs of Richard Nixon*. New York: Simon and Schuster, 1990.

▶ Perret, Geoffrey. *Jack: A Life Like No Other*. New York: Random House, 2001.

▶ Rorabaugh, W. J. *Kennedy and the Promise of the Sixties*. New York: Cambridge University Press, 2002.

▶ White, Theodore H. *The Making of the President, 1960*. New York: Atheneum Publishers, 1961.

Periodicals

▶ Schaffer, Michael. "Behind Nixon's Decision to Concede." *U.S. News and World Report,* November 20, 2000, p. 35.

▶ Matthews, Christopher. "Dark Mirror: The Kennedy-Nixon Friendship," *Vanity Fair,* February 1996, p. 114.

▶ Morrow, Lance. "Of Myth and Memory; Dreaming of 1960 in the New World." *Time,* October 24, 1988, p. 21.

▶ "The Making of the Presidents: 1969-1988." *Life,* September 1988, p. 50.

▶ Ambrose, Stephen (interview). "The Best and Worst of Presidents." *U.S. News and World Report,* May 4, 1987, p. 67.

On the Web

▶ "1960: Kennedy vs. Nixon." *The Living Room Candidate: A History of Presidential Campaign Commercials. 1952–2000.* American Museum of the Moving Image. **http://www. ammi.org/livingroomcandidate/.**

▶ Kennedy, John F. "Inaugural Address, Friday, January 20, 1961." Inaugural Addresses of the Presidents of the United States. Washington, D.C.: U.S. Government Printing Office, 1989; Bartleby.com, 2001. **http://www.bartleby.com/124/ pres56.html.**

▶ Wooley, John and Gerhard Peters. "The American Presidency Project." University of California, Santa Barbara, Department of Political Science. Links to presidential papers of John F. Kennedy and others. **http://www.presidency.ucsb.edu/site/ docs/index_pppus.php.**

▶ "U.S. Presidential Election of 1960." Questia (online library). Links to digitized published sources; some require paid subscription. **http://www.questia.com/Index.jsp?k=presidential_ election_1960.**

1964

Lyndon Johnson (Democrat) vs. Barry Goldwater (Republican)

The ultra-conservative wing of the Republican Party suffered a devastating defeat at the hands of the Democratic incumbent, Lyndon Johnson, in 1964. Republican senator Barry Goldwater successfully dominated the party's nominating process and became the nominee, but he seemed to lose his bearings in the general election campaign and went down to ignominious defeat. Even so, he did pave the way for later conservatives, such as Ronald Reagan.

The Context

On November 22, 1963, an assassin killed President John F. Kennedy in Dallas, Texas. Vice President Lyndon Johnson became president in the wake of a national trauma, slightly under one year from the next presidential election. As the Democratic majority leader in the Senate, Johnson had a more conservative record than did Kennedy, but after the assassination he vowed to promote Kennedy's domestic goals, and in the process became a more liberal Democrat. Nevertheless, in his personal manner Johnson could not hope to match the youthful vigor and glamour of Kennedy.

The African American civil rights movement was in full swing in 1964. Throughout the South African Americans had adopted the non-violent tactics of India's independence leader, Mahatma Gandhi, to press their campaign for equal rights. Sit-ins and marches were often met with violence by white police forces in the South, which helped bring the status of African Americans to the front page of newspapers throughout the country. The Kennedy administration had sent federal troops to enforce Supreme Court decisions that required public institutions, particularly schools and universities, to abandon racial segregation. On July 2, Johnson signed the Civil Rights Act of 1964, regarded as the most sweeping legislation in a century. The bill guaranteed African Americans equal access to all places of public accommodation, such as hotels and restaurants. Johnson did not just sign the act; he used his knowledge of the Senate and his considerable political influence as president to overcome southern resistance to its passage.

In Vietnam, Johnson was presented with a dilemma. Communist guerrillas, the Vietcong, supported by North Vietnam, were making progress in their fight against the non-Communist government in Saigon despite the presence of U.S. military "advisors." On August 5, 1964, Johnson asked Congress for a resolution supporting an increased U.S. combat role after North Vietnamese torpedo boats attacked a U.S. Navy destroyer in the Gulf of Tonkin. This resolution, and the steady erosion of the position of the anti-Communist government in Saigon, set the stage for a U.S. combat role in the war,

FlashFocus: 1964

Candidates

Lyndon B. Johnson & Hubert H. Humphrey, Democrat
Barry M. Goldwater & William E. Miller, Republican

Issues

Vietnam. The conflict in Southeast Asia presented a challenge to both parties during the campaign, especially within the context of the Cold War with the Soviet Union. Republicans criticized the Democrats for not taking a strong enough stand against Communism, and accused them of losing the region to Communist forces. However, they did not want to alienate moderates by appearing too extreme in their pursuit of the war. Democrats wanted to reassure voters of their toughness against Communism, but at the same time wanted to seem measured in their responses to the perceived threat.

Civil rights. Johnson and Goldwater had agreed not to discuss civil rights during the campaign, because both were afraid of alienating particular groups of voters; Johnson feared losing support among white southerners by pursuing black voters, and Goldwater wanted to avoid accusations of racism that might result if he pursued white Southerners too eagerly. However, their positions on the issue were well established: Johnson had passed the Civil Rights Act, which Goldwater had voted against on supposedly Constitutional grounds. Although civil rights were not discussed, the candidates' respective records on racial issues were an important part of the campaign.

Outcome

Popular Vote

Johnson	43,129,566	61.1% ✓
Goldwater	27,178,188	38.5%

Electoral College

Johnson	486 ✓
Goldwater	52

and pushed the issue into the presidential election. The long-simmering debate over the Cold War, and whether the United States was "winning" or "losing" to Communism around the world, became focused on Vietnam.

The Candidates

The narrow defeat of Richard Nixon in the presidential election of 1960, followed by another defeat in a bid to become governor of California in 1962, had the effect of leaving the Republican Party without an obvious candidate for the election in 1964. Ultra-conservative Republicans, who had backed

FlashFocus: Lyndon Baines Johnson

36th President, 1963–1969

Born: August 27, 1908, Stonewall, Texas
Died: January 22, 1973, San Antonio, Texas
Family: Son of Sam Johnson, a businessman and state legislator, and Rebekah Baines; married Claudia (Lady Bird) Taylor.
Education: Southwest State Teachers College.
Political career: Democrat. U.S. representative from Texas, 1937–49; U.S. senator from Texas, 1949–61; vice president, 1961–63

Johnson was elected the House of Representatives in 1937, during the New Deal era of President Franklin Roosevelt, and to the Senate in 1948. He was the Senate majority leader from 1955–60 and by all accounts was a brilliant arm-twister, universally credited with having great powers of persuasion. In 1960 the Democratic presidential nominee, Senator John F. Kennedy, chose Johnson for his running mate.

After Kennedy's assassination, Johnson was sworn into office and began his successful push for passage of the Civil Rights Act of 1964, giving African Americans free access to public accommodations. He established the Office of Economic Opportunity as the key building block of his War on Poverty. He was elected president in 1964 by the biggest margin of any candidate—61.1 percent against Republican Barry Goldwater's 38.5 percent.

Johnson asked Congress to pass the Gulf of Tonkin Resolution in 1964, authorizing retaliation for North Vietnam's alleged torpedo attacks on a Navy destroyer off the coast of Vietnam. In 1965 U.S. combat troops entered the war between Vietnamese Communists and the anti-Communist government in Saigon. By 1968 the controversy over U.S. participation in the Vietnam war overshadowed the Johnson Administration's achievements. With his every public appearance marked by anti-war protests, Johnson declined to seek the nomination for president in 1968.

In November, 1968 Johnson halted bombing of North Vietnam in a bid to negotiate a peace agreement, but the move failed.

Johnson left office after Richard Nixon's narrow victory over Vice President Hubert Humphrey. Johnson died on January 22, 1973.

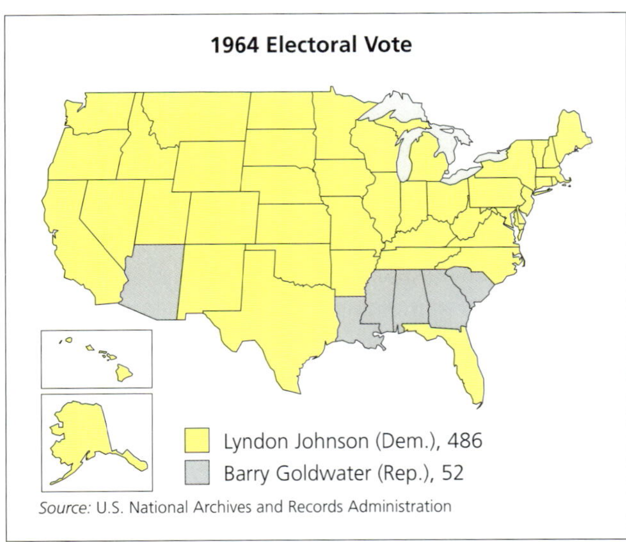

Source: U.S. National Archives and Records Administration

Ohio senator Robert Taft against Dwight Eisenhower for the nomination in 1952, saw a new opportunity to steer the party onto a more conservative path. To do so they needed a viable candidate, which they believed they found in Barry Goldwater, a senator from Arizona.

Goldwater had been running his family's department store in Phoenix when he entered politics. In 1952 he was elected to the Senate. Like many conservatives, he thought the federal government had become too powerful in domestic affairs and too weak in combating Communist influence, especially in underdeveloped countries like Vietnam. Although Goldwater had a personal history of supporting civil rights for African Americans (his store was the first in Phoenix to hire African Americans as sales clerks), he voted against the 1964 Civil Rights Act on grounds that the law went beyond Constitutional limits on federal power.

For many months a group of conservatives had been building an organization inside the Republican party to steer the nomination towards Goldwater, who was reluctant to run for president for fear he lacked financial and political support from the populous Northeast. Nevertheless, in January 1964 Goldwater set aside his concerns and announced he would run for the nomination. He surrounded himself with a group of long-time supporters who lacked experience in national campaigns.

Moderate Republicans were concerned that Goldwater could never be elected, and coalesced around New York Governor Nelson Rockefeller, heir to the Standard Oil fortune and a liberal Republican. Two other Republican governors, George Romney of Michigan and William Scranton of Pennsylvania, also entered the race for the nomination, but their campaigns fizzled before the Republican convention in San Francisco. At the convention, conservative Goldwater supporters booed Rockefeller so loudly that he was unable to deliver his speech on the party's platform, and shortly afterwards Goldwater became the nominee. He selected a virtually unknown conservative Congressman from upstate New York, William Miller, as his running mate.

The Democratic nomination was never in doubt: it was Johnson's if he wanted it. Even so, Johnson waged a vigorous campaign to ensure support, fearful that President Kennedy's younger brother, Attorney General Robert Kennedy, might try to win nomination as his brother's natural heir. Before the convention, Johnson and Kennedy met and agreed that Kennedy would not seek the nomination. For his vice presidential running mate Johnson decided on Senator Hubert Humphrey of Minnesota, a well-known liberal Democrat and strong supporter of civil rights. (It was Humphrey who had helped push through a civil rights plank in the 1948 platform, resulting in the decision by Southern "Dixiecrats" to run their own candidate.) Humphrey brought another advantage to the ticket: his nomination was designed to help assuage the anger by civil rights activists after an all-black delegation from Mississippi (the Mississippi Freedom Democratic Party) was refused seats at the convention. The seats went instead to the all-white regular Democratic delegation.

The Issues

Race and civil rights. For a century, the Democratic Party had been two parties disguised as one. In the states of the former Confederacy, the Democrats were the party of whites who opposed Republican efforts to "reconstruct" southern society by giving rights to former slaves freed after the Civil War. In the North, the Democrats were, after 1932, the party of Franklin Roosevelt's New Deal, representing the working class against business interests. The election of 1964 was the last time these two "parties within a party" were able to overcome the growing tensions between them and unite behind a single candidate. Nevertheless, Johnson's strong support for the Civil Rights Act of 1964 was a major wedge between the two factions. An indication of the future was a campaign by the governor of Alabama, George Wallace, who campaigned in three Democratic primaries (Wisconsin, Indiana, and Maryland), drawing a surprising number of votes. Wallace decided to drop out of the contest, and Johnson and Goldwater agreed to avoid racial discussions in the campaign, but the progress of the civil rights movement was nevertheless an unavoidable issue.

States' rights. In the South, those who opposed rights for African Americans could politely hide their true motives beneath the umbrella of "states rights" arguments. For Goldwater, however, states' rights stood for opposition to growing federal influence in daily life. He had opposed the Civil Rights Act of 1964 not out of personal racism, but out of the belief that the federal government should be kept to a more limited role. Goldwater represented a form of libertarianism, the political philosophy of maximum personal freedom from government control. Democrats, on the other hand, saw no evidence that civil rights would ever come for African American citizens if it were left up to the governments of southern states.

War on Poverty. A month after signing the Civil Rights Act, Johnson signed another bill, the Economic Opportunity Act, which established a new Office of Economic Opportunity (OEO). The act was the first in a series of bills passed as part of what Johnson called the war on poverty. The OEO established educational and training programs designed to help lift poor Americans, many of whom were African Americans, into the ranks of the employed.

Vietnam. Americans did not play a major combat role in Vietnam until 1965. Goldwater was critical of what he perceived as a low level of U.S. military support for anti-Communists

in South Vietnam. Johnson, who had taken a significant step in the war by securing passage of the Tonkin Gulf resolution, defended the level of American involvement.

The Campaign

The election of 1964 pitted one of the most savvy politicians in the country, Johnson, against one of the most naïve, Goldwater. While Goldwater continued to rely on an inexperienced political staff, and often made statements that were used against him, Johnson ran an aggressive campaign that involved scores of speeches across the country. Johnson succeeded in making Barry Goldwater a campaign issue, focusing particularly on a Goldwater statement that "extremism in the defense of liberty is no vice; moderation in the pursuit of justice is no virtue." Goldwater's political foes helped make sure the first half of the statement was widely publicized, while usually ignoring the second half, with the result that many voters concluded Goldwater was a potentially dangerous extremist.

Television advertising again played a key role in the campaign. The Democrats produced one of the most notorious political advertisements of all time, the so-called "Daisy" commercial. It showed a young girl picking petals from a daisy while counting each one aloud. A male voice-over suddenly broke in, intoning a count-down: "Ten, nine, eight . . . " At zero, the screen was filled with the picture of a nuclear explosion. There was was no voice or tag line connecting the image to Goldwater, but most viewers understood the implication: Goldwater could not be trusted to keep his finger off of the nuclear trigger. (This commercial can be viewed from the Web at the American Museum of the Moving Image's "Living Room Candidate," http://www.ammi.org/livingroomcandidate/.)

The Outcome

Lyndon Johnson won 61.1 percent of the popular vote, the highest percentage of any presidential candidate, to Goldwater's 38.5 percent. In the Electoral College, Johnson won 486 votes; Goldwater won 52. Significantly, however, Goldwater broke the Democrat's hold on the "solid South," the states of the former Confederacy that had voted for the Democratic candidate since the era of Reconstruction. The Republican's electoral votes came from South Carolina, Georgia, Alabama, Mississippi, Louisiana, and his home state of Arizona.

On the other hand, the margin of Johnson's victory in many large industrial states of the North was even more impressive than his overall popular vote: 64.9 percent in Pennsylvania, 68.6 percent in New York, 76.2 percent in Massachusetts, and 66.7 percent in Michigan.

The irony of the 1964 election was that an overwhelming victory by the Democratic incumbent foreshadowed four turbulent years, culminating in 1968 when Johnson was forced to drop any plans he might have had for reelection.

More Information

▶ Bell, Jack. *Mr. Conservative: Barry Goldwater.* Garden City, NY: Doubleday, 1962.

▶ Caro, Robert A. *The Years of Lyndon Johnson.* 3 vols. to date. New York: Alfred A. Knopf, 1982–. *The Path to Power* (1982); *Means of Ascent* (1990); *Master of the Senate* (2002).

▶ Conkin, Paul K. *Big Daddy from the Pedernales: Lyndon Baines Johnson.* Boston: Twayne Publishers, 1986.

▶ Dugger, Ronnie. *The Politician: The Life and Times of Lyndon Johnson.* New York: W. W. Norton, 1982.

▶ Edwards, Lee. *Goldwater: The Man Who Made a Revolution.* Washington: Regnery, 1995.

▶ Evans, Rowland, and Robert Novak. *Lyndon B. Johnson: The Exercise of Power.* New York: New American Library, 1966.

▶ Goldberg, Robert Alan. *Barry Goldwater.* New Haven: Yale University Press, 1995.

▶ Perlstein, Rick. *Before the Storm: Barry Goldwater and the Unmaking of the American Consensus.* New York: Hill and Wang, 2001.

▶ Goldwater, Barry Morris. *The Conscience of a Conservative.* (reprint) Washington: Regnery Gateway, 1990.

▶ ———. *Where I Stand.* New York: McGraw-Hill, 1964.

▶ Goodwin, Doris Kearns. *Lyndon Johnson and the American Dream.* New York: St. Martin's Press, 1991.

▶ Johnson, Lyndon B. *My Hope for America.* New York: Random House, 1964.

▶ Mann, Robert. *The Walls of Jericho: Lyndon Johnson, Hubert Humphrey, Richard Russell, and the Struggle for Civil Rights.* New York: Harcourt Brace, 1996.

On the Web

▶ "The Living Room Candidate: A History of Presidential Campaign Commercials 1952–2000." American Museum of the Moving Image. **http://www.ammi.org/livingroomcandidate/.**

▶ Johnson, Lyndon B. "Inaugural Address, Wednesday, January 20, 1965." Inaugural Addresses of the Presidents of the United States. Washington, D.C.: U.S. Government Printing Office, 1989; Bartleby.com, 2001. **ttp://www.bartleby.com/124/pres57.html.**

▶ Wooley, John and Gerhard Peters. "The American Presidency Project." University of California, Santa Barbara, Department of Political Science. Links to presidential papers of Lyndon Johnson and others. **http://www.presidency.ucsb.edu/site/docs/index_pppus.php.**

1968
Richard Nixon (Republican) vs. Hubert Humphrey (Democrat)

The election of 1968 came at the end of a traumatic year filled with military setbacks in Vietnam, political assassinations, and street riots in the United States. The winning candidate was later accused of sabotaging a peace initiative in the Vietnam War in order to hold on to a slippery lead in the last days of the campaign, while the loser saw his reputation transformed from champion of civil rights to war monger, and was met at every appearance by chanting crowds of angry antiwar protesters. In the larger context the Democratic party's iron grip on the South was broken for the first time since the Civil War.

The Context

By 1968, American combat troops had been fully engaged in the Vietnam War for three years with little progress to show in their fight against Communist guerrillas, the Vietcong, and the government of North Vietnam. On the morning of January 30, 1968, coinciding with the Vietnamese New Year holiday, Tet, Communist forces launched a series of attacks against American and South Vietnamese forces. The ferocity and early success of the attacks (which were eventually driven back) shocked many Americans, who had assumed that U.S. troops were making headway in their battle against Communist domination of South Vietnam. In the end the military significance of the Tet offensive was less important than the blow struck against American confidence in the war effort.

Two months later, on April 4, a sniper in Memphis, Tennessee assassinated Reverend Martin Luther King, the charismatic leader of the African American civil rights movement. King had preached the gospel of nonviolence, and his murder touched off rioting in urban black neighborhoods, as if to say that the death of King meant the end of the nonviolent approach in the search for equality.

On June 5, in Los Angeles, another assassin murdered Robert F. Kennedy, younger brother of the slain President Kennedy and a leading candidate for the 1968 Democratic presidential nomination. Kennedy had just delivered a statement in a hotel ballroom following his victory in the California presidential primary and was passing through the hotel's kitchen when a Palestinian immigrant, Sirhan Sirhan, shot him.

For many voters, these three events were part of an atmosphere of chaos enveloping the United States. In some parts of the country, the civil rights movement had changed social patterns between whites and blacks that had existed since the nation was founded. In many cities African American neighborhoods broke out in a frenzy of rioting and looting in the summers from 1965–67. The non-violent philosophy of Martin Luther King was challenged by militant advocates of "Black Power," Stokeley Carmichael and the Black Panthers.

Nixon	31,785,480	43.4% ✓
Humphrey	31,275,166	42.7%
Wallace	9,906,473	13.5%

Electoral College

Nixon	301 ✓
Humphrey	191
Wallace	46

In white communities the profound cultural revolution of the 1960s was in full swing. Psychedelic drug use, premarital sex, and long hair on boys as well as girls, all symbolized a decade in which the "baby boomer" generation challenged authority on every level. There was an inescapable and widespread sense that events had spun out of control.

The Candidates

For Republicans memories of the crushing defeat of Barry Goldwater in 1964 were still fresh. Party leaders sought a moderate candidate who could challenge an incumbent president. Richard Nixon, vice president from 1953 to 1961 and the unsuccessful Republican nominee in 1960, seemed to have the qualities Republicans were looking for.

Two Republican governors, George Romney of Michigan and Nelson Rockefeller of New York, had also expressed interest in the nomination. Romney's candidacy died of a self-inflicted wound when he declared that during a visit to Vietnam he had been "brainwashed" by military officials.

FlashFocus: Richard Milhous Nixon

37th President, 1969–1974

Born: January 9, 1913, Yorba Linda, California

Died: April 22, 1994, New York, New York

Family: Son of Francis Nixon and Hannah Milhous; married Thelma "Pat" Ryan

Education: Whittier College; Duke University Law School

Political career: U.S. representative from California, 1947–50; U.S. senator from California, 1950–53; vice president 1953–61

Nixon entered politics as a rabid anti-Communist, winning seats in the House and Senate by accusing his opponents of Communist sympathies. Nixon gained fame investigating allegations that State Department official Alger Hiss was a Soviet spy in World War II (Hiss was jailed for perjury, but not for espionage.).

Dwight Eisenhower chose Nixon as his vice president in 1952 and 1956. Nixon ran for president against John Kennedy in 1960, losing narrowly. He then lost a race for governor of California in 1962.

Nixon returned to politics in 1968 as the Republican presidential nominee, beating Democrat Hubert Humphrey. In the waning days of the campaign, Nixon sabotaged a peace initiative of President Lyndon Johnson by persuading South Vietnam to refuse to participate in peace talks. As president, Nixon presided over a gradual withdrawal of U.S. troops from Vietnam while continuing to bomb North Vietnam and neighboring Cambodia until the Vietnam War ended in 1973.

Nixon opened talks with the Communist government of China in a visit to Beijing in 1972, and later negotiated a nuclear weapons control treaty with the Soviet Union. That year, Nixon was reelected in a landslide over Democrat George McGovern.

A break-in at Democratic National Committee offices in the Watergate complex in 1972 was Nixon's downfall. Although Nixon had denied any White House involvement in the plot, intended to install bugging devices, reporters at the Washington Post revealed evidence that Nixon had knowledge of the break-in and had tried to cover it up. Faced with evidence of personal involvement in a cover-up, Nixon resigned from office in August, 1974 to avoid impeachment. He was pardoned the next month by his successor, President Gerald Ford.

Nixon spent the next twenty years trying to recover his reputation, often commenting on foreign affairs and even advising President Bill Clinton. He died in New York in 1994.

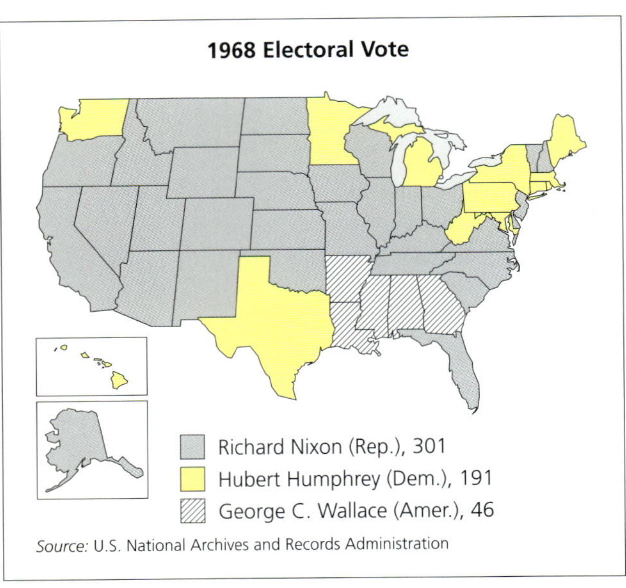

Source: U.S. National Archives and Records Administration

The Republican convention opened in Miami on August 7 with Nixon and Rockefeller still in contention. A third candidate, actor Ronald Reagan of California, announced at the last minute that he, too, would be a candidate. Reagan represented the ultra-conservative wing formerly represented by Goldwater. Nixon, however, had been endorsed by Strom Thurmond of South Carolina, the 1948 Dixiecrat nominee who had switched from the Democratic Party to the Republicans and who could be counted on to bring over other southern delegates. In the voting, Nixon did get support from southern states and won the nomination on the first ballot with 692 votes. Rockefeller had 277 votes and Reagan had 182. Nixon chose Maryland's governor, Spiro Agnew, as his vice presidential running mate. Agnew had previously endorsed Rockefeller, making his nomination a sop to liberal Republicans.

The Democratic convention, in sharp contrast, was a wild and chaotic affair held in Chicago at the end of months of bitter infighting for the 1968 nomination. In December 1967 Minnesota Senator Eugene McCarthy declared he would challenge President Lyndon Johnson for the nomination as a protest against Johnson's Vietnam War policies. Thousands of college students had turned out to help McCarthy campaign in presidential primaries. In the first primary, in New Hampshire, Johnson had defeated McCarthy, but by a much smaller margin than expected. A week later, Senator Robert Kennedy of New York, brother of the assassinated President John F. Kennedy, also declared his candidacy for the Democratic nomination. Consequently, at the end of March Johnson delivered a speech on television announcing a new peace initiative in the war, and also declaring that he would not seek, or accept, the party's nomination for a second full term. Following Johnson's decision, Vice President Hubert Humphrey jumped into the contest, proclaiming the "politics of joy" as his theme.

Rockefeller, representing the Northeastern liberal wing of the Republican party, first said he would not be a candidate, then changed his mind and entered the race at the end of April. In the meantime Nixon had scored uncontested victories in three state primary elections, and had won nearly enough delegates to ensure his nomination.

The three remaining candidates–McCarthy, Kennedy and Humphrey—battled for the nomination through the handful of primaries left after May 1. On the night of the California primary, June 5, 1968, an assassin murdered the New York senator.

As if political turmoil in the Democratic party were not enough, the nominating convention turned into a combination of political brawl and street riot. Thousands of anti-war protesters gathered in Chicago, chanting anti-war slogans outside the convention center while delegates meeting inside behind barbed-wire barriers debated the war. In what an investigating committee later called a "police riot," Chicago police attacked the war protesters with clubs and Mace gas, chasing them inside hotels where delegates were staying. The melee was broadcast live on television, as was Chicago's Mayor Richard Daley mouthing of an anti-Semitic slur while Senator Abraham Ribicoff was denouncing the police from the podium.

Humphrey left the convention with the nomination thanks largely to Democratic organizations like the one controlled by Mayor Daley, but it was a dubious victory.

There was a third party candidate in 1968, former Alabama Governor George Wallace, who launched a campaign for the American Independent Party in February. Wallace was a former Democrat whose campaign revolved around "law and order," a euphemism for controlling African Americans who benefited from the civil rights legislation passed in the Johnson administration. He gained national attention by symbolically "standing at the schoolhouse door" in a futile attempt to maintain racial segregation at the University of Alabama. In 1968, Wallace posed a further strategic challenge to Democrats, who were trying to hold on to southern voters, and to Nixon, who was trying to make inroads into the "solid South." Wallace chose as his running mate retired Air Force General Curtis LeMay.

The Issues

Vietnam war. Johnson's war policy—a steady increase of U.S. forces, called "escalation," to defeat the Vietcong guerrillas and the regular North Vietnamese army—had become highly unpopular by 1968, not just with young adults, but across the entire spectrum of Americans. The Tet offensive challenged claims by the administration that it was making progress. Middle class parents resisted seeing their sons drafted into the military to fight a war that was beginning to seem hopeless.

The Republicans counted on public discontent with Johnson's war policy to help them win the presidential election. At the end of October, Johnson announced a new peace initiative: the United States would stop bombing North Vietnam and peace talks would start with the North Vietnamese on November 6. In a highly controversial move, the Republicans contacted the government of South Vietnam and persuaded officials not to participate in the peace initiative by Johnson, promising them a "better deal" in a peace agreement Nixon would negotiate if he won the election. On November 2, the South Vietnamese government announced it would boycott

peace talks arranged by Johnson. The initiative failed, and a momentary surge of support for Humphrey sparked by Johnson's announcement quickly evaporated. The Vietnam war continued for four more years, a period in which 20,000 more American soldiers died.

Civil rights. The Johnson years saw significant progress in achieving equality of opportunity for African Americans, as well as government-financed programs designed to improve the lives of the poor, many of whom were African American. Initially, the civil rights movement was concentrated in the

South, led by Martin Luther King. By 1968 King was also focusing on northern urban areas, where there was also discrimination, although it was less obvious, against black Americans. George Wallace in particular capitalized on white resistance to equality for African Americans, appealing especially to white working class voters who felt threatened by laws guaranteeing equality of opportunity for all people regardless of race. Demands by more militant groups, such as the Black Panthers, for "black power" made whites even more nervous.

Law and order. Resistance to civil rights in the North was connected to riots in black neighborhoods of many cities, such as Newark, New Jersey, Los Angeles, California, and Detroit, Michigan, during the Johnson years. The riots were accompanied by widespread arson and looting of white-owned stores, and made some white residents of these cities concerned about their own security. Wallace tried to exploit such fears with the euphemistic call for "law and order," by which he really meant a return to the peaceful years of the 1950s, before the dual revolutions of the "hippies" and civil rights.

Nixon and Wallace both played on the dual issues of civil rights and domestic peace. Nixon insisted he backed civil rights while deploring crime. Wallace tied the two together, suggesting that civil rights advances were the root cause of disorder in black urban ghettos. Outside the deep South, Nixon's approach proved more palatable to voters.

The Campaign

Humphrey's Democratic campaign was hindered by President Johnson's insistence that Democrats support his war policy. Coming out of the chaotic convention, Humphrey also supported Mayor Daley and the violent tactics of the Chicago police. McCarthy, the defeated challenger, refused to endorse Humphrey at first. Anti-war protesters plagued Humphrey's every public appearance. By late September, Humphrey's support was fifteen percentage points behind Nixon's, and only seven percentage points ahead of Wallace.

On September 30, Humphrey announced a new Vietnam war policy: he promised that as president he would stop bombing North Vietnam in order to get peace negotiations started. Almost immediately, anti-war Democrats began supporting Humphrey and his standing in the polls rose.

In the meantime, Wallace's running mate, LeMay, hurt the American Independent campaign by threatening to bomb North Vietnam "back to the stone age," which made the Wallace ticket seem potentially dangerous in the field of foreign relations.

By the last week in October, Humphrey had reduced Nixon's margin in the polls to eight points, while Wallace's sup-

port had slipped. Nixon, perhaps remembering his poor showing in the 1960 campaign's debates against Kennedy, refused to debate Humphrey, which elicited taunts from the Democrats.

The biggest potential development came when Johnson announced a temporary halt in bombing North Vietnam and the opening of peace talks in November. Fearful that this move could further strengthen Humphrey, Nixon sabotaged the talks by persuading the South Vietnamese not to participate.

The Outcome

The election was held on November 5, and it was extremely close. Nixon received 31.8 million votes, or 43.4 percent of the total, to Humphrey's 31.3 million votes, or 42.7 percent. Wallace received 9.9 million votes (13.5 percent).

In the electoral college, Nixon won 301 votes to 191 for Humphrey and 46 for Wallace.

Wallace won his home state of Alabama, plus Arkansas, Louisiana, Georgia, and Mississippi, plus one electoral vote from North Carolina. Humphrey held on to four New England States (Connecticut, Massachusetts, Rhode Island, Maine), a swath of northeast and Midwestern industrial states (Michigan, Minnesota, New York, Pennsylvania), plus the District of Columbia, Maryland, Washington, Texas, and West Virginia.

More Information

- Ambrose, Stephen E. *Nixon*. New York: Simon and Schuster, 1987.
- Berman, Edgar. *Hubert: The Triumph and Tragedy of the Humphrey I Knew*. New York: Putnam, 1979.
- Eisele, Albert. *Almost to the Presidency: A Biography of Two American Politicians*. Blue Earth, Minnesota: Piper, 1972.
- Humphrey, Hubert H. *The Education of a Public Man: My Life and Politics*. Garden City, NY: Doubleday, 1976.
- Mazo, Earl and Stephen Hess. *Nixon: A Political Portrait*. New York: Harper and Row, 1968.
- McGinniss, Joe. *The Selling of the President, 1968*. New York: Trident Press, 1969.
- Nixon, Richard M. *RN: The Memoirs of Richard Nixon*. New York: Simon and Schuster, 1990.
- Wills, Garry. *Nixon Agonistes: The Crisis of the Self-Made Man*. New York: New American Library, 1979.

On the Web

- The Richard Nixon Library and Birthplace. **http://www.nixonfoundation.org/**.
- "The Living Room Candidate," American Museum of the Moving Image. (Campaign commercials.) **http://www.ammi.org/livingroomcandidate/**.

1972

Richard Nixon (Republican) vs. George McGovern (Democrat)

Eight years after the Republican Party suffered an overwhelming defeat by nominating an ultra-conservative, Senator Barry Goldwater of Arizona, for president to run against Democratic incumbent Lyndon Johnson in 1964, the Democratic Party experienced a similar debacle when it nominated an ultra-liberal, Senator George McGovern of South Dakota, to challenge the incumbent Republican Richard Nixon. Ironically, despite their overwhelming victories, both Johnson and Nixon left office with their popularity in tatters.

The Context

During his first term President Nixon pursued a policy of "Vietnamization," dedicated to turning the ground war in Vietnam over to Vietnamese forces while American involvement in the war was increasingly limited to providing air support. By 1972 American ground forces in Vietnam had been reduced by more than ninety percent, even as U.S. planes continued to bomb North Vietnam and, on occasion, neighboring Cambodia, where Communist Vietcong and North Vietnam were suspected of storing weapons.

In the first half of 1972 Nixon made two historic trips overseas. In February, Nixon visited Beijing, China, ending two decades of American refusal to have high-level communications with the Communist government of China. In May, Nixon visited Moscow and signed the Strategic Arms Limitation Treaty (SALT) limiting the number of nuclear weapons held by the United States and the Soviet Union; the trip also produced a new trade agreement.

Domestically Nixon had pursued moderate policies aimed at strengthening the position of the Republican Party in the South and among labor unions. Nixon's steadfast opposition to the use of school busing to achieve integration won widespread approval in North and South. Blue-collar workers generally supported the president in his Vietnam policy, and often clashed with student anti-war protesters. Nixon attempted a decisive move to combat inflation by imposing a freeze on wages and prices, an action at odds with the traditional Republican aversion to government intrusion into the economy, but one that made Nixon seem proactive in combating the leading economic ailment of his first administration. Riots in urban black ghettos had come to an end, and Nixon had taken policies that established him as a strong supporter of "law and order," a code phrase understood to mean "controlling African Americans."

In other areas, too, the Republican president had pursued moderate to liberal policies, even at the cost of infuriating his own party's conservative wing. In his first term Nixon signed an environmental protection law in 1969, an extension of the

FlashFocus: 1972

Candidates

Richard M. Nixon & Spiro T. Agnew, Republican
George McGovern & R. Sargent Shriver, Democrat
John G. Schmitz & Thomas J. Anderson, American

Issues

The Eagleton incident. Democratic candidate George McGovern had originally chosen Thomas Eagleton as his running-mate. When it was discovered that Eagleton had spent time in a hospital for "nervous exhaustion" and had received electroshock therapy, McGovern was supportive of Eagleton and kept him on the ticket. However, when a journalist alleged that Eagleton had a history of arrests for drunk driving, McGovern's staff pressured Eagleton to withdraw from the campaign, which he did. This was seen by the public as an indication of indecisiveness on the part of McGovern, and he lost credibility with voters due to this incident.

Vietnam. The war in Vietnam still had not reached any conclusion, until just days before the election when there was a breakthrough in negotiations with the North Vietnamese. McGovern criticized the way Nixon was handling the situation in Vietnam. Nixon repeated promises to end the war and to bring peace to the region.

Amnesty for draft evaders. McGovern was in favor of extending an amnesty to all those who had evaded the draft during the Vietnam War. Republicans succeeded in painting this stance as being overly liberal.

Outcome

Popular Vote

Nixon	47,169,911	60.7% ✓
McGovern	29,170,383	37.5%
Schmitz	1,099,482	1.4%

Electoral College

Nixon	520 ✓
McGovern	17

Voting Rights Act in 1970, and an education act in 1972 that prevented discrimination in schools that received federal aid.

The Candidates

While the Nixon administration symbolized regaining government control, the Democratic Party had launched a program of broadening the participation of women and minorities. A special Democratic Commission on Party Structures and Delegate Selection, headed by South Dakota's Senator George McGovern, changed the way delegates to the 1972 convention were selected, giving more influence to constituencies thought to have been underrepresented in 1968. Another commission had changed procedures at the party's convention, limiting demonstrations on the convention floor and establishing new procedures for challenging the right of delegates to represent their respective states.

In the months leading up to the convention the Democratic Party had a dozen contenders for the nomination. Maine's Senator Edmund Muskie was an early leader, but was forced to withdraw after an incident in New Hampshire in which he appeared to cry in the midst of denouncing a newspaper attack on his wife. Governor George Wallace of Alabama, who ran as an independent in 1968, was shot and paralyzed during a campaign appearance in Maryland. Hubert Humphrey, the 1968 nominee, lost the California primary and came into the convention trailing McGovern. Other contenders included Senators Vance Hartke of Indiana and Henry Jackson of Washington, Mayors John Lindsay of New York and Sam Yorty of Los Angeles, and Representative Shirley Chisholm of New York.

McGovern had established himself as the front-runner during the presidential primaries as the natural heir to the 1968 candidacies of Eugene McCarthy and Robert Kennedy. The South Dakota senator, a well-established and vocal critic of the war in Vietnam, won ten of the twenty-three primaries he entered. By the time the Democratic convention opened in Miami Beach on July 10, McGovern was within a few votes of capturing the nomination.

As a result of changes proposed by McGovern's commission on delegate selection, the convention saw an unprecedented number of challenges to delegations, including the one headed by Mayor Richard Daley of Chicago, the leading symbol of Democratic "machine" politics and the man blamed for the "police riot" at the 1968 convention in Chicago (see p. 175). Daley and the delegates he controlled were denied seats, on grounds the process by which they were chosen had violated the party's new rules.

After a series of other challenges the resulting composure of the convention contained far more women and minority delegates than ever before, and it was not a surprise when McGovern won the nomination on the first ballot. The nominee tried to persuade Senator Edward Kennedy of Massachusetts, whose older brothers John and Robert had both been assassinated, to run as his vice president. Kennedy refused, at which point McGovern chose Senator Thomas Eagleton of Missouri, who was to play a pivotal role in the campaign.

On the Republican side there was no question that incumbent President Nixon would be nominated. The convention, also held in Miami Beach, had more the appearance of a television program than a political convention. Compared to the Democratic meeting in the same hall a few weeks earlier, the Republicans were a model of order and organization. Nixon was nominated on the first ballot with all but a single vote, the one held by Senator Paul McCloskey Jr. of California, a sharp

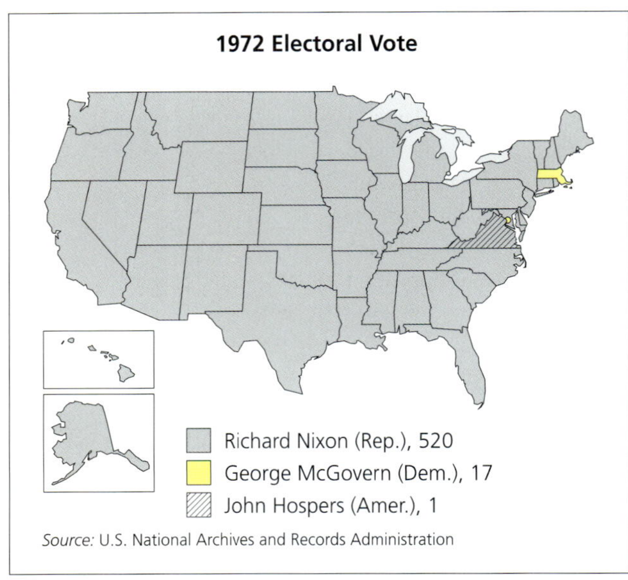

Source: U.S. National Archives and Records Administration

critic of Nixon's Vietnam policy. The convention also renominated Spiro Agnew as vice president.

The Issues

The Eagleton Affair. Less than two weeks after he was nominated to be McGovern's running mate, Eagleton told reporters that he was once hospitalized for depression and had undergone electric shock therapy. The next day, a national newspaper columnist, Jack Anderson, claimed Eagleton had been charged with driving under the influence of alcohol (the claim was soon retracted by Anderson as being untrue). At first, McGovern responded by saying he backed Eagleton "a thousand percent." But within days, McGovern accepted Eagleton's resignation, and Eagleton was replaced in August by Sargent Shriver, a brother-in-law of John and Robert Kennedy and former director of the Peace Corps. McGovern's seeming reversal of positions on Eagleton's candidacy raised doubts about his decisiveness, and McGovern's character became a major issue for the rest of the campaign.

"Extremism." Arizona Senator Barry Goldwater had been labeled a conservative extremist in 1964, and McGovern was labeled a liberal extremist in 1972. McGovern had advocated several positions that underlined this image: an amnesty (pardon) for people who had evaded the military draft in the Vietnam era, and a program to send $1,000 to every American as part of an anti-poverty welfare initiative. In the eyes of many, the Democratic convention's new rules on choosing delegates, rules drafted under McGovern's supervision, also fit the category of "extremely" liberal. Other McGovern positions judged to be "extreme" included legalization of both abortion and marijuana.

Vietnam. Although American involvement in ground fighting in Vietnam had been reduced, the continued bombing of North Vietnam kept the issue alive for many war opponents. The fact that the Nixon administration had secretly bombed Cambodia, a neutral country adjoining Vietnam, seemed to be an unlawful expansion of the war. Withholding from the public the decision to bomb underscored Nixon's reputation for untrustworthy behavior in the eyes of his foes. On the other hand, and more important in the election, blue-collar workers and their unions supported the administration's policy and opposed McGovern's plan for an immediate cease-fire without necessarily obtaining concessions from North Vietnam and the Vietcong. On balance, Vietnam worked to the advantage of Nixon rather than McGovern.

The Campaign

Before either of the nominating conventions had taken place, a group of five men had broken into the headquarters of the Democratic National Committee in Washington, DC in an effort to plant eavesdropping "bugs." An alert watchman had called police, resulting in the arrest of the burglars. The incident had no measurable impact during the campaign, but it proved to be of monumental importance later on.

The 1972 campaign was always a one-sided affair. Nixon began the campaign far ahead of McGovern in public opinion polls. Moreover, the Democratic convention had alienated many traditional Democratic stalwarts, such as Mayor Daley's Chicago Democratic organization that had been denied seats. Many southern Democrats, backbone of the Democrats' "solid South" for a century, were disaffected with the party's insistence on greater representation of African Americans. Organized labor, another traditional Democratic ally, largely supported Nixon's Vietnam policy and opposed McGovern's. The circumstances of the Eagleton affair severely damaged McGovern's reputation as a potential national leader.

On October 26, the Nixon administration and the North Vietnamese disclosed a breakthrough in peace negotiations underway in Paris. Nixon's national security advisor (and later secretary of state) Henry Kissinger announced that "peace is at hand," undercutting one of McGovern's key campaign issues.

There were no debates in the 1972 campaign because Nixon refused to participate. In general, Nixon was absent from the campaign; his few public appearances were highly orchestrated and left little room for verbal mistakes. McGovern, on the other hand, was unusually open to the press, which opened him to closer scrutiny.

The Outcome

The 1972 election was an overwhelming landslide for the Republicans. Nixon won over 47 million votes, or 60.7 percent of the total, compared to 29 million, or 37.5 percent, for McGovern. In the electoral college, Nixon won 520 votes. McGovern won just one state, Massachusetts, and the District of Columbia, for 17 electoral votes. Nixon's margin was just slightly below the Democratic landslide of 1964; his electoral college

FlashFocus: George Stanley McGovern

Democratic Candidate for President, 1972

Born: July 19, 1922, Avon, South Dakota
Family: Son of Joseph McGovern, a Methodist minister, and Frances McLean; married Eleanor Stegeberg
Education: Dakota Wesleyan University; Northwestern University
Political career: McGovern earned the dubious distinction of racking up the biggest loss in the modern two-party system, winning just one state (Massachusetts) and the District of Columbia in his campaign against incumbent Richard Nixon in 1972.

McGovern flew 35 missions as a bomber pilot in Europe, winning the Distinguished Service Flying Cross. After returning to South Dakota, he was elected to the U.S. House of Representatives in 1956, and 1958. In 1960, he became the first director of President John Kennedy's Food for Peace program. McGovern ran again for the Senate in 1962, winning the first of three terms.

In January, 1965, he delivered a speech denouncing the Vietnam War policy of President Lyndon Johnson, one of the first national politicians to do so, and never relinquished his status as the country's leading "dove" and most respected advocate for an end to American participation in the Vietnam War.

McGovern was the Democratic nominee for president in 1972, running on a promise to bring American troops home. He courted young voters by condemning Nixon as a servant of the military and big business and proposing a guaranteed minimum income for everyone and an amnesty for youths who refused to be drafted for service in Vietnam. McGovern and his running mate, Sargent Shriver, carried only Massachusetts and the District of Columbia, winning 17 electoral votes to Nixon's 520.

McGovern was reelected to the Senate from South Dakota in 1974, but lost his seat to Republican James Abdnor in 1980.

In July, 2000 President Clinton awarded McGovern the Medal of Freedom, the country's highest civilian honor.

See also: Richard Nixon, p. 174.

margin was the biggest since 1936, when the Republican candidate, Alf Landon, won just eight electoral votes against Franklin Roosevelt (see p. 144).

The Republican victories across the South underscored the permanent change in American politics that was evident in 1968. States that had voted for the Democratic candidate for a century following the Civil War and Reconstruction were now firmly in the Republican fold.

On the other hand, there was little question that McGovern was the principal issue. In Congressional races, the Democrats won decisively, retaining control of Congress. In races for governor, Democrats won eleven of the eighteen governor's chairs up for election, bringing their national total to 31.

Richard Nixon's nose is caricatured as belonging to Pinocchio, the puppet whose nose kept growing every time he told another lie. Secretary of State Henry Kissinger is Jiminy Cricket, Pinocchio's conscience.

The irony of the overwhelming victory by Nixon and Agnew in 1972 was that neither man would still be in office in 1976. Agnew resigned the vice presidency in 1973 after being accused of corruption in an earlier job as Baltimore County, Maryland chief executive, and Nixon resigned office in 1974 in the face of almost certain impeachment for his role in covering up involvement in the Watergate burglary affair.

More Information

▶ Emery, Fred. *Watergate: The Corruption of American Politics and the Fall of Richard Nixon*. New York: Times Books, 1994.

▶ McGovern, George S. *An American Journey: The Presidential Campaign Speeches of George McGovern*. New York: Random House, 1974.

▶ McGovern, George S. *Grassroots: The Autobiography of George McGovern*. New York: Random House, 1977.

▶ Nixon, Richard M. *In the Arena: A Memoir of Victory, Defeat, and Renewal*. New York: Simon and Schuster, 1990.

▶ Reeves, Richard. *President Nixon: Alone in the White House*. New York: Simon and Schuster, 2001.

▶ White, Theodore. *The Making of the President, 1972*. New York: Atheneum Publishers, 1973.

▶ Wicker, Tom. *One of Us: Richard Nixon and the American Dream*. New York: Random House, 1991.

▶ Witker, Kristi. *How to Lose Everything in Politics Except Massachusetts*. New York: Mason and Lipscomb, 1974.

On the Web

▶ "The Living Room Candidate: A History of Presidential Campaign Commercials 1952-2000." American Museum of the Moving Image. http://www.ammi.org/livingroomcandidate/.

1976
James Earl "Jimmy" Carter (Democrat)
vs. Gerald Ford (Republican)

No presidential election before 1976 had offered voters an incumbent president who had never been elected to a national office running against a one-term governor who was virtually unknown outside his home state. The election took place in the wake of the nation's worst political scandal, and came on top of an international humiliation in Vietnam and economic turmoil at home.

The Context

In August, 1974, President Richard Nixon resigned from office, faced with the certainty of impeachment and the likelihood of becoming the first president ever turned out of office. For two years Nixon had been battling to keep secret the involvement of the White House in the break-in at the Democratic Party's national headquarters in the Watergate office complex in Washington. The scandal had captured the nation's attention for months, first as the *Washington Post* revealed details of how the investigation was leading directly into Nixon's office at the White house, then as it was revealed that Nixon had installed a system in his office to tape record all conversations there. Upon Nixon's resignation, Vice President Gerald Ford became president. Ford had been appointed to the job to replace Spiro Agnew, who had resigned in 1973 faced with charges of evading U.S. income taxes. (Agnew later pleaded guilty to tax evasion and was fined $10,000 and sentenced to probation.) Ford, the Republican leader in the House of Representatives, became the first person to serve as president without having run in a national election. Although Ford was never implicated in the Watergate scandal, he tarnished his image in September 1974 by granting Nixon a presidential pardon, thereby avoiding any future criminal prosecution of the former chief executive.

Ford's two years in office were somewhat tumultuous. In January, 1975, the Organization of Petroleum Exporting Countries (OPEC) raised global oil prices by ten percent, adding to already acute inflationary pressures on the economy. In October, OPEC imposed an embargo on shipments, causing severe fuel shortages in the United States, where motorists could only buy gasoline every other day and had to wait in long lines at stations to pay much higher prices than ever previously experienced. The higher prices and oil embargo added fuel to the list of economic problems plaguing the country.

In April, 1975, Communist forces seized control of Saigon, the capital of South Vietnam, effectively ending the Vietnam war with a stinging defeat for the United States. (The next year, North and South Vietnam were merged into a single country, governed by Communists.) In May, 1975, Cambodia seized an American ship, the Mayaguez, which was later rescued by U.S. Marines at the cost of 38 lives. In September, President Ford survived two assassination attempts.

The calm promised by a second term for Richard Nixon was shattered on every front.

FlashFocus: Gerald Rudolph Ford

38th President, 1974–1977

Born: July 14, 1913, Omaha, Nebraska

Education: University of Michigan; Yale Law School

Family: Son of Leslie King and Dorothy Gardner; stepson of Gerald Ford; married Betty Warren

Political career: Republican. Ford served in the U.S. House of Representatives from 1949 to 1973, the last eight as the minority leader. On December 6, 1973, he was appointed vice president after the resignation of Spiro Agnew; on August 9, 1974, inaugurated president, succeeding Richard Nixon, the only president ever to resign from office. One month later, Ford granted Nixon a full pardon for all offenses committed during his administration, allowing him to escape accountability in the Watergate scandal. Ford was accused of misuse of power since he made the move without consulting Congress or any other political leaders. The previous year Ford had indicated that he would not consider a pardon, since Americans "would not stand for it." He spent months refuting the charge that he may have made a deal for the pardon beforehand, and found himself besmirched by the same scandal that had brought down so many others.

In this political climate, Ford announced a conditional amnesty for Vietnam era draft evaders. Americans were again dissatisfied, as those who were against the Vietnam War thought there should be a full amnesty with no conditions, and those who were in favor of the war were angry at the thought of any amnesty at all.

When Ford turned his attention to the economy, he declared inflation "domestic enemy No. 1" and urged Americans to buy less and save more. Inflation came down, but the economy went into full recession with production plunging and unemployment spiking.

Internationally, U.S. prestige was running low, especially after the fall of South Vietnam to Communist forces in 1975. Ford continued Nixon's policy of détente with the Soviet Union and with China.

Ford lost the 1976 presidential election to Democrat Jimmy Carter.

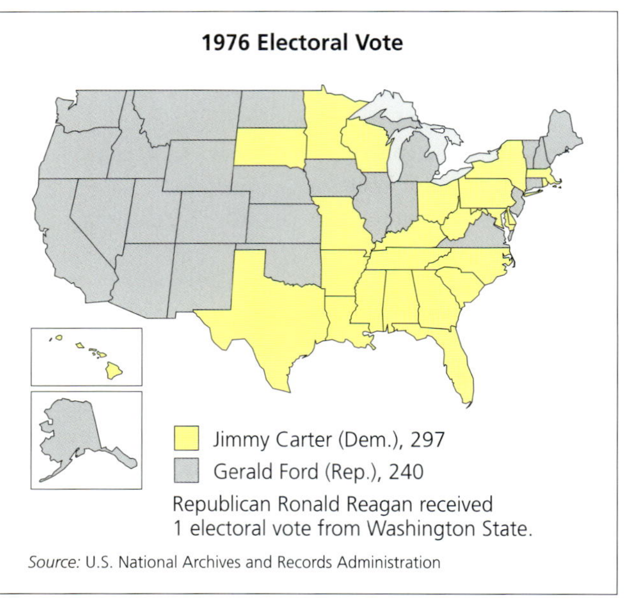

Source: U.S. National Archives and Records Administration

The Candidates

Having lost the 1972 election in a Republican landslide, the Democrats were without a clear leader for the presidential nomination in 1976. As a result of reforms in the party, however, presidential primaries became critical for anyone wishing to gain the nomination; the days when party leaders could select delegates to the national convention, and effectively determine the candidate for president, were long over. Moreover, most of the party's previous presidential contenders, such as George McGovern and Senators Edmund Muskie, Edward Kennedy, and Hubert Humphrey, had chosen to stay out of the race. On the other hand, a slew of newcomers were interested. These included Governors James "Jimmy" Carter of Georgia, Milton Schapp of Pennsylvania, and Edmund "Jerry" Brown of California, Senators Henry "Scoop" Jackson of Washington, Frank Harris of Oklahoma, Birch Bayh of Indiana, and Frank Church of Idaho, and Representative Morris Udall of Arizona. Many of the contenders were little known across the country, and none was more obscure than Carter of Georgia.

But the Georgia governor, who announced his intention to run in December 1974 just before his term as governor ended, was able to use his obscurity to good advantage. To an electorate tired of political scandal, Carter appeared to be an honest, straightforward candidate without a shred of scandal in his past. The fact that Carter spoke often about his religious faith as a Baptist seemed to underscore his honesty. Backed by a strong campaign organization, Carter worked at building recognition and support in the early primary states of Iowa and New Hampshire, and entered the 1976 campaign season by winning a fourth of the Iowa delegates, then winning the New Hampshire primary with 30 percent of the vote, ahead of Udall's 24 percent.

Over the next six months the field of Democrats battled in primary elections. Carter demonstrated his ability to do well in the South by beating former Alabama Governor George Wallace in the Florida primary, then won the Illinois primary a week later. In North Carolina, another southern state judged critical for success in the presidential election, Carter achieved his first majority of the primary season. A Carter victory in Pennsylvania effectively ended the candidacy of Senator Jackson. In four other states—Maryland, Rhode Island, New Jersey, and California—the Georgia governor lost to Brown of California, and he lost to Senator Church of Idaho in Nebraska, Oregon, Montana, and Idaho.

A Carter win in Ohio on June 8, the last of the primary elections, was regarded as decisive, and Mayor Richard Daley of Chicago, excluded from the convention in 1972, swung the Illinois delegation to Carter, virtually guaranteeing him the nomination at the convention in July. For his vice president, Carter chose Senator Walter Mondale of Minnesota, an ally of Hubert Humphrey and representative of the northern, liberal wing of the party.

The Republican nomination might have been expected to be a shoo-in for the incumbent, President Ford, but he actually needed to fend off a challenge from conservative candidate Ronald Reagan of California. Reagan, governor of California from 1967–75, had been a supporter of the ultra-conservative Arizona Senator Barry Goldwater in 1964. He campaigned for the Republican nomination unofficially for several months before announcing his candidacy in late 1975. In the first Republican primary election in New Hampshire, Ford beat Reagan, but by just 1,300 votes out of over 100,000 cast. Ford won the Florida and Illinois primaries by convincing margins. Reagan refused calls to withdraw from the election, and beat Ford in the North Carolina primary and later in the Texas primary. In Texas many conservative Democrats were able to vote in the Republican campaign; for them, Reagan was a substitute for the disabled George Wallace of Alabama.

Entering the Republican convention at the end of July, Ford was still short of the number of delegates needed to win nomination. The president was ahead of Reagan, but only by about a hundred votes. Reagan tried to force Ford to show his hand by announcing that if he, Reagan, were the nominee, he would name Pennsylvania senator Richard Schweiker as his vice presidential running mate. Reagan challenged Ford to say whom he would nominate, and even tried to pass a resolution at the Republican convention forcing Ford to name his choice. The Reagan move failed to win a majority, however, and Ford narrowly won the nomination on the first ballot. Reagan declined to be considered for the vice presidency, after which Ford turned to Kansas senator Robert Dole.

The Issues

Economy. The economy had undergone a series of shocks during Ford's presidency. An oil embargo had driven prices for gasoline and other petroleum products much higher, as well as inconveniencing millions of Americans and sparking a serious economic downturn. Unemployment had affected nine percent of the adult workforce, and inflation had soared to 12 percent. The Ford campaign insisted that the way to stimulate economic growth was to cure inflation by reducing government spending and cutting taxes. The Democrats said that unemployment was the biggest problem facing the economy, and proposed the large-scale hiring of people to staff a public service program. Democrats also advocated mandatory wage and price controls if necessary, the same remedy chosen by former President Nixon in his first term.

Foreign relations. The issue of Vietnam had faded by the 1976 election. Carter campaigned on the proposition that American foreign policy should be more in keeping with American ideals of democracy and equality, while at the same time insisting that the United States must take a firm line towards the Soviet Union. Ford, the incumbent, defended the role of Secretary of State Henry Kissinger, a Nixon appointee, and defended his handling of foreign policy.

Character. Although the disgraced Nixon was not in the race, the personal morality of Jimmy Carter was an issue in the campaign. The Republicans depicted Carter, who owned a peanut farm in Georgia, as too inexperienced, even naïve, to take responsibility for foreign policy.

Social issues. Two social issues separated the party: school busing to achieve racial balance in public schools and a woman's right to abortion. Republicans generally opposed both busing and abortion, and in this respect their positions were in line with conservative blue-collar workers. Carter, the Democratic candidate, favored voluntary school busing to achieve racial integration of schools. Ford advocated a Constitutional amendment barring school busing to achieve racial segregation. Ford also advocated leaving it to the individual states whether to permit abortions.

The Campaign

Carter, still largely unknown in the country, waged an aggressive public campaign which sometimes put him at a disadvantage. For example, he agreed to be interviewed by Playboy magazine, and remarked that "in his heart" he had committed adultery "many times." Carter was widely ridiculed for his statement, although it may have struck just the right chord among some voters who also took their religious beliefs seriously.

Ford, on the other hand, followed the example of his predecessor, Richard Nixon, and stayed close to the White House, using the power and influence of his incumbency to his advantage. Ford was often seen receiving dignitaries or signing legislation—acting the role of president.

There were three face-to-face debates between Carter and Ford, the first such debates since the Nixon-Kennedy debates of 1960 and the first ever between an incumbent president and his challenger. The debates were largely inconclusive, with neither candidate committing a gaffe or outdoing the other.

Toward the end of the campaign, economic statistics suggested the economy was taking a turn for the worse, which helped buttress the very slender lead Carter had going into election day. Having started well ahead of Ford in the opinion polls, Carter ended the campaign in a race that polls said was too close to call.

The Outcome

The outcome of the popular vote was not known until after midnight. Carter received 40.8 million votes, or 50.1 percent, to Ford's 39.1 million (48 percent). In the electoral college, Carter won 297 votes to Ford's 240.

A number of states were so close that a shift of few thousand votes could have taken electoral votes from Carter and given them to Ford, changing the outcome. In Ohio, for example, Carter won the state's 25 electoral votes by less than 11,000 votes out of over four million cast. On the other hand, Ford won Oregon's six electoral votes by just 1,713 votes out of just under one million.

Carter restored the "solid South" to the Democratic column, and won a swath of industrial states in the Northeast and upper Midwest. Ford won all the states west of the Mississippi except Texas.

More Information

▶ Cannon, James M. *Time and Chance: Gerald Ford's Appointment with History*. New York: HarperCollins, 1994.

▶ Ford, Gerald. *A Time to Heal: The Autobiography of Gerald R. Ford*. New York: Harper and Row, 1979.

▶ Greene, John R. *The Presidency of Gerald R. Ford*. Lawrence: University Press of Kansas, 1995.

▶ Jordan, Hamilton. *Crisis: The Last Year of the Carter Presidency*. New York: Putnam, 1982.

▶ Stroud, Kandy. *How Jimmy Won: The Victory Campaign from Plains to the White House*. New York: Morrow, 1977.

▶ *The Presidential Campaign, 1976*. Compiled under the direction of the Committee on House Administration, U.S. House of Representatives. Washington: U.S. Government Printing Office, 1978–79.

▶ Wheeler, Leslie. *Jimmy Who? An Examination of Presidential Candidate Jimmy Carter: The Man, His Career, His Stands on the Issues*. Woodbury, New York: *Barron's* Educational Series, 1976.

▶ Wooton, James T. *Dasher: The Roots and the Rising of Jimmy Carter*. New York: Warner, 1979.

On the Web

▶ "The Living Room Candidate: A History of Presidential Campaign Commercials 1952-2000." American Museum of the Moving Image. **http://www.ammi.org/livingroomcandidate/.**

1980
Ronald Reagan (Republican)
vs. James Earl "Jimmy" Carter (Democrat)

In 1976, California Governor Ronald Reagan had mounted a strong challenge to President Gerald Ford for the Republican presidential nomination. Four years later, after Ford had lost the White House to a little-known governor of Georgia, Jimmy Carter, Reagan returned for a second, successful effort. Reagan's nomination marked the ascent of the ultra-conservative wing of the Republican Party, and came in the midst of a series of national crises that seemed to overwhelm President Carter.

The Context

Voters wish to believe that the president is in control of events, rather than rather than at their mercy. During the Carter administration, those expectations were shattered. In 1979, the United States was repeatedly rocked by events that seemed to overwhelm Carter's ability to act.

The biggest event took place in Iran, where Islamic radicals stormed the U.S. embassy and took 66 Americans hostage. The United States had long backed the autocratic rule of the Shah of Iran, who was overthrown by fundamentalist Islamic leaders; seizing the American embassy was, in some sense, payback for years of harsh rule by the Shah. Carter's efforts to solve the hostage crisis through negotiations failed, and a military rescue mission also failed. Night after night, Americans watched on television as the power and prestige of the United States were mocked in Tehran.

Making matters worse was a spate of economic problems related to the sharp rise in oil prices brought on by actions of the Organization of Petroleum Exporting Countries (OPEC). An embargo on shipments by OPEC had driven up the price of petroleum products in 1973 and touched off a severe recession from 1975–76. The Islamic revolution in Iran sparked another oil crisis, sending prices spiraling. Between 1977 and 1979, the price of gasoline doubled. Prices of other consumer goods also soared at an annual rate of 18 percent, causing higher unemployment and slower growth. In one famous response, Carter appeared before voters from the White House, wearing a cardigan sweater and urging conservation. The impact of his appearance was to suggest that the only thing Americans could do was to shiver in an effort to save expensive oil products.

In parallel with Carter's perceived failings as a chief executive, Americans' confidence in government as a mechanism to solve problems was declining. Public opinion polls showed that three-quarters of Americans did not trust the government in 1980, the result of eight years of government scandal during the second term of President Richard Nixon (see p. 181); oil shocks from the OPEC embargo and Iranian revolution and consequent economic recession; the end of the Vietnam war

with a Communist victory; and the perceived decline in American prestige as a result of the Iranian hostage crisis.

The Candidates

Carter's prestige as the incumbent president suffered another blow in 1980 with a challenge by Senator Edward Kennedy of Massachusetts for the Democratic presidential nomination.

FlashFocus: Ronald Wilson Reagan

40th President, 1981–1989

Born: February 6, 1911, Tampico, Illinois
Died: June 5, 2004, Los Angeles, California
Family: Son of John Edward "Jack" Reagan, a small businessman, and Nellie Wilson; married Jane Wyman, an actress (divorced), Nancy Davis
Education: Eureka College (Illinois)

Political career: Ronald Reagan was a radio announcer, then a Hollywood studio actor. He was elected head of the Screen Actor's Guild in 1947, maintaining a staunch anti-Communist stance amid allegations of Communist influence in the film industry. In 1964, Reagan supported ultra-conservative Republican Senator Barry Goldwater; Reagan later emerged as a leading spokesman for Republican conservatives.

Reagan was elected governor of California in 1966 on a promise to crack down on civil unrest on campuses and in cities. He made a last-minute bid to snatch the 1968 Republican presidential nomination from Richard Nixon, and tried again in 1976, losing to incumbent President Gerald Ford.

Reagan was the Republican nominee in 1980, and defeated incumbent Jimmy Carter in the midst of a diplomatic crisis in which American diplomats were held hostage in Iran.

Reagan named the first woman to the U.S. Supreme Court (Sandra Day O'Connor), and initiated tax cuts and increased defense spending that caused the federal deficit to balloon. He also supported an anti-missile defense system, dubbed "Star Wars," plus a host of socially conservative causes such as endorsing prayer in public schools. His smooth television style earned him the nickname "the Great Communicator."

Reagan was reelected in 1984 by a landslide. In his second term, federal budget deficits continued to soar, but Reagan refused to consider cutting defense spending. In 1986, revelations that White House aides had illegally sold arms to radicals in Iran, and used profits from the sales to fund right-wing "Contras" in Guatemala, caused some serious controversy regarding the possibility of a White House role in the affair. However, the suspicions did not tarnish the "Teflon president," and Reagan left at the end of his second term still highly popular and a hero to conservatives.

In the mid-1990s, Reagan announced that he was suffering from Alzheimer's disease, which attacks the brain. He stopped making public appearances. He died in June 2004.

mary in March, in Pennsylvania in April, and in California in June. Carter, on the other hand, won primaries in Florida, Illinois and Texas.

After thirty-four Democratic primaries, Carter emerged with enough delegates at the Democratic convention to win renomination on the first ballot. But his victory had been difficult and had further diminished his stature as a national leader. The convention agreed to renominate Vice President Walter Mondale for a second term as well.

During the Democratic convention, an effort by Kennedy to change the rules and allow delegates to vote for whomever they liked, rather than the candidate who had won their state's primary, failed. In an effort to satisfy disaffected Kennedy supporters, Carter allowed the Massachusetts Democrat to have his way on many planks in the party platform—planks that Carter did not agree with, and which were more liberal than the Georgian thought wise. At the end of the convention, with Carter on the stand as the nominee, Kennedy also appeared, but obviously not enthusiastic about Carter's nomination. The split between Carter and Kennedy deprived the Democrats of strong enthusiasm going into the campaign.

On the Republican side, a long list of contenders emerged. Although former President Gerald Ford made it known he would like the nomination, he declined to mount an aggressive campaign. The list of challengers included former Texas Governor and Nixon Treasury Secretary John Connolly, former U.N. Ambassador and CIA Director George H. W. Bush; the 1976 vice presidential candidate, Senator Robert Dole of Kansas; Illinois Congressman John Anderson; and former California Governor Ronald Reagan, who had come close to beating Ford for the nomination in 1976.

Reagan was 69 years old in 1980, the oldest of the Republican contestants but also the most popular. Reagan was heir to the ultra-conservative support enjoyed by Senator Barry Goldwater, the unsuccessful 1964 Republican nominee (see p. 169). He was a familiar figure to many Americans, having served as the television host of a popular program sponsored by General Electric in the 1950s. As an actor and experienced television personality, Reagan had mastered the art of communicating through the TV set. He also delivered a simple message: America's problems could all be solved by shrinking the size of government through simultaneous cuts in spending and taxes.

Reagan got off to a strong start even before the New Hampshire primary, where his main opponent was Bush, in a television debate in which Reagan seemed to take a strong stand when challenged by the hired moderator of a paid-for television debate. When the moderator tried to cut Reagan off, he replied: "I'm paying for this microphone," and kept on talking. It seemed like the decisive action Americans were looking for in the White House.

By May, Reagan had won twenty-eight of the thirty-four Republican primaries, and gained enough delegates to assure nomination. At the Republican convention in Detroit, Reagan

Kennedy, brother of the slain President John Kennedy and Senator Robert Kennedy, represented the liberal wing of the Democratic Party which had reached a high point during the Administration of Lyndon Johnson and passage of the Great Society social welfare legislation from 1963–68.

Kennedy's campaign got off to a weak and slow start with losses in Iowa and New Hampshire, but the Massachusetts senator came roaring back with victories in the New York pri-

first offered the vice presidential spot to former President Ford, who declined, then turned to Bush, who accepted. Bush had won six primaries and, despite his New England roots, was a resident of Texas. Republicans thought Bush's extensive Washington resume would compensate for Reagan's lack of national political experience.

Representative Anderson, who lost the Republican primary in his home state of Illinois to Reagan, decided to run as an independent. Anderson represented the liberal wing of the Republican party, and organized what he called a "national unity campaign" directed at disaffected Democrats and liberal Republicans alike.

The Issues

Economy. Years of economic weakness, high unemployment, high inflation and repeated jolts from rising oil prices made the economy the dominant issue for most Americans. For Carter, the actions of OPEC in raising oil prices seemed to be beyond reach of the government to solve, but Reagan proposed a solution that seemed both simple and alluring: reduce the size of government by cutting spending and taxes. During the primary season Bush had ridiculed Reagan's formulation as "voodoo economics," but it was incorporated into the Republican platform and to a great extent became policy during the Reagan administration. The Democratic platform, largely influenced by Kennedy, took the opposite approach, proposing a $12 billion job-creation program and an expansion of public housing, among other social initiatives.

Oil. The Republicans called for aggressive efforts to increase energy production and more efficient use of existing supplies. The Democrats vowed to make energy conservation "our highest priority."

Social issues. The Supreme Court decision supporting women's right to abortion, *Roe v. Wade,* continued to be the focus of strong opposition by Republicans. The issue was also a route to support from voters with conservative religious beliefs, including Catholics and Christian fundamentalists. The Republicans supported a constitutional amendment to outlaw abortion. The Democratic platform declared that "reproductive freedom (is) a fundamental human right" and opposed government interference. The Democrats also endorsed passage of an Equal Rights Amendment to the Constitution, guaranteeing women equality with men; the Republicans, who had previously endorsed such an amendment, settled for a plank supporting women's rights without endorsing an amendment, a concession to Reagan's opposition to such an amendment.

National security. In the campaign Reagan deplored what he regarded as a decline of American military power compared to the Soviet Union, and he opposed a second Strategic Arms Limitation Treaty proposed by Carter. The Republicans rejected Carter's theory of Mutual Assured Destruction (with both the U.S. and U.S.S.R. having sufficient nuclear weapons to assure the destruction of the other side, as a deterrent to starting a nuclear war), and urged enough American nuclear

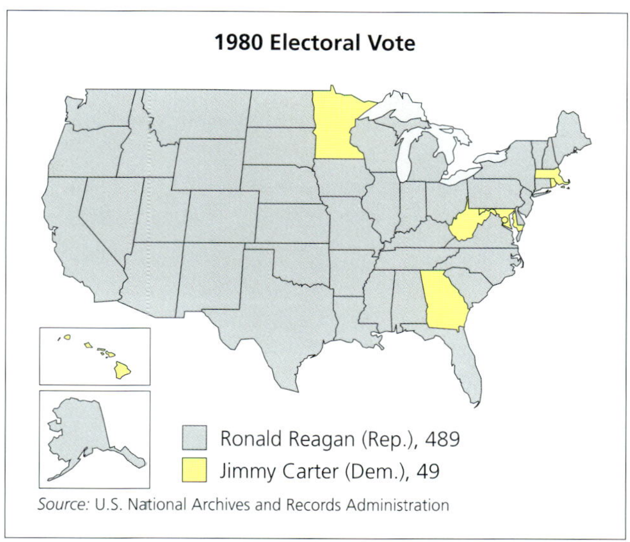

Source: U.S. National Archives and Records Administration

power to guarantee that the United States could "win" a nuclear contest. Both parties endorsed a rise in military spending.

The Campaign

Carter entered the campaign trailing Reagan. Even Democratic polls concluded that Carter was widely unpopular. The Democratic campaign strategy was therefore aimed at undermining Reagan's popularity by portraying him as potentially dangerous—a strategy similar to the one used against Barry Goldwater in 1964. It proved to be a difficult strategy for Carter to execute however, since it stood in contrast with his image as a Baptist Sunday School teacher.

For the Republicans Reagan was a master at communicating via television, but also prone to making mistakes in casual, off-the-cuff conversations. Reagan had a special advisor who traveled with him to help prevent such errors.

Initially Carter tried to conduct the campaign from the White House, the so-called "Rose Garden" strategy, which maximized his advantages as the incumbent. As his ratings in the polls continued to lag behind Reagan's, Carter agreed to a more aggressive campaign, and even to a debate against Reagan on October 28, just a week before the election. In the debate Carter aggressively challenged Reagan's record. Reagan responded with a good natured phrase, "There you go again," as if to imply that Carter was distorting the truth. In the context of television and in terms of how voters perceived the outcome, Regan clearly bested the president.

Reagan's most effective slogan during the campaign was, "Are you better off now than you were four years ago?" Given the battering of the economy during the Carter administration, most voters answered, "No."

The Outcome

Reagan won both the popular vote and the electoral vote. The Republican ticket won 43.9 million votes, or 50.8 percent, to the Democrats' 35.5 million votes, or 41 percent. Anderson, the moderate Independent, won 5.7 million votes, or 6.6 percent of the total, one of the strongest showings for an Independent since George Wallace won 13.5 percent of the popular vote in 1968.

In the electoral vote Reagan received 489 to just 49 for Carter. The incumbent won his home state of Georgia, his running mate's home state of Minnesota, plus Rhode Island, West Virginia, Maryland, Hawaii, and the District of Columbia. Anderson carried no states.

Part of Reagan's victory was attributed to disaffected Democrats who voted for Reagan. Carter won only two-thirds of the votes from people who identified themselves as Democrats; by comparison, Reagan got the votes of over 90 percent of people who identified themselves as Republicans. Among Independents Reagan out-polled Carter by a margin of 58–27 percent.

Post-election polls showed that the economy was the most important issue, and one which cost Carter votes. Social issues also cost the Democrats support, especially among socially conservative blue-collar workers. On the subject of the Iran hostage crisis most voters thought Carter had projected an image of American weakness and looked to Reagan to restore American prestige.

More Information

▶ Barrett, Laurence. *Gambling with History: Ronald Reagan in the White House*. Garden City, New York: Doubleday, 1983.

▶ Cannon, Lou. *President Reagan: The Role of a Lifetime*. New York: Simon and Schuster, 1991.

▶ Dallek, Matthew. *The Right Moment: Ronald Reagan's First Victory and the Decisive Turning Point in American Politics*. New York: Free Press, 2000.

▶ Evans, Rowland and Robert Novak. *The Reagan Revolution*. New York: Dutton, 1981.

▶ Germond, Jack and Jules Witcover. *Blue Smoke and Mirrors: How Reagan Won and Why Carter Lost the Election of 1980*. New York: Viking, 1981.

▶ Jordan, Hamilton. *Crisis: The Last Year of the Carter Presidency*. New York: Putnam, 1982.

▶ Morris, Edmund. *Dutch: A Memoir of Ronald Reagan*. New York: Random House, 1999.

▶ Ranney, Austin (ed.) *The American Elections of 1980*. Washington: American Enterprise Institute for Public Policy, 1981.

▶ Reagan, Ronald. *An American Life*. New York: Simon and Schuster, 1990.

Periodicals

▶ Emerson, Steven and Jesse Furman. "The Conspiracy That Wasn't: The Hunt for the October Surprise." *The New Republic*, November 18, 1991, p. 16.

▶ "How the Land Slid." *Newsweek*, November 17, 1980, p. 31.

On the Web

▶ "The Living Room Candidate: A History of Presidential Campaign Commercials 1952–2000." American Museum of the Moving Image. **http://www.ammi.org/livingroomcandidate/**.

1984
Ronald Reagan (Republican) vs. Walter Mondale (Democrat)

Ronald Reagan's campaign for reelection in 1984 resulted in one of the least dramatic presidential elections since Franklin D. Roosevelt ran against Republican Alf Landon in 1936 and Lyndon Johnson ran against Republican Barry Goldwater in 1964. Reagan won reelection against Democrat Walter Mondale by one of the biggest landslides in American presidential election history. Reagan was sometimes called the "Teflon President," since setbacks that occurred during his terms did not seem to stick to him, as they had in the case of his predecessor, Democrat Jimmy Carter.

The Context

In 1980 Reagan had presented an economic program that combined tax cuts, spending reductions, and increased military spending, all intended to cure an economic recession. Reagan's eventual vice presidential candidate, George H.W. Bush, had previously dubbed it "voodoo economics." During the course of the first Reagan administration, the combination had resulted in unprecedented deficits (spending more than the government collected in taxes) as had been widely predicted by Reagan's political foes.

In foreign affairs an effort by the U.S. Marines to restore peace to Lebanon effectively ended when 241 Americans died in a terrorist bombing of their camp near Beirut. The bombing caused a withdrawal of American forces that might have seemed like a U.S. humiliation but was not perceived that way by the electorate.

For Reagan neither the soaring deficits nor reverses in foreign policy diminished his popularity. He was able to maintain a certain distance from the policies of his administration, using television effectively to project the image of a strong, caring chief executive somewhat in the mold of President Dwight Eisenhower from 1953–61. The answer to the question whether that image was the result of effective leadership, or merely a reflection of Reagan's earlier career experience as a motion picture and television actor, depended largely on whether the answer came from a Republican or a Democrat.

The Candidates

In 1984 there was never a question that Ronald Reagan would be the Republican nominee. Reagan stuck with his vice president, George H. W. Bush. The Republican convention in Detroit was an opportunity for the Republicans to open the 1984 campaign with a unified front, united behind a candidate who asked again, "Are you better off now than you were four years ago?" With both inflation and unemployment reduced, Reagan knew that most voters could answer, "Yes."

The Democratic nominating process was far more complex. Mondale, a senator from Minnesota who had been the

vice presidential running mate of Jimmy Carter in the losing 1980 election, was challenged by so-called New Democrats, and especially Senator Gary Hart of Colorado. Hart's strategy was to combine more conservative economic policy, including reductions in spending, with a set of liberal social policies.

Hart succeeded in scoring an impressive victory in the New Hampshire primary followed by victories two weeks later in Massachusetts, Rhode Island, and Florida. Mondale won primaries in Alabama and Georgia. Civil rights leader Jesse Jackson also entered the race, drawing support from African Americans that might have been expected to go to Mondale.

The effect of Hart's challenge was to push Mondale into defending the set of "old" Democratic policies that had been prevalent since Franklin Roosevelt's New Deal in the 1930s. When Mondale won primaries in Illinois, Pennsylvania, New Jersey, and New York, it limited Hart's likelihood of gaining the nomination, but Hart's very presence in the race made it impossible for Mondale to style himself as a "new" Democrat.

At the Democratic convention in San Francisco Mondale was nominated on the first ballot, but this did not mean that the divisions in the party were instantly healed. Mondale was faced with a need to bring dissident factions together for the general election, a handicap made even more critical by the unity of the Republicans behind Reagan. Even after the convention Jackson insisted as a condition for his support that African Americans have prominent roles in the Democratic party and election campaign. The result was to make the Democrats seem more like a shaky coalition of special interest groups than a coherent political party.

Mondale scored a public relations coup at the convention by selecting as his running mate Representative Geraldine Ferraro of New York, the first woman nominated to run for national office by a major party. In the early days of the campaign the advantage of having Ferraro on the ticket was diminished when questions were raised about financial dealings of her husband, John Zaccaro. Rather than providing Mondale with a boost the Ferraro nomination presented another obstacle to be overcome.

The Issues

Economy. In the 1980 election the combination of high inflation and high unemployment had helped propel the Republicans back into the White House. An improved economy in 1984 helped keep them there.

Deficits. The flip side of a strong economy in 1984 was rapidly rising government borrowing. Mondale tried to make the point that high government deficits sowed dangerous economic seeds for the future, since the borrowed money would have to be repaid. But in 1984 the public's relief over economic recovery over-shadowed more abstract concerns about how future generations would have to cope with paying back government debts.

Taxes. Reagan had lowered taxes as promised, and government deficits had risen as predicted, making it necessary to borrow to fund the rise in military spending occasioned by a renewed arms race with the Soviet Union. Mondale pledged at the Democratic convention that if elected he would raise taxes. His promise was based on his belief that deficits would come back to bite the economy in the future but his position enabled Reagan to portray Mondale as a "tax and spend" Democrat. A vow to raise taxes cost Mondale support just as Reagan's promise to cut taxes even further proved highly attractive.

Arms race. Mondale and Reagan vied with one another over who would be tougher in meeting military and diplomatic challenges raised by the Soviet Union. Mondale tried to portray Reagan as another Goldwater: someone who could not be trusted to avoid nuclear war. The fact that Reagan had already been president for four years without getting into a

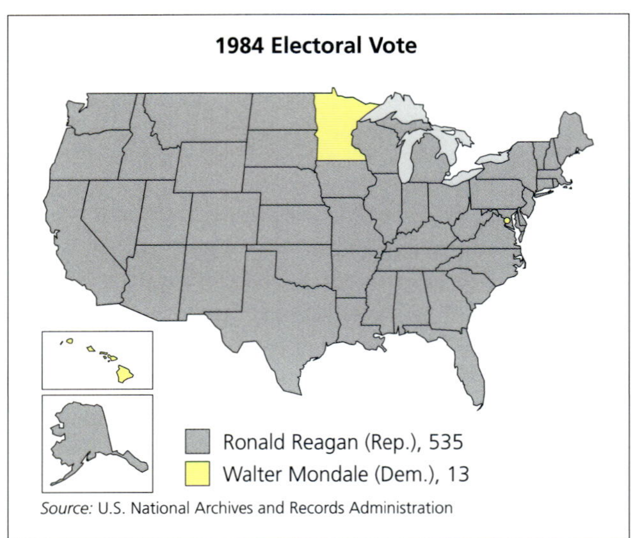

Source: U.S. National Archives and Records Administration

confrontation blunted this argument. The debates included differences over a missile defense system, dubbed "Star Wars" by Mondale, that Reagan had proposed. Mondale urged that the United States should vow to "keep the heavens free" of the arms race.

Age. Reagan was the oldest candidate ever elected president. The Democrats tried to hint that Reagan was too old, at 73, to serve another four-year term. Reagan neatly sidestepped the issue in a debate with Mondale when he promised not to raise the issue of fitness for office against the much younger, and less experienced, Mondale.

The Campaign

The Reagan campaign revolved around a general "feel good" slogan, "It's morning again in America." Republican campaign ads emphasized improvements in the economy and portrayed images of small-town America where young couples were getting married and buying new houses, where people were working once again in factories that had been closed. "Why would we ever want to go back?" the ads asked, without mentioning the ballooning federal deficits.

Democratic ads emphasized "fairness" in taxation and raised questions about the Reagan administration's foreign policy, calling it reckless. One television spot showed a suburban homeowner digging a shelter for protection against a nuclear attack. Another suggested that rising deficits would benefit foreign lenders and rich corporations at the expense of ordinary people.

In effect, the television campaigns of the two parties pitted bright, optimistic images (Reagan) against predictions of gloom and doom (Mondale). Reagan's ads emphasized that times were good; Mondale's warned that if Reagan were re-elected the future would be bad.

The two candidates engaged in two debates during the campaign. In the first encounter Reagan appeared to be relatively weak compared to Mondale, which the Democrats tried to capitalize on by reiterating concerns about Reagan's age. Reagan's performance was considerably stronger in the second debate which thwarted the Democrats' effort to gain from the fitness issue, and in fact left Mondale defending his own fitness to lead the nation.

The Outcome

Reagan's margin of victory in 1984 was a landslide on a par with Franklin Roosevelt's victory in 1936, Lyndon Johnson's in 1964, and Richard Nixon's in 1972. Reagan won 54.5 million votes, or 58.8 percent of the total compared to Mondale's 37.6 million votes, or 40.6 percent (In 1936 Roosevelt had won 60.8 percent of the popular vote; in 1964 Johnson won 61.1 percent; in 1972 Nixon won 60.7 percent.).

In the electoral college Mondale won just 13 votes—his home state of Minnesota (but only by 3,761 votes out of over two million cast) and the District of Columbia. In all but a handful of states, Reagan's margin over Mondale reflected the landslide proportions of the national totals.

More Information

▶ Gillon, Steven M. *The Democrats' Dilemma: Walter F. Mondale and the Liberal Legacy.* New York: Columbia University Press, 1992.

▶ Hayward, Steven F. *The Age of Reagan: The Fall of the Old Liberal Order, 1964–1980.* Roseville, California: Forum/Prima, 2001.

▶ Johnson, Haynes B. *Sleepwalking Through History: America in the Reagan Years.* New York: W. W. Norton, 1991.

▶ Lewis, Finlay. *Mondale: Portrait of an American Politician.* New York: Perennial Library, 1984.

▶ Ranney, Austin. *The American Elections of 1984.* Durham, North Carolina: Duke University Press, 1984.

Periodicals

▶ Greider, William. "The Year in Politics: Reagan Turns Dangerous. The 1984 Presidential Election is a Battle for the Soul of America." *Rolling Stone,* January 5, 1983, p. 7.

On the Web

▶ "The Living Room Candidate: A History of Presidential Campaign Commercials 1952-2000." American Museum of the Moving Picture. (Digital campaign commercials.). **http://www.ammi.org/livingroomcandidate/.**

FlashFocus: Walter Frederick Mondale

Democratic Presidential Nominee, 1988

Born: January 5, 1928, Ceylon, Minnesota
Family: Son of Theodore Mondale, a Methodist minister, and Claribel Cowan; married Joan Adams
Education: Macalester College, 1951; University of Minnesota, law degree 1956
Career: "Fritz" Mondale was elected Minnesota attorney general in 1960, then named to fill the Senate seat vacated by Hubert Humphrey's election as vice president in 1964. Mondale won two full terms in the Senate (1966 and 1972) before his election as Jimmy Carter's vice president in 1976.
Political life: Democrat. In the Senate Mondale supported the social and welfare initiatives of President Lyndon Johnson's Great Society program. On the subject of Vietnam Mondale was loyal to the Johnson administration even after the war became highly unpopular among liberals. In September, 1968, Mondale broke with the administration and urged an immediate halt to bombing of North Vietnam.

Mondale was elected to a second full Senate term in 1972, declining to run as George McGovern's vice presidential nominee. He became a harsh critic of President Richard Nixon's pursuit of the Vietnam war and his conservative domestic policies.

In 1976 Mondale was elected vice president on the ticket led by Georgia Governor Jimmy Carter and assumed a variety of diplomatic responsibilities. In 1980, Carter and Mondale lost their reelection bid to Republicans Ronald Reagan and George H. W. Bush.

Mondale joined a Washington law firm while successfully maneuvering for the 1984 presidential nomination. He chose New York Rep. Geraldine Ferraro as his running mate, the first time a woman ran on a major party's national ticket. They lost to the incumbent Republicans.

Mondale left politics and returned to his Washington law firm. He was named ambassador to Japan by President Bill Clinton in 1993, and staged a brief, unsuccessful run for the Senate after the death (in a plane crash) of Sen. Paul Wellstone (D-MN) in 2002.

See also: Ronald Reagan, p. 186.

1988
George H. W. Bush (Republican) vs. Michael Dukakis (Democrat)

Ronald Reagan was prevented by the Twenty-second Amendment from running for a third term although his broad popularity was intact at the end of his second term. Instead his two-term vice president, George H. W. Bush, was nominated to run against Democrat Michael Dukakis, governor of Massachusetts. Their contest was oddly devoid of substantive issues and revolved instead on a series of campaign ads and symbols that put the little-known Dukakis on the defensive against Bush.

The Context

On the surface, events leading up to the 1988 election favored the incumbent administration. Decades of Cold War tensions with the Soviet Union were greatly reduced with the rise of Mikhail Gorbachev as a Russian leader eager to reach new accommodations with the West. Employment was high, inflation low, and there was reasonable economic growth. The 1980 taunt of Ronald Reagan, "Are you better off today than you were four years ago?" again worked to the advantage of the Republicans.

True, the government had run unprecedented deficits by following Reagan's formula of cutting taxes while increasing military spending. A policy that had, in effect, pushed the Soviet Union into bankruptcy had also driven the United States deeply into debt, to the extent that loans from abroad were needed to enable the government to pay its bills. The Iran-Contra affair also emerged, a scandal in which government agents were caught selling arms to the regime in Iran that had seized Americans hostage in 1979. The proceeds of the arms sales were used to fund anti-Communist guerrillas in Nicaragua, in direct violation of an American law prohibiting such aid. President Reagan and Vice President Bush both declared they had been unaware of these activities—"out of the loop," in the words of Bush—an explanation that was seemingly accepted by the American people. Once again the "Teflon president," and his vice president, escaped accountability.

On October, 19 1987, the Dow Jones Industrial Average fell 508 points, its biggest one-day fall in its history, equivalent to 22.6 percent of its value. The fall would lead to economic recession but this was not evident during the 1988 election.

The Candidates

In the midst of general satisfaction with the state of the nation, the nomination of Reagan's vice president to succeed him in the White House might have seemed a foregone conclusion except for the fact that the last time an incumbent vice president had been nominated for the presidency was in 1836, when Martin Van Buren succeeded Andrew Jackson. Indeed, Bush faced five challengers for the Republican nomination, not all of whom were credible. Senator Bob Dole of Kansas, the vice presidential nominee in 1976, was close to Bush on most policies but lacked Bush's upper-class, prep-school background. Pat Robertson, a television evangelist, tried to turn the contest into a religious revival by appealing to "Christian soldiers" to support his candidacy. Senator Pierre du Pont of Delaware and New York Congressman Jack Kemp attacked Bush from the right while Alexander Haig, a former general and secretary of state, tried to make foreign policy the main issue in the contest.

None of the challengers seemed to have much chance of beating Bush, but in caucuses held in Iowa (a variant on the presidential primary) Bush came in third, trailing Dole and

Robertson. The Iowa results spurred Bush into action in the New Hampshire primary, which was held eight days later and which Bush won. The vice president went on to win the South Carolina primary along with a series of primaries in other southern states. By April 26, with victory in Pennsylvania, Bush had secured enough delegates to be assured of the Republican nomination.

Attention then turned to Bush's vice presidential nominee. Bush kept quiet about his choice until the Republican convention in New Orleans when he announced his choice: Senator J. Danforth Quayle of Indiana, age 41. The choice immediately raised controversy after reports that Quayle had used family connections to avoid service in Vietnam by settling into a desirable and safe position in the National Guard.

On the Democratic side there was no clear front-runner for the nomination at the beginning of 1988 after Walter Mondale's crushing loss to Reagan four years earlier. The early front-runner was Dukakis, whose campaign was the best-funded of any of the contenders. His competitors for the Democratic nomination included Colorado Senator Gary Hart, who had been George McGovern's campaign manager in 1972 and was a self-described "new Democrat;" Senator Al Gore of Tennessee; Senators Paul Simon of Illinois and Joseph Biden of Delaware; Representative Richard Gephardt of Missouri; Governor Bruce Babbitt of Arizona; and civil rights leader Jesse Jackson. One by one most of the contenders were forced out of the race. Evidence of marital infidelity knocked out Hart in May, 1987 (although he reentered the race briefly in December); accusations of plagiarism eliminated Biden in the autumn of 1987. By early March poor showings in early primary elections had effectively eliminated all but Dukakis, Gore and Jackson. Of these, Jackson was not taken seriously by many party professionals because he was African American, a perception that was challenged when Jackson won the Michigan caucus contest on March 26, the first time Jackson had come in first in a contest among mostly white voters. Gore finished a weak third in the key New York primary and withdrew from the campaign. Jackson also was effectively eliminated by failure to win in New York but stayed in the race until the end. Dukakis was finally guaranteed the nomination after winning the last four primaries, in California, Montana, New Jersey, and New Mexico.

At the Democratic convention in Atlanta from July 18–21, Dukakis was nominated on the first ballot. Jackson made it known that he would like the vice presidential nomination, but Dukakis turned instead to Senator Lloyd Bentsen of Texas in hopes of providing geographical and ideological balance to the ticket of the liberal New Englander.

The Issues

Taxes and deficits. Federal borrowing (budget deficits) had reached historic highs in the Reagan administration as a result of a combination of tax cuts and increased military spending. Despite this, Republican Bush declared in the campaign: "Read my lips: no new taxes." The Democrats, on the other

Born: June 12, 1924, Milton, Massachusetts
Family: Son of Prescott Bush, Republican senator from Connecticut, and Dorothy Walker; married Barbara Pierce
Education: Phillips Academy; (Andover, Massachusetts); Yale University
Political career: George Bush was a Navy pilot in World War II. After graduating from Yale he settled in Odessa, Texas, and worked in the oil industry, eventually founding an oil drilling company.

Bush became chairman of the Republican Party in Houston, Texas, then ran for the Senate in 1964 but lost to Senator Ralph Yarborough. In 1966 Bush won the first of two terms representing a Houston suburb in the House of Representatives.

In 1970 Bush lost his second Senate campaign, to Democrat Lloyd Bentsen. President Nixon awarded Bush's party loyalty with an appointment as U.S. Ambassador to the United Nations.

Nixon's successor, Gerald Ford, sent Bush as chief U.S. representative to China from September, 1974 to January, 1976. Bush returned to Washington as Director of the Central Intelligence Agency for a year.

After Jimmy Carter was elected president in 1976 Bush began his own quest for the 1980 Republican presidential nomination. His campaign was unsuccessful, and he accepted the vice presidential nomination under Ronald Reagan and served for two terms.

Bush won the Republican presidential nomination in 1988 and capitalized on Reagan's popularity to win the White House over Democrat Michael Dukakis.

Shortly after Bush took office, Iraq invaded Kuwait. Bush organized a successful campaign to drive Iraq out of Kuwait, resulting in widespread public support. After the Gulf War the U.S. economy slipped into a sharp recession. Bush seemed insensitive to the economic suffering of Americans and he lost his bid for reelection to Governor Bill Clinton of Arkansas.

Eight years later Bush's son, George W. Bush, was elected president by beating Clinton's vice president, Al Gore.

hand, accused the Reagan administration of taking the United States from being "the number one lender nation in the world to the number one debtor nation in the world."

"Liberalism." The Bush campaign focused on the record of Dukakis as governor of Massachusetts, lampooning the state as "Taxachusetts" and accusing Dukakis of being a "tax and spend liberal." The accusations were in large part the Republican response to Democratic accusations that Republican tax cuts, in combination with military spending, had resulted in ballooning government debt.

Military spending. The Reagan administration had sharply increased military spending on grounds that the United States

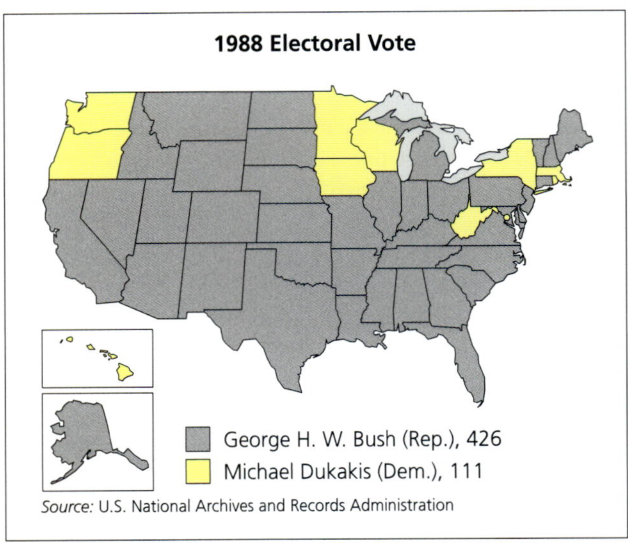

Source: U.S. National Archives and Records Administration

publicans in particular turned to a series of television commercials attacking the record and suitability of Dukakis to be president. The Bush campaign commercial with the biggest impact featured a convicted murderer, William ("Willie") Horton. During a weekend release from a Massachusetts prison Horton had traveled to Virginia and killed a man and woman. Although both the federal government and other states had similar weekend-release programs, the Bush campaign focused on the Horton case to suggest that Dukakis was soft on crime. The commercial was magnified by extensive discussion in news stories, and in a television interview Dukakis was asked about his opposition to the death penalty. What if his own wife was raped and murdered, he was asked. Would he still oppose the death penalty? Dukakis, who had a reputation as a somewhat emotionless bureaucrat, harmed himself by not expressing emotion or anger at the thought. Instead he dryly replied that he opposed the death penalty and that studies showed it was ineffective at preventing crime. The commercial, and Dukakis' bland response to an emotionally charged question, amounted to little less than a fiasco. Another Bush commercial showed Dukakis wearing a helmet and driving in a tank. The candidate looked faintly ridiculous—too small for his helmet and for the tank—even as the narration accused Dukakis of opposing new weapons system. As with the Horton ad, the tank commercial effectively undercut the Democratic candidate on an emotional level while nominally discussing defense policy.

In his campaign Dukakis was never able to reply effectively to the Bush attacks, or to launch counter-attacks against Bush. Instead Dukakis was permanently on the defensive during most of the fall campaign. Although public opinion polls showed that the position of Dukakis was more consistent with the majority of Americans than that of Bush on many issues, ranging from social equality, reducing nuclear weapons, and protecting civil liberties, the Bush campaign was much more effective in undercutting its opponent than were the Democrats.

had fallen behind the Soviet Union, a longstanding debate during the Cold War. In the 1988 campaign Republicans continued to support a high level of spending on the military, while the Democrats advocated reduced spending. The emergence of Gorbachev as leader of the Soviet Union in 1985 seemed to open a new chapter in the Cold War. Gorbachev advocated two new policies: glasnost (openness) and perestroika (restructuring), resulting in a freer society inside Russia and a gradual relaxation of the Soviet grip on Communist countries in Eastern Europe. In 1988, though, the full results of Gorbachev's policies had not yet been seen and Republicans insisted on their traditional support for military spending.

The Campaign

Without a compelling set of circumstances, such as war or economic depression, to differentiate the two candidates, the Re-

The Outcome

Bush beat Dukakis in the popular vote, 48.9 million (53.4 percent) to 41.8 million (45.6 percent), a far smaller margin than Reagan's in 1984, but still a convincing victory. In the electoral college Bush collected 426 votes to just 111 for Dukakis (and one vote for Lloyd Bentsen, the vice presidential candidate). Dukakis carried ten states—his home state, Massachusetts, plus Rhode Island, New York, West Virginia, Iowa, Wisconsin, Minnesota, Oregon, Washington, Hawaii—and the District of Columbia.

Perhaps reflecting the lack of substantial issues in the campaign, only about 50 percent of eligible voters bothered to come to the polls on election day, the lowest turnout since 1924.

Nor did Bush have "coattails" as a presidential candidate. His party lost three seats in the House of Representatives and one seat in the Senate, leaving both halves of Congress under Democratic control.

More Information

- Black, Chris and Thomas Oliphant. *All By Myself: The Unmaking of a Presidential Campaign*. Chester, Connecticut: Globe Pequot Press, 1989.
- Bush, George, with Victory Gold. *Looking Forward*. New York: Bantam Books, 1988.
- Duffy, Michael and Dan Goodgame. *Marching in Place: The Status Quo Presidency of George Bush*. New York: Simon and Schuster, 1992.
- Hinck, Edward A. *Enacting the Presidency: Political Argument, Presidential Debates and Presidential Character*. Westport, Connecticut: Praeger, 1993.
- Kenney, Charles and Robert L. Turner. *Dukakis: An American Odyssey*. Boston: Houghton Mifflin Co, 1988.
- Nyhan, David. *The Duke: The Inside Story of a Political Phenomenon*. New York: Warner Books, 1988.

Periodical

- Dowd, Marreen. "The Right Fluff," *Washington Monthly*, July–August, 1992, p. 44.

On the Web

- "Debate History: The 1988 Debates." Commission on Presidential Debates. (Includes transcripts of two Presidential debates and the vice-presidential debate.) **http://www.debates.org/pages/trans88b.html.**
- "The Living Room Candidate" American Museum of the Moving Image. (campaign commercials) **http://www.ammi.org/livingroomcandidate/.**

1992
William "Bill" Clinton (Democrat)
vs. George H. W. Bush (Republican) vs. H. Ross Perot (Independent)

"It's the economy stupid" was the internal slogan of Bill Clinton's Democratic campaign against incumbent Republican George Bush in 1992, and it proved prophetic. Despite Bush's earlier popularity following victory in the 1991 Gulf War to liberate Kuwait from Iraqi occupation, an economic recession and widespread fears about job security contributed to Bush's defeat in 1992, an election which also saw the strongest showing (18.9 percent of the popular vote) for a third party candidate since Theodore Roosevelt's Progressive Party in 1912.

The Context

In 1991 President Bush had launched an attack on Iraqi forces occupying the oil-rich kingdom of Kuwait. The Americans and their allies scored a rapid, decisive victory, sending the Iraqis fleeing back into Iraq. Bush's popularity, measured by polls, rose to stratospheric levels of around 90 percent. With the next presidential election just over a year away Bush appeared to be a shoo-in.

However, the economy was mired in a recession. The economic downturn was not severe but it did affect middle class, white-collar workers to a greater extent than previous downturns. The president had reacted in part by denying that things were so bad and assuring the public that an upturn was just around the corner. More importantly, faced with huge federal budget deficits, Bush violated his unambiguous promise in 1988 ("Read my lips: no new taxes") and raised taxes. As the election neared Bush seemed unable to cope with the economy, and voters interpreted his inaction as indifference.

For the first time in nearly half a century the Cold War was not an issue in 1992. The Soviet Union had collapsed, seemingly eliminating any imminent threat of nuclear war between the former "superpowers." Countries of Eastern Europe, formerly dominated by the Soviet Union, were free to choose their own governments. The end of the Cold War also had an impact on military spending and on the future role of the United States in a world where there was only one superpower left.

The Candidates

Like most incumbents Bush was the presumed Republican candidate for reelection in 1992. Only one person, journalist and talk-show host Patrick Buchanan, launched a challenge for the Republican nomination. Buchanan's challenge was based on so-called "social issues," notably abortion and immigration (he opposed both) as well as a tougher stand on crime and more influence for organized religion in government (Buchanan favored both). Buchanan entered the New Hampshire Republican presidential primary in February and won 37 percent of the vote. Although Bush scored 53 percent in New Hampshire, the challenge by Buchanan was surprisingly strong and made Bush appear relatively weak. Over the next three months, Bush continued to win primaries even as Buchanan's contributions declined and his campaign ran out of money. He dropped out of contention in early May, after Bush had won enough delegates to guarantee nomination, but in the process the incumbent president had been wounded.

Bush was easily nominated by the Republican convention, which turned into a prolonged television ad for Bush and the Republican platform. However, suspicions about Bush from the conservative wing of the party muted his support coming from the convention.

Counter to the advice of many party professionals Bush again chose Dan Quayle as his vice presidential running mate. During the 1988 election Quayle had achieved a reputation, never entirely overcome, as an intellectual lightweight and was viewed as attracting few votes in his own right.

For Democrats, hoping to win back the White House for the first time since Jimmy Carter's single term in 1976, there were five contenders for the nomination none of whom began the race with national name recognition. Former Senator Paul Tsongas of Massachusetts focused on the troubled economy. Senator Tom Harkin sought support in the traditional Democratic coalition of labor unions and the economically disadvantaged. Former California Governor Edmund "Jerry" Brown ran a low-budget populist campaign. Senator Bob Kerrey of Nebraska focused on healthcare as a signature issue. William "Bill" Clinton, governor of Arkansas, led an effort to steer the Democrats into a more moderate position on such issues as welfare.

Tsongas won the primary in New Hampshire; Clinton came in second. For Clinton, however, the outcome in New Hampshire was a victory, since it came after a string of news stories about marital infidelities (specifically with a woman named Gennifer Flowers) and evading the draft during the Vietnam War. Clinton had dealt with both issues by appearing on television programs to assure voters that his marriage was sound and to deny evading the draft. After New Hampshire Clinton dubbed himself "the Comeback Kid," effectively claiming a victory from a second-place finish.

In the primary elections following New Hampshire Clinton accumulated a string of victories in southern states, his natural base of strength, as most of the other contenders failed to catch fire with voters and withdrew. Tsongas, Clinton's main competitor, had refocused his campaign to attack Clinton, a tactic that backfired by making the Arkansas governor seem like the strong front-runner while doing little to enhance Tsongas' own reputation. After March 19 only Clinton and Brown were still in the contest. Brown's somewhat quirky campaign did not seem serious although the Californian did win the Connecticut primary on March 24, and won more votes in New York than any other candidate. Clinton made a point of responding to attacks against him, and assured voters that he could "feel your pain" in the economy. For Clinton, the second half of the primary election season was an opportunity to present himself to voters as a sensitive, caring politician from the small town of Hope, Arkansas who was more in touch with voters than the elitist President Bush.

Clinton had secured the Democratic nomination well ahead of the party convention. He chose as his vice presidential running mate Tennessee Senator Albert Gore who, like Clinton, was a moderate-to-conservative Democrat with a reputation as a strong supporter of environmental protection.

FlashFocus: *William Jefferson Clinton*

42nd President, 1993–2001

Born: August 19, 1946, Hope, Arkansas
Family: William Jefferson Blythe, who died in an accident before his son was born, and Virginia Kelley. Clinton's mother married Roger Clinton when her son was eight; William changed his last name to Clinton at age 15; married Hillary Rodham

Education: Georgetown University; Oxford University (Rhodes Scholar); Yale University Law School
Career: Democrat. Attorney general of Arkansas, 1976; governor of Arkansas, 1978–80, 1982–92

In 1991 Clinton became chairman of the Democratic Leadership Conference, a group dominated by Southern Democrats determined to shift control of their party away from the liberal Northeast. In October 1991 Clinton announced he would run for the Democratic presidential nomination in 1992.

He gained nomination despite charges of inexperience in foreign affairs and of personal indiscretions in his sexual life. He lost the early primaries but bounced back on "Super Tuesday" (the day in March when several large states held primaries) and by June 2 had enough primary victories to assure the nomination.

Clinton's two administrations (1993–2001) were marked by strong economic growth, spurred by the boom in new Internet-related companies, and by continuing scandals over his sexual life. Early efforts to create a comprehensive federal health care insurance program failed conspicuously, but the government deficit withered and turned into a surplus by the end of his administration. He was instrumental in negotiating a cease-fire in Northern Ireland between warring Protestants and Catholics, but could not finalize a Middle East peace agreement between Israel and the Palestine Liberation Organization despite strong efforts.

Clinton survived an effort by Republicans to impeach him on grounds of lying to a grand jury about his affair with a White House aide, Monica Lewinsky, but the impeachment shadowed the unsuccessful 2002 presidential campaign of Clinton's two-term vice president, Albert Gore.

An independent candidate also appeared in 1992—H. Ross Perot, a billionaire founder of a computer services company, who played on voter dissatisfaction with both political parties. Perot's approach was entirely unconventional. He did not enter the race, but said he would run if his supporters could collect enough signatures to put his name on the ballot in every state. Unlike many third party candidates Perot drew serious attention from the news media, and polls in the spring showed that he was preferred by up to a fourth of the voters, far more than typical for third party candidates, especially one who had never held office before. Perot campaigned through appearances on radio and television talk shows, where he presented the image of a tough-minded businessman equipped with charts showing the scope of problems with government borrowing and a negative balance of trade. Perot's support peaked in early summer, after which news stories about how his company had thrived on government contracts and his tendency to hire private detectives to look into the private lives of business colleagues caused his support to wane. In mid-July, just after the Democratic convention, Perot announced that he was dropping out of the campaign.

The Issues

Economy. Bush advocated repealing tax increases passed with his approval in 1990. In so doing, he seemed to be trying to make good on his 1988 pledge not to increase taxes; but at the same time his new pledge was a reminder that he had broken his previous promise. Bush accused Democrats of playing a "shell game" by supporting a balanced federal budget while simultaneously increasing spending. For Clinton the economy was by far the strongest issue; the fact that the country seemed mired in a recession was an argument in itself for a change in administrations. Clinton proposed a tax credit for some investments to help build new companies and thus produce new jobs, as well as restructuring income taxes to make the wealthy pay more in taxes—"their fair share") and the lower- and middle-class pay less. He promised to make government more efficient and limit budget increases to the rate of growth of the average paycheck. Of all the issues in the campaign, the economy was by far the most important in determining the outcome.

Social issues. Abortion in particular was a strongly emotional issue in 1992 for many voters. Bush advocated a constitutional amendment to outlaw abortion. Clinton supported women's right to choose abortion. Bush opposed proposals to include sexual orientation as a protected right; he also thought AIDS, a disease that struck homosexuals disproportionately, should be treated like any other disease. Clinton supported laws to protect homosexuals, including ending a ban on gays and lesbians in the military, as well as a "war on AIDS."

Health care. The cost of health care was rising rapidly, adding significantly to the federal budget deficit. Clinton advocated making access to health care a right, rather than a privilege, as well as instituting controls on health care costs. Bush opposed handing health care coverage over to government, and advocated a tax policy to help individuals and small companies pay health insurance premiums.

Environment. Clinton and his vice presidential running mate, Gore, argued that environmental protection was needed and was not inconsistent with economic growth. They focused on protecting so-called "old growth" forests from logging, and on banning new oil drilling off-shore. Bush argued that environmental controls had to be tempered to protect economic growth.

The Campaign

After the nominating conventions Clinton started the general campaign with a comfortable lead over Bush. On all the important issues—the economy, health care, education, and the environment—opinion polls indicated that the Democratic positions were favored by voters. Clinton's campaign strategist, James Carville, insisted that in 1992, Clinton should remember that "it's the economy, stupid."

Lacking a strong positive issue on which to base his campaign, Bush attempted to discredit his opponent, much as he had four years earlier when he faced Michael Dukakis. However, the Republican campaign did not come up with a strong theme, such as the "Willie Horton" commercial that implied Dukakis was soft on crime (see p. 194). A variety of approaches ranging from attacking Clinton's wife Hillary to belittling his record as governor of Arkansas, fell flat.

In October a nonpartisan commission invited Clinton and Bush to debate one another. Clinton accepted but Bush declined—until Clinton supporters started showing up at Bush

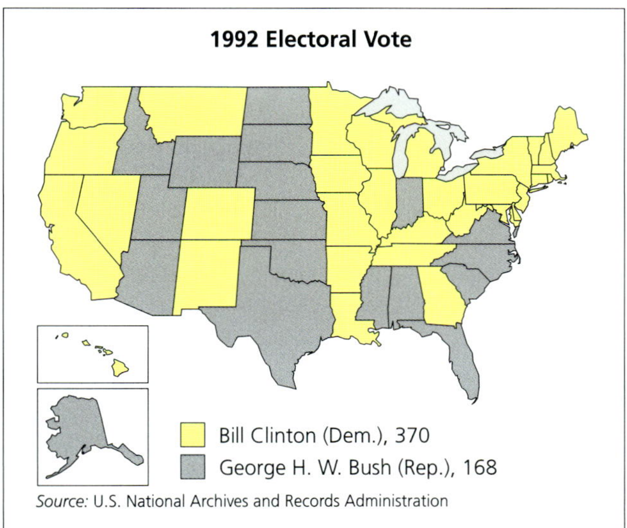

Source: U.S. National Archives and Records Administration

rallies wearing chicken costumes. Belatedly Bush reversed course and agreed to debate Clinton in October.

It was at this point that Perot reentered the contest, promising to focus attention on the economy and also threatening to hurt both Clinton and Bush. In Bush's case Perot put even more attention on the issue on which Bush was most vulnerable. In Clinton's case Perot threatened to divide the anti-Bush vote between Democrat Clinton and Independent Perot.

In a series of three-man debates Perot emerged as the "winner" and Bush was the "loser." Clinton was viewed as having avoided defeat. After the debates Perot's standing in opinion polls started rising—until debates between the vice presidential candidates. In those debates the Republican, Quayle, surprised many voters by avoiding the sort of misstatements that characterized his campaigning in 1988. Gore came across as intelligent and knowledgeable but also stiff and humorless. Perot's running mate, retired Admiral James Stockdale, seemed confused and poorly prepared.

The end of the campaign threatened to make the election a cliff-hanger. Perot's standing in the polls was steadily rising while Bush was closing in on Clinton, largely the result of a frenetic schedule of appearances during which Bush labeled Clinton "Slick Willie," called Gore "Ozone," and called the Democratic ticket "bozos."

The Outcome

Despite the last-minute surges of both Perot and Bush, Clinton won the popular vote with 44.9 million votes (43 percent) to Bush's 39.1 million (37.4 percent) and Perot's 19.7 million (18.9 percent). Clinton swept the electoral college with 370 votes to 168 for Bush. Perot did not carry any states.

The map showing Clinton's victory shows that the Democrats captured the heavily populated northeastern quadrant of the country with the sole exception of Indiana, plus the West Coast and selected states in the South (Arkansas, Clinton's home state, Louisiana, and Georgia). Bush's support lay in a vertical swath of farm states in the Midwest, running from North Dakota south to Texas, the Rocky Mountain states (except Montana, Colorado and New Mexico), and the South.

Perot drew his greatest support in the western half of the country, especially the Rocky Mountain states, and was relatively much weaker in the South and Northeast. Perot's strongest showing was in Maine, where he beat third-place finisher Bush by 315 votes but trailed Clinton by about 57,000 votes (out of 679,000 cast). Perot's 18.9 percent of the popular vote was the highest third party share since former President Theodore Roosevelt's Progressive Party won 27.4 percent in 1912. It was not, however, indicative of a trend or of Perot's staying power. Four years later Perot captured only 8.4 percent of the popular vote.

More Information

- Brown, Gene. *The 1992 Election*. Brookfield, Connecticut: Millbrook Press, 1992.
- Greenstein, Fred. *The Presidential Difference: Leadership Style from FDR to Clinton*. New York: Martin Kessler Books, 2000.
- Halberstam, David. *War in a Time of Peace: Bush, Clinton and the Generals*. New York: Simon and Schuster, 2002.
- Hamilton, Nigel. *Bill Clinton: An American Journey*. New York: Random House, 2003.
- Heagerty, Leo E. (ed.) *Eyes on the President, George Bush: History in Essays and Cartoons*. Occidental, California: Chronis Publishing, 1993.
- Parmet, Herbert S. *George Bush: The Life of a Lone Star Yankee*. New York: Scribner, 1997.
- Schier, Steven E. (ed.) *The Postmodern Presidency: Bill Clinton's Legacy in U.S. Politics*. Pittsburgh: University of Pittsburgh Press, 2000.

On the Web

- "The Living Room Candidate" American Museum of the Moving Image. (campaign commercials) **http://www.ammi.org/livingroomcandidate/.**

1996
William "Bill" Clinton (Democrat)
vs. Robert "Bob" Dole (Republican) vs. H. Ross Perot (Independent)

Bob Dole was almost certainly the last member of his generation to run for president. It was a generation that grew up during the Great Depression of the early 1930s, then fought in World War II. Dole's campaign came in the midst of a strong economic recovery when the problems of earlier years—the Cold War, Communist subversion, and even economic doldrums—seemed passé in light of the new age of personal computers and the Internet.

The Context

In 1994 Republicans won majorities in both the Senate and House of Representatives for the first time in four decades, posing a serious challenge to President Clinton. In the House Republicans chose Representative Newt Gingrich of Georgia as Speaker. Gingrich was a firebrand on the right, determined to change the direction of government and push through a set of proposals Gingrich called the "Contract with America." The plan was aimed at significantly reducing the role of the federal government. Some of the Gingrich programs were popular and President Clinton agreed to sign them into law, but when Gingrich invited business lobbyists actually to draft legislation deregulating their own industries, or to weaken environmental protection laws, Clinton resisted. In so doing Clinton cemented his image as a moderate and made Gingrich and his fellow House Republicans seem all the more extremist by comparison.

Clinton's strategy was demonstrated in the autumn of 1995 when the Republican Congress sent Clinton a budget that cut funding for many programs favored by the president. Clinton refused to sign the budget, preferring instead to close down many government offices for several days in late November. The Republicans sent another budget to the president in December; again, Clinton vetoed the budget and closed government offices for three weeks at the end of December and into January (Eventually, Congress relented and modified the budget so that Clinton would sign it.) Clinton had succeeded in portraying Gingrich and his House supporters as extremists willing to go to virtually any length, including shutting down basic government functions, in order to get their way. The budget battle, which might have been a political defeat for the president, instead turned into a memorable victory.

The Candidates

President Clinton faced no challenge in obtaining the Democratic nomination, nor did his vice president, Al Gore. Saved from having to spend energy or money on obtaining the nomination, Clinton was able to plan for the general election without having made any promises or gaffes that might come back to haunt him in the fall.

On the Republican side at least nine candidates entered the race to achieve the presidential nomination. Five Senators—Phil Gramm of Texas, Richard Lugar of Indiana, Arlen Specter of Pennsylvania, Lamar Alexander (a former senator) of Tennessee and Robert Dole of Kansas—were joined by three conservative journalists—Patrick Buchanan, Alan Keyes and Steve Forbes—and U.S. Representative Bob Dornan of California. Of these only three lasted beyond the first three weeks of primary elections: Dole, Forbes, and Buchanan. The others failed to attract support and/or ran out of money.

Dole, the Senate Majority Leader since 1994, was not always regarded as the front-runner. He won the Iowa caucuses, but by a smaller-than-expected margin, then lost the New Hampshire primary to Buchanan. Forbes, armed with a huge inherited fortune from the magazine his father founded, stayed in the race partly because he could afford to. Dole recouped his front-runner status by winning a string of primaries, and after the Arizona primary, Dole had won enough delegates to guarantee his nomination.

Ross Perot, the Texas businessman who won over 18 percent of the popular vote in 1992, organized the new Reform Party in September, 1995, to back a second bid for the White House. The new party was different from both the Republican and Democratic Parties; it was organized more as a marketing device for Perot and omitted many of the procedures built up over years by the established parties. Perot did not announce his candidacy for the Reform Party's nomination until July, 1996. Perot's running mate was Pat Choate, who had never held elective office.

A fourth national candidate was Ralph Nader, a well-known activist for consumer rights, who ran as the candidate of the Green Party. Nader effectively ruled himself out of contention by announcing that he would spend a mere $5,000 on his campaign, a statement about the role of fund raising in the major party campaigns.

Before the campaign began in the fall Clinton already had a substantial lead over Dole; Perot was the preference of about seven percent of people polled in September.

The Issues

Character. Clinton was constantly dogged by accusations of personal immorality, especially marital infidelity. Dole was a generation older, a World War II veteran whose withered right arm was a constant reminder of his sacrifice during the war. On the other hand, Clinton was successful in projecting an image of a caring president who understood the problems of ordinary people, whereas Dole's personality tended to be acerbic in public. Clinton seemed comfortable in displaying and discussing emotional issues; Dole backed off from any display of emotion, which tended to make him seem more distant, especially to many women voters.

Economy. After a sluggish start early in the Clinton administration, the economy had rebounded and was growing strongly in 1996. Just as presidents are inevitably blamed for economic downturns, regardless of their cause, so do they get credit for good times, and Clinton benefited greatly from the strong economy in 1996. On economic policy both candidates advocated a balanced budget by 2002. The heart of Dole's economic plan was a proposed 15 percent tax cut for all tax pay-

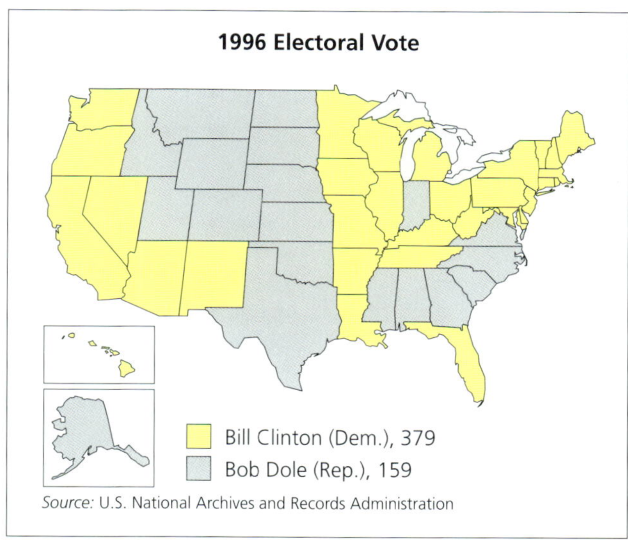

Source: U.S. National Archives and Records Administration

ers, plus repealing taxes on Social Security benefits and lowering taxes on capital gains (the increase in value of stocks and other property). Clinton preferred more targeted tax policies, such as tax credits for parents who adopt a child and eliminating the capital gain on the sale of a home.

Education. Clinton supported continuation of the federal Department of Education; Dole advocated abolishing the federal department in favor of turning over all responsibility for education to the states. Clinton opposed spending "vouchers" that parents could use at private (including religious) schools; Dole supported such vouchers. Proponents of vouchers felt that poorer parents should be given help in financing private schools; opponents felt that such vouchers would simply subtract from the funds available for public schools.

Foreign policy. Absent an imminent threat to the United States, the debate over foreign policy was subdued. Clinton favored working through the United Nations; Dole favored more unilateral action by the United States. Clinton favored American involvement in Arab-Israel peace negotiations; Dole opposed what he characterized as intervention in domestic Israeli politics (i.e. by encouraging Israel to make more concessions in order to achieve peace). Clinton advocated more treaties with Russia to reduce the number of nuclear weapons held by both sides; Dole favored a "Star Wars" missile defense system, first proposed by Ronald Reagan.

The Campaign

The 1996 campaign was largely a story of Dole trying to focus on a theme that would catch the attention of voters in a year when the country was at peace and the economy strong. As a candidate Dole often strayed from the political message laid out for him by his campaign advisors, preferring instead to tell voters about his record in Congress, a tactic that tended to remind voters of Dole's age without scoring major points in the campaign.

FlashFocus: Robert Joseph Dole

Republican Candidate for President, 1996

Born: July 22, 1923, Russell, Kansas
Family: Son of Doran Dole, a creamery operator, and Bina Talbott, a sewing machine saleswoman; married Phyllis Holden (divorced), Elizabeth Hanford
Education: Washburn University; Washburn University Law School
Political career: Kansas state house of representatives, 1951–53; prosecutor, 1953–61; U.S. House of Representatives, 1961–69; U.S. senator, 1969–1996

Bob Dole grew up in the hard-scrabble life of a financially struggling family in a small town in rural Kansas. That background, plus ghastly injuries suffered in the final weeks of World War II (he required years of physical therapy to recover), came together in a personality best known for a sharp tongue and short temper. He was elected to Congress four times starting in 1960, and to the Senate for three terms starting in 1968. He ran for vice president on the losing 1976 Republican ticket, then served as a Republican leader in the Senate (including two stints as Majority Leader).

In Congress Dole faithfully represented his conservative, mostly rural constituents and opposed most of Lyndon Johnson's Great Society programs, while supporting civil rights legislation. He arrived in the Senate in the same year that Richard Nixon was elected president and for most of the Nixon Administration Dole served as a loyal lieutenant.

In 1976 Gerald Ford chose Dole as his vice presidential running mate to appeal to the conservative wing of the party. Dole's famously short temper cast him in the role of the campaign's "hatchet man"—a quality that tripped him up in a televised debate with Walter Mondale when Dole referred to "Democrat" wars, including World War II.

Dole entered a short run for the presidential nomination in 1980 and again in 1988. In 1996 Dole finally won the Republican nomination, running against, and losing to, President Bill Clinton. He is now a partner in a prestigious Washington law firm.

Other biographies from 1996:
William Clinton, p. 197.

Stories about Clinton's personal life seemed to some Republicans like one of the few fruitful areas in which to attack the incumbent president. On social issues Clinton said he supported capital punishment and the right of students to pray in school; on social welfare Clinton reminded voters that he supported reforms to encourage recipients to get jobs, while at the same time supporting a higher minimum wage so that ex-welfare beneficiaries could support themselves.

During the campaign stories emerged that the Democratic Party had received contributions from foreign sources, raising the suggestion of foreign influence over the government. But since the contributions had been made to the Democratic Party, rather than to the Clinton campaign, the candidate managed to sidestep the issue by issuing assurance that his campaign was entirely separate from the Party.

Clinton and Dole participated in debates which reflected the nature of the rest of the campaign: Dole failed to score a significant victory while Clinton was able to use his ability as an effective communicator to project an image of a sympathetic, caring and competent leader. In one of the debates, Clinton disregarded a "rule" and stepped from behind the podium, interacting with an audience in the television studio in a natural, friendly way. Dole seemed frozen behind his podium.

The Outcome

Clinton's victory in the popular vote was significantly larger than it had been when he won in 1992. In 1996 Clinton won 47.4 million votes, or 49.2 percent of the total, compared to Dole's 39.2 million (40.7 percent). Perot, as the Reform Party candidate, received fewer than half as many votes as in 1992. His 1996 total, eight million, represented just 8.4 percent of the total, down from 18.9 percent four years earlier. Nader received 684,871 votes, less than one percent.

In the electoral college Clinton won 379 votes to Dole's 159. Dole carried the Midwest farming states and Rocky Mountain states in a vertical stack starting with Montana and North Dakota in the north, straight south to Texas. He also won a band of southern states from Virginia to Mississippi, excluding Florida, and Alaska.

Clinton won all the northern states east of the Mississippi River, except for Indiana, as well as the Pacific coast states, Arizona, New Mexico and Hawaii, and two southern states, his home state of Arkansas and Louisiana.

Because the 1996 election was largely "non-ideological," insofar as it did not revolve around major issues of political philosophy, it did not seem to mark a turning point in the nation's political history. Instead the election was a testament to Clinton's successful use of professional political advisers who shaped the campaign much like a company might sell a product or service—by appealing to specific groups in the population, such as women, with a combination of personal appeal and orientation on issues that might never come up on the agenda of Congress. The downside to this approach was that neither candidate aroused excitement or commitment from voters, and when Clinton's affair with a White House intern subsequently led to his impeachment by the House of Representatives (but not his removal from office by the Senate), he had little deep commitment from the public to draw on for support.

More Information

▶ Carville, James. *Stickin': The Case for Loyalty*. New York: Simon and Schuster, 2000.

▶ Cramer, Richard Ben. *Bob Dole*. New York: Vintage Books, 1995.

▶ Eszterhas, Joe. *American Rhapsody*. New York: Vintage Books, 2001.

▶ Hilton, Stanley G. *Bob Dole: American Political Phoenix.* Chicago: Contemporary Books, 1988.

▶ Hilton, Stanley G. *Senator for Sale: An Unauthorized Biography of Senator Bob Dole.* New York: St. Martin's Press, 1996.

▶ Klein, Joe. *The Natural: The Misunderstood Presidency of Bill Clinton.* New York: Doubleday, 2002.

▶ Thomas, Evan. *Back From the Dead: How Clinton Survived the Republican Revolution.* New York: Atlantic Monthly Press, 1997.

▶ Woodward, Bob. *The Choice.* New York: Simon and Schuster, 1996.

Periodicals

▶ Mashek, John. "Election a Yawner, Partly Because of the Media." *The Masthead,* Spring 1997, p. 5.

▶ "On the Campaign Trail" (panel discussion). *Brookings Review,* Winter, 1997, p. 42.

On the Web

▶ "The Living Room Candidate 1996," American Museum of the Moving Image. (Selected campaign commercials) **http://www.ammi.org/livingroomcandidate/.**

2000
George W. Bush (Republican) vs. Albert Gore (Democrat) vs. Ralph Nader (Green)

FlashFocus: 2000

Candidates

George W. Bush & Dick Cheney, Republican
Albert Gore, Jr. & Joseph Lieberman, Democrat
Ralph Nader & Winona LaDuke, Green

Issues

Morality. After the sexual scandals involving President Clinton, both candidates promised to bring integrity to the Oval Office. Gore distanced himself from Clinton, refusing his offers of campaign help. Bush struggled to divert public attention from his record of arrest for drunk driving and allegations about past drug use. Both candidates emphasized their Christianity.

Personality. Bush and Gore held very similar, moderate positions on most issues, differing only in details and subtleties of policy, so increased focus was placed upon their personalities. Although Gore was more knowledgeable on issues of foreign policy and had more political experience he often came across as stiff and preachy. Bush was more relaxed and related better to voters.

The Florida vote. On election day major controversy arose over voting procedures in Florida. Hand recounts of ballots were ordered in several counties and the two campaigns filed numerous lawsuits to either enforce or block the recounts. Weeks later the Supreme Court ordered an end to the recounts, and Bush was declared the winner in Florida by under 600 votes, giving him the state's 25 electoral votes, and the presidency.

Outcome

Popular Vote

Gore	50,999,897	48.4%
Bush	**50,456,002**	**47.9%** ✓
Nader	2,882,955	2.7%

Electoral College

Bush	**271** ✓
Gore	266

One elector from Washington, D.C. abstained.

The outcome of the 2000 election was the most complex and controversial of any presidential election. While Democrat Al Gore received about 500,000 more popular votes than Republican George W. Bush, the United States Supreme Court eventually determined the outcome by ordering a halt to recounting ballots in Florida while Bush was ahead, thus giving the Republicans all 25 Florida electoral votes, and pushing Bush over the top in the electoral college tally, 271–266.

The Context

Oddly the 2000 campaign focused on a man who was not in the race: President Bill Clinton. In 1999 Clinton had been impeached by the House of Representatives, but not convicted by the Senate, for his handling of a sex scandal. Clinton had been accused of having an affair with a White House intern, Monica Lewinsky. The president at first denied the accusations, then admitted to improper behavior. The scandal, which included minute details of the president's behavior released to the public by a special prosecutor, Kenneth Starr, seemed to overshadow every other issue for the last two years of Clinton's presidency and had a major impact on the 2000 campaign.

In other respects Clinton's second term was nearly idyllic. The U.S. economy was at the end of an extraordinary cycle of growth and wealth creation, although no one realized the end was near. Prices for shares in companies had reached unprecedented levels. Particularly in the area of technology and the Internet, new companies were attracting large investments and their share prices were highly valued, making owners and employees alike paper millionaires. As stock prices soared, middle- and working-class people began participating as well in a frenzy of investing reminiscent of the 1920s before the crash of 1929.

The most serious foreign policy issue was the disintegration of Yugoslavia and the outbreak of fighting between ethnic groups there. Eventually the United States, with European nations, sent soldiers to keep the warring sides apart, but it was not the sort of military action that seemed to threaten the security of the United States.

The Candidates

Democratic Vice President Al Gore had been part of the Clinton administration since 1993. Gore was not personally tainted by the scandal involving Clinton and he emerged as the most likely Democratic presidential nominee in 2000. He faced one significant challenge, from former New Jersey Senator (and former basketball star) Bill Bradley, who staked out positions more liberal than Gore's. In the first primary election, in New Hampshire on February 1, Gore beat Bradley by a margin of only five percent. It proved to be the high point of Bradley's campaign. Gore went on to win the Delaware primary as well as a string of primary elections held on "Super Tuesday," March 7. Voters who had supported Clinton in 1992 and again in 1996 viewed Gore as the logical successor and the man most likely to extend the Clinton record for another four, or even eight, years.

Bradley dropped out of the contest after Super Tuesday leaving Gore to focus on a running mate. He selected Senator Joseph Lieberman of Connecticut, one of the most conservative Democrats in Congress and regarded as a morally upright individual. (Lieberman was a strictly observant Orthodox Jew, the first member of his faith to be nominated for president or vice president.) Lieberman had also been one of the first Democrats to criticize Clinton's behavior in public.

On the Republican side Texas Governor George W. Bush, son of the forty-first president, quickly emerged as a leading contender for the nomination. His most formidable opponent was Arizona Senator John McCain, whose personal background (as a Vietnam prisoner of war) and progressive views on limiting the influence of corporations on election campaigns put him in a category similar to Theodore Roosevelt a century earlier. Steve Forbes, heir to a magazine publishing fortune, entered the contest, as he had in 1996, and used his personal funds to fight for the election long after his chances had diminished to none. A handful of other Republicans also entered the race early on: Elizabeth Dole, head of the Red Cross and a former cabinet member in the Ford administration; Utah Senator Orrin Hatch; former Education Secretary Lamar Alexander of Tennessee; and former Ambassador Alan Keyes.

McCain won a significant victory in the New Hampshire primary, putting Bush on the defensive. The Texas governor then went to South Carolina, whose primary was next, and made a speech at Bob Jones University, a private school that insisted on racial segregation. Bush's appearance at the controversial school seemed to many as a signal to ultra-conservative southerners who still longed for segregation that George W. Bush was their candidate. Bush won the South Carolina primary on February 17, beating McCain by eleven percentage points.

Bush attracted support among Republicans around the country while McCain appealed largely to Independent voters and some Democrats. In states where voters were free to cast ballots in either the Democratic or Republican elections, McCain did well. In states where only enrolled Republicans could vote in the Republican primary, Bush dominated. In early March McCain dropped his efforts to win the nomination, giving Bush a clear path to the nomination in August. For his running mate Bush chose Richard Cheney, a former defense secretary and chief of staff for Gerald Ford (see p. 182). Cheney was a man of wide-ranging experience in national politics, in contrast to Bush who had none. Cheney's nomination helped reassure voters who worried that Bush demonstrated little knowledge about world affairs or leaders.

The candidates for both parties, chosen without a serious fight, both lunged for the political center, obscuring the difference between themselves in the process. Trying to take advantage of the faint differences between Gore and Bush, a well known campaigner for consumer safety regulations, Ralph Nader, again became the candidate of the Green Party. The Green Party's signature issue was environmental protection, but it also stood for reform in the way presidential elections were financed, largely with contributions from large corporations with an interest in future legislation, and opposition to "globalization," the free import of goods manufactured by American companies in countries where wages were extremely low. In 1996, Nader had also been the Green candidate, pledging to spend only $5,000 on his campaign. In 2000, Nader attracted a significant army of volunteers and mounted a much more credible campaign.

FlashFocus: George Walker Bush

43rd President, 2001–

Born: July 6, 1946, New Haven, Connecticut

Family: Son of George Bush, 41st president, and Barbara Pierce; married Laura Welch

Education: Yale University; Harvard Business School

Political career: Republican. Governor of Texas, 1995–2000

George W. Bush spent much of his childhood in Midland, Texas and later in Houston. After graduating from Yale in 1968 he returned to Houston, where he served as a pilot in the Texas Air National Guard. After graduating from Harvard Business School he settled in Midland, Texas where he entered the oil and gas business. Reacting to what he perceived as a threat to the oil industry by the policies of President Carter, Bush ran for Congress in 1977, but was defeated.

In 1985 Bush experienced what he referred to as a "personal conversion," swearing off alcohol and drugs and declaring himself a "born again" Christian. His new devotion to religion became significant in later political campaigns.

Bush worked on his father's presidential campaigns in 1988 and 1992. He served two terms as governor of Texas from 1995–2000, the first Texas governor elected to consecutive terms. He was the Republican consensus candidate for president in 2000, running against Vice President Al Gore, Jr.

The election proved to be highly controversial as questions arose over voting practices in Florida. The results were contested in Florida courts and eventually the Supreme Court ruled in favor of Bush, providing him just enough electoral votes to beat Democrat Al Gore.

He was president when Islamic terrorists attacked the World Trade Center in New York and the Pentagon in Washington on September 11, 2001. Bush responded by ordering military attacks on Afghanistan, where the terrorist leader Osama bin Laden was thought to be hiding. In 2003 Bush ordered U.S. forces to invade and occupy Iraq on grounds that the country posed a threat to the United States.

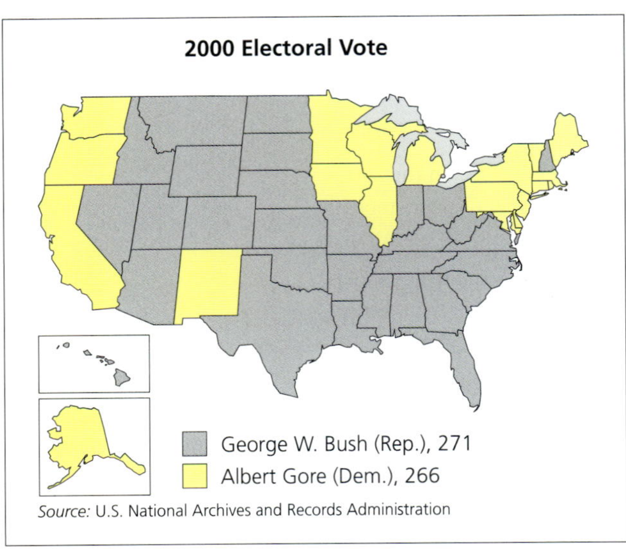

Source: U.S. National Archives and Records Administration

Pat Buchanan, a former speechwriter for President Richard Nixon and communications director for President Ronald Reagan, also entered the 2000 election as the candidate of the Reform Party (founded by Ross Perot in 1996). Buchanan ran on a platform of social conservatism: opposition to abortion under any circumstances, opposition to immigration, opposition to gun control, and opposition to free trade.

The Issues

In their efforts to claim the broad middle part of the electorate, Bush and Gore seemed close together on many issues; the distinctions between the candidates' positions lay in relatively fine details of complex programs. Nevertheless, the two sides took distinctly different positions on some key issues.

Environmental protection. Environmental protection was long an issue associated with Al Gore. He advocated stricter air pollution controls as a means of combating "global warming," the gradual rise in temperature in the earth's atmosphere that many scientists believed would result in drastic climate changes. Bush denied that there was sufficient evidence of global warming to justify preventive actions.

Energy. Energy was the flip-side of the environment. Gore emphasized the need to burn fewer fossil fuels, such as oil and coal, to protect the environment. Bush, who had spent some years in the oil business (as had Cheney), advocated more aggressive efforts to find new sources of oil, especially in a portion of Alaska set aside as a wildlife refuge.

Campaign finance. Gore proposed sweeping reforms of campaign financing including an outright ban on "soft money," the largely unregulated contributions to political parties (as opposed to specific candidates). It was a stand partly calculated to appeal to supporters of McCain, and also to distance Gore from a controversy surrounding "soft money" contributions to the Democratic Party at a meeting held in 1996 in a Buddhist temple where Gore had spoken. Prosecutors alleged that donations from participants in the meeting had later been reimbursed and that the contributions were really from Asian business interests. Bush, for whom fund raising was never a problem, emphasized the rights of people, and groups, to express their political opinions, including by means of contributions, while at the same time calling for an end to "abuses" of "soft money" contributions to political parties and involuntary use of union dues to support political candidates.

Social Security. Gore emphasized the importance of protecting funds in the national retirement system from being spent on other programs; he called for the funds to be placed in a "lock box." Bush advocated introducing an element of privatization, allowing citizens to direct the investment of funds deducted for Social Security in the rapidly rising stock market.

The Campaign

The biggest issue in the 2000 campaign was personal morality. Both Gore and Bush repeatedly stressed their dedication to "family values," a euphemism for putting distance between themselves and President Clinton. Gore refused to let Clinton campaign on his behalf for fear that his name could become more closely attached to the disgraced president. To help explain his former bouts of drinking Bush emphasized that he was a "born again" Christian who had changed his ways when he experienced a mid-life religious awakening. Gore, too, portrayed himself as a deeply religious man. Gore emphasized his wife Tipper's well-known role in regulations to put warning labels on music CDs and videos with explicit sexual or violent contents; Lieberman's own well-known religiosity was well known, and appealed even to conservative Christians.

Competence was another strong campaign theme. Gore reminded voters of his many years of experience as a Representative from Tennessee, then a Senator, then eight years as vice president; his record in this regard was much stronger than Bush's terms as Governor of Texas, a position with prestige but limited political power. Democrats also played on Bush's many verbal gaffes during the campaign: a tendency to misspeak, or an inability to name the leaders of foreign countries.

On the other hand, Bush proved to be a more adept campaigner than Gore. Time after time observers described Gore as "stiff" and unable to relate to his audience. Bush, on the other hand, had a much more casual, friendly manner. These differences were especially apparent during the three television debates between the two candidates. While Gore seemed to be in better command of the facts behind the issues, Bush's manner was more appealing to many voters. Gore scored more "points" for his answers but Bush "won" the debates on style.

The Outcome

The outcome of the election was unprecedented. Eventually it was determined that Gore won 50,999,897 popular votes, or 48.4 percent, to Bush's 50,456,002, or 47.9 percent, a difference of 543,895 votes. Nader, of the Green Party, won 2,882,955 votes, or 2.7 percent, and Buchanan won 449,120 (0.4 percent) and Harry Browne of the Libertarian Party won 384,440 (0.4 percent).

It was on the electoral vote, however, that the outcome hinged. The popular vote in several states was extremely close—in New Mexico, Gore beat Bush by just 366 votes; in Oregon, Gore won by 6,765 votes out of 1.5 million cast; in Iowa, Gore won by 4,144 votes out of 1.3 million.

But nowhere was the vote closer, or more crucial, than in Florida, which had 25 electoral votes. By the morning after election day, it became apparent that the next president would be the man who won in Florida.

At first, it seemed that Bush had won Florida by a razor-thin margin, and Gore conceded the state, and the election, to Bush on election night. An hour later, Gore called back and retracted his concession.

Because the Florida vote was close—at first, it was reported that Bush won by about 140,000 votes—election officials in Florida counties recounted the ballots to make sure. On November 10, three days after the election, Bush's lead stood at just 327 votes.

In the recounting process, numerous problems arose. Some ballots required voters to punch little holes; when the voter failed to fully penetrate the ballot, the confetti-like "chads" could be left dangling, or merely dented. Automatic vote counting machinery tended to reject such ballots, but with the thin margin, election workers began examining the ballots with magnifying glasses, trying to determine voters' intentions.

In other cases a "butterfly" ballot was designed with check-off boxes grouped down the middle of a folded paper, with the selections to either side. Some voters said the design, which was new, had confused them. Ballots were rejected because voters had voted for two candidates—perhaps mistaking a box as belonging to a choice on the other "wing" of the "butterfly." In some heavily Jewish districts many votes were recorded for Buchanan, despite his penchant for anti-Semitic remarks. The confusing butterfly design was a plausible explanation.

Republicans were anxious to stop the recount while Bush was ahead; Democrats insisted on continuing the process. Both sides went to court. Gore won a court order to keep counting; Bush asked a federal court to order the process stopped. The state official in charge of tabulating the votes, Republican Katherine Harris—who had been the co-chair of Bush's campaign in Florida—also went to the Florida Supreme Court, requesting an end to hand counting of some ballots. The Florida Supreme Court refused the request, letting hand-counting of ballots continue. The Bush team then went to federal court, trying to stop the counting. Rebuffed at first, Bush's lawyers went to the U.S. Supreme Court.

Finally on December 12, over a month after the balloting, the U.S. Supreme Court overruled a federal appeals court and the Florida state supreme court and ordered a halt to the recount. At that stage, Bush was still 527 votes ahead of Bush (out of 5,963,110 votes counted in Florida), and received Florida's 25 electoral votes, pushing him five electoral votes ahead of Gore and into the White House.

The official end of the counting did little to quell the controversy. Observers noted that absentee ballots that had been postmarked after November 7 were being counted in some counties, but not in others. Subsequent studies by The New York Times and other newspapers strongly suggested that the outcome was determined less by political corruption than by confusion and even incompetence.

It was the first time since 1888 that the loser in the national popular vote was declared the winner in the electoral college vote.

More Information

- Bruni, Frank. *Ambling Into History: The Unlikely Odyssey of George W. Bush*. New York: HarperCollins, 2002.
- Burns, James MacGregor and Georgia J. Sorenson. *Dead Center: Clinton-Gore Leadership and the Perils of Moderation*. New York: Scribner, 1999.
- Correspondents of the New York Times. *36 Days: The Complete Chronicle of the 2000 Presidential Election Crisis*. New York: Times Books, 2001.
- Kaplan, David A. *The Accidental President: How 413 Lawyers, 9 Supreme Court Justices and 5,963,110 (Give or Take a Few) Floridians Landed George W. Bush in the White House*. New York: William Morrow, 2001.
- Milbank, Dana. *Smashmouth: Two Years in the Gutter with Al Gore and George W. Bush: Notes from the 2000 Campaign Trail*. New York: Basic Books, 2001.
- Moore, James. *Bush's Brain: How Karl Rove Made George W. Bush Presidential*. New York: Wiley, 2003.
- Political Staff of the Washington Post. *Deadlock: The Inside Story of America's Closest Election*. New York: Public Affairs, 2001.
- Sammon, Bill. *At Any Cost: How Al Gore Tried to Steal the Election*. Washington: Regnery Publishers, 2001.
- Simon, Roger. *Divided We Stand: How Al Gore Beat George Bush and Lost the Presidency*. New York: Crown Publishers, 2001.
- Turque, Bill. *Inventing Al Gore: A Biography*. Boston: Houghton Mifflin, 2000.

On the Web

- "In Their Own Words: Sourcebook 2000." Political Communications Lab, Stanford University (texts of speeches and policy papers for both candidates.). **http://pcl.stanford.edu/campaigns/campaign2000/sourcebook/.**

Set Index

"cross of gold" speech **1:**107–108, 110; **2:**82–84
Crusade for Justice **2:**184
Cruzan v. Director, Missouri Department of Health (1990) **3:**175–176
Cuba, and the election of 1900 **1:**109
Cuffe, Paul **4:**11, 13
Cumming v. Richmond County Board of Ed. (1899) **3:**78–79
Curley, James, biography **2:***112*
currency
  paper
    banknotes **2:**30
    greenbacks **2:**77, 88, 92
  political parties and
    Democratic Party (1900–32) **2:**111
    see also Greenback Party; National Silver Party; Silver Republicans
    silver **1:**106–107; **2:**77–78, 80, 81–82, 92, 98, 111–112
    see also gold standard
Curtis, Benjamin **3:***37*
Curtis, George **1:**70
Cushing, William **3:**2–3

D

Daley, Richard J., biography **2:***146*
Dallas, George **1:**54
Daniel, Peter **3:***34*–35
Dartmouth College v. Woodward (1819) **3:**13, 23–24
Daugherty, Harry **1:**132
Davis, Benjamin **2:***129*
Davis, David **3:***39*–40
Davis, John
  biography **1:***134*
  presidential candidate (1924) **1:**132–135; **2:**114, 133
Dawes, Charles **1:**133
Day, William **3:***71*–72
Dean, Jim **2:**187
death penalty *see* capital punishment
Debs, Eugene V. **2:**116
  biography **1:***110*
  presidential candidate
    in 1900 **1:**109–112; **2:**102
    in 1904 **1:**113–116; **2:***118*
    in 1908 **1:**117–120
    in 1912 **1:**121–124; **2:**117
    in 1920 **1:**128–131; **2:**102, 117
    see also In re Debs
debts, Union Party (1936–39) and **2:**149
Declaration of Rights for Women **4:**158–160
Declaration of Sentiments and Resolutions **4:**155–157
defense, Union Party (1936–39) and **2:**149
De Jonge, Dirk **3:**113
De Jonge v. Oregon (1937) **3:**113–114
DeLeon, Daniel **2:**95, *96*
Democratic-Farmer-Labor (DFL) Party **2:**127
Democratic Leadership Council (DLC) **2:**165–166
Democratic Party (1828–60) **1:**44; **2:**17–20
  funded, by Customs employees **2:**6

National Convention (1860), and the breakaway Southern Democrats **2:**20, 52
presidents *see* Buchanan, James; Jackson, Andrew; Pierce, Franklin; Polk, James; Van Buren, Martin
and slavery **2:**4, 17, 19–20
Democratic Party (1860–76) **2:**61–65
  Copperheads (Peace Democrats) **1:**76; **2:**56, 62
  during the Civil War **2:**62
  and the election of 1864 **1:**76
  platform (1864) **2:**64–65
  post-Civil War **2:**62–64
Democratic Party (1876–1900) **2:**80–84
  convention (1896), Bryan's "cross of gold" speech **1:**107–108, 110; **2:**82–84
  election (1876) **2:**80
  platform (1876) **2:**82
  presidents *see* Cleveland, Grover
Democratic Party (1900–32) **2:**111–115
  platform (1912) **2:**114–115
  presidents *see* Roosevelt, Franklin; Wilson, Woodrow
Democratic Party (1932–68) **2:**3, 137, 141–148
  platform (1932) **2:**145–146
  platform (1948) **4:**85–86
  presidents *see* Johnson, Lyndon; Kennedy, John; Roosevelt, Franklin; Truman, Harry
  see also States' Rights Democrats (Dixiecrats)
Democratic Party (1968–2004) **2:**163–168
  platform (1992) **2:**167–168
  presidents *see* Carter, James "Jimmy"; Clinton, William "Bill"
Democratic-Republican Party (Antifederalists) **1:**7, 9, 10–11, 12, 17; **2:**3–4, 9, 13–16
  and the election of 1820 **1:**30
  and foreign affairs **2:**14
  presidents *see* Adams, John Quincy; Jefferson, Thomas; Madison, James; Monroe, James
Dennis, Eugene **2:***129*
depression, economic
  and the election of 1896 **1:**105, 106
  see also Great Depression
Dewey, Thomas
  biography **1:***152*
  and the election of 1940 **1:**147
  presidential candidate (1944) **1:**151–153; **2:**158
  presidential candidate (1948) **1:**154–157; **2:**137
"direct democracy" **1:**121, 123–124
Dixiecrats *see* States' Rights Democrats
Dole, Robert "Bob"
  biography **1:***202*
  presidential candidate (1996) **1:**200–203
Dorr's Rebellion **2:**38
Dorr, Thomas **2:**38, *40*
  biography **2:***39*
"double jeopardy" **3:**114
Douglass, Frederick **2:**72; **4:**33–34
  biography **4:***33*
Douglass, Sarah Mapps **4:**37

Douglas, Stephen
  biography **1:***71*
  and the election of 1852 **1:**61
  presidential candidate (1860) **1:**68–73; **2:**61
  and slavery **2:**19
Douglas, William **3:***108*–109, 119
Dow, Neal **1:**92
Dred Scott case *see Scott v. Sanford*
Drew, Timothy **4:**142
Duane, William **1:**46
Dubinsky, David **2:**152, 153, *158*
Du Bois, W.E.B. **1:**135; **4:**6, 60, 63–64
  biography **4:***64*
  quoted on Marcus Garvey **4:**140
Dukakis, Michael
  biography **1:**194
  presidential candidate (1988) **1:**192–195; **2:**165, 171–172
Duke, David **2:**178
Duvall, Gabriel **3:***16*

E

Eagleton incident **1:**177, 178
Eagleton, Thomas **1:**177, 178; **2:**164
Eastland, James **4:**110
economics
  depression
    and the election of 1896 **1:**105, 106
    see also Great Depression
  laissez-faire **2:**107
  supply-side **2:**170–171
Edmunds, George **1:**95
Edmund v. Florida (1982) **4:**77–78
education
  affirmative action in, violates the rights of whites? (SC) **3:**155, 166–167
  censorship of student newspaper (SC) **3:**168, 173–174
  and the election of 1876 **1:**86
  and the election of 1996 **1:**201
  Green Party and **2:**190
  Liberal Party and **2:**157
  Natural Law Party and **2:**193
  segregation in *see* segregation, in education
  see also schools
Edwards v. California (1941) **3:**117–118
Eighteenth Amendment **1:**128; **3:**xiv
  Prohibition Party and **2:**66
Eighth Amendment **3:**xiii
Eisenhower, Dwight
  biography **1:***159*
  health **1:**162, 163, 164
  as president **2:**138, 144
    and the Civil Rights Act (1957) **4:**104
    and the Civil Rights Act (1960) **4:**110
    and Little Rock High School **4:**101, 102
  presidential candidate (1952) **1:**158–161; **2:**137, 138, 144
  presidential candidate (1956) **1:**162–164; **2:**144
election campaigns, paying for **2:**6–8
Electoral College **1:**1
Eleventh Amendment **3:**xiii, 1, 3, 6
Ellsworth Court **3:**9–12
Ellsworth, Oliver **3:**9–10

Emancipation Proclamation (1863) **1:**70, 74; **2:**36, 55, 56, 58; **4:**42–44
Embargo Act (1807) **1:**19
employment
  hours worked by women (SC) **3:**66, 82–83, 88
  see also child labor
energy, and the election of 2000 **1:**206
Enforcement Act (1870) **3:**56, 62, 63; **4:**56
Engel v. Vitale (1962) **3:**143–144
environment
  and the election of 1992 **1:**198
  and the election of 2000 **1:**206
  Green Party and **2:**190
  Natural Law Party and **2:**193
  Progressive Party (1912–16) and **2:**121
Equal Opportunity Act (1964) **1:**171
Equal Rights Amendment **4:**178, 179, 181
Equal Rights Party **2:**72–74; **4:**163–165
  platform (1872) **2:**73
Esch-Cummins Act (1920) **2:**113
Escobedo v. Illinois (1964) **3:**147–148
Espionage Act (1917) **3:**84, 91
Essex Junto **1:**17
Everett, Edward **2:**50
Evers, Medgar, assassination **4:**90, *121*
Everson v. Board of Education (1947) **3:**122
Executive Order 8802 **4:**73, 79
Executive Orders 9980 and 9981 **4:**83–84, 184
Ex Parte Milligan (1866) **3:**48
extradition, interstate (SC) **3:**31, 45–46

F

Fall, Albert **1:**132
Family Reinforcement Act **2:**173
Fard, Wallace Dodd **4:**142
Farmer, James **4:**80, *81*
Farmer-Labor Association **2:**125–126
Farmer-Labor Party **2:**4, 125–127
Farmers' Alliance **2:**90, 98–99
Farmer's Non-Partisan League **2:**125
farming *see* agriculture
Farrakhan, Louis **4:**144, *145*, 149
  biography **4:***150*
Faubus, Orval **4:**101–102
  biography **4:***102*
Featherstone, Ralph **4:***136*
federal budget, Reform Party and **2:**196
Federal Corrupt Practices Act (1910) **2:**7
Federal Election Campaign Act (1971) **2:**7–8
federal government
  Executive Order ending racial discrimination in **4:**83
  and river navigation (SC) **3:**27–28
  supremacy over states? (SC)
    see Brown v. Maryland; Gibbons v. Ogden; McCulloch v. Maryland; Ware v. Hylton
  versus state powers **2:**10, 11–12
Federalist Party **1:**8, 9; **2:**9–12
  attacks on Jefferson **1:**11
  and the election of 1804 **1:**17–18
  and the election of 1816 **1:**27–28
  and the election of 1820 **1:**30